PSYCHOLOGY AND THE WORLD OF WORK

PSYCHOLOGY AND THE WORLD OF WORK

DAVID A. STATT

MACMILLAN

First published 1994 by
THE MACMILLAN PRESS LTD
Houndmills, Basingstoke, Hampshire RG21 2XS
and London
Companies and representatives
throughout the world

ISBN 0–333–58460–0 hardcover
ISBN 0–333–58461–9 paperback

A catalogue record for this book is available
from the British Library.

Copy-edited and typeset by Povey–Edmondson
Okehampton and Rochdale, England

Printed in Great Britain by
Antony Rowe Ltd, Chippenham, Wiltshire

To Bert Cooper
who taught me most
about the meaning of work

Contents

x   *Contents*

List of figures

xii   *List of figures*

List of tables

Preface

When you tell your students that you learn more from them than they do from you, they tend to look at each other and smile. Nevertheless every experienced teacher knows that it's true. This book is the product of what I have learned during the past five years of teaching in the Edinburgh University Management School. My hope is that it might therefore be user-friendly for both teachers and students, with teachers finding the coverage and detail they require and students the level of explanation and writing style.

Each chapter has been designed to stand by itself, so that chapters may be read out of sequence if teachers so desire. At the same time there should be a cumulative learning gain in reading the book all the way through, whether in sequence or not, as familiarity grows (aided by cross-referencing) with the most important themes and ideas.

The book has a psychodynamic orientation, most explicitly set out in Chapter 6: 'The "unconscious" at work', but also informing the discussion of many other areas such as motivation, leadership, mental health, selection, learning and the role of women. The perception of time is also used as a means of integrating a great deal of diverse research. 'The time dimension' is the specific topic of Chapter 4 but it is also used throughout the book as a running motif to help illuminate some familiar material in a rather unusual way.

I would like to thank my publishing editor, Stephen Rutt, for suggesting this book to me. It turned out to be more absorbing and enjoyable to write than I had anticipated! Finally I would like to record a huge debt of gratitude to my wife Judith who not only typed every word of this manuscript but improved it with some tactful editing of my more ill-advised comments and phrasing. The final product is my responsibility alone.

Edinburgh   DAVID A. STATT

Acknowledgements

The author and publishers wish to thank the following for kindly giving permission for the use of copyright material:

Cartoonists and the Writers Syndicate for the Harris cartoon in Chapter 14
HarperCollins for Table 15.2
Jossey-Bass Inc. for Figure 6.5
The Psychological Corporation for Figures 10.3, 10.4 and 10.5
Penguin Books Limited for Figures 6.3 and 6.4
Pergamon Press Limited for Figure 5.1
Tavistock Publications for Table 4.1
Times Newspapers Limited and Professor Cary Cooper for Figure 5.2
John Wiley Inc. for Figures 3.3 and 3.4
Routledge for Figures 2.2 and 9.3

Every effort has been made to trace all copyright-holders, but if any have been inadvertently overlooked the publishers will be pleased to make the necessary arrangement at the first opportunity.

PART I

THE ORIGINS OF THE WORLD OF WORK

The single chapter that forms Part I introduces the major ideas and themes of the book, and does so by placing them in their historical and cultural context. It is primarily concerned with developments that took place at the end of the nineteenth century and the beginning of the twentieth. These developments have formed the basis of both professional psychology and the world of work itself as they have been experienced throughout the twentieth century.

Parts II and III then form the detailed examination of this legacy, and in Part IV its possible future is considered as we move into the twenty-first century.

CHAPTER 1

Out of the nineteenth century

The world of work before psychology

Introduction

Both psychology and the world of work, as we think of them today at the end of the twentieth century, are largely products of the nineteenth century. In order to understand our present situation and how it is likely to change as we enter the twenty-first century we need to turn back a page of history therefore, to consider the roots of modern psychology, of the world we work in, and how the two are connected.

The scientific study of psychology is usually dated from the 1870s. That is an appreciable length of time and in the course of it the study of psychology has developed greatly. But the world of work is, of course, vastly older: as old indeed as human society. While it is probably true to say that the changes which occurred in the world of work during the nineteenth and twentieth centuries have been far greater than anything which occurred before then, the hundreds of thousands of years of human history and prehistory that led up to our modern world are worth at least a glance before we immerse ourselves in the details of that world.

The pre-industrial world

In the space available here it is possible to provide only the merest sketch of the most basic features commonly held about the pre-industrial world. This will require us to skip lightly over vast tracts of intellectual territory, and risk causing offence thereby to the professional anthropologist and historian. Yet I would argue that for our purposes this hazardous journey is worth attempting, for *psychologically* we are still linked to the pre-industrial world in several important ways that I will refer to at various points in the coming chapters.

For all but the last 10 000 years or so of human society the world of work was technologically at the level of the Stone Age. That is, the tools (and weapons) people had were made of no material more durable than stone. They could work with wood, bones, skins and bark but they had not yet learned how to work with metal and manufacture metal implements. This technological restriction meant that human society was composed of small nomadic communities which subsisted by what anthropologists call 'hunting and gathering'. They hunted wild animals, and followed them on their migrations; they gathered wild fruits and vegetables in their seasons. They did not domesticate animals for their food supply nor did they cultivate any crops.

The vestiges of this way of life are still to be found in some remote parts of the world. The Aborigines of Australia, for example, still contain communities whose way of life probably goes back about 40 000 years. By studying such living communities anthropologists have been able to supplement the fossil record and the remains of ancient cultures studied by archaeologists and enabled us to reconstruct at least the outlines of the earliest world of work.

Perhaps the most striking aspect of this world is that work as we understand it is not separated off from the rest of people's lives. In fact, no word exists in these societies for what we call 'work'. It was something that everybody, men, women and children participated in as part of the community's ongoing existence. The community made the tools that it needed to provide itself with food and shelter, and given the nature of their food supply this was a continual round of activity. There were no surpluses of food, there was no money economy where reserves could be built up for hard times and there was little if any trade.

In these communities there was only the simplest division of labour; the men generally did the things that were physically hardest and most dangerous, like hunting and the building of homes, while the women usually gathered food and prepared meals. This is another aspect of Stone Age society that has left traces in our modern world, but as we shall see later on in this book these are *psychological* traces which take the form of a myth that women cannot (or should not) do hard or dangerous work. Children, as far as we know, did not have the separate existence they usually have today. They were probably treated like small adults and given tasks appropriate to their size and stage of development. The only schooling they received was in the ways of the community.

The Stone Age began to end around 8000 BC with the development of agriculture in those parts of the world, such as China or the Middle East, that had a climate and a soil conducive to the planting of crops, like wheat or barley, and the domestication of livestock, like goats or sheep. This development was probably more widespread than has long been thought, extending to such unlikely places as Northern Scotland which at one time had a mild and temperate climate. Climatic conditions have, of course, changed a great deal in the past 10 000 years, and indeed are still changing.

The development of agriculture marked a radical change in the world of work. The cultivation of crops required a community to stay in the one place all the year round and to build permanent homes. To this day the lives of farmers and farming communities revolve around their land. The working of the land stimulated the development of more efficient tools and led to the use of metals, of bronze and then iron. Domesticated animals were used both for food and as a source of muscle-power greater than that of human beings. Surpluses could now be stored for hard times and traded for other goods. A simple money economy developed.

Though the immediate and continual necessity of working for sheer survival was now less crucial, work was still a totally integrated part of the community's life (Thomas, 1964). This is the way most of the world still lives and vestiges of this life can still be seen in farming and fishing communities even in the most highly industrialised countries. Songs of these communities and the work that people did in them have formed an important basis of Western folk, blues and popular music for instance. (On the other hand there are not a great many songs written in our day about the lives of systems analysts or computer programmers!)

Out of these settled agricultural communities grew the first towns and cities to act as trading, administrative, cultural and religious centres for the surrounding areas. From about 2500 BC onwards there emerged the first complex civilizations of city states, nations and empires, and in them we can recognise the idea of 'work' as a separate activity from the rest of life. With this development came a division of labour that we are more familiar with. Most kinds of manual work whether on the land, in mines or in small workshops was soon regarded as degrading and something to be avoided. It was usually assigned to the people with the lowest status in the society, often slaves.

People with technical skills or abilities that others did not possess were usually more highly regarded and rewarded, as for example scribes in Ancient Egypt or Mandarin civil servants in China. But the highest status and rewards usually went to the elites and aristocracies who often inherited land and other sources of wealth. The work that these people did lay essentially in looking after their estates and other holdings, that is in following their self-interest rather than the interest of the community as a whole. Thus, socially and psychologically, a potential for conflict of interest was created with the split between those who owned a society's resources and those who depended for their subsistence on their own skills and labour.

By the fifth century BC the civilization of Ancient Greece was flourishing and this civilization has been crucial in shaping Western ideas about all aspects of society, including psychology and including the world of work. Although *experimental* psychology is not much more than a century old the first attempts to ask psychological questions, particularly about mental processes like learning, thinking and perception were actually made in Ancient Greece, and most of them are attributed to Aristotle (Hearnshaw, 1987; Watson, 1978).

The Greek thinkers were obsessed with epistemology, with the search for true knowledge, and they regarded the study of philosophy and the arts as the highest and most desirable activities of mankind – a view of the world that was to have great influence on Western systems of education. Manual labour was reserved for people unfit for these pursuits, like the slaves who made up about half the population of Athens. This division of labour also allowed the Athenian (male) citizen to take a great interest in politics and government. Even craftsmen like potters and sculptors whose skills were greatly admired were regarded none the less with distaste if they received wages from an employer rather than working for themselves (Murray, 1986).

In time these attitudes towards work were taken over (along with the rest of the Greek culture which they admired so much) by the Romans, and spread throughout the Roman Empire. With the fall of the Roman Empire and the rise of the feudal system of social organization in Europe these ideas about the world of work became even more entrenched. The landholding nobility who owned the feudal system regarded all work as servile and degrading and to be done only by the lower orders. In a word, work was *ignoble* (Neff, 1985).

Yet there was one very important countervailing view in the medieval world of work, that of the monastic orders who regarded both mental and physical work as a religious duty. Work was seen by them as a form of worship, a way of serving God and disciplining the human soul. In a word, work was *ennobling* (Neff, 1985). However, by the later Middle Ages the monastic orders, and the Church in general, had become very rich and powerful throughout Europe. The Church became a pillar of the feudal system along with the nobility and aligned its interests more with them than the labouring commoner. Thus the Church regarded mental labour with more approval than physical labour, and this at a time when virtually all educated men – there were few educated women – were clerics of one kind of another.

By the end of the Middle Ages, around the fifteenth century, the Church had come a long way from its simple religious roots and was widely regarded as a thoroughly corrupt institution. A series of religious reformers appeared throughout Europe in reaction to this corruption, most notably Martin Luther in Germany and John Calvin in Switzerland, in a movement known as the Protestant Reformation.

The growth of industry: a change in the psychology of work

The Protestant reformers revived the idea of the ennobling power of work and of earning one's own living while saving one's soul, an idea which struck a ready chord among various groups of people. Trade had increased greatly during the medieval period and merchants of substance were soon persuaded by a creed that honoured their diligence in contrast to the landowning nobles or the landholding Church officials. The master craftsmen of the urban crafts guilds were often quite wealthy men in the exercise of their skills and they too were attracted to Protestantism. Finally the growing towns and cities contained a rapidly increasing group of people who had left, or been forced off, the land and who had to provide for themselves by their own labour outside the protective, if harsh, feudal system run by the lord of the manor (Neff, 1985).

The set of values and attitudes that emphasised the moral worth of work for its own sake, along with honesty, sobriety and thrift in the performance of that work, became known as the Protestant Ethic. The Protestant Ethic therefore represented a radical psychological shift in orientation towards the world of work. Those parts of Christendom that rejected the Catholic Church and became Protestant, such as Scandinavia, Switzerland, the United Kingdom, Holland and North Germany, were marked by their adherence to the Protestant Ethic and by rapid economic development and the beginnings of industrialization.

In Britain particularly the sixteenth, seventeenth and eighteenth centuries saw far-reaching changes, with the end of feudalism, in the way the world of work was organised, particularly in the urban craft workshops but even, eventually, on the land. At one end of the scale these changes allowed more and more individuals to work for wages, giving a day's labour for a day's pay.

At the other end of the scale there was an increase in the number of people who went from being merchants or craftsmen to being owners of businesses and employers of labour. They did this by investing the surplus capital they had accumulated from the successful exercise of their trade or craft (Dobb, 1963). The enterprise of these small businessmen combined with changing attitudes to work in the population at large helped prepare the way for large scale industrialization, starting at the end of the eighteenth century.

These changes were accompanied by the most massive shifts of population ever seen. In England in the year 1200 AD, for example, about ninety per cent of the population lived on the land and about ten per cent in towns. By the year 1900 AD these figures were virtually reversed. Today less than three per cent of the population lives on the land and is able to supply food for the other ninety-seven per cent. The vastly increased productivity represented by this agrarian revolution was an essential underpinning for the Industrial Revolution that was to follow. It meant that the world of work became largely urban rather than rural. The transfer of population resulted in densely packed and hugely expanded towns and cities, each with a large pool of available labour.

Other countries had different experiences of the urbanization and industrialization processes. These were often compressed into a shorter period of time. In the United States, for example, about half the population still lived on the land at the start of the twentieth century and in France a little less than half were still on the land at the end of the Second World 'War. But the fundamental *psychological* effects of urbanization and industrialization on the world of work were the same everywhere.

The Industrial Revolution and the modern world

The start of the Industrial Revolution is often dated as 1769, the year James Watt patented the first steam engine. Large-scale historical movements can rarely, if ever, be traced back to a single event but in this case it is more appropriate than most for it was steam that powered the whole process of the Industrial Revolution. Watt's invention was immediately adopted in textiles and mining in Britain then spread to all areas of manufacturing and production. Every factory that could afford one had a steam engine. With the coming of the railways early in the nineteenth century, first for goods haulage and then for passengers, and the invention of steamships, steam power also revolutionised transport and the means of distribution on a global scale.

Even for people who already lived in towns the world of work went through a radical transformation after the Industrial Revolution. Instead of a small workplace run by a master craftsman and his extended family there were factories, owned by the new entrepreneurs, which eventually contained hundreds of people crammed into them alongside noisy, dirty and dangerous machinery – the 'dark satanic mills' described by the poet William Blake.

However there is some evidence that the new technology of work was of secondary importance to a change in the psychological relationship between employers and employees. The factory system pre-dated the introduction of steam-powered machinery, and indeed even flourished in its absence. The impetus behind the rise of the factory system seems to have been the desire by employers to control the working lives of their employees as closely as possible, in the interest of maximising their profits (Marglin, 1974).

Given the physical existence of the factory environment it made economic sense to site the new technology in it. E. P. Thompson, the well-known historian of the English working class, has shown how employers used their factories to control, for the first time, every aspect of the production process and, more importantly, of the working life of their employees. This involved the use of impersonal forms of regulation, like the clock to measure punctuality for instance, the imposition of a detailed system of discipline, and the close, visual *supervision* of each worker's behaviour (Thompson, 1967). This supervisory function was later to form the basis for the job of the professional manager and of his associate the industrial psychologist.

Working conditions in these early factories were indeed as hellish as Blake suggested, for men, women and even children. A report on child labour in 1832 gave examples of children starting work at the factory at 3.00 am where they worked until 10.00 pm or even later. During these nineteen hours they had a 15 minute break for breakfast, 30 minutes for dinner and a further 15 minutes to have something to drink (Smith, 1952). These children were also liable to receive corporal punishment for any 'transgressions'. Sanitation was, of course, rudimentary. The work itself was so hard and dangerous that many children died from their experiences.

We think of these working conditions now as 'Dickensian' and Dickens was, after all, writing largely from his own observations of mid-nineteenth century England. In fact the conditions of work in the early factories were virtually slave labour. Indeed people were often legally bound to their employers and unable to take their labour elsewhere. Psychologically their condition may have been even worse than slavery. There was no guarantee whatsoever of employment and if there was a slump in demand they could be dismissed at any time, a difficult enough fate now but quite calamitous then. Where slaves might hope for a benevolent master, some kind of personal relationship (however subservient) and a permanent place in the household, the factory worker was usually denied even these meagre psychological comforts.

These appalling conditions eventually improved largely for the same reason that slavery fell into disuse; it was no longer a profitable way to organise the world of work. Factory owners found that paying people just enough to keep them hungry without actually starving them to death, while running the workplace with tyrannical authority and brutal discipline, was simply counter-productive. For terrible though these conditions were they did not stop people being late, drunk, or absent from work or even from sabotaging the machines in a desperate revolt against the way they were treated. Nor did it prevent them from slowing down the production process or turning out poor quality goods. Working conditions were not only bad for the workers they were bad for business.

The change in the dominant mode of working from small farm and craft workshop to large factory had the effect of detracting from the individuality of workers. Not only were individual work skills lost as the division of labour meant that factory workers served the machines in the simplest ways that could be organised, but individual differences between the workers themselves were erased as far as possible. Ideally under the factory system the workers would become a set of entirely interchangeable pairs of hands. Part of the plant, just like machines. And even when the physical conditions of workers improved, the seductive and powerful idea that they were simply a less reliable kind of machine remained. As indeed, in many workplaces, it still does.

Taylor's shovel and scientific management

The simplification of jobs mentioned above was the earliest workplace strategy for organising work. The earliest account of this strategy goes right back to the classical economist Adam Smith (Smith, 1982) and the very beginning of the Industrial Revolution. Smith's argument was that if a complex production process can be divided into very simple steps, each of which requires little if any skill or training, then costs (of wages, materials and so on) are minimised. Charles Babbage (Babbage, 1835), the computer pioneer, took the division of labour idea a stage further by relating human labour to the most effective use of machines, and this way of organising the industrial workplace was to remain virtually unchallenged until the mid-twentieth century. But it was Frederick W. Taylor who had the most profound influence on the practical applications of the division of labour.

Taylor was born in Philadelphia in 1856 and started work as a labourer in the Midvale Steel Company. By the age of 31 he was the company's chief engineer, and his astonishing rise was due in large part to the powers of observation he brought to the industrial processes that he was part of. He later moved to Pittsburgh to work as a consultant for the huge Bethlehem Steel Company. Taylor carried out the first systematic studies of industrial work ever undertaken (Taylor, 1911. See KEY STUDY 1).

In 1885 Taylor began to examine the way men carried out one of the very simplest of all the tasks in the steel mill, the shovelling of sand.

What he discovered was quite astonishing. He found they were doing it all wrong. Indeed he found that every step of the process was marked by inefficiency and waste. For example, the shovels were the wrong size, shape and length, the amount of sand carried was often too little or too much for the worker's stamina and the receptacles they were supplying were in the wrong place.

After Taylor had analysed each step of the process thoroughly (stopwatch in hand) he redesigned it, shovel and all, and found that productivity shot up through the roof. People had been using shovels inefficiently ever since the things had been invented and no one had realised it. As Peter Drucker, the grandaddy of all business gurus puts it, Frederick Taylor was 'the first man in history who did not take work for granted, but looked at it and studied it' (Drucker, 1988, p. 29).

If you can demonstrate a technique for improvement as simple and dramatic as this you can be sure the world will beat a path to your door. Taylor's findings had a speedy and far-reaching impact on the world of work. Taylor called his approach to work 'scientific management' and with it he figured out a detailed set of principles to be applied to the workplace (Taylor, 1911). He was concerned not only with the division of work into the smallest and most efficient units possible but with the *management* of all these units.

Taylor was the first person to suggest that the management (including supervision) of the work process should be separated from the operations themselves. Control of, and responsibility for, the work process should not, he felt, be in the hands of the operator. Once the individual worker had been ('scientifically') recruited, selected and trained it was the manager's role to organise the labour force and supervise the workers' performance.

Taylor was most concerned about the relations between workers and management. He had been deeply influenced by his own experiences on the factory floor where he saw not only gross inefficiency in the use of men and machines but men deliberately working as slowly as possible. He attributed these industrial ills to bad management and the practice of letting workers do their jobs as they wanted. Management, he felt, was not doing enough proper managing. Taylor, however, was also very concerned about the quality of each worker's job. He thought that everyone was entitled to as much money and advancement as he was capable of earning.

In a sense he wanted to reintroduce individuality into the workplace, and he stressed that managers should always deal with individual workers rather than groups. But Taylor also felt strongly that workers and management were dependent on each other and that unless they recognised and respected this mutual dependency they could not achieve their common goal of maximum prosperity for both employer and employee. This goal could only be achieved by getting the maximum productivity out of each worker and each machine.

'Taylorism' became very popular with many employers, though not always in the way that Taylor had intended. They often tended to see it mainly as a technique for getting more work out of their workforce for the same wages. Conversely it was never accepted by the labour force or their union representatives, who regarded the man with the stopwatch as an enemy to be outwitted.

When factories were still run by their owners the basic conflict was seen as an ideological one between capitalists and workers. In the course of the twentieth century owners have given way to managers in the running of most enterprises. The conflict now seems to have taken on a more psychological aspect, as between managers and managed, or 'doers' and 'done to'. That is why this basic and intrinsic conflict of interests, which Taylor never recognised, has been as true of many other countries, including the former Soviet Union, as it was of the late nineteenth century United States. And the conflict persists to this day, with widespread management attempts (both conscious and unconscious) to use Taylorism in practice, whatever modern theoretical flag happens to be flying over the workplace. This is a topic to which we will return at various points in our examination of the world of work.

Taylor's approach came to be known as 'time-and-motion study', amongst other things, but his own use of the term *scientific* management is important (Hollway, 1991). Science was, if anything, even more revered in the nineteenth century than it has been in the twentieth. With the tremendous development of physics and chemistry especially, it looked to many people as if all human problems could, in principle, be solved by the appropriate application of science. This is often described as the philosophy of *positivism*. The steady stream of nineteenth century inventions, technical improvements and increased understanding of the natural world coincided with industralization and economic expansion to produce an ethos of irresistible progress in human affairs. 'Scientific' was almost a synonym for 'good'.

When Taylor described his approach as 'scientific', therefore, he was laying claim to some powerful social and psychological support. In effect he was saying 'My approach is self-evidently correct; it is modern, rational, objective and it works. If you're against it you're against progress'. Not surprisingly organised labour disagreed profoundly with this approach, considering it exploitative, autocratic and, in the long run, inefficient. Moreover they saw its claim to be scientific as quite spurious, 'scientific' meaning whatever an employer chose it to mean.

You would expect organised labour to say something like that but there is also support for their viewpoint from other sources. A contemporary behavioural scientist who studied Taylor's work noted that:

. . . the changing methods and conditions of work and the setting of tasks by time study with its assumption always of scientific accuracy put the individual worker at a disadvantage in any attempt to question the justice of the demands made upon him . . . There are no simple, definite, recognised and permanent standards of work and earnings to which he can appeal. The onus of proof is upon him and the standards of judgement are set up by the employers, covered by the mantle of scientific accuracy. (Hoxie, 1915, p. 104)

Further support comes from a well-known contemporary British employer, the chocolate manufacturer Edward Cadbury (a Quaker, like Taylor himself incidentally). Cadbury was distressed by:

the reduction of the workman to a living tool, with differential bonus schemes to induce him to expend his last ounce of energy, while initiative and judgement and freedom of movement are eliminated . . . (Cadbury, 1914, p. 105)

If the general treatment of workers was no longer quite as brutal by the turn of the twentieth century as it had been in the early days of the Industrial Revolution, the essential psychological relationships between workers and their work and between workers and management was not so much changed as 'modernised' in style. And that was one important aspect of Taylor's legacy. Although he was never trained in psychology Taylor's stress on the individual was very much in tune with that new science, as we shall see below. For this reason Taylor is sometimes referred to as the first industrial psychologist.

Oddly enough Taylor's legacy lives on not only in the world of work but in the world of leisure too. While he was still at college he demonstrated how the recently developed sport of baseball could be improved by changing the pitching action from an under-arm to the more efficient over arm delivery. The authorities were sufficiently impressed by this demonstration to change the rules. However he was unable to persuade the more conservative tennis authorities that their game could benefit from increased efficiency in the form of a spoon-shaped racket!

Scientific psychology and the modern world

The sciences of physics, chemistry and biology, which achieved such great prominence in the nineteenth century, went on growing and developing and changing throughout the twentieth century. The Newtonian universe as physicists understood it in the nineteenth century, for instance, was radically altered in the early twentieth by the theories of Einstein. In turn the picture of the universe and its laws presented by Einstein is being challenged by later developments.

These theories, in a sense, provide pictures or stories about the material universe that attempt to use all the available knowledge in a given field to explain convincingly what still remains unknown. Specific tests of these new theories are then devised and if they are successful the new, and inevitably more subtle, picture is accepted.

However this account of the way the natural sciences are driven has not applied to psychology. As one historian of the subject has put it:

> in contemporary psychology, not only have the problems of the nineteenth century survived, but so have many of the methods developed in that century. More important than even this fact is that the contemporary perspective is largely the one bequeathed by the scholars of that time. (Robinson, 1976, p. 308)

The author points out that of all the great psychologists usually credited with having formed modern psychology only one, B. F. Skinner, was born in the twentieth century. The two most important perspectives on the human condition produced by the nineteenth century are Behaviourism and Psychoanalysis and we will consider shortly the relevance of each to the world of work. First though we should consider what other relevant currents of thought there were in nineteenth century psychology.

Materialism

A lot of the advances in nineteenth century science were made in German laboratories. To the dominant cultural ethos of positivism that we noted above German scientists added that of *materialism*, the belief that all scientific advances can be described in terms of physics and chemistry. Thus scientists working in the fields of medicine and physiology reduced the study of the human body and its processes to a set of physical and chemical laws. A few scientists in this area were interested in matters that we would now call psychological, and they in turn believed that anything psychological could be reduced to physiology.

Two foreign students who were trained in this German scientific tradition were to have the greatest influence of all in the development of modern psychology, Ivan Pavlov (from St Petersburg) and Sigmund Freud (from Vienna). We will examine the work of these great psychologists in more detail below when we discuss Behaviourism and Psychoanalysis. For the moment we might just note that neither man started out as a psychologist. Indeed Pavlov never considered himself anything other than a physiologist. While Freud started out as a neurologist he did eventually accept that his interests were really psychological in nature, though even then he always used hydraulic, physical and other metaphors drawn from natural science.

Psychophysics

In 1879 psychology became a modern and experimental science when Wilhelm Wundt, a physiologist whose interests had taken him out of physiology, opened the first laboratory, in Leipzig. Wundt felt that studying the external workings of a living system was physiology but any attempt to study its internal workings was psychology and should be recognised as a separate science. The experiments that Wundt and other German scientists carried out were on the workings of the senses, first of all examining things like reaction time and auditory acuity. Later on they studied what psychologists called the 'higher mental processes' of learning and memory. Given the prevailing dominance of physics it is no surprise that these early steps in scientific psychology were known as *psychophysics*.

Psychophysics was seen as a way of examining the contents of the mind – the conscious mind – and the methods of examination were the techniques of experiment and introspection. Introspection in this context was not simply the response given by a subject to a stimulus task, like distinguishing colours or sounds, but a rigorous procedure that sought to heighten the subject's attention and his awareness of what was going through his mind.

This definition of what psychology was about was to be comprehensively challenged with the dawn of the twentieth century. As we shall see below the major challenges to this view of the new science were in relation to two aspects of it in particular: the exclusive study of the *conscious* mind and the use of *introspection* as the technique for studying it.

Individual differences: Francis Galton

Another important psychological current is directly related to one of the most celebrated scientists of the nineteenth century, Charles Darwin. It is Darwin's cousin, Francis Galton who is usually credited with having founded the study of individual differences in psychology, and Galton based his work on his cousin's theory of evolution. Darwin's theory that species of animals, including man, evolved over time had a tremendous impact on nineteenth century intellectual life, far beyond the science of biology.

The argument that the animals of each generation had to struggle for survival against their fellows, and that those who made it were therefore best fitted to do so by nature, was a particularly potent part of Darwin's theory. It formed the basis for the view of human society known as Social Darwinism. According to this view those people who did well in the competitive environment fostered by industrialisation did so because they were best fitted to survive. Those who couldn't cope and went under, whether they were competing as entrepreneurs or as workers, were therefore simply not fitted to survive.

In other words both winners and losers in society were selected as such by Mother Nature, and who would argue with Her? Certainly not employers of flourishing enterprises in the United States or Great Britain. Nor even some enthusiastic academic proponents of the doctrine like the American sociologist William Graham Sumner who concluded that millionaires were a product of natural selection.

It was this social interpretation of his cousin's theory of evolution that most intrigued Francis Galton. In particular he was concerned with the observable differences between individual human beings and how these differences arose. With Darwin's findings he felt he had the answer: individual differences are determined by genetic inheritance. The best and the brightest have been naturally selected by the process of evolution.

This being the case it followed that if you wanted to make people brighter and better it was pointless doing anything about their social environment, like training or educating them. The only way to improve people was by working with the process of nature: the best and the brightest should be encouraged to breed with each other so that eventually, after enough generations of mating, a super-race would emerge. As for the least gifted members of society they should be discouraged from breeding at all so that eventually their unfortunate weaknesses would die out. He called this process *eugenics* and it's not difficult to see why it became so popular with social thinkers like Adolf Hitler.

Galton set about demonstrating his cousin's evolutionary theory by studying the families of eminent men of his day (Galton, 1869). Galton himself came from a family of prosperous landed English gentry containing several eminent men and Social Darwinism was intuitively appealing to him. The 977 eminent men he included in his sample produced 332 close relatives of equal eminence. By chance alone a group of people of this size would have been expected to produce only one eminent relative. Galton therefore concluded that this demonstrated how ability ran in families, with the eminent begetting eminence. The major problem with Galton's demonstration is, of course, the circularity of his argument: the implicit assumption that because men are eminent they are naturally intellectually gifted and if they are intellectually gifted they will, just as naturally, become eminent.

It is clear that Galton did not live in an age of television talk shows. One evening's viewing would surely have shattered his serene faith that people in positions of eminence must naturally be intellectually gifted. In the prevailing ethos of Victorian society his views were accepted without question. What was also accepted without question was that female children from eminent families did not grow up to become eminent women. But then everyone 'knew' that women were physically and mentally inferior to men, and Galton's finding that men performed better than women at tasks of sensory discrimination merely lent empirical support to an unquestioned assumption.

One of the most important developments from Galton's work was an emphasis on measurement. As he put it, 'wherever you can, count'. He applied this dictum first to collecting and examining physical measurements of human differences, like height and weight, then moved on to measurements of differences in mental abilities, inventing what were in fact the first mental tests or *psychometrics*. We will discuss this topic in some detail in Chapter 10 but it is worth noting here that not only did Galton influence the emergent science of psychology in the direction of studying individual differences but he suggested the tools of statistical analysis for examining them and drawing conclusions from them. In fact his statistical contributions are still quoted in textbooks of work psychology today (for example Landy, 1989).

Behaviourism

The beginning of the twentieth century saw the publication of the first writings in the two most important schools of thought in psychology, Behaviourism and Psychoanalysis. The birth of Behaviourism was announced by J. B. Watson in the journal *Psychological Review* in the following uncompromising tones:

> Psychology as the behaviorist views it is a purely objective branch of natural science. Its theoretical goal is the prediction and control of behavior. (Watson, 1913, p. 158)

Watson's forthright views were a reaction to the German psychophysics pioneers who had adopted the technique of introspection as the best way to study the mind. Not only did Watson not care for introspection as a method, he didn't believe in the existence of a mind to be studied.

There was nothing else to be studied but someone's observable physical behaviour, he argued. Watson, in other words, was firmly of the opinion that in psychology what you see is what you get, and what you can't see and don't get doesn't exist. The experimenter provided the *stimulus*, noted the *response* to it which the subject made, and didn't worry about what happened in between.

Pavlov

The question of what occurred between stimulus and response was, however, something that greatly concerned Ivan Pavlov. We noted earlier that Pavlov was not a psychologist. He was, in fact, a very distinguished physiologist who won the Nobel Prize in 1904 for his work on digestion. But in the course of his research on the digestive system of dogs he came to demonstrate the working of a process that was clearly psychological.

Pavlov had known for a long time that when dogs are fed, their digestive glands start to function and they salivate. What he began to observe in the course of his research was that the dogs in his lab began to salivate *before* they were fed, as soon as they recognised the man who was coming to feed them. This aroused Pavlov's curiosity, and he designed an ingenious series of experiments to find out what was going on (Pavlov, 1927).

A dog salivating when he is given food displays a perfectly automatic inborn response. It does not depend on any other conditions being present, so that both the *stimulus* of presenting the food to the dog and the dog's *response* of salivating are *unconditional* – unconditional stimulus (US); unconditional response (UR).

A dog salivating when he is merely shown food or simply sees someone bringing him food is not producing an inborn response because there is a condition attached to it. The condition is that the dog be able to associate what he now sees with what he has previously tasted; that he be able to recognise it as food. When the dog recognises food, his brain flashes a message to his digestive system and he starts to salivate. Thus, the *stimulus* of seeing the food (or even food provider) and the *response* of salivating are both *conditional* – conditional stimulus (CS); conditional response (CR).

What Pavlov now wanted to find out was what kinds of conditional stimuli could produce the conditional response of salivating. After starting out by simply showing the animal food and getting it to salivate, he substituted a whole host of conditional stimuli like bells, buzzers, metronomes, and lights and found that with any of them he could produce the conditional response and get the dog to salivate. The experimental procedure he used is known as *conditioning*:

1. Food (US) leads to salivation (UR).
2. The sound of a bell (CS) by itself leads to nothing.
3. The sound of a bell (CS) followed by the presentation of food (US) leads to salivation (UR).
4. When this process has been repeated often enough that the dog begins to associate the bell (CS) with the food (US), he will salivate (UR) at the sound of the bell alone.
5. At this point, the animal's salivation has become conditional on hearing the bell rather than unconditional on being given food. Thus, the bell (CS) now results in salivation (CR) just as effectively as the food (US) had resulted in salivation (UR). The animal, in other words, has been *conditioned* to salivate at the sound of a bell.

J. B. Watson was very taken with Pavlov's work and incorporated it into his theory of Behaviourism. Here was a clear and objective way of understanding why a given stimulus produced a given response without recourse to talk of introspection or the conscious mind. Moreover it should be possible using the conditioning method to *change* someone's behaviour in a desired direction, an exciting prospect indeed and one we will return to in Chapter 12.

This view of what psychology should be about had an immediate and powerful impact on psychologists, particularly in the United States. Indeed the effect of Behaviourism on American life was to go far beyond psychology or the academic sphere. In its clearly stated, no-nonsense style concentrating on an objective and apparently common sense view of the human condition, it seems to me reminiscent of the recently introduced principles of Taylorism in the world of work. Both 'isms' seemed to have a similar appeal for many people in early twentieth century American society, with its roaring economy and the sense of endless opportunity that attracted millions of immigrants from all over the world. Behaviourism was part of a simple 'can-do' philosophy for a time and place that was growing impatient with its European heritage. It was a vigorous antidote to Social Darwinism and its denial of environmental influences. It was an affirmation of the fundamental American belief that people could better themselves by their own efforts.

Henry Ford and the 'assembly line'

The year 1913 also saw the emergence of a third 'ism' that complemented the other two in its effects on the world of work. In that year Henry Ford introduced the first moving assembly line to his small automobile factory, and with it began the era of mass production.

'Fordism' was essentially an application of Taylorism to the process of production. The pace of the assembly line determined the rate of productivity and the workers had to adjust to that pace. Each worker performed a simple operation, lasting a few seconds, as the line passed him. Henry Ford was very much in favour of Taylor's ideas of job fragmentation and the most intensive use of labour and machines. He was perhaps most strongly influenced by Taylor's idea of high wage incentives and paid his operatives the unheard-of sum of $5 a day – at least twice as much as his rivals. He had to pay such high wages. The conditions of the job were so awful that he had a staggering 400 per cent turnover of staff in his first year of operation (Littler and Salaman, 1985).

Paying people more money for the job rather than trying to improve their working conditions was typical of Fordism. Henry Ford's approach to the psychology of his workers was similar to J. B. Watson's approach to his subjects; here is the stimulus ($5), there is the response (a pair of hands at the assembly line for a day). If it works why worry about anything else? And Henry Ford's invention did indeed seem to work, with brilliant success. Like F. W. Taylor's redesigned shovel the effect on productivity seemed like magic.

Within a decade of Ford introducing his assembly line he owned the largest and most profitable manufacturing company in the world with cash reserves of one billion dollars. All other manufacturers felt obliged by Ford's spectacular success to introduce the assembly line process of production wherever possible. Indeed the assembly line became a symbol, an icon, of the twentieth century workplace. Although there were always many other ways in which people made a living the assembly line became widely accepted as the very essence of the world of work. It has certainly been the working situation most intensively studied by psychologists in the twentieth century.

Ford may have made one further contribution. I suspect that because his way of solving a problem by throwing money at it seemed to be so successful, it may have been a major reason for it becoming such a favoured strategy of American business. Looked at from this viewpoint the assembly line was undoubtedly the most successful technological 'fix' in the world of work since the Industrial Revolution.

Psychoanalysis

The other great school of modern psychology was largely developed by Sigmund Freud who was born in 1856, the same year as F. W. Taylor. The birth of Psychoanalysis is usually dated from the publication of Freud's book *The Interpretation of Dreams* in 1900 (Freud, 1953). Many of the dreams he interpreted in this book were his own, part of the self-analysis that he began on the death of his father in 1896.

Psychoanalysis was radically different in its approach and its methods both from Behaviourism and from the recently emergent experimental psychology. Where the former denied the very existence of mind and the latter studied only the contents of the conscious mind, the essence of psychoanalysis is the working of the *unconscious* mind.

Freud was trained in medicine, then did some research in physiology and neurology. It was as a neurologist that he then went into private practice. But although he was making a reputation in this field the physical aspects of neurology did not hold much interest for him. However, most of the patients who came to see him were not really suffering from any physical problems of the nervous system so much as emotional problems, or *neuroses*, and these did interest Freud greatly.

At this point in his career Freud became friendly with a very successful Viennese physician called Joseph Breuer who had discovered that hypnosis was a useful method for dealing with a form of neurosis called *hysteria*. In this neurosis physical symptoms appeared which could not be linked to any malfunctioning of the nervous system. The most striking of these symptoms was paralysis, often of arms or legs. Breuer had found that the hysterical symptoms of one of his patients disappeared when she was able to deal with her emotional conflicts while under hypnosis.

Freud was intrigued by the apparent evidence that visible medical symptoms could be due to emotional factors that the patient was not consciously aware of. Moreover when these emotional factors were brought to consciousness and dealt with, the medical symptoms seemed to disappear as suddenly as they had appeared. Freud quickly moved on to other ways for tapping into a patient's unconscious mind, notably free association and dream interpretation. In free association the patient was encouraged to talk spontaneously about a significant matter until the flow of associations to it ceased. Then another issue would be taken up and the process repeated until an area of particular emotional sensitivity and concern was identified.

Freud often combined these two techniques by taking the patient's dreams as a starting point for free association. He called the interpretation of dreams 'the royal road to the unconscious'. The particular importance of dreams was that they were the patient's own unique production and contained matters of significance to them which would not occur to their conscious mind.

The material in the unconscious is placed there by the process of *repression*. Repression is not simply a passive business of not wanting to know certain things. It is a very active process that takes up a huge amount of psychic energy to hold things down in the unconscious. For this reason Freud referred to the 'dynamic' unconscious, and the psychological processes involved in it are often referred to as *psychodynamics*.

The psychoanalytic or psychodynamic view of the human condition, that the most powerful causes of human behaviour are unconscious and therefore unavailable to external observation, was a powerful one that attracted an important following around the world, first in a clinical or psychiatric setting and later in virtually every area of life. We will look specifically at the role of the unconscious in the workplace in Chapter 6 but we will also trace the influence of the unconscious on many other aspects of psychology and the world of work including motivation, leadership, unemployment, mental health, work-group relationships, the role of women and even on learning and personnel selection.

The tension that has existed throughout the twentieth century between Behaviourism and Psychoanalysis is reflected in the different views that managers and management writers have of the behaviour of workers and the reasons for that behaviour. The behaviourist view has been a particularly congenial one for management though, as we shall see, managers have had to take more and more account of the psychodynamic viewpoint.

This is not to say that Behaviourism is now either outmoded or wrong – its contributions will be apparent at various points in the following chapters – so much as that the causes of human behaviour are much more complex and difficult to understand than a purely behaviourist interpretation by itself can cope with. The behaviourist viewpoint frequently provides a good *description* of human behaviour in the workplace, but it has little to say about the life of the emotions that underlie the particular form that behaviour may take. Just as managers are often made uneasy by talk of emotional life in organizations, so are textbook writers. But the tide seems to be turning in that direction and I make no apology for including it as a major theme in this book.

PART II

THE WORKPLACE SETTING

Part II takes the workplace as its focus and the next seven chapters therefore view the diverse psychological forces that influence and inform the world of work which we inhabit.

We begin with an examination of the way organizations are structured and how they operate, then consider the actual physical setting in which work takes place (Chapters 2 and 3). The far-reaching, and often overlooked, dimension of time in the world of work is dealt with next (Chapter 4). The following two chapters deal primarily with the influence of the emotions on our interpersonal relations and our orientation towards the workplace (Chapters 5 and 6). Chapter 7 is concerned with our behaviour in groups and the unique psychological properties that small groups have. Finally, in Chapter 8 the importance to people of being involved in the world of work is considered, along with the implications of being outside that world.

CHAPTER 2

Organizations

Introduction

For the vast majority of workers whatever their physical workplace may be like their psychological workplace is an *organization* of some kind. For the 10 per cent or so of the working population of industrialized countries who are self-employed this may not always be the case, particularly if they work from home. Even here, though, people must deal with work organizations, for example in marketing their skills and services. And of course there are many family business organizations – especially in the most profitable economic sector, organised crime – where the family home is also the workplace, as it was in pre-industrial times. It would not be too much of an exaggeration, therefore, to describe work organizations as practically ubiquitous. Which leads us to the obvious question.

What exactly is an organization?

This is a simple enough question, you might think, but like many simple questions in the behavioural and social sciences, it does not have a simple answer. 'Organizations are difficult to define' says a leading British textbook on the subject (Buchanan and Huczynski, 1985, p. 3). 'It is surprisingly difficult to give a simple definition of an organization' says a leading American text (Schein, 1988, p. 12).

Why this should be so may become clearer if we start off with a few preliminary definitions and see where that leads us. The British textbook quoted in the above paragraph has the following definition 'Organizations are social arrangements for the controlled performance of collective goals' (Buchanan and Huczynski, 1985, p. 5) while the American one says, in part, 'An organization is the planned coordination of the activities of a number of people for the achievement of some common, explicit purpose or goal . . .' (Schein, 1988, p. 15) and The Penguin Management Handbook defines an organization as 'A social group deliberately created and maintained for the purpose of achieving specific objectives' (Kempner, 1987, p. 361). There seems to be a large measure of agreement in these definitions. They all include three main factors, as follows:

(a) Social Identity   An organization is composed of people who all share a sense of belonging to it in some way.

(b) Coordination   The activities of these people are arranged so that they will interact with each other in what is intended to be a supportive and complementary fashion.

(c) Goal-directed   The reason for the arrangement of these activities is to accomplish the stated goals of the organization.

It is very important to note at the outset that although an organization is composed of individual people these people are not (with rare exceptions) what the organization is supposed to be about. That is an organization is interested only in what its members *do*, not who they are, what they want or how they feel about things. Organizations exist independently of any and all individual members. Thus as we saw in the last chapter the 400 per cent staff turnover of the Ford Motor Company in 1913 left the existence of the company completely unaffected. The members of the organization may have changed several times within a 12-month period but the organization itself continued to exist.

As far as organizations are concerned individual members are interchangeable. Indeed from an organizational point of view they have no individual existence at all. What the organization – any organization – is concerned with is the *role* that a given person plays, whether the role is floor sweeper, assistant production engineer, mother, teacher, doctor, team captain or chief executive. Whether the role is performed by Tom, Dick or Harriet is immaterial to the organization though, as we shall see later in this book, hiring and promotion decisions are subject to all sorts of psychological factors and are not always taken on strict objective organizational criteria.

Although organizations are not about the people in them they do not, of course, run themselves. This is one source of the difficulty in defining an organization and understanding how it works, for everyone brings his or her individual personality to the role that they play, and the interlocking pattern of roles that looks so neat on an organizational flowchart is a lot more messy in real life. And the picture is further clouded by the fact that we all appear on more than one flowchart. We can simultaneously be a member of a family, a company, a sports team, a religion, a choir and a political party.

These memberships will be of varying importance to us: our family may be salient to us every single day of our lives and our political party only once every four years. In middle age the company we work for may become more important to us than any other organization; and in old age it may be the religion we belong to.

The organizations we belong to, and therefore our fellow members, will have a set of expectations of us depending on what role we are supposed to fulfil. We in turn will have certain expectations of other people, and it is in the network of these interlocking sets of expectations that organizational life – and indeed all the life of a society – occurs.

Types of Organization

Organizational theorists usually distinguish two forms of organization in the world of work, formal and informal. The simple definitions of an organization given above are usually applied to what are called *formal organizations* and these include work organizations. Formal organizations, sometimes known as 'bureaucratic' organizations, represent the earliest scientific thinking about organizations that appeared at the beginning of the twentieth century. The bureaucratic model of organizations is associated primarily with the Germany sociologist Max Weber.

The term 'bureaucratic' has a negative ring to our modern ear. We tend to use it in everyday speech to describe an organization that is obstructive, rigid, ineffective and wasteful both of its own staff time and resources and those of its customers. But the bureaucratic model that Weber suggested was intended to combat nepotism, favouritism, corruption and personal whim in the running of organizations and to encourage a more professional and efficient administration. Weber proposed that organizations should ideally contain four essential features (Weber, 1922):

- a hierarchy of authority with power flowing from the top down.
- a division of labour into specialised tasks.
- the existence of written rules and procedures.
- the rational application of these rules and procedures.

We can see how this kind of thinking fitted well with Frederick Taylor's contemporary ideas about scientific management. Both adopted the viewpoint of the *manager* within the organization. His or her job was to administer the rules and procedures in an impersonal, objective and rational fashion as this was considered the ideal way to pursue the organization's goals.

The formal bureaucratic model represents the way organizations are *supposed* to run, and the behaviour that is officially expected of people. This is encapsulated in the public face that organizations present to the world via their annual reports, brochures, rulebooks, organizational charts and so forth.

But as most people who work in organizations have swiftly realised, what is supposed to happen is not always what does happen and research has revealed the great extent and diverse nature of this gap (see for example Pugh, 1971). People form their own groups within the organization based on friendships and common interests as a way, for instance, of overcoming the rigid, impersonal nature of the formal system. These groups can sometimes cut across both functional and hierarchical lines and indeed may even be used in preference to the formal system as a more efficient way of giving and receiving information.

These groups make up what has been called the *informal organization* and this is a universal feature of formal organizations. Indeed there are times when they could not function without the informal organization, for instance when staff voluntarily do far more than they are officially contracted to do in order to help the organization through a crisis. However there are also times when the needs and values of the informal organization may be different from and even opposed to the formal one, for example if a new method of working is imposed from above without prior consultation.

Though a great deal of research has been done since the 1920s on the way the informal system can affect the output and productivity of an organization (which we will discuss later, particularly in Chapter 7), the formal system still remains the basic model for work organizations – to many of the people who are supposed to run them as well as to organizational theorists.

One important outcome of using this model is that organizations and the people in them tend to be treated as if they were two distinct entities each with a separate existence of their own. It seemed to behavioural scientists the most practical way to study something very complex, and it was also in line with general managerial thinking and practice. This has led to great stress being laid on studying *either* the individual *or* the organization. In the former case individual behaviour and personality and the motivation behind it is regarded as paramount and the organization is regarded as a static, fixed background. In the latter case how the organization is structured and the way it functions is seen as all-important while the behaviour of any given individual within it is regarded as simply the product of these organizational forces.

These two approaches have been described respectively as the 'individualistic fallacy' and the 'culturalistic fallacy' (Allport, 1963). What is sometimes added to this model, to link it into society in general, is a third entity, the *environment*. This results in what has been characterised as a 'Russian doll' approach, where each entity is contained within a larger one and is treated as if it can be removed without affecting the shape of the others, as illustrated in Figure 2.1 below (see for example Hosking and Morley, 1991).

While the Russian doll model may have had some use as a way into studying behaviour of enormous complexity by focussing on one entity and holding everything else constant it also had one crucial flaw; that nothing about human behaviour is static. It is now generally accepted that what makes us human is our social existence, our relationships with other people. And all human relationships are a two-way process. Whether the relationship is between husband and wife, worker and boss, teacher and student or customer and salesman, each must always affect the other – however equal or unequal that relationship may be. (This is a topic we will examine in more detail in Chapter 9.)

Organizing rather than organization

It is often remarked by business gurus discussing the importance of staff that 'an organization is its people', and this sentiment is usually received with pious nods of approval by the people who run organizations. But

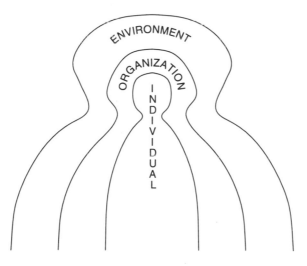

FIGURE 2.1   The 'Russian doll' approach to organizational behaviour

despite its modern status as a megacliché it is literally true none the less. When behavioural scientists talk of 'organizational behaviour' they are not referring to the actions of some mysterious creature hidden away on the top floor. Organizations do not, of course, behave. What we are being asked to look at are the actions of various members of the organization at certain times and places and in certain ways. Their collective actions represent organizational behaviour.

Thus although the Ford Motor Company continued to exist over the period when it experienced a four-fold turnover of staff, the nature of the organization inevitably changed with the changing membership. Indeed the Ford Motor Company at the end of the twentieth century is a very different organization from the one that Henry Ford started at the beginning of the century. Similarly the experience of being a member of that organization has been a very different one over the course of the century.

Within the continuity of the company, therefore, there has been constant change, and that, of course, is the nature of the human condition. An individual may have the same name for 100 years but he will look, and be, a quite different person at different points in that century. Why? Because as he goes through life he not only changes physically he also changes psychologically as he interacts with the people around him. He affects them and they affect him and in the process he comes to be the unique individual he is. It is the same with organizations. An organization is the product of the interrelationships that its members have with each other, including their individual views of what the organization is about. And each member therefore affects, and is at the same time affected by, the organization and its environment.

This is a much messier model to deal with than these neat Russian dolls but it's also much closer to what actually happens in real life. It also has two other important aspects:

- it emphasises that individuals are always in some sort of relationship to each other within the organization.
- it discards the managerial viewpoint.

By emphasising relationships between people we are drawing attention to the process of *organizing* rather than to an entity called an organization that has no separate existence. This process is continuous and ever-changing whereas the entity is an idealised snapshot at any given point in time. The process is really the way in which people make sense of their work environment by comparing, discussing and modifying their individual views and understanding of the organization. Making sense of ourselves and our lives is the most basic psychological process there is and it is not something that we can do alone: it has to be done in conjunction with other people (Statt, 1977). At times of stress or crisis when the identity and *raison d'être* of the organization becomes salient – reorganization, takeover bids, mergers and so on – this process will become quite overt. But normally it proceeds in an unspoken, and even unconscious, manner.

To focus on the process of organizing is also to set aside the managerial viewpoint on organizations which, as we have seen, has always dominated both thought and practice in this field. Central to this viewpoint is the unquestioned assumption that managers are the 'doers' in an organization and non-managerial staff are there to be managed, or 'done to'. The implication of this approach for the use of psychology and other behavioural sciences in the workplace is therefore plain: how can an understanding of organizational behaviour be used to manipulate people in a desired direction? There is nothing necessarily sinister in such attempted manipulation, which is often covered by phrases like 'showing leadership qualities' or 'improving motivation'. It is regarded as part of a manager's role and done in what are seen to be the interests of the organization as a whole, which of course includes the people being managed. None the less, apart from the serious ethical issue involved in trying to manipulate people's behaviour, this approach (as we will see in later chapters) is both a misunderstanding and a misuse of psychology – as well as being counter-productive.

This is where we can begin to see the difficulties presented by the definitions of an organization that I quoted at the beginning of this chapter. It was assumed by these definitions that every member of the organization identified with its goals and values and was committed to achieving them. But we have already seen that the organizations of which they are members play different roles at different times in the normal course of people's lives. A young woman in her first job, a middle-aged man, and an older man coming up for retirement have very different needs and expectations and will inevitably view the same work organization quite differently.

Conflicts of interest

Moreover it has been clear for a long time that members of work organizations do not always share the same goals and values. The differences between management and workforce, and the turbulent history of industrial relations in many countries, are the most obvious example. Indeed in the case of Henry Ford and his assembly line workers it is difficult to see much that they could have had in common, and with a 400 per cent staff turnover in one year whatever they had in common didn't last very long.

The specialisation of jobs and division of labour found in large organizations led also to the emergence of special interests and divisions within the organization along functional lines. This is an inherent conflict in work organizations to this day and it remains largely unacknowledged. For example a company's Research and Development division might promise the appearance of a world-beating widget if only their budget was doubled and they had ten years to work on it, while the Sales and Marketing people would be happy with a bog standard widget that works, just as long as they can hire extra salesmen and show it to the customers by next Tuesday. What does the organization do? Does it decide whether its goals and values imply a long-term or short-term strategy and act accordingly (leaving one group of staff very unhappy) or does it fudge the issue? I'll give you three guesses.

Even the basic, and apparently obvious, issue of just deciding who the members of an organization are, throws up serious difficulties of definition. Everyone would presumably agree that the staff of a company are members, but does that apply to all staff, including part-time or temporary people or people on fixed-term contracts? How about consultants on long-term contracts? Or people who work in the field offices on the other side of the world? How about retired employees with a company pension and company shares? In fact how about shareholders in general who might legally own the company but who have no other contact with it whatsoever? Other than wanting the company to stay in business what possible agreement could all these people reach on its particular goals and values, let alone the everyday running of the organization?

So not only is organizational life untidy and difficult to predict and deal with, it has the potential for internal conflict built into its *normal* pattern of working, quite apart from the particular stresses caused by unusual situations. As we will see at various points throughout this book this is a very difficult issue for the people who run organizations to deal with, and it is indeed a very difficult issue. But pretending that it doesn't exist, the We're-All-One-Big-Happy-Family-Here syndrome, is a good way of guaranteeing a steady flow of organizational problems. And it is only the symptoms of these problems that can then be dealt with – absenteeism, high staff turnover, low productivity and so on – because the real sources of the problems have already been denied a hearing.

Power and political behaviour

One of the most striking aspects of our everyday experience of organizations is that some people seem to have more influence over what happens than other people. The exercise of this influence is often referred to as having *power*. This is another of those complex terms in social and behavioural science that we need to unpack for a closer look. However it has been suggested that the common-sense view of power – I have power over you to the extent that I can get you to do something you wouldn't do otherwise – might be a good place to start (Dahl, 1957).

Power

There is more than one source of power and various writers in this field have attempted to identify and catalogue them, notably French and Raven (1968) who distinguished five kinds or bases of power. They called these reward, coercive, legitimate, referent and expert power:

(a) Reward power   is the ability to give people something they value, such as promotion, more money or a bigger office

(b) Coercive power   is a kind of negative reward power, the ability to punish, for example by demotion or the withholding of a salary increase, and these two kinds of power are usually held by the same person

(c) Legitimate power   is what is usually meant by having authority as a consequence of one's position in the organization and, very importantly, the willingness to accept that authority that is shown by people of inferior position

(d) Referent power   is often thought of as the possession of charisma such that people identify with someone because of his personal qualities and are then happy to be his followers

(e) Expert power   depends on the possession of knowledge or skills that other people happen to value particularly highly, for example in areas like law, finance, science and technology.

The most obvious source of power we encounter in an organization is, of course, *legitimate* power. The more hierarchical the organization the more evident is this type of power. In the army or the civil service one may encounter a dozen or more different levels in the hierarchy, each with its own carefully defined amount of authority over the levels below it. This is sometimes described as a 'tall' organization (see Figure 2.2).

In the late nineteenth century, when the factory system was coming to its peak, the tall organization was regarded as a model for the running of a large commercial enterprise. The focus was on hierarchy, discipline

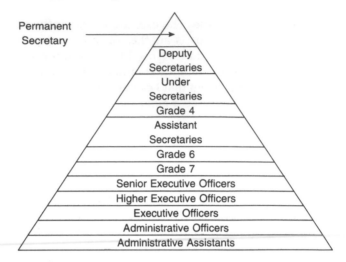

Permanent
Secretary

Deputy
Secretaries

Under
Secretaries

Grade 4

Assistant
Secretaries

Grade 6

Grade 7

Senior Executive Officers

Higher Executive Officers

Executive Officers

Administrative Officers

Administrative Assistants

FIGURE 2.2   Tall organization (the British Civil Service)

and control. By the late twentieth century the worldwide decline in heavy industry and traditional forms of manufacturing, together with the rise of professional specialization to be found in organizations, may have resulted in a certain shift in power with an increase in *expert* power at the expense of the *legitimate* power of management.

This shift has been particularly pronounced for two groups of experts, those in computing and in *accountancy*. It has been argued that personnel managers are a third such group and we shall discuss them in Chapters 11 and 12. In the second half of the twentieth century the world of work has seen a relatively slow but steadily increasing level of computerization. This is true of the manufacturing sector as well as the service sector and administration. Consequently many organizations may well become more and more dependent on their computer systems and the people who design, install, run and maintain them. However people do not give up power willingly in organizations and senior management will often try to undermine the computer experts' power (Pettigrew, 1973).

The source of the expert's power within the organization actually comes from outside it, from his professional skills, knowledge and experience. Indeed his first loyalty may be to his profession, which is the source of a lifelong form of identity, and source of employment, as opposed to his particular work organization of which he may be a member for only a few years. The expert is not part of the hierarchy of line management and may even report directly to the chief executive. To the extent that an organization is dependent on its expert members, and sometimes built round their expertise, its reliance on the traditional use of legitimate power is correspondingly curtailed. Thus it is not surprising that, for example, computer software companies or design consultancies tend to have very few levels of hierarchy, and to be 'flat organizations'.

If anything the position of accountants in organizations has become even more powerful than computer experts for they now exert great influence on the daily life of many organizations and the very language of organizational discourse. Regardless of the organization's purpose, its goals and values, the *costs* of its current operations and of its possible future activities are usually accepted as the dominant factor in its decision-making process after the recessions and restructurings of the 1980s. Often 'the bottom line' is the only factor that really matters whether the organization is providing a public service, making washing machines or producing films. And as 70 per cent to 90 per cent of an organization's costs typically are staff salaries the implications of the accountant's expertise for an organization's members are obviously profound.

When power of this kind is found in an organization it suggests something much more important than simply a victory for expertise. The ability to set an organization's agenda, define the issues it should deal with and the language used to discuss these issues, confers on the group in question the power to see off any potential opposition without a fight, perhaps even without the opposition being aware of it. In these circumstances the controlling group has succeeded in identifying its own interests with those of the organization as a whole (Bachrach and Baratz, 1962).

So, far from being something unsavoury, or a distracting annoyance, the way power is distributed and used in an organization is at the very heart of organizational life. It is integral to the way people behave in organizations that they will use whatever power they have to further their own interests (Hickson, 1990). Sometimes these uses of power will be in line with the formally stated interests of the organization and sometimes they won't. But there need be nothing cynical or reprehensible about this and if we are to understand the psychology of organizational behaviour we need to take a dispassionate look at what people actually do and why they do it (Dror and Romm, 1988).

As well as behaving in an individual capacity members of organizations usually belong to a particular section or department of the organization. Often the political behaviour they are involved in concerns the interests of their department. But just as individuals are unequal in power, so are departments:

Some may be involved in most major decisions, others only in a few . . . Production, sales and finance, by whichever titles they may be known in different forms of organization, are a core trio through whose hands most decisions must pass. (Hickson, 1990, p. 175)

In both their individual and representative capacity members of organizations will form alliances and coalitions with each other to further mutual interests. The pattern of these coalitions will shift over time and with changing circumstances. This behaviour takes place within the informal network that underlies every formal organization and which exists alongside the more static distribution of power as described by French and Raven (Kotter, 1982).

Just as the distribution and use of power in society is the stuff of politics the same is true of life in the organization. When people exercise power over others and over resources by virtue of their formal authority or their expertise or their personal qualities or the coalitions they join, they are acting politically. Political behaviour is thus an integral and routine part of organizational behaviour and not a flaw (usually described as 'office politics') that detracts from the otherwise smooth functioning of the organization. (For a fuller discussion of this topic see also Bacharach and Lawler, 1980.)

Communicating and the use of information

Another and related key area of our experience in organizations is that of internal communication where there is a widespread concern about the way the transmission of information takes place. Some organizational theorists think that this aspect of an organization's life is the most important, and the most problematic one that it has. The old cliché 'information is power' is widely believed in organizations and the use of information – who has access to what and when – is often regarded as the organization's power structure in action.

In traditional, formal organizations, information usually mirrors the legitimate power structure of authority by flowing downwards from the top of the organization. A serious problem with this form of communication is that over 80 per cent of the contents of a message may be lost in its path from the top to the bottom of a hierarchy comprising five or six levels – which is only about half the distance it would have to travel in the civil service (Nichols, 1962).

It has been suggested that attempts to communicate in the reverse direction are even more problematic because people are very aware that the recipients of their messages have power over them and often use information to control them, and they may be afraid of presenting their boss with bad news or unwelcome information. While people may be very keen, indeed desperate, to communicate upwards they often feel that they have to tailor their presentation of the information very carefully, to such an extent that the essence of the message may very well be lost (Katz and Kahn, 1978).

Such distorted communication on the formal level invariably leads to an increased reliance on informal communication. The information that members of an organization receive verbally via the 'grapevine' is transmitted far more quickly, is often regarded as more trustworthy and, as we have seen, is unlikely to be any less accurate. Although the grapevine usually operates horizontally, via people at more or less the same level in the hierarchy, it can be used quite effectively to pass messages up and down the line where formal, written communications might be seen as more rigid or threatening and lead to fixed positions being taken up on either side of a conflict of interests.

There can also, of course, be *too much* communication or, more usually, too much of the wrong kind of communication, where people are snowed under with information they do not really want or need while the information they are most interested in may not be given them. Management consultants are fond of telling organizations that they generate far too much paper and too much of it is marked 'Secret' or 'Confidential', thus clogging up the arteries of communication.

The process of communication is a very complex one which has profound implications for diverse areas of the world of work, and we shall examine some of them in detail later in this book. For example we will consider how individuals process information (Chapter 12), how work groups do so and make decisions based on that information (Chapter 7) and the part that communication plays in changing people's attitudes (Chapter 14).

Organizational culture(s)

The term 'organizational culture' has become very widely used in recent years but it is also used in a wide variety of different ways in both the popular and the scientific literature. A leading management scientist has identified six different usages (Schein, 1985). To my mind the most helpful use of the term is one which combines the anthropological idea of shared beliefs, values, attitudes and expectations together with the psychological notion of the unquestioned assumptions that everyone has about the organization's ways of doing things, its traditions, etc.

As we saw earlier in this chapter, however, there is often very little that *all* the members of a work organization can agree on and I would therefore suggest that we really need to use the plural and talk about 'cultures', and indeed 'sub-cultures', in organizations. Thus as well as interaction and relationships at the individual level in an organization there seems to be a parallel process involving the different cultures to be found there. Seen from within there may be as many different cultures in an organization as there are interest groups. These will often be determined by function (for example Sales and Research) or hierarchy (senior management and shop floor) although they may arise through other factors like location (headquarters and field office) or even length of service (old timers and new hands).

When looking at an organization from outside we are often likely to be struck by a broad general set of characteristics that forms what is usually referred to as a 'corporate culture'. We can see immediately that the civil service has a vastly different corporate culture from a small market research firm for instance. Even in the same field there may be great differences between two corporate cultures, like the traditional buttoned-down image of IBM compared with the laid-back Californian image of Apple.

With the growing importance of multinational organizations we should also note that there are many differences of *national* culture to be found in the world of work (Hofstede, 1980). Japanese companies do not operate in New York or Glasgow in quite the same way as they do in Tokyo. Differences in national culture can show up quite strikingly in an organization's everyday functioning. For example:

> The readiness to joke even about business matters is distinctively British . . . take the production director who reacts to the suggestion that the firm manufacture rather than buy-in a simple component with: 'Let's stick to what we're good at . . . losing vast sums of money.' This is not a universal phenomenon. Such irreverence in the business context from American lips is unthinkable. In the American case, corporate humour is constrained by the intensity of feeling and seriousness of organizational purpose. (Barsoux and Lawrence, 1990, p. 111)

The psychological contract

We conclude this brief look at organizations and how they operate by focussing specifically on the nature of the psychological relationship between an individual and a given organization that he or she is a member of.

In any organization its members, whatever their formal agreement or contract, enter into an unwritten (and often unspoken) *psychological contract*. This psychological contract consists of a set of *expectations* which the particular member and the organization have of each other, and each member has a different contract. On the degree of fit between these two sets of expectations rests the health and happiness of both. Members of a family, for example, expect love and support: if they receive mental or physical abuse instead the psychological contract has been broken and the health and happiness of the organization jeopardised. Management normally expects employees to perform their jobs competently and conscientiously and, if possible, enthusiastically: that is, to be well motivated in coming to work. If employees do not perform in this fashion the people who run the organization might well consider them in breach of their psychological contract.

In work organizations there are many ways in which the sets of expectations held by member and organization may not fit. Often the public face of an organization may be highly misleading to a new member. Employers claiming in their job advertisements to be 'progressive' 'innovative' or 'forward-looking' and offering a job both 'challenging' and 'rewarding' may proudly believe these descriptions to be quite true (or want to believe them); or then again they may simply be parroting the fashionable buzz words to sugarcoat a dead-end soul-destroying non-job in an organization that is going nowhere. In any event the description may not be realistic, and eager new recruits looking for the 'challenge' and the 'reward' can soon find themselves sadly under-employed, but trapped, and getting more resentful every day.

Conversely, an employer may genuinely wish to give someone more responsibility and authority but be faced by an employee who interprets his psychological contract as putting in the minimum effort necessary to keep the job he's got. Or perhaps a conscientious employee is offered a promotion to a new role which she would like to accept but feels that the travelling involved would imply a different and unacceptable psychological contract for her.

The psychological contract will also change over time with the changing circumstances of both individual and organization. The expectations of a 22-year old beginning a career are very different from that of a 42-year old in the midst of a mid-life review or a 62-year old thinking about retirement. Similarly, organizations have different expectations of their employees if they themselves are younger and expanding as opposed to older and contracting.

Organizations always demand loyalty of their members as their side of the psychological contract. That is their most crucial requirement (see for example Barnard, 1938; and Gouldner, 1958). In return members' demands, though often couched in terms of pay and conditions, can usually be boiled down to being taken seriously and treated with respect. Contempt and lack of respect by employers is guaranteed to produce employee discontent – and more quickly than any other cause. While the specifics of any psychological contract are subject to change from time to time as individual or organizational needs change, the underlying relationship of loyalty – respect, I would argue, remains constant.

The greatest difficulty in maintaining this psychological contract, in my experience, is that it is not even-handed, usually reflecting a vast disparity in power. Respect must come first for loyalty to develop. Employers who do not show respect for their employees, whether in direct relationships or in dealing with their representatives, simply cannot expect any loyalty from them. They might be able to coerce them; they might be able to buy them off. But loyalty they will not get, and without it any organization is doomed, in time, to decay, disintegrate and disappear.

CHAPTER 3

The work environment

Introduction

In this chapter we shall be concerned with the physical environment that people inhabit at work, how they relate to that environment and how it affects them. In Part IV when we turn to the future of work we will return to the work environment (in Chapter 10) to consider the effects upon it of introducing new technology, and the changes that can entail for our working lives. Central to everyone's physical work environment are the machines and equipment that we use, from pencils to cranes, microscopes to video screens, pocket calculators to supercomputers. And all the furniture, furnishings and fittings that surround us.

It seems glaringly obvious to say that the first point of contact we have with our physical environment is through our senses but it needs saying none the less because we need to understand what our brain does with the sensory information it receives before we can appreciate the psychological interaction we have with our environment. And only then can we think about improving that environment to help us work better. So before we consider how we deal with machines we will examine how we deal with our own senses.

The senses

Information about the environment is conveyed to the brain from the eyes, ears and other sense organs. Traditionally people have referred to the five senses of vision, hearing, touch, taste and smell. We now know that this is an oversimplified description of the human senses. The sense of touch, for instance, is really four different senses – pressure, pain, cold and warmth. There are four senses of taste – salt, sweet, sour and bitter. Even the sense of vision has to be divided into two senses – colour vision and black-and-white vision. In addition to these familiar senses, psychologists would now add two less familiar ones: bodily movement and balance.

Our senses are wide-ranging, complex, delicate and sensitive and in everyday life we normally use only a fraction of their power. Thus on a clear dark night we are capable of seeing a candle flame over 30 miles away, and in a quiet room the tick of a watch can be heard at a distance of 20 feet. But each of our senses, however acute, can nonetheless be bettered by some member of the animal kingdom. A hawk, for example, has sharper vision than we do and a dog can hear sounds inaudible to us. It is thus the *range* of the human senses together with their sensitivity that provides us with a unique quantity and quality of information about the environment.

The senses we know most about are vision and hearing. These senses have long been of great interest to scientists from several disciplines, and the relevant sense organs (the eyes and ears) are readily accessible to observation, experimentation and measurement. Less is known about the other senses but some recent work has added to our understanding of them as well.

Common properties

Before we say a few words about each of the senses, we need to look at some important phenomena common to all of them. Before we can become aware of any stimulation from the environment, a stimulus has to be strong enough for our sense receptors to pick it up. Below a certain level of intensity, we simply won't experience the stimulus. A point of light in a dark room, for example, has to be bright enough to cross our threshold of vision before we can see it.

This threshold is known as the *absolute threshold* because it marks the difference between sensing and not sensing. Different people have different absolute thresholds, however, and a person's ability to sense a certain stimulus may also vary depending on his psychological and physiological condition at the time.

There is another sensory threshold that operates when we try to discriminate between two stimuli. Suppose there are two slices of cake left and you're trying to decide which is bigger. In order for you to decide, there has to be a difference between them sufficiently large for you to notice. The minimum amount of difference that you can detect is called the just noticeable difference, or j.n.d. Once you have detected a j.n.d. between one stimulus and another, you have crossed the *difference threshold* between them.

Difference thresholds are also quite variable, depending on the two stimuli in question, and not only sensory experience. We can see this in our everyday experience. A one dollar increase in the price of a night at the Waldorf-Astoria is probably not a j.n.d.; the same increase in the price of a hamburger certainly would be. As you read this book you are probably not aware of any pressure on your skin. Yet if you wear a watch or clothes with elastic in them you will find your skin marked by their pressure when you take these things off. If you have ever visited a fish market you may have wondered how the people who worked there could stand the smell. Had you asked them, they might have replied 'What smell?' and assured you that people got used to it in time.

In both these cases the sense organs involved did the same thing – they adapted. Just as people in fish markets get used to the smell, you can get used to the feel of what you wear, until you stop feeling pressure on your skin. The sensory adaptation involved helps us live through everyday situations without the mind-boggling necessity of stopping to examine the meaning of every stimulus from the environment that our sense organs pick up. In fact if the stimulus is constant and familiar the sense organs become insensitive to it and stop sending information about it to the brain. If the stimulus changes, the sense organs are back in business. You are probably most familiar with the visual form of adaption between conditions of light and dark – and so are psychologists. We will discuss this process further in the next section on vision.

There is a limit to sensory adaptation, of course – if your watch strap is so tight it causes you discomfort, you won't adapt to it; you'll change your environment by loosening the strap. But below the level of pain, our senses can adapt very efficiently to a wide range of environments.

Vision

The working of the human eye is often compared to that of a camera. Light falling on the eye is focused on the retina, the sensitive lining at the back of the eye, in a similar manner to a photographic film. The retina contains an enormous number of nerve endings that are sensitive to light. These nerve endings form an image on the retina of whatever the eye is looking at, and eventually this image is transmitted via the optic nerve to the brain.

The retina contains two kinds of nerve endings, known by their shape as rods and cones. The cones react to the stimulus of daylight falling on them by being sensitive to both chromatic colours (blue, green, red, etc.) and achromatic colours (black, white and grey). The rods, functioning in a dim light, are sensitive only to achromatic colour.

If we move abruptly from light to darkness, as when entering a basement room from the sunshine outside, the rods in our retina have to take over from the cones which become only slightly sensitive to the fainter light. After seven or eight minutes, the cones have reached the limit of their sensitivity, but the rods increase their sensitivity for a further thirty minutes, by which time the process of dark adaptation is largely complete and we can see as well as is possible in the dark. This process is reversed when we come out into the sunshine again and adapt to the light, but light adaptation is much more rapid, taking only about fifteen minutes.

Hearing

Hearing and seeing provide us with the information about our environment that we rely on most. Our experience and our ability to make sense of the world is largely shaped by these senses. In both seeing and hearing, our sense organs react to waves of energy from the environment: our eyes to light waves and our ears to sound waves.

Just as light waves are made to activate the optic nerve at the back of the eye, sound waves are focussed by the outer ear on the eardrum where they stimulate nerve endings that send messages to the auditory nerve, and from there to the brain.

Unlike our visual (and other) senses, the sense of hearing can be markedly affected by living in an increasingly technological civilization. With advances in technology have come increased levels of loudness and intensity in the sound stimuli that reach our ears. In fact, people living and working in a modern city are in real danger of having their sense of hearing impaired. There is no question that people who live in quiet environments have better hearing than people who live in noisy environments. Prolonged exposure to intense noise levels leads to partial or total deafness, and even lower levels of noise can cause permanent damage.

Nor is there much evidence that we get accustomed to noise and stop hearing it the way we can stop smelling unpleasant odours by the process of sensory adaptation. It is more likely that people who claim they no longer notice screaming sirens or roaring motorbikes have simply lost part of their sense of hearing.

The table that follows illustrates the loudness of our environment. Notice how much of our daily lives are lived around the 85-decibel level which represents the danger point of our sense of hearing (see Figure 3.1).

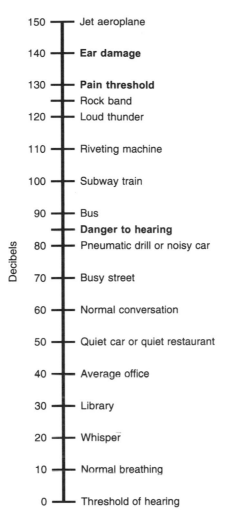

150	Jet aeroplane
140	**Ear damage**
130	**Pain threshold**
	Rock band
120	Loud thunder
110	Riveting machine
100	Subway train
90	Bus
	Danger to hearing
80	Pneumatic drill or noisy car
70	Busy street
60	Normal conversation
50	Quiet car or quiet restaurant
40	Average office
30	Library
20	Whisper
10	Normal breathing
0	Threshold of hearing

Decibels

FIGURE 3.1   Loudness of normal sounds

The skin senses

What used to be called the sense of touch is now known to be four senses: pressure, pain, cold and warmth. It is not hard to see why these senses were long considered to be one and the same, for in everyday life they are often intermingled into the same sensation. Pain, heat and cold, for instance, are often accompanied by a sensation of pressure. Sensations of tickling and itching are caused by variations in the stimulation of these senses.

Sense receptors are found all over the surface of the skin, although they are not distributed uniformly either in amount or in type. Some areas of the skin are generally more sensitive than others; and some areas contain more of one kind of receptor than another.

Our senses are where we make contact with the environment and a striking illustration of their importance to our functioning is the sense of pain. The stimulation of pain receptors is usually an unpleasant experience, but if they didn't work the result might be much more unpleasant, and even fatal. There are rare cases of people who don't seem to have any sense of pain, and the lack of this warning device has often resulted in their doing physical damage to themselves before they realised what was happening.

Smell and taste

The senses of smell and taste, which we normally think of as being quite different, are even more closely tied to each other than are the four skin senses. In fact if we didn't have a sense of smell the food we eat would have very little taste. You've probably experienced this yourself when you had a head cold and your nose was blocked. If not, try holding your nose while you taste a piece of raw potato and a piece of raw apple. You probably won't be able to tell the difference.

The receptors for the sense of smell are high up in the nasal cavity – too high, in fact, to be in the direct line of the airflow through the nose and down into the lungs. Unless the odour is very strong, therefore, we have to sniff in order to force the air up the nose to the small receptors which are then activated and pass their message along to the brain.

The receptors for the taste sensations are found mainly in the taste buds on the tongue. The tip of the tongue is most sensitive to sweet and salt, the sides of the tongue are most sensitive to sour, and the back of the tongue to bitter. Combinations of these four senses, together with the sense of smell, provide us with the potential for a great variety of taste sensations.

Bodily movement

A sense that most of us don't realize we have is the sense of bodily movement that keeps track of the changing position of our limbs. There are sense organs embedded in the muscles, the tendons connecting muscle to bone and the linings of the joints between the bones. These sense receptors respond to the environment by moving various parts of the body in an appropriate manner. Our sense of bodily movement makes it possible to walk steadily without looking carefully at each step to see where our feet are. When we go to lift a package, the same sense tells us how much muscle power we need to exert and whether we are using too little or too much. The sense of bodily movement is most useful in situations that call for rapid and closely coordinated behaviour and without it most sports we engage in would be quite impossible.

Balance

The sense of balance is linked to the sense of bodily movement. It too is a sense that we are not aware of normally. It is concerned with movements of the whole body rather than the limbs. The organs of balance are composed of three semicircular canals located in the inner ear. These canals are filled with fluid that moves when the head is moved and they keep us oriented to the force of gravity, thereby maintaining our balance when we move.

As the sense organs are our point of contact with the environment, the information they provide us with forms the basis of everything we do. In discussing the various sense organs we noted that they pass their information along to the brain. In the brain the information is sorted into the patterns that seem to make the most sense to us.

Perception

The sense organs provide our brain with a steady flow of information about our environment and the brain's task is then to take this raw material and use it to help us make sense of that environment through the process of perception. And the brain does its job so smoothly and well that we're not even aware of what it does.

Occasionally we come across incidents in our daily lives where the 'sense' we have made of our environment is seen to be illusory. Walking home late at night we turn a corner and jump as we see a mugger lurking in the shadows. A split second later we realize the 'mugger' is actually a tree. Why did we make the mistake and what did we actually see? Well, what we saw was a tree but what we *perceived* was a mugger.

Presumably if we lived in an environment where there were no muggers, and only sabre-toothed tigers lurked in shadows, we might well have seen a sabre-toothed tiger as we turned the corner. The raw material provided by our sensory apparatus is thus a very important component of perception, but it is not the only one. What we see, hear and feel is quite unlearned but if we had to rely only on these sensations to make our way about the world we would be as helpless as an infant.

We have to learn how to interpret and order these sensations in such a way that the environment becomes secure and predictable.

Not only does our past experience of dealing with the world enter into our perceptions but so does our current emotional state and our needs, wishes, fears and desires. Some people are more likely than others to mistake trees for muggers (or sabre-toothed tigers). There are times and places in which we would all make the same mistake.

Focussing and attention

Given the enormous amount of stimuli picked up by our sense organs why is our perceptual process not continually swamped? The answer seems to be that, as very few of the stimuli that impinge on us at any given time are of any importance, we filter out the ones which are important simply by paying attention to them and we ignore the rest.

We focus on whatever stimuli are most important in the environment at any given time. We ignore a constant hum from an air conditioner, for instance, but immediately focus on the machine if it suddenly stops, providing us with a new and possibly important stimulus. If the steady hum returns, the sound of the air conditioner becomes unimportant once more and it recedes to the edge of our awareness. It is this process of focussing our perceptions, bringing them in from the edge, that we refer to as *attention* and attention is crucial in learning something and committing it to memory.

By attending to certain sensory stimuli and not to others, we give them access to our sensory memory, the first stage of the memory process, and they can then move from there to short-term and to long-term memory. Underlying this series of psychological processes are corresponding physiological processes. Thus when one channel of communication between a sense organ and the brain is occupied and has our full attention, the other physiological pathways to the brain are apparently blocked so that we don't become confused and overwhelmed by the other sensory messages.

Selective perception and distortion

We have seen that in order to make sense of our sensations our perceptions have to be selective. But how do we go about making the selection? In order to perceive something we have to give it our attention. But we know from our own experience that our attention is continually shifting. What determines which stimuli will capture our attention?

Psychologists refer to external and internal factors in trying to understand attention-getting and selective perception.

External factors

In our example of the air conditioner we noted that the sound of the machine stayed at the edge of our awareness until it stopped whereupon it captured our attention. It is the stimulus provided by *change* in the environment that is most important. The change can take many forms. Contrast (between sound and silence, for example) is one of them. A man seven feet tall stands out much more on the street than he would on a basketball court. A white television newscaster wearing a see-through dashiki would attract more attention than one in a dark pin-striped suit.

Movement in the environment is another important kind of change. People are very responsive to visual movement, quite automatically. Even the youngest infants will try to follow movements with their eyes and adults will have their attention caught by moving neon signs rather than by stationary ones.

The repetition of a stimulus can sometimes be effective – a phenomenon well known to mothers calling their offspring in from play. Size can also be an important factor, hence newspapers grade the importance of their headlines by the size of the type. The intensity of a stimulus can also catch our attention, so bright colours and loud sounds are often effectively used to gather a crowd to a public event or to sell a product.

Internal factors

The external factors outlined above refer to the stimuli from the environment. However the person perceiving these stimuli does not do so as a neutral observer; different people react to the same sensations in different ways. A woman may put on a sweater because the room is too cold, while her husband throws open the windows. She may sleep through the ringing alarm that wakes him up for work but is instantly awake at the baby's first whimper. When they read the same magazine she will pick out the sales of women's clothing and he the men's.

This man and woman have different interests and motives that they bring to each situation they share. Their emotional and their physical states will change and if they don't happen to feel the same way at the same time they may well have different reactions. But the most important internal factor in perception is what people *expect* to see or hear in each situation. The woman has a mental set to hear her baby cry. She expects it to happen. The man has a mental set to hear the alarm go off at the same time each morning – so much so that he has come to wake up a few seconds before it goes off.

Sometimes this set may be so habitual or so important to a person that he may perceive things that aren't there – like the tree we mistook for a mugger at the beginning of this chapter. Psychologists have discovered some striking examples of such perceptual distortion.

In one study a group of white people who were known to be highly prejudiced against blacks were shown a picture and asked to describe it from memory (Allport and Postman, 1947). The picture depicted a subway carriage with several people in it. The central characters in the scene were a black man and a white man. One of these men was well-dressed and standing quietly in the middle of the carriage. The other was poorly dressed and rough-looking and he was standing in front of the first man threatening him with an open razor. The first man was black; his attacker was white. But the prejudiced white subjects in this study did not have a set to see what the picture showed and so they reported a rough-looking black man threatening a well-dressed white. They had distorted their perception to fit what they expected to see.

Illusions

Internal factors can thus lead us to perceive things differently from the way they really are. But so can external factors. The important difference is that while each person brings a unique group of internal factors to a perceptual situation, the external factors for all the members of a given society are the same. There are some perceptual situations, for example, where we will all react the same way, perceive the same thing, and be completely wrong.

In Figure 3.2 the top line is obviously longer than the bottom line. But if you measure them you'll find they are exactly the same length.

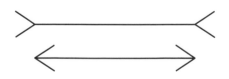

FIGURE 3.2   Length of line illusions

Would you believe that the brim of the top hat in Figure 3.3 is the same length as the height?

And how about the impossible tuning fork in Figure 3.4?

Organizing perceptual cues

These perceptual illusions are very exceptional however and in our daily lives our perceptions are normally accurate and perfectly reliable. But the existence of such illusions has been helpful to psychologists interested in the normal process of perception. Out of a vast number of careful studies has emerged the understanding that the way in which we perceive is highly organized and well ordered. We do not live in a world of changing sound and light waves but in a world of objects, people, music and events. With our perceptions we make sense of our sensations according to some well-established principles that are partly learned and partly due to the structure of the brain and the nervous system. These principles allow us to navigate our way through the world, but they are not perfect – hence impossible tuning forks and trees as muggers.

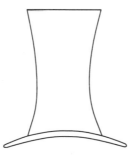

FIGURE 3.3   The vertical-horizontal illusion

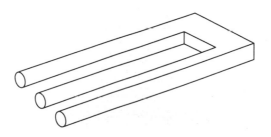

FIGURE 3.4   The impossible tuning fork

(A) FIGURE AND GROUND

Perhaps the most basic of these perceptual principles is the way we perceive things against a background; the way we need a background before we can pick out an object in the environment. Where we cannot separate figure and ground in this way we are unable to see the object we may be looking at; it is hidden or camouflaged. Many animals make use of this principle to evade their predators, like the chameleon that changes colour to blend in with its background.

You are also making use of this principle in reading this book. You are perceiving black print against a white background. When you close the book and put it on the desk it doesn't disappear. You can see it clearly outlined against the background of the desk. We can separate figure and ground in this fashion because of our ability to perceive contour. Contours mark off one thing from another, an object from its background and even a musical theme from its surrounding chords. Figure and ground are both necessary for our perceptions and, as Figure 3.5 shows, they can be interchangeable at times.

When you perceive the white figure, the vase, the black part is the ground. When you perceive the black profiles, the white part becomes the ground. Notice that you can't see both figures at the same time and that no matter how hard you try to focus on one of these figures your attention will shift after a time and focus on the other.

(B) GROUPING

Another important way in which we structure our perceptions is by grouping things into patterns. In Figure 3.6 we see six single lines on top but three pairs of lines on the bottom.

FIGURE 3.5   Vase and profiles

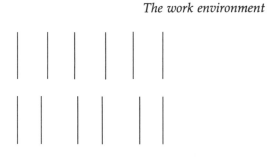

FIGURE 3.6   Organization of lines

(C) CLOSURE

Despite the fact that they are incomplete you recognise the three drawings in Figure 3.7 as a triangle, a square and a circle. If certain things are familiar to us our perceptual process will close the gaps in the picture, thereby providing the necessary contour lines for us to perceive it as a distinct object. We do much the same thing with our language when we read a telegram or a newspaper headline.

(D) GESTALT

The principles of perception we have been discussing are due mainly to the work of a school of German psychologists who took the view that what we perceive is more than just the sum of the sensory stimuli that impinge on us from the environment. We perceive something, they argued, as a *gestalt*, a German word meaning 'form' or 'configuration'. Each gestalt has a lot more meaning to the perceiver than just its sensory properties of size, colour or weight. An apple, a book or a painting may have meaning for us (and be able to affect our behaviour) far beyond a cataloguing of its physical properties no matter how detailed.

Therefore, in perceiving, not only is the whole greater than the sum of its parts but the parts in themselves are not important, or even perceived.

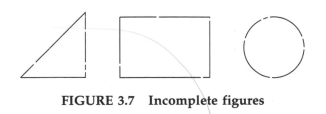

FIGURE 3.7   Incomplete figures

We search constantly for patterns, for order, for wholes that make sense of the parts.

Perceptual constancy: colour, size and shape

There are several other factors we must consider in discussing the way our perceptions are organized. One of these is the fact that while the sensations we receive from the environment are ever-changing, our perceptions of things remain constant. You know for instance that as the eye operates like a camera, images of the objects you look at will appear on your retina as they would on a photograph. So if you set your coffee cup down in front of you and take a picture of it, the picture will show what you see – an elliptical object. But you know your coffee cup is not an ellipse. It's round. How do you know that?

When you're surrounded by people on the street it's quite easy to judge how tall each person is and you would be accurate to within a few inches if you did so. When you're on a country road and you see someone coming towards you from a great distance the image of him on your retina would make him about as tall as an insect. How do you know he's not?

Apparently what we see is not always what we perceive, not just in visual illusions but in our everyday perception. We have to learn the meaning of what we see. Among the things we learn are that black snow at night is really white, that an opening door does not disappear into a vertical line and that buildings seen from the air are really bigger than matchboxes.

Depth and distance

Just as perceptual constancy is so completely a part of our lives that we take it for granted until it is pointed out to us, so the fact that we see a three-dimensional world seems totally unremarkable until we realize that the retina, like the lens of a camera, is a two-dimensional surface. How do we use the two-dimensional information of right-left and up-down that our eyes see to perceive a world of objects, of depth and distance?

It appears that in judging the distance of objects we are very sensitive to various cues from the surrounding environment in a fashion similar to the figure-ground phenomenon we noted above. These cues include the play of light and shadow, perspective and the positioning of other things in the environment. The fact that we have two eyes which give us slightly different images of what we're looking at also plays a part in judging distance.

Movement: movies and the phi phenomenon

The final area of perception we should examine in trying to make sense of what we see is that of movement. Some of the movement we perceive, like a bird flying past the window, can be explained simply as visual stimuli moving across our visual field and stimulating different parts of the eye. However, much of the movement we perceive is also quite illusory and cannot be explained in this fashion.

The most common illusion of movement is perceived in watching a film. A film consists of a series of still photographs, each one slightly different from the preceding one, flashed on to a screen at the rate of about twenty frames per second. At this speed we don't perceive a series of stills, we perceive movement on the screen.

This illusion was studied extensively by the Gestalt psychologists at the beginning of this century when movies were first introduced. They were able to isolate the simplest form of the illusion and examine the conditions under which it appeared.

They discovered that if they flashed two lights on and off in quick succession, given the right time interval between the flashes, people perceived the light as moving between two points. They called this illusion of movement the Phi phenomenon and in addition to being active in our perception of films, it underlies the effectiveness of the moving neon light displays that attract our attention in big cities.

Sex and the single triangle

In dealing with our environment we not only perceive many different objects we also perceive interactions between these objects. We see rain beating on the roof, birds searching for worms, a man chopping wood for the fire, buses halting at stop signs and countless other interactions involving people, animals and inanimate objects.

Central to the way we make sense of these interactions is our need to explain things that happen in terms of cause and effect. By placing yourself at a bus stop (cause), the driver will see you and stop the bus to let you get on (effect). Now how about my neighbour chopping firewood? Unlike myself he doesn't live in a house with a fireplace, he lives in a modern apartment. He's not chopping firewood at all, as it turns out, he's making splints to support the potted plants on his terrace. I have attributed the wrong cause and effect to his behaviour. However I could have been right and until I knew where he lived my explanation of his behaviour was at least plausible.

We have already seen how our need to make sense of our perceptions can lead us to see things that aren't there and to give false explanations for certain events. Fritz Heider took this problem into the laboratory where he devised an animated cartoon consisting of a large triangle, a smaller triangle and a small circle arranged in a series of different positions (Heider and Simmel, 1944).

Because of the animation people saw the three figures moving about. But they saw a lot more than that. When they were asked to describe the cartoon they reported an 'aggressive' triangle 'bullying' a smaller one in 'rivalry' over a 'shy, timid female' circle. Not only did they perceive causation but they saw causation in human social terms.

The Belgian psychologist Albert Michotte has taken this work a step further by trying to isolate the conditions under which people will attribute causality in this way (Michotte, 1954). He gave his subjects a very simple situation to deal with, consisting of a slot with two rectangles, A and B (see Figure 3.8).

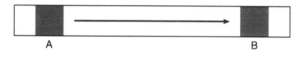

A   B

FIGURE 3.8   Illusion of movement

Michotte moved the rectangles back and forth within the slot at different speeds and in different ways then asked the subjects what they saw. If A was moved quickly to B and then both were moved together to the end of the slot, A had pushed B. If A was moved quickly to B then slowed down while B was moved quickly to the end of the slot, A had hit B. If A was moved slowly to B then stopped, they were getting together.

These examples from Heider and Michotte show quite clearly the tremendous influence of the social context in which we live on the process by which we make sense out of what we see. Without that social context we would have little idea of what it was we were seeing.

Ergonomics/human factors

Introduction

With this background in the processes of sensation and perception we can now introduce the interaction of people at work with machines and equipment and their physical environment in general. As we saw in Chapter 1 with the story of Taylor's shovel this is an area of study that goes back to the late nineteenth century. It is an area now known by various names. In the United States the terms 'human factors', 'human factors engineering' and 'human performance factors' are all used and so, less frequently, are the terms 'human engineering' and 'engineering psychology'. In much of the rest of the world, however, the term most commonly used is 'ergonomics' and, for the sake of simplicity, that is the term which will be adopted in this book.

Though we approach ergonomics here from a psychological viewpoint it is an area of study that makes use of several other sciences in combination with psychology, chiefly anatomy, physiology, engineering and mathematics but including also contributions from such disparate sources as toxicology, sociology and anthropometry.

Though the term 'ergonomics' was first used in 1950 the biggest single impetus to the development of this field took place during the Second World War. One of the less nasty side effects of large-scale war is the great leap in research and development of many areas of psychology. Thus we noted in Chapter 1 how mass intelligence testing arose during the First World War. The Second World War was longer and the use of psychology was even more intense.

A field like ergonomics was obviously of particular relevance to war ministries with the widespread use of ever-more complex forms of technology, like tanks and aircraft, which had increased greatly in speed and power since their introduction in the First World War, and the invention of new technologies like radar and sonar. It was literally a matter of life-and-death to their operators that the ergonomics of these technologies be as efficient and effective as possible. With the return to civilian life for most ergonomists in 1945, the lessons learned in the intensive days of wartime were applied more systematically to the world of work.

The man-machine interface

This frequently used term originated in the early 1960s and focusses on the point of contact between workers and the machines and equipment which they use – a central aspect of ergonomics. The man-machine interface has two such points of contact of particular importance and they are known as *displays* and *controls*. In the case of the former, information is being provided by the machine to the operator; in the latter it is the operator who provides information to the machine.

(A) DISPLAYS

Given the processes of sensation and the limits of human perception which we noted earlier in this chapter it is obviously important for ergonomists to design displays that take these factors into account. Most displays (clocks, dials, telephones, etc.) depend on vision and hearing. Vision is considered to be the more effective modality when there is a great deal of complex information to be perceived and time is not a pressing factor. Obviously when the information is in the form of a design or diagram the display would have to be visual. Auditory displays are preferred when a relatively small amount of simple information is required urgently (Chapanis, 1976).

Both visual and auditory displays take many forms. The most common visual displays include clocks (circular and digital), counters, scales, moving pointers and screens. Research in this area has given rise to a number of simple but important principles in the design of displays, for example that the numbers of a scale should increase only in a clockwise direction, as this is what we would normally expect to see based on our previous experience (Chapanis, 1976).

Another important principle (based on the Gestalt psychology we examined earlier) is the use of different colours for arranging information, for example on a cluttered radar screen. It is much easier for an operator to spot a target object if it is coloured red while everything else is coloured green (Carter and Cahill, 1979). Similarly we can spot a number on a page of letters very quickly, long before we could have recognized each of the letters (Duncan, 1983).

Auditory displays are usually categorised as *signal* or *speech*. Signalling systems are used when something simple, secret or speedy needs to be transmitted to someone able to decode the signal. Examples of this are navigational systems or burglar alarms linked to a police station. Speech is considered more appropriate when the information is complex or may require some kind of interaction. As in the case of the cluttered radar screen a variety of different sound sources can confuse an operator unless, for example, the one she is listening for comes from one direction and the rest (the 'noise') from a different direction. This again is an example of the 'figure and ground' principle of gestalt psychology in operation.

(B) CONTROLS

The fundamental principle for the design of controls (levers, buttons, wheels and so on) is that they should fit as harmoniously as possible with the design of the human anatomy. Controls that are difficult to reach, grasp or operate put undue strain on the arms, legs and trunk and are obviously inefficient.

Controls in everyday use, such as those on a car or truck, are usually well designed, though they can always be improved. But as Taylor showed us, even such a simple and common instrument as a shovel can be badly designed in the demands it makes on the human anatomy. Moreover we now know that controls designed for one kind of usage may be badly designed for another. This is what happened when typewriters gave way to word processors, the resultant changes in office procedure leading (as we shall see in Chapter 16) to Repetitive Strain Injury, a new form of industrial injury.

As we saw in discussing displays it is crucial psychologically for controls to be compatible with our expectations and our sensory experience of the world. That is why it is much easier to learn to steer a car where the steering wheel turns in the direction of movement than a small boat whose tiller must be moved in the opposite direction of movement. The more compatible a control is with our expectations the quicker and more accurately will we be able to use it (Chapanis, 1976).

Finally in this account of the man-machine interface it might be useful to summarize the things that people and machines each do best:

> There are many things that machines can do better than people. They (1) provide power and physical force, (2) engage in repetitive activity without tiring, (3) make calculations and analyse large amounts of data, (4) are capable of long-term monitoring, and (5) can detect small sensory or other signals . . . At present humans are better than machines at (1) dealing with other people in supervision, selection, training and so on, (2) designing new work systems and machines, programming computers, planning new products, (3) making use of a wide range of past experiences in making decisions, as in the case of doctors and research workers, and of being able to learn by experience, (4) being able to deal with a wide range of stimuli or information, as in driving a car or flying a plane, and (5) being able to deal with emergencies, new situations and problems which have not been met before. (Argyle, 1989, pp. 36–7)

This list represents an ideal situation. In practice the relative use of people and machines at work is usually cost-driven. Where labour is cheaper than equipment people will continue to perform tasks that a machine could do more efficiently.

The physical ambience

The man-machine interface is itself contained within a physical work environment, or ambience. This ambience comprises the total sensory stimulation we receive in the form of temperature, light, humidity, air pressure, noise and so on. As we have already seen, the senses we rely on most are vision and hearing and so the ambient sensations we are most responsive to are light and noise.

(A) LIGHT

Different types of work require different amounts of illumination for safety and efficiency, ranging from the dim light that is sufficient for halls or stairways to the brightness required in an operating theatre. Lighting arrangements should also avoid glare and flicker which can affect accuracy of vision and concentration and cause headaches.

(B) NOISE

Defining what constitutes noise in a given situation is a particularly subjective process. One man's music, after all, may well be another man's noise, so it might be best simply to classify noise as any sound the listener doesn't want to hear. What is clear, as we saw in the section on hearing earlier in this chapter, is that prolonged exposure to high decibel levels (Figure 3.1) leads to impaired hearing (La Benz *et al.*, 1967). Noise also creates stress and discomfort, thereby impairing performance at work.

It has long been thought that music which people like can have a beneficial effect on their work. Indeed this was tried on a mass scale during the Second World War when a radio programme called 'Music While You Work' was played in factories all over the United Kingdom. It is certainly true that many people prefer to have music in their workplace, especially young people engaged in monotonous, repetitive and simple tasks but there is little evidence that performance improves as a result. Indeed if anything music may be somewhat more likely to impair performance of a task (Uhrbrock, 1961).

Fatigue and hours of work

Though ergonomics received its greatest boost during the Second World War another important aspect of the work environment had come to prominence during the emergency conditions of the First World War. This was the issue of worker *fatigue* and its relationship to the number of hours worked.

It had actually been established in the middle of the nineteenth century that reducing a mill worker's hours from twelve a day to eleven did not lead to a reduction in output (Smith, 1952). But it was not until the issue of fatigue and performance in factories was specifically examined by British psychologists during the First World War that any general conclusions were drawn for the world of work. In fact it was found that decreasing working hours in heavy industry could actually lead to an *increase* in output. In one case a decrease of hours worked per week from 58.2 to 51.2 resulted in output being increased by 22 per cent (Hearnshaw and Winterbourn, 1945). These findings were later supported by research on American workers during the Second World War (Kossoris *et al.*, 1947).

As well as sheer length of time worked another factor in fatigue and performance is that of rest breaks during the working day. Again it has generally been found that providing rest breaks does not diminish output and can sometimes lead to an increase in output (Miles and Skilbeck, 1944). The frequency and duration of rest breaks depends mainly on the type of work being done. Tasks that require a very high degree of alertness might benefit from a few minutes rest every half hour or so.

Apart from the physical tiredness we have been considering there are also aspects of fatigue that are psychological and probably referred to most commonly as boredom. Boredom may arise, for example, when people have too little work to do and are desperately trying to fill in time, a process every bit as fatiguing as overwork which we will discuss further in Chapter 5. As the visible effects on work of this kind of fatigue are the same as for the subjective feeling of physical tiredness it is very difficult to disentangle the two. Indeed it has been found that both boredom and tiredness are reported by (female) office workers to peak just before lunchtime and the end of the working day (Nelson and Bartley, 1968).

A final factor that adds to the complexity of fatigue and performance for some workers is that of shift work and loss of sleep, and we shall consider these factors in the next chapter when we examine the significance of time on the world of work.

Accidents and human error

In discussing the human senses in the first part of this chapter we glimpsed both their limitations and their fallibility. What the use of increasingly complex equipment at work has done is to map out the boundaries of these limitations and that fallibility in many areas. This has often been done by simply following a process of trial-and-error to see how human operators coped with a particular machine or process or piece of equipment before any attempt was made to modify it.

We noted above how the growth of ergonomics was given a tremendous impetus by the Second World War. Because of wartime conditions technology was put into operation as soon as it was available. Initially it was found that the technology frequently failed, and this was usually put down to 'human error'. In effect what this meant was that the new radar or sonar systems or whatever were simply too complex for the sensory, perceptual and informational processing capacities of their human operators. As the operators could not be redesigned their capacities had to be taken as a starting point and the technology redesigned around them. When this was done human error became a rare occurrence and happened when people and/or equipment were under unusual pressure or suddenly confronted with a new situation.

The term 'human error' is frequently used in connection with accidents. In the attempt to find *the* cause of an accident, particularly a transport accident involving the public like a plane or train crash, human error will often be cited in reports. However it is often difficult to pinpoint any one cause of an accident and there is a danger of blaming *only* the highly visible pilot or driver and ignoring less visible design faults or equipment failure or adverse conditions. There are even rare occasions, as we will see when discussing training in Chapter 12, when the automatic human responses that result from extensive training in complex systems can themselves help cause accidents.

Some people are labelled as 'accident prone' because they seem to be involved in more accidents than their colleagues. Certainly people who are depressed or under unusual stress may be less attentive and able to concentrate on their work, which could have disastrous consequences in a dangerous situation. But these are not the most deep-seated aspects of personality and all of us are liable to experience them at one time or another. Much more important in causing accidents at work are factors like the nature of the job itself, the amount of risk people are asked to take, how much provision and supervision there is of safety measures and equipment and the level of fatigue the individual is experiencing (Stevenson, 1980).

CHAPTER 4

The time dimension

'We live in a time of unprecedented change.'
I. L. Tellem-Howe (business guru)

Introduction

The above 'quotation' could have been taken from almost any of the leading Western business gurus of the day. It is the currently accepted wisdom. And for that reason alone we should, of course, be highly sceptical about it. 'Unprecedented' is a very big claim to make for anything. Applying it to present economic and social conditions is, I would suggest, to betray a lack of awareness about history and the effects of time which is both self-limiting and, ultimately, self-destructive. This chapter will attempt, on the contrary, to heighten that awareness by following the thread of time through many different aspects of psychology and the world of work.

What do we mean by change?

When we talk about 'change' (any kind of change) we really mean *change over time* for comparing the same thing, or person, at different times is the only way we have of knowing that any change has occurred. This is as true of the life and death of stars and sub-atomic particles as it is of commerce and society, or the life and death of individuals.

Economic and social change is usually measured in terms of years, if not decades or even centuries. These seem like long periods of time to us and difficult to grasp. Even more difficult to understand is geological change, measured in millions of years, and cosmological change measured in billions. We are therefore used to thinking of the heavens and the earth as fixed and unchanging because our senses cannot detect any change occurring. In fact change is a constant feature of everything in the universe. Only the time-scale of change differs.

We seem to have a similar difficulty, psychologically, in dealing with the past, where things occurred prior to our own experience. Think how difficult we find it, for instance, to see our parents as the children we know they once were. Photographs and films undoubtedly help but it still takes a leap of imagination to envisage in a different form the people we know as adults. Perhaps we just think of the child and the adult as different people who are in some way related to each other.

How much more difficult will it be then for us to imagine ourselves working for a medieval craftsman, or even on Henry Ford's assembly line, and to relate these experiences to our own working life? It is therefore very tempting to take the line of least resistance and simply not make the effort. And we can do this by seeing the past as perhaps interesting but quite different and of no real relevance to our own life and times, which means it contains no precedents for us to learn from, and therefore our own experience becomes literally, *unprecedented*.

The interacting layers of time

It might be useful to explore this issue of 'unprecedented change' by looking at some of the changes that have occurred in the past century or so, and considering the impact they may have had on people's lives. In Figure 4.1 I have distinguished four major processes (four Is) that can occur over the same periods of time at different levels. These are:

- the level of the *Individual* lifecycle
- the level of *International* or global activity
- the level of technological *Innovation*
- the level of the *Institution*.

These four levels in the flow of time are constantly interacting to form a complex web that links an individual with his or her time and place. At the Individual level I have illustrated the lifecycles of three fictional generations, the grandfather born in 1890, the son in 1920 and the grandson in 1950. We can see that this latter generation, now moving into senior positions in the world of work, has certainly lived through a number of great changes in International activity and the introduction of technological Innovation, and continues to do so.

But let us now look at the grandfather's experiences. He was born into the Victorian age, fought in the trenches of the First World War as a

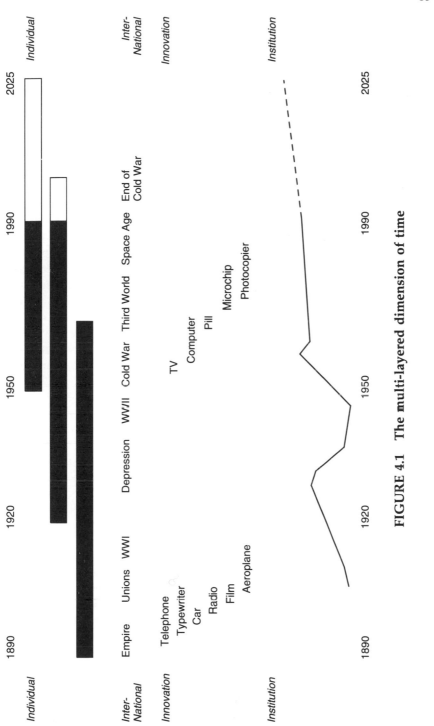

FIGURE 4.1 The multi-layered dimension of time

young man, returned from 'the war to end all wars' to 'a land fit for heroes' where he struggled to raise his family during the Great Depression and recovered from that just in time to endure the Second World War. At work he saw the introduction of the telephone and the typewriter, and the company he joined when it started in 1908 went through many ups and downs as did he. The world he lived in was changed by the car and the aeroplane, by films, radio and television. He grew up with the horse and buggy and he lived to see men walk on the moon. I don't know how you feel about it but that seems like a fair amount of change to me, and a lot more than anything we are ever likely to experience ourselves.

Perhaps it is the tremendous *pace* of technological change in the workplace and in the life of organizations generally that our current gurus have in mind? Well when Henry Ford introduced the assembly line to his car factory in 1913 it may have been the single most revolutionary change in the history of commerce. It was so immediately and spectacularly successful that every other manufacturer of consumer goods tried to copy it. Within ten years the Ford Motor Company had amassed cash reserves (*cash* – none of your leveraged buyouts or mergers or other funny money) of one billion dollars. Yet a few years after that Ford was overtaken by General Motors and by 1929, when the last of 15 000 000 Model Ts trundled off the assembly line, the company was in dire trouble and heading for oblivion. Again, that seems like an awful lot of change – both technological and organizational – in a fairly short period of time.

Well then, maybe the 'unprecedented change' of modern times refers to the great innovations in information technology? Have not the process of computerisation and the invention of the microchip been responsible for radical changes in the way we communicate at work? Well yes and no. A fairly recent review of research in this area, while suggesting that new computer technology would become an integral part of working life at some unspecified future date, also admits that: 'At present the penetration of new technology into work organizations is uneven and in general not high' (Wall, 1987, p. 270).

So about forty years after the introduction of the computer into the workplace this exciting information revolution in the world of work was still vaguely to be glimpsed some time in the uncertain future. The introduction of the telephone at the end of the nineteenth century was a lot more successful than that in the transmission of information, and it had a radical effect on people's lives both at work and outside it. Just try to imagine life without telephones.

For an even greater example of an information revolution I would suggest we look at what may have been the most influential technological innovation of all time for the whole of society, printing.

The printing process was invented in the middle of the fifteenth century in Germany and quickly spread throughout the Western world. It immediately became a powerful contributor to the intellectual, political and religious upheavals of Europe and an agent of great change in people's attitudes to knowledge, its transmission and its reception (for example see Small, 1982).

It is worth noting that between the years 1517–1521 Martin Luther, the Protestant reformer, sold about 300 000 copies of his works. Even today that would almost make him a best-selling author. With a population that was a small fraction of the current one and few people who could read, it was a staggering achievement and it highlights the success of what was really the first application of machine methods to the mass production of consumer goods.

Which still leaves us scratching our heads about the reason for the practically universal claim that change in our time is 'unprecedented'. Why is the claim made, and made so strongly? The answer, I think, lies in the psychology of the current business culture which, as we have seen already and will explore further below, has little sense of the past and is thus unable to put current events in the perspective of time and to make a comparative judgement.

The historian A. J. P. Taylor once pointed out that a series of books on the-death-of-civilization-as-we-know-it began to come out of Oxford just after the First World War. Oddly enough this was just when the upheaval in the labour market meant that domestic servants were a lot more expensive to maintain than they had been previously. And Oxford professors found they now had to do their own washing up . . .

I think a similar psychological process is at work in the world of business, and therefore of the business guru, and it can be encapsulated in the following newspaper headline: JAPAN OVERTAKES UNITED STATES AS WORLD'S RICHEST NATION. The post-World War II generation has grown up with the (justified) belief that the United States was the richest and most powerful nation the world had ever seen. This was accompanied (especially, of course, in the States) by the implicit and unquestioned assumption that it would always be that way. And this made for a perceived business environment of stability and order; of what seemed to be timelessness and changelessness. Commentators had known for quite a few years that Japan was becoming a very wealthy country and in trade terms it was clearly perceived as a serious rival to the United States. But the publication of economic statistics in 1989 making this official came as a psychological shock none the less.

This, I would suggest, is the real 'unprecedented' change that forms the (mainly American) business guru's unspoken agenda. The end of the American economic and political hegemony, the United States becoming one large power among others, the realisation that American wealth and power is not limitless, is certainly an unprecedented situation in this century and it will indeed require a swift and a radical change of attitudes, not least among the American business community. However it is not the first dominant economic power to be overtaken by others and it might profitably think again about Henry Ford's unfortunate dictum that 'history is bunk'.

If the present situation is truly 'unprecedented' then we really would be in the realm of the unknown with nothing to guide us. As we will see more than once in later chapters people find that very upsetting psychologically and are prone to clutch and do all sorts of irrational things in order to feel more comfortable. I would suggest that the overreaction by business gurus to the International situation is perhaps one such irrational response. But irrationality has its psychological roots and in this case they lie deeply buried in our conception of time itself.

The psychology of time

Only a philosopher or a physicist would attempt a definition of time. It is a very complex phenomenon indeed, a fundamental part of human existence; and the more you think about it the more complex it gets. We will confine ourselves to those aspects of time that are relevant to psychology and to work, but even these limits encompass a vast amount of material which we can only attempt to summarise and highlight.

The psychology of time deals with our attitudes towards time and our subjective experience of it. A leading writer on the subject has called it 'the framework within which our personality is organized. When it is absent we are disorientated' (Fraisse, 1964, p. 289). And these attitudes and that experience is intimately bound up with the world of work. The introduction to a recent scholarly review of the subject puts it thus:

> Time is one of the central preoccupations in contemporary industrial society: enormous effort is expended in designing ways to increase the amount of activity which can be done in a given time . . . for our industrial society, a primary determinant of the experience of and attitudes to time is the experience of work . . . The kind of work individuals are in, the kind of work-organizations they belong to assume a primary importance when it comes to issues concerning individual and collective time. (Blyton *et al.*, 1989, p. 1)

We will deal with the nature of time under three main headings, *linear time, cyclical time* and *steps, stages and seasons*.

Linear time

Linear time is probably our most salient view of time. In it we view time as flowing, in a straight line, from the past to the future via the present. One assumption – often unconscious – which accompanies this view of time is that the future, whatever it may be, will naturally be different from the past. Therefore to the extent that our present life involves planning for, and being influenced by, our view of the future, our attention will necessarily be deflected from a past which might seem (almost by default) of little relevance.

Allied to this view of time is that of 'progress' as also being linear. This view is heavily influenced by the development of science and technology, where steady progress over time in understanding and knowledge is self-evident. Until very recently it was widely accepted that this was also true in social and material terms. It seemed that at every level from the Individual to the International people were getting healthier, living longer and enjoying greater prosperity with each succeeding generation. Indeed one of the psychological engines driving the industrial machine was that of people working towards a better life for their children than they had had themselves.

For the first time, perhaps, since the Industrial Revolution this unconscious assumption of continuous progress over time is being widely questioned. The effects of political and economic policies leading to unemployment and lack of job security (or work alternatives), as well as social upheavals and environmental concerns, have forced upon many people throughout the world the conclusion that not only is the present worse than the past but the future for their children may be even worse than the present. Psychologically this can be a devastating realisation, and that is why governments will stand on their heads to persuade their citizens that there really is hope for the future.

Clock time

The way we usually experience linear time in our everyday lives is via the clock. Clock time is the basis upon which we order and organize practically everything we do, from when we get up to when we go to sleep. While the clock as a way of measuring the passage of time is not a modern invention – it was known, for example, to the Ancient Egyptians – its universal usage and its measurement of time in ever smaller and more accurate segments dates from the Industrial Revolution. Before then the single (hourly) hand on the sundial sufficed for all of a society's needs. We now have atomic clocks that can measure time in nanoseconds (billionths of a second).

The development of clock time was crucial to the process of industrialization. Indeed the clock has been considered even more important than the steam engine in that respect because, as we noted in the first chapter, it allowed for the external control of the work process and the coordination of the work force who were involved in it (Mumford, 1934). In the pre-industrialised work of work people would normally work at a task until it was finished, with the duration of the task a secondary issue. After industrialization work became organized by the clock, with workers starting and stopping work at a pre-arranged time, often regardless of the task in hand. Punctuality and regularity of timekeeping by workers became crucial aspects of the world of work.

For the factory owners who organized the work process there were two financial incentives involved in the use of work time. One was to get people to work as many hours as possible for as low a rate as possible and the other was to obtain maximum productivity for the hours that were worked (and paid for).

As we saw in Chapter 3 these two goals could be mutually contradictory at a certain point when a *reduction* in hours could actually lead to increased productivity. In any event work time became a commodity, to be bought and sold like any other. Time, in other words, became money. Given the limited nature of human capacity and the unlimited desire for profits the commodity of work time inevitably became a scarce resource for both individuals and organizations. And as a combination of social pressure, trade union activity and self-interest led employers to agree on a shorter working week so they became increasingly concerned to obtain the maximum output from the hours worked.

THE EXPERIENCE OF TIME AND WORK

The workers' experience of time at work has clearly been different from that of their employers'. This experience is usually divided into three closely interlinked *qualitative* factors, *duration, pace* and *intensity* .

(a) Duration   Duration refers to the *subjective* judgement of a period of time rather than the objective measurement of it. That is, how long does a period of time feel like as opposed to how much time has elapsed on the clock? As Einstein is supposed to have said in the course of explaining his theory of relativity to a young man 'a few hours spent with your girlfriend can seem like a few seconds but a few seconds sitting on a hot stove can seem like hours'.

There is evidence that for people in particularly boring and monotonous jobs the eight, ten, twelve hours stretching ahead of them at the start of the day can feel like an unbearable eternity with no horizon in sight. The way that workers in such a situation make it bearable psychologically is by imposing some meaning on their largely meaningless experience (Roy, 1960; Burawoy, 1979. See KEY STUDY 2).

This imposed meaning takes the form of breaking the work day up into several artificially created time horizons by organizing a series of social interactions at regular times throughout the day for talking, eating, horseplay and so on. The day thus consists of a series of bite-sized time chunks which can be 'eaten' one at a time. This is a form of the gestalt psychology we encountered in Chapter 3 when discussing the process of perception and the way people make sense of their environment. In this case workers are creating artificial sense out of nothingness.

However in other occupations, particularly managerial ones, duration can seem very short indeed. There has been a trend, beginning at the turn of the twentieth century, for time intervals in managerial work to shorten, in meetings and telephone conversations for instance (Kern, 1983). This has tended to make for a very fragmented work day (see for example Stewart, 1967 and Mintzberg, 1973) and many managers have the opposite problem to the workers mentioned above, that is how to *lengthen* their time horizons and impose some coherence on their working day.

(b) Pace   Pace has to do with the feeling of how quickly or slowly time is passing. 'Is that the time already?' is a frequent cry of the busy manager. 'Is that all it is?' would be more likely from the shop floor workers with longer time horizons. It is closely related to judgements of duration.

(c) Intensity   Intensity is the term given to the experience of time as being relatively empty or full. The more there is happening over a period of time, and where we are involved in the work, the more quickly time seems to pass. Empty time, where little is happening, seems to drag. However if we are performing a task that demands great attention time seems to stretch so that the more intense the attention required the longer we feel the period of time to be (Fraisse, 1964).

We have seen that work organizations have come to exert pressure for greater intensity of work time as the official hours worked have decreased. But this trend has encouraged many white collar workers unofficially to extend their hours of work by filling non-work hours bordering the working day. Working lunches, dinners and even breakfasts are a prominent example of this phenomenon. So is the filling of otherwise empty time spent in travelling to or from work. This trend can only increase with the widespread use of technology like mobile telephones and lap-top computers.

The intensification of time has encouraged organizations to try to eliminate as much empty time at work as possible. This process can take various forms. Activities may be scheduled as tightly as possible so that, for example, a minimum amount of time is spent on waiting for machines to be made ready or computers to come on line. And any such waiting time may be filled with activities like filing or checking which are less time-constrained.

In manufacturing industry the 'Just-in-Time' system of production and stock control is now widely used to eliminate empty time. This system attempts to organize the flow of materials so that items only appear on line at the time they are required, so minimising time spent in obtaining them from suppliers or stockrooms for example. When it works well this system is capable of delivering a car seat to an automobile assembly plant at twenty-minute intervals (Blyton *et al.*, 1989).

But there can also be a downside to such efficiency in the use of time. The unremitting intensity of some jobs that result from it can seriously affect the physical and mental health of workers, as we will see in Chapter 5 and Chapter 6. Moreover it has been suggested that valuable thinking and decision making time may be lost by having virtually instantaneous electronic communication, and this may well have contributed to the stock market crash of 1987. The absence of the accustomed time lags in communication between world financial centres leaves no time for reflection and puts a premium on instant reaction (Blyton *et al.*, 1989).

OCCUPATIONAL DIFFERENCES

We noted above that one of the primary effects of industrialization was to make work time-driven rather than task-driven. Psychologically this meant that a worker no longer ordered his own time and organized his own work according to the demands of a particular task, whether it was harvesting a crop or making a table, or even teaching students. After industrialization his work time was ordered by the impersonal, rigid and abstract agency of the clock. It has often been said that for many workers, especially those in industry or large bureaucratic organizations, this led to a feeling of being alienated from their work.

There are still, of course, great occupational differences in people's ability to order their own time. At one end of the scale workers on assembly lines probably have least freedom in this respect. At the other end of the scale professionals such as college teachers, despite the constrictions of scheduled classes and meetings, appear to have most freedom. It is probably not entirely coincidental that, as we will see in later chapters, these two types of work are also widely divergent on scales of job satisfaction, stress and so on.

However other professionals, where there are few schedules to be kept, are often paradoxically less free in their experience of time. This is especially true of self-employed people, all of whose time can theoretically be ordered at their discretion, but who often feel compelled to devote almost all their waking hours to work. It is as though these people have given up their freedom of choice and instead of being masters of the clock they have become its slaves (Pahl and Pahl, 1971). It is also possible, though, to find professionals who feel they have enough money for their needs and are willing, consciously, to exchange further income for more time.

Cyclical time

As its name implies the cyclical view of time is concerned with repeated events that occur at regular and predictable intervals. Unlike linear time, therefore, it is *ahistorical* and anticipates that a given experience will be the same in the future as it was in the past. As we noted in Chapter 1 pre-industrial societies were primarily ordered by cyclical time events like the seasons, the phases of the moon and the alternation of night and day.

While our lives are so greatly affected by linear time this does not mean that we have no contact with cyclical time. It is not as though our society has outgrown it. And while we can turn night into day with technology, for instance, and work at any time, we will discover below that there can be psychological costs to doing so. We may be similarly unaffected at work by the seasons yet summer is still when most vacation time is taken. Our experience of linear time thus overlays rather than replaces that of cyclical time.

CIRCADIAN RHYTHMS

Our experience of cyclical time is most salient in the area of our physiological systems. The obvious ones are the menstrual cycle – linked to the moon's phases of course – and the cycle of sleep and waking, one of our *circadian* rhythms. The term 'circadian' is Latin, meaning 'about a day', and is used to describe our various daily physiological cycles of activity. Circadian rhythms include the secretion of hormones, blood pressure, temperature and so on. They are like internal biological clocks. For instance our daily body temperature is lowest around 4.00 am and rises to its peak in the afternoon or evening.

While we are not normally aware of most of these circadian rhythms our sleep/waking cycle is of continuous salience in our lives, and indeed has been the subject of research since the mid-nineteenth century. It has long been recognised that biologically we are a diurnal species which has evolved to be active during daylight and to sleep at night. But as we have seen, the process of industrialization has led to this situation being reversed for increasing numbers of people and for an increasing proportion of the industrialised workforce.

Psychologists have been studying the way people perform tasks at different times of the day since the end of the nineteenth century, originally from the managerial viewpoint of optimizing work schedules (Folkard, 1987). A more recent finding to emerge from this area of research is that there seem to be two different types of daily rhythm that divides people into 'morning' and 'evening' types (Kerkhoff, 1985). Morning types wake early, get up quickly and feel tired early, while evening types wake up later and take longer to get going but stay up late at night. The performance of morning types on a simple task tends to deteriorate as the day goes on while that of evening types improves (Horne *et al.*, 1980).

It would obviously be most efficient for morning and evening types – or 'larks' and 'owls' as they are also known – to arrange their workday in accordance with their individual predilection. But for a lot of people this is simply not possible. In any event the world of work is organized mainly for the benefit of larks, who are apparently in a majority. There is also social pressure in this direction, with the unquestioned presumption that getting up early is A Good Thing.

The sleeping/waking cycle is usually synchronized with our other circadian rhythms. But this cycle is not quite synchronized with the external 24 hour clock. If we were isolated from all external clocks our internal clock would be more likely to average a 25 hour cycle of sleeping/waking. We make the necessary adjustment to external social demands without being aware of it.

Jet lag

Our circadian rhythms are not always synchronized however. In particular, body temperature and sleeping/waking cycles may get out of synch, for example when we travel through different time zones and our biological clock is giving us different messages from the external clock. If we fly from Europe to the United States, for instance, we will arrive with our circadian rhythms between five and nine hours too early for the local clock.

We may get to sleep all right at the usual time but will probably be woken up in the middle of the night by our body temperature telling us it's morning. The temperature rhythm usually takes about a week to adjust and until then it will probably disturb our sleeping/waking rhythm (Klein *et al.*, 1972). Circadian rhythms being out of synch with each other underlie the kind of symptoms of tiredness and disorientation that we refer to as 'jet lag'.

Jet lag is usually more pronounced in eastward rather than westward flights. The reason for this is that bringing forward our biological clock is more difficult for our body to handle than delaying it. Our natural 25-hour cycle means that if we are removed from our usual time framework of activities our circadian rhythms will tend towards delaying rather than advancing (Folkard, 1987). (At least that's the theory. Personally I'm always shattered travelling in either direction.)

Shiftwork

Unless your work regularly takes you on flights across time zones the disorientation and minor physical symptoms associated with jet lag are only temporary. On the other hand people who *are* regularly in this kind of situation will be called upon to make a profound adjustment to their lives, both physiologically and psychologically. In this respect they will face similar issues of adjustment and coping as people on 24-hour shiftwork. People who find it difficult to cope with shiftwork do so because their body temperature and sleeping/waking cycle are out of synch (Reinberg *et al.*, 1984).

Only a minority of shiftworkers seem to have long-term problems however. Most people seem able to cope reasonably well psychologically with the different sleeping patterns and unsocial hours, particularly of the night shift. None the less, given the pressure to utilise resources as fully as possible, shiftwork has become increasingly common throughout the world over the course of the twentieth century, and so in absolute terms more and more people are having difficulties. It has also been found that the effects of shiftwork can be chronic and may not show up in the form of poorer health for a good many years (Kundi *et al.*, 1979).

There is also some evidence that people working the night shift generally tend to be less productive and also more prone to errors and accidents (Folkard, 1987). The cumulative effects of lost sleep can apparently lead to the kind of temporary muscle paralysis that is found in certain phases of the sleep cycle, as well as a general impairment of functioning at work. There is therefore a serious question as to whether the advantages of 24-hour shiftwork – in occupations where there is a choice – outweigh the disadvantages (Folkard, 1987).

One way of coping with the sleep disturbances of shiftwork is by changing the timing of sleeping periods. In particular a four-hour sleep in the afternoon might be very helpful. As many people can testify from their own experience at work, our biological clock seems already set for us to take a sleep after lunch (Folkard, 1987). Perhaps the Latin countries have their working hours most in tune with human biology, with the work day bisected by the afternoon siesta.

Links between linear and cyclical time

We have already noted that linear time and cyclical time are closely interwoven and not to be regarded as totally discrete and separated from each other. It is worth taking a closer look at some of the forms this interweaving can take.

THE RHYTHMS OF WORK

We noted in Chapter 1 that vestiges of the pre-industrial world of cyclical time survived in working communities like farmers and fishermen who live closer to the seasons than other people. We also noted that the work of these communities is often recorded in song. Many of these songs are written in a rhythm that mirrors the rhythm of the work itself, like sea shanties on sailing ships for example.

Indeed the origin of much rhythm and blues music lies in the work of field hands and railroad workers going back to the time of slavery in the Southern States of America. The point of these songs is *synchronization*, making sure that everybody in the work group performs their tasks as a unit at the same time (Moore, 1963).

Such synchronization is easy to see in this form but in fact it exists in all organizations where close coordination of workers is required, in making widgets or music and producing television programmes as much as building pyramids and hauling fishing nets (Moore, 1963). In other words it is embedded in what we think of as a linear time frame.

Different occupations also have a different annual rhythm to their work. In many countries the income tax year is not the same as the calendar year, for instance, so accountants and revenue officials may have a year that runs from April to April, with peaks and troughs of work that differ accordingly. Or take academics and teachers whose year may begin in September/October and end in May/June, with a long break between years.

Service industry suppliers like telephone companies may have peak and off-peak rates for their services on different days of the week and different times of day. And the travel industry has several peak seasons, in July and August and at Christmas and Easter, plus lesser peaks at weekends and public holidays.

It is clear that at any given point in the year people in different organizations may have very different time horizons. In fact as we noted in Chapter 2 even people within the same organization can have different time horizons, with the sales and marketing people having a much shorter horizon than the research and development people. And these differences may be reflected in the way they regard their jobs, their interests and the organization they all work for.

WORKER/MANAGER TIME

We also noted in Chapter 2 that a potential conflict of interests existed in organizations where there was a clear distinction between workers and management. It has been suggested that this inherent conflict is reflected in different time orientations at work, with management oriented towards linear time and workers towards cyclical time (Ditton, 1979).

Management seems obsessed by the dictates of the clock and the machinery. Workers on the other hand can use their intimate knowledge of the recurrent cycles of work events to manipulate time and exercise some control over it. This includes the pacing of the work so as to create strategies for taking time out in the form of unofficial breaks for refreshment. Where the job is monotonous, undemanding and boring, and time drags, the worker's only thought is to put in his time and get it over with – until the next day when the cycle starts all over again.

The manager's criteria of increasing production and improving quality are alien, in this context, to the worker's needs, for he works in a different time. Where there is never enough time for the manager and he chases it ceaselessly, for the worker there is nothing *but time and he can see no end to it*.

Steps, stages and seasons

So far we have looked at two of the interacting layers of time in Figure 4.1, the International and Innovation layers. In this section we will look at the other two, the Individual and Institution layers. We will examine them in terms of the different periods of time that both individuals and organizations pass through in the course of their life cycle, from birth and growth through maturity to eventual decline and death.

INDIVIDUAL LIFE STAGES

When psychologists talk of *stages* they are referring to a process of development that takes place in a series of sequential and progressive *steps* where each step subsumes all the preceding ones. These stages may deal with the largely physical behaviour of infant development (Gesell and Amatruda, 1947) or the cognitive development of children and adolescents (Piaget, 1953) or emotional development over the whole lifespan (Erikson, 1963).

We will look at this work in more detail when we discuss personality factors in Chapter 9. What concerns us here is the idea that there are timetables of development; physical, mental, emotional and social, which everyone goes through roughly in the same way and (very roughly) at a similar age. In modern industrial society, moreover, these timetables are almost invariably out of synch with each other. Young women are biologically capable of bearing children, for instance, when they are still at school being treated as children themselves.

Nevertheless industrial societies are organized as if all these different timetables *were* synchronized and applied to everyone at exactly the same age. So children start school at the same age and normally progress through the educational process in age-graded classes. Most people who go on to higher education are aged around eighteen. And there are legal minimum ages for buying alcohol, getting married, voting, military service and all the other public activities that a society considers important.

The world of work is similarly age-graded. A widely accepted series of lifecycle stages in one's orientation towards work would be something like that shown in Table 4.1, though the specified ages are merely intended as a guide.

This is of course an ideal model, as its proponents recognise. There are great variations between individual timetables, though the broad stages are thought generally to hold good. It is also clearly based on the male rather than the female experience of work. And on the white, middle-class experience of work rather than that of poor people or minorities, who may count themselves lucky to have any kind of employment at all. Neither does it take account of the case of people changing careers or being made redundant.

So at any given time it probably applies to no more than a fraction of the labour force of industrial societies. Yet this model is still seen as being the social norm, with the psychologically important corollary that people whose working lives do not follow it are therefore regarded as unusual, abnormal and out of synch with social expectations.

We learn the 'correct' age for doing things very early in our lives and being out of synch with social expectations, and what other people are doing, can be a source of anxiety and stress (Hagestad and Neugarten, 1985). People will often worry about not being married by the age of thirty or not having children by the age of forty for instance, as if that made them psychologically abnormal. The same is true of the world of

TABLE 4.1   Life stages and the world of work

---

1. *Growth stage* (Birth to 14 years)
    (a) Fantasy (4–10 years) ● play includes role-playing and fantasy about work
    (b) Interests (11–12 years) ● a liking for particular kinds of work develops
    (c) Capacity (13–14 years) ● abilities and job requirements are considered

2. *Exploration stage* (15–24 years)
    (a) Tentative (15–17 years) ● tentative choices of occupation made and discussed
    (b) Transition (18–21 years) ● reality effects of first contacts with work or training
    (c) Trial (22–24 years) ● trying out first job with a view to finding appropriate work

3. *Establishment stage* (25–44 years)
    (a) Trial (25–30 years) ● making appropriate field permanent; perhaps changing jobs
    (b) Stabilization (31–44) years ● creating secure place in world of work

4. *Maintenance stage* (45–64 years)
    Consolidating what has been established

5. *Decline stage* (65–70 years)
    (a) Deceleration ● age of official retirement; perhaps part-time work
    (b) Retirement (71+) ● work ceases completely, either voluntarily or involuntarily

---

Source: Super and Bohn (1971).

---

work where, for example, many people feel pressure to be at least at the same level in the organizational hierarchy as their peers of the same age.

COHORTS

People born in the same year or so are said to belong to the same age *cohort*. If we look at Figure 4.1 again we will see that the three individual lifecycles illustrated represent three different cohorts spaced a generation apart from each other. Each cohort will go through the biological lifecycle at the same time, of course, but they will also experience historical time together. Social and political events, technological inventions and so on will all be experienced by these people – and the people a year or two older or younger – in the same season of their life.

This simple fact can have a marked difference in the way people of different generations feel and think about the same historical events. For example the generation of 1890 was middle-aged and living at home during the Second World War, while the generation of 1920 was actively engaged in it, often overseas. And to the generation of 1950 it was already in the past, to be read about as history. The lives of the middle generation were most directly affected by this event, the 1890 generation less so and the 1950 generation only indirectly.

Or take a cultural example. The 1950 cohort grew up with television, the 1920 cohort with radio and the 1890 cohort with neither – but with newspapers. The way each of these cohorts views the world through these different media of communication, including the world of work, will therefore probably be systematically different – though in ways at which we can only guess.

Another way in which historical differences can affect people's lives is in the growth and spread of new forms of understanding. This is particularly marked in the field of health, for example (Nadien, 1989). It is now widely understood that the risk of illnesses like strokes and heart disease can be greatly reduced by appropriate diet and exercise, by not smoking, and by avoiding excess alcohol. Our 1950 cohort is in a position to take advantage of this understanding, and has benefited from it, but it may well have come too late for their parents. Similarly the 1950 cohort was protected from the crippling effects of polio by the invention of a vaccine that was unavailable to earlier generations who suffered badly from the disease.

THE SEASONS IN THE LIFE OF THE ORGANIZATION

The final layer of time in Figure 4.1 – our fourth 'I' – is that of the Institution. While nothing is forever some institutions last longer than others. Compare for instance the British monarchy with that of Iran, which came and went in two generations during the mid-twentieth century. Work organizations are institutions whose longevity follows the monarchical example. Public sector organizations in industrial societies tend to follow the British model of preserving continuity through periods of great change (though how long this will continue – in either public sector or monarchy – is an open question). Commercial organizations on the other hand tend to follow an Iranian model. It is a rare company that maintains an independent identity for more than a couple of generations.

However such a long-lived organization is represented by the graph in Figure 4.1: the Wizard Widget Corporation, loosely based on an actual company. We can see how WWC has grown enormously since its birth in the early years of the twentieth century. And its prospects for continued growth look healthy well into the twenty-first century. But there have been some serious problems along the way and indeed the company almost died in the 1940s.

Our three-generation family each worked for WWC from their late teens onwards. Grandad was there in the exciting days when the company was just taking off. They were young and vigorous together. The first twenty years were ones of great expansion and growth. Profits soared and the labour force increased enormously. Then the competition caught up with them, senior management ran out of ideas and the company went into a steep decline. Then came the Great Depression. Grandad was laid off – after twenty years' service.

By the early 1940s the company was barely in existence, though by then the son had joined the organization. Even with his family connection the son had to accept a job that did not match up to his abilities and for a very poor salary at that. It was a bleak introduction to the world of work, but WWC was a local employer and the son was glad just to have a job.

During the Second World War the son served in the army and returned to WWC in 1945 to find a changed company. The depressed and depressing atmosphere had gone and the company was expanding rapidly once again. A new and more enlightened senior management had taken over in his absence. Lucrative contracts had been widely available from a war-time economy that was desperate for widgets and this was immediately followed by a post-war boom in civilian applications of widgets. Profits increased even more steeply than they had in the company's youth. New export markets were entered successfully and the company became a multinational corporation. It thrived, and so did the son.

By the time the grandson was ready to enter WWC in the late 1960s it was a very different organization from the one his grandad had joined nearly sixty years before. It was now a very large and complex organization with an intricate management structure. Although its profits had recently taken a dip due to some poor marketing decisions, compared to the company's previous collapse in profits this was just a blip in a story of continuous progress, even if that progress was now slow and steady rather than spectacular.

The organization the grandson entered afforded him neither the excitement his grandad had first experienced nor the depression his father had suffered. He experienced his first work organization as steady, secure, cautious, ordered and complex.

We can describe these periods of expansion, contraction or consolidation as the seasons of an organization's life. They are related to internal developments in the way the organization is run and to external developments like the economic and political situation worldwide, the effects of new technology, the appearance of new markets and so on. All these developments are situated in the flow of time, as are the lifecycles of the individuals who work in them. What young people want from a job when they first enter the world of work is quite different from what they will want from a job in 20, 30 or 40 years' time. Moreover what they will bring to a job at different ages will also be very different. The expectation is that youth will bring energy and openness while maturity will bring experience and judgement.

JOB LONGEVITY

The final layer of time that we should consider runs through both individual and organizational life history. This is simply the amount of time someone spends in a job. It has been found that different aspects of the job are important to people at different periods (Katz, 1978. See KEY STUDY 3). The suggestion is that there are three broad periods of time involving different orientations towards doing the same job:

(i)   *socialization* (0–6 months)
     ● the task itself and how one is doing it is all important.
(ii) *innovation* (6 months to 5 years)
     ● all aspects of the job are important.
(iii) *adaptation* (5+ years)
     ● the context of the job becomes most important, ie. pay, benefits, relations with colleagues and supervisor.

The factor of job longevity appears to have these effects on the behaviour of a given worker over time *other things being equal*. But as we have seen all the way through this chapter, in the time dimension other things are never equal. The different layers of time that we have tried to disentangle and examine never operate in isolation. We need only draw a vertical line at any point in Figure 4.1 to see that every individual is affected by all the layers of time at almost any point in his or her life.

Finally we should note that people acquire their basic orientation to time from their culture, and this orientation is reflected in the language used to describe time. In the African language of Schambala, for instance there are no words for past or future. There is only a 'today' and a 'not-today'. In English time *flies*; in Spanish it *walks*. British politicians *stand* for office, but Americans *run*.

In our brief look at the hugely complex dimension of time we have highlighted the major aspects that apply to psychology and the world of work. But that is not the end of the story for us. It is more of an introduction, for the effects of the time dimension will come up in a wide variety of contexts throughout the rest of this book.

We began this chapter with a quote from a contemporary guru: 'we live in a time of unprecedented change'. We have seen how this simplistic linear view of time is only one part of the jigsaw. It is *literally* true, in the sense of the Greek philosopher who pointed out that you can never step into the same river twice because the water continues flowing on between times. But psychologically that is hardly a profound truth, and we end this chapter with a quote from a much older and somewhat wiser guru, in the Old Testament:

> The thing that hath been, it is that which shall be; and that which is done is that which shall be done; and there is no new thing under the sun. (Ecclesiastes 1, 9)

CHAPTER 5

Work and mental health

Health and sickness at work: learning from the Mad Hatter

It has commonly been known for thousands of years that certain occupations carried health hazards. Tanners and dyers were always prone to skin diseases, for example, and coal miners to black lung disease. More recently we have learned that building workers who deal with asbestos are at risk of lung cancer and there is current concern about the possible radiation hazards faced by operators of Visual Display Units.

Perhaps the most striking instance of an occupational hazard has entered the English language through the phrase 'mad as a hatter'. But what made hatters act strangely and appear 'mad' had nothing to do with their emotional life. It was not a psychological problem at all. In fact it was caused by the effects of inhaling vapours, from the mercury used in the felting of the hats, on the workers' central nervous system. In other words, a form of brain damage. But until the effects of the mercury was discovered it could plausibly be assumed that only odd people went in for hatmaking. We will explore some of the links between personality and occupation later in this chapter and, from a different perspective, in Chapter 9, but let us just note here that we are justified in being a little suspicious of any such neat-looking links between the two.

Occupational hazards such as these are the easiest aspects of ill health and work to identify. However they account for only a small part of the working days lost each year through ill health. Many millions of working days, costing many billions of dollars, are in fact lost each year in industrialized countries. That is many times as much as is lost to industrial action, though you'd never know it from the amount of media attention devoted to each (Steers and Rhodes, 1984). But the majority of lost working days are probably due to problems of what is usually called mental health rather than physical health.

Health and mental health

Just as the relationship between mind and body has long been thought to be both complex and close, so has the relationship between physical and mental health. Psychological or mental health is usually taken to be a state of emotional, cognitive and behavioural well-being. Mental ill-health involves the malfunctioning of these aspects. In the past century or so more and more physical diseases have been recognised as having a strong psychological component to them. These are now known as *psychosomatic* illnesses from the Latin 'psyche' (mind) and 'soma' (body).

Psychosomatic illnesses take three forms:

(a) *stress*
   - where people have difficulty in coping with occupational or personal pressures, for example coronary heart disease, stroke and stomach ulcers. Much of this chapter will be devoted to exploring stress and its effects.

(b) *triggers*
   - where people have sensitivities or allergies to particular environmental conditions, foods and so on which are triggered off by psychological factors.

(c) *personality*
   - where someone's basic personality predisposes them to certain illnesses, for example abnormally anxious people and respiratory problems. It has become difficult in some cases, as we shall see, to distinguish between (a) and (c).

There is a growing school of psychological thought which believes that *all* physical illness is also psychological to a greater or lesser extent. If we accept this hypothesis it would mean that virtually all absences from work which are attributed to ill health – other than the occupational hazards described above – have psychological causes. That is, for all practical purposes 'health' in the workplace means mental health.

We may even add many injuries due to workplace accidents to this category because, as we saw in Chapter 3, people who are emotionally upset are more accident-prone than usual. Indeed this may even be true of people who take time off work because they are 'bored' or 'fed up'.

Some jobs are, of course, mind-numbingly boring by any standards and the wonder there is that people can stand to be present at all rather than occasionally absent. But nevertheless people can describe themselves as being bored or fed up in any job, no matter how exciting others might find it.

The crux of this issue lies in the way people use the term 'bored'. To a clinical psychologist an expression of boredom where there is no apparent reason for it suggests a mask for underlying emotions that are not being dealt with, and the suspicion is that they may be negative ones like anger and frustration. Feelings like these don't simply disappear if they are bottled up. They get up to all kinds of mischief in the unconscious and often break out to affect our behaviour in very unhelpful ways, as we will see in the next chapter.

What does work do for mental health?

For people of both sexes and all ages paid employment, generally speaking, is expected to provide some measure of independence and autonomy, a feeling of competence, achievement and self-worth, a feeling of being valued, of making a contribution and of belonging. Whether any of these feelings are justifiable or supported by an objective appraisal of the situation is neither here nor there. If these feelings are genuinely felt then they are real enough to the people concerned and they are all vital to the kind of psychological climate that fosters good mental health.

Thus it is that people enter the world of work with optimism and hope, and though sometimes little remains of these positive feelings after a while, the alternative of not being in paid employment is usually *perceived* as being worse. The only major exception to this rule is that of retirement, and we shall see why in Chapter 8. The basic importance of work to mental health thus being stated we will discuss, in the remainder of this chapter, the interaction of different occupational and personality factors and their effects on mental health.

Anxiety: reasonable and unreasonable

Anxiety is the most common form of mental health problem there is. Everybody experiences it and the physiological symptoms that accompany it. The Penguin Dictionary of Psychology defines anxiety as: 'a vague, unpleasant emotional state with qualities of apprehension, dread, distress and uneasiness.' (Reber, 1985, p. 43).

Psychologists are generally agreed that the root cause of anxiety is a feeling of *uncertainty* about what will happen. During the Second World War it was discovered that Londoners, who suffered regular and heavy bombing attacks, displayed little anxiety about them. People who lived in the surrounding countryside however where bombing was infrequent, and therefore *unpredictable*, displayed a great deal of anxiety (Vernon, 1941). In everyday life we have all observed that 'knowing the worst' is more bearable than hanging about waiting to know. Once we know what's going to happen we can mobilise our physical and psychological resources to deal with it.

Even more important to us than certainty and predictability about future events may be the feeling that we are in *control* of them. Another important discovery about anxiety from the Second World War concerned the reactions to danger of different kinds of airmen. Fighter pilots, who had higher casualty rates than bomber pilots, none the less reported less fear of danger (Rachman, 1978).

The reason for this seemed to be that fighter pilots had more flexibility of operation than bomber pilots who had to sit tight as part of a safer, but rigid, formation. The degree of actual control that we have over a given situation doesn't determine how anxious we will feel about it. Throughout our mental life what matters most is what we *perceive*, and our anxiety will therefore be related to the degree of control we perceive ourselves as having. This is presumably why people often feel safer in driving a car than being a passenger in an aeroplane, despite the statistical evidence that they are much safer in the air than on the road.

Neurotic anxiety

If the head of your organization calls the workforce together and assures you that, despite the forthcoming merger/takeover/efficiency drive/ reorganization your job is perfectly safe, you will naturally become very anxious about it. That is a reasonable *state* of anxiety to be in and everyone would share it. Psychologists regard this as 'realistic' anxiety. But if none of these things are to happen, and you are well thought of and appreciated by your superiors, and you are *still* afraid of losing your job then that anxiety is unreasonable. It is what psychologists refer to as 'neurotic' anxiety and neurotic anxiety is more likely to be a continuing *trait* of someone's personality than a transient state which anyone could experience.

The need for definiteness in our everyday environment which we all have becomes, in neurotic anxiety, the inability to tolerate even a little uncertainty or ambiguity. Generally speaking, given that life itself is so unclear, uncertain and complex, the higher your tolerance for ambiguity the better your mental health is likely to be.

Effects of anxiety

Intolerance for ambiguity is particularly evident at times of organizational change. Anxiety about the unknown will naturally heighten people's reluctance to change, or even to contemplate change. But people who suffer from neurotic anxiety may simply find the prospect paralysing and be quite unable to cope with any change at all.

Anxiety will also get in the way of rational decision making. Distortions caused by wishful thinking for instance, that tries to deny the source of the anxiety, will often creep into what is supposed to be an objective assessment of a situation whether it is the likely profitability of a new product, the effect of interest rates on inflation, or the scoring potential of a new member of a professional sports team.

Stress

Introduction

The modern term 'stress' has been traced to its linguistic origins by psychologists working in this field. One version has its origin in the Latin *stringere*, meaning 'to draw tight' (Arnold *et al.* 1991). Another version traces it back to the Old French word *destresse* meaning 'to be placed under narrowness or oppression' (Fontana, 1989). The connotations of being constricted and put upon does seem to be a graphic description of what most people probably think of as the experience of stress.

However it is important to note that there are other ways in which the word 'stress' is used. It may be used in a neutral way, as when engineers talk about the stress on load-bearing walls or beams for instance. It may also be used in a positive way, for example when poets and linguists talk about using different levels of stress on certain words or syllables.

When we look at the psychological effects of stress we will find positive, negative and neutral aspects of the term used, illustrating once more that in psychology so much depends on the context of the phenomenon in question and the nature of the individual reaction to it. However we shall focus our attention mainly on the negative aspects of stress as this seems to be the dominant mode in which we experience it.

The physiological experience of stress

We have already seen that the workings of mind and body affect each other closely so we will take a brief look at the physiological reactions to stress before considering the more specifically psychological issues.

The human body is biologically programmed to react to challenges from the environment by mobilising its resources. We can either confront the challenge and fight it or get away from it as fast as possible. The choice in other words is 'fight or flight', whichever we deem to be more appropriate in the situation. But in order to prepare us for such emergency action the body has to go through a series of *automatic* changes (Fontana, 1989).

We don't have any choice in this matter. If our brain, that is our central nervous system, perceives an imminent challenge (from, say, a sabre-toothed tiger) the message it passes to our autonomic nervous system results immediately in a series of automatic changes including the following:

- The hormones adrenalin and noradrenalin are released into the bloodstream where they speed up our reflexes, raise the level of blood sugar and increase our blood pressure and heart rate. These changes mean extra blood supplies to tense our muscles with and to help us breathe more quickly, while the pupils of the eyes dilate to let us see more clearly.
- The digestive system closes down, allowing the blood used in the normal process of digesting food to be re-routed to the muscles and lungs. In addition our mouth goes dry and the saliva stops flowing so that the digestive system doesn't have to deal with it.
- Endorphins are released from the hypothalamus into the bloodstream which reduce pain and sensitivity to bruising and injury.
- Cortisone is released from the adrenal glands into the bloodstream which slows the body's immune system and shuts out possible allergic reactions that might interfere with body functioning.
- The blood vessels constrict while the blood thickens, flows more slowly and coagulates more quickly than normal if a wound causes it to flow.

The sum of these changes is to prepare us to deal with a short-term emergency situation. The changes happen subconsciously and virtually instantaneously, and if they didn't happen as intended our very survival would be endangered. When we are in an emergency situation we use our mobilised resources in either fight or flight, then after the emergency has passed our body de-mobilises and gradually returns to normal functioning.

Now imagine what it would be like if we perceived a challenge sufficient to activate the primary stress response outlined above, mobilised our resources to deal with it – then couldn't actually deal with it. What if the source of stress was not a sabre-toothed tiger but a boss who was just looking for a chance to fire you? Given that you wanted (or needed) to stay in the job you might not be able to engage in either fight or flight. Yet the stress wouldn't go away and so your resources would have to stay mobilised while it was there.

The physical consequences of not being able to resolve a stressful situation directly by using our emergency resources in fight or flight can be very serious – in fact life-threatening. Increasing heart rate and blood pressure for a short-term emergency only, for example, is the body's natural way of coping, but on a long-term basis it is a prime cause of strokes and heart disease and can also lead to kidney damage. Increasing blood cholesterol level can lead to arteriosclerosis (hardening of the arteries) and subsequent heart disease. Altering blood sugar levels over a lengthy period increases the risk of diabetes, and slowing down the immune system leaves us vulnerable to a wide range of infections, possibly including cancer.

It is in this sense that stress can be a killer. Our physiological responses to the perception of a challenge in the environment have evolved over millions of years and served our ancestors well. But they did not have to work for a living in high-pressured, high-tech jobs for a highly complex organization within a still more complex society.

To the extent that our sources of stress have their origins in the world of work and *are an ongoing part of that world*, our natural defences against stress are not only rendered useless, they are positively dangerous. We therefore need to create new defences against work stress. As we will see below these are social and psychological rather than physiological, and they are desperately needed. A recent review of this topic states that 'stress in the workplace has become the black plague of the twentieth century' (Arnold *et al.*, 1991, p. 301). And as we move into the twenty-first century stress at work is generally considered to be on the increase.

General causes of stress

Stress is usually associated with anxiety; particularly in our response to stressful change. In this context stress is normally taken to be the condition where external pressures, or *stressors*, threaten our ability to cope with our life and work. These stressors, and therefore stress, form a normal part of everyday life, and in the mid-1960s a group of psychologists drew up a rating scale from 0–100 to try to grade the different amounts of stress that result from a list of 43 commonly experienced life events. This scale is reproduced as Figure 5.1.

There are great individual differences, of course, in people's perceptions of what is stressful, and in their reactions to these

Rank	Life event	Value
1	Death of spouse	100
2	Divorce	73
3	Marital separation	65
4	Jail term	63
5	Death of close family member	63
6	Personal injury or illness	53
7	Marriage	50
8	Fired at work	47
9	Marital reconciliation	45
10	Retirement	45
11	Change in health of family member	44
12	Pregnancy	40
13	Sex difficulties	39
14	Gain of new family member	39
15	Business readjustment	39
16	Change in financial state	38
17	Death of close friend	37
18	Change to different line of work	36
19	Change in number of arguments with spouse	35
20	Large mortgage or loan	31
21	Foreclosure of mortgage or loan	30
22	Change in responsibilities at work	29
23	Son or daughter leaving home	29
24	Trouble with in-laws	29
25	Outstanding personal achievement	28
26	Wife begins or stops work	26
27	Begin or end course of study	26
28	Change in living conditions	25
29	Revision of personal habits	24
30	Trouble with boss	23
31	Change in work hours or conditions	20
32	Change in residence	20
33	Change in place of education	20
34	Change in recreation	19
35	Change in church activities	19
36	Change in social activities	18
37	Small mortgage or loan	17
38	Change in sleeping habits	16
39	Change in number of family get-togethers	15
40	Change in eating habits	15
41	Vacation	13
42	Christmas	12
43	Minor violations of the law	11

FIGURE 5.1   General stress scale

Source: adapted from Holmes, T. H. and R. H. Rahe (1967) 'The social readjustment rating scale', *Journal of Psychosomatic Research*, 11, 213–18 perceptions. So these numbers should not be treated as holy writ, though they are none the less useful in helping us to understand the effects of stress in general. There are some important points to note.

The first point to strike us is that by far the most stressful life events are ones that take place in our private life outside of work. In particular they deal with the most important relationship we can have; to our spouse (or partner). Of course we expect events like death and divorce to be stressful, but perhaps the next most striking point about the list is that even positive and joyful life events like marriage can also be very stressful. And even going on vacation to get away from all that stress can be stressful. What are we to make of this?

An important clue to this apparent contradiction is offered by the fifteen items that begin with the word 'change in . . .' In fact all of the life events listed involve change. The very fact of change – whether in connection with an unpleasant event like being fired or a pleasant one like getting married – is itself apparently a stressor. As we saw earlier in this chapter we find uncertainty threatening and difficult to deal with. It makes us anxious. And what could be more uncertain than a single person about to become part of a couple?

The final point to make about Figure 5.1, therefore, is that it brings home the crucial insight that the only way to avoid all stress in life is to stop living. Our aim must therefore be not the avoidance of stress but the *management* of it. And stress – or at least pressure – does have its positive side. Without the excitement and stimulation of opening a new chapter in our life we would never get married – certainly not for the second time – or change jobs. As we will see in more detail below it is the pressure involved which often gives a zest to meeting a new challenge. In a sense, therefore, stress can be both life-enhancing and life-threatening – occasionally, as with mountain climbers and racing drivers, at the same time.

Causes of stress at work

Some occupations are, of course, inherently more stressful than others. A ten-point rating scale of occupational stress has been devised by psychologists who came up with the following league table shown in Figure 5.2.

As with Figure 5.1 on general stress we should not regard these numbers, or the exact order in which these occupations are listed, as gospel. But the table does give us a useful insight into the level of stress that seems to be prevalent in different *kinds* of occupation, and how different occupations compare with each other.

Miner	8.3	Farmer	4.8
Police	7.7	Armed Forces	4.7
Construction worker	7.5	Vet	4.5
Journalist	7.5	Civil servant	4.4
Pilot (civil)	7.5	Accountant	4.3
Prison Officer	7.5	Engineer	4.3
Advertising	7.3	Estate agent	4.3
Dentist	7.3	Hairdresser	4.3
Actor	7.2	Local Government	
Politician	7.0	officer	4.3
Doctor	6.8	Secretary	4.3
Taxman	6.8	Solicitor	4.3
Film producer	6.5	Artist, designer	4.0
Nurse, midwife	6.5	Architect	4.0
Fireman	6.3	Chiropodist	4.0
Musician	6.3	Optician	4.0
Teacher	6.2	Planner	4.0
Personnel	6.0	Postman	4.0
Social Worker	6.0	Statistician	4.0
Manager (commercial)	5.8	Lab technician	3.8
Marketing (export)	5.8	Banker	3.7
Press Officer	5.8	Computing	3.7
Professional		Occupational	
footballer	5.8	therapist	3.7
Salesman,		Linguist	3.7
shop assistant	5.7	Beauty therapist	3.5
Stockbroker	5.5	Vicar	3.5
Bus driver	5.4	Astronomer	3.4
Psychologist	5.2	Nursery Nurse	3.3
Publishing	5.0	Museum worker	2.8
Diplomat	4.8	Librarian	2.0

FIGURE 5.2   Occupational stress scale

Source: Cooper, C. L. (1985) 'Your place in the stress league', *The Sunday Times*, 24 February.

The job titles on this list are also very general ways of describing what people actually do for a living. If we look more closely at doctors, for example, we find some striking and significant differences in the amount of stress experienced by different branches of the medical profession as measured by psychologically induced illness. General practitioners, for instance, have a much higher rate of heart disease than dermatologists or pathologists (Russek, 1960). Indeed heart disease among middle-aged GPs is twice as common as it is in the rest of the medical profession (Morris *et al.*, 1952).

Responsibility

Why should there be such a striking difference within the same profession? For the same reason that air traffic controllers have four times as much hypertension (high blood pressure) as other airport employees doing different kinds of work: *responsibility for other people* (Cobb, 1973). In fact the busier the airports they have to deal with the more likely are air traffic controllers to suffer from hypertension, as well as peptic ulcers and increased levels of cholesterol and blood pressure (Kasl, 1978). This may also be why civil pilots of passenger aircraft have a much higher stress level than military pilots responsible mainly for themselves. And similarly lawyers in general practice suffer more stress induced disease than, for example, those working in patent law (Russek, 1960).

Responsibility for others is probably why first-line supervisors in industry generally suffer more from the effects of stress than the people they supervise (Cobb, 1973). Indeed managers at all levels tend to suffer more from stress than professionals of similar status who do not have any supervisory responsibilities (French and Caplan, 1970; Baron, 1986). It is interesting to note that university teachers tend to have very low levels of stress – until they move into administration (French *et al.*, 1982).

Control

Another important occupational difference in stress is the feeling of having a *lack of control* of one's working life. Our classic picture of this situation is the manual worker trapped on the treadmill of a never-ending assembly line (think of Charlie Chaplin in *Modern Times* for instance). But, while the stressful assembly line is by no means extinct, the present-day victim of such monotony and the constant pressure of someone else's timetable is more likely to be a VDU operator.

There is a lot of evidence that the current industrial restructuring, accompanied by the introduction of new technology and ways of using it, has led to increased levels of stress among workers who do not have control of it (Warr, 1987a). Conversely, the ability to retain a high degree of control of their work life may be why stress and ill health are relatively low among the self-employed (Curran *et al.*, 1987). And this despite the pressure, that we noted in the previous chapter, for them to work longer hours than other people.

Overload

At the same time the most obvious cause of stress at work, regardless of occupation, is sheer *overload*. That is where there is simply too much to do in the time available for it. There are three factors involved here – quality and quantity, as well as time – and the individual is faced with a choice among doing less work than expected, doing the work less well, and taking more time to do it. People tend to take the constraint of time as a given in this type of situation and see the conflict as between quantity and quality (Sales, 1969). People also tend to underestimate the amount of overload they are being subjected to, and seem to treat it as though it was their sole responsibility, thereby increasing the amount of stress they are under (Kraut, 1965).

Underload

But perhaps the most serious cause of stress at work, in both individual and organizational terms, is *underutilization* of people's abilities. We have already seen in the last chapter how workers in jobs with little or no stimulation feel that they have to provide their own to retain their sanity. In terms of both manual and mental skills many jobs use only a tiny fraction of a person's capabilities, to say nothing of their emotional commitment.

We will examine this issue in some more detail in the next chapter but for now let us note that the frustration caused by underutilization of skills and abilities, and lack of appreciation in general, is the most corrosive kind of stress for both individual and organization. It is the quickest way to foster alienation from the organization – and even the deliberate sabotage by workers of its objectives and its production process (Kornhauser 1965; O'Brien, 1986). It is also why people near the top of a hierarchy tend to suffer *less* stress than those at the bottom (Cooper and Smith, 1985).

Emotional labour and role conflict

A more recently identified source of stress, and one which is becoming more prevalent because of its location in the service sector, has been described as *emotional labour* (Hochschild, 1983). It has been estimated that 25 per cent of men's jobs and 50 per cent of women's jobs call for some kind of emotional labour (Hochschild, 1983). Emotional labour is asked of people when they have to manage their emotions so as to present a particular face to the customer on behalf of the organization; for example the ever-smiling, friendly air hostess or the coldly business-like debt collector.

As these different sets of feelings are paramount in performing the role of either air hostess or debt collector it is practically inevitable that such people will often be alienated from what they really feel about the job and the public they deal with in performing it. But an air hostess who expressed her true feelings, even after many hours in the company of some obnoxious passengers, would not last long in the organization, and neither would a debt collector calling on a poor widow with young children who was emotionally moved by her plight to overlook the debt. However as we will see in the next chapter there is always a heavy psychological price to pay for being alienated from one's true feelings.

Burnout

At its extreme the performance of emotional labour for a living can lead to a condition described as *burnout*. This condition is found among people in what are called the 'caring' or 'helping' professions like medicine, social work or counselling. The clients of people in these professions are themselves often under stress and will therefore make emotional demands on the professionals they deal with because they are feeling frightened or angry or depressed (Maslach and Jackson, 1982).

Burnout has been studied quite widely in the medical professions. Doctors and nurses suffer a high incidence of emotional exhaustion compared to other occupations. Nurses may also suffer from reduced personal accomplishment and doctors may be prone to depersonalise their patients and treat them in what seems to be a cold and unfeeling manner (Maslach and Jackson, 1982). The medical professions also have much higher rates of suicide, alcoholism, drug abuse and depression than other professions.

While the stress of client or patient demand is probably the major cause of burnout there may be some other factors involved (Argyle, 1989):

● feelings of failure and helplessness when clients or patients don't improve or recover
● feelings of not being in control of the situation caused by uncooperative clients or colleagues
● becoming depressed simply by too much listening to other people's troubles.

Stress and working conditions

Finally in this section we will look at the main environmental factors involved in causing stress at work. There is often a tendency to overlook their effects in the search for more subtle psychological causes. In Chapter 3 we saw how badly designed workplaces can have an adverse effect on the way a job is performed. Unpleasant working conditions that are noisy, badly lit and so on are stressful (Kornhauser, 1965). So are jobs where workers are regulated by a fast-moving assembly line (Cooper and Smith, 1985).

Simply working long hours can be an important cause of stress. It has been found, for instance, that a group of middle-aged American workers in light industry who worked more than 48 hours a week had twice as much risk of dying from coronary heart disease as colleagues working no more than 40 hours a week (Breslow and Buell, 1960). Indeed it has now been officially accepted in Japan that people can die of overwork, a cause of death known as *karoshi*.

Specialists in this area now believe that working for more than 40 hours a week becomes increasingly unproductive (Arnold *et al.*, 1991). As we saw in the last chapter this clashes with the modern managerial ethos that more is better than less when it comes to spending time at work – despite the long-established research findings to the contrary for shop-floor workers.

In the last chapter we looked at some of the effects of shiftwork on performance. We noted that most people seem able to deal adequately with the physiological and psychological problems involved. However there is no doubt that shiftworking is a source of some stress for everyone and can result in serious problems for a sizeable minority of people. The longer the shift the greater seems to be the stress, for example in oil rig workers doing four weeks on, four weeks off as opposed to two weeks on and two weeks off (Sutherland and Cooper, 1987).

As we noted previously problems are particularly found in the night shift, though if anything working rotating shifts seems to be a greater problem than working a fixed night shift (Tasto *et al.*, 1978). A study of nurses on shiftwork found that those on rotating shifts suffered significantly more depression and anxiety than those on fixed shifts. Unlike the nurses on fixed shifts they did not seem able to adapt to the necessary changes.

Coping with stress psychologically

To help us cope with stress, or indeed any mental health problem, it is very important that we receive all the social support we can get, both in our private lives and at work. In our discussion about stress in general we noted how vitally affected people are by their closest personal relationships. If someone experiencing stress in his work life has a supportive home environment the effects of the stress can be greatly reduced, as measured by lowered cholesterol level, or tendency to develop arthritis, or speed of recovery from surgery, or even the risk of dying prematurely (Cobb, 1976; Berkman and Syme, 1979).

This is also true of alcohol consumption, a widespread if under-discussed symptom of stress at work. Many people drink more under stress, but with supportive personal relationships this tendency is often reduced (Cobb, 1976). The basis of this support is the conveying of positive feelings like concern, liking, respect and trust for the person, and perhaps also the affirmation of their basic beliefs about themselves and about life in general. Social support thus forms a *buffer* between the individual and the effects of stress. This buffering effect is also known as the 'suntan lotion' model because it's only applied when needed.

Equally important is the social support given to a person under stress by colleagues at work. Such support, from peers, supervisors and subordinates can lead to a reduction in blood pressure, for instance, and even the number of cigarettes that someone smokes (Katz and Kahn, 1978). It has been found possible to organize this kind of social support at work in such a way that people suffering from stress have been able to keep on working while the problems were sorted out. The support of one's partner is most important when a radical change occurs, like the loss of a job, but colleagues are more important when there is ongoing stress at work, probably because they are directly and continually involved (Henderson and Argyle, 1985).

The social support outlined above is the best way we know to cope with stress but it is an ideal and, for many individuals and organizations, the reality falls short of this. Not everyone is fortunate enough to have warm and emotionally supporting relationships at home or at work. However there are still ways in which stress at work can be managed, or at least alleviated.

Stress management workshops can often help (Meichenbaum and Jaremko, 1983). Typically they will help participants to realise that stress is not an inevitable consequence of a particular situation and that the way they perceive the situation contributes to how much stress is experienced. Specific techniques can also be helpful including simple relaxation and exercise (it is amazing how many of us walk around with tensed neck muscles or clenched stomach muscles) to help people feel better physically, and therefore mentally. Helping individuals deal with stress helps the organization too, of course. It has been calculated that every dollar spent on treating stress at work yields an organization $5.52 in improved job performance (NIOSH, 1987).

More complex psychological techniques can also be employed, like teaching people how to be assertive of themselves without becoming aggressive, or how to plan coping strategies for future stressful situations. In addition individual clinical counselling and psychotherapy is increasingly being made available, and proving helpful, for job-related problems of mental health (Firth and Shapiro, 1986).

Incidentally it doesn't seem to matter what kind of psychotherapy is used: all those used seem to be equally helpful. What seems important is that serious attention is being paid to the individual and his problems. Clinical psychologists are puzzled by this finding but I would suggest that it has something in common with similar findings elsewhere in psychology, like the Hawthorne Effect that we will consider in Chapter 7.

Personality factors

Clearly there is a self-selection factor involved in the way people wind up in certain occupations, and this is related to the kind of people they are. Journalists and librarians are at opposite ends of the occupational stress scale, for example, yet their educational backgrounds and skills are not that dissimilar. Presumably journalists regard library work as too slow, dull and boring and perhaps librarians regard journalism as too fast, noisy and trivial. People considering either of these two occupations would have a pretty good idea of the stress levels involved and would choose accordingly. If the choice is arrived at fairly freely a relatively high degree of stress and pressure can be an attractive aspect of a job to some people. And such occupations are often regarded as glamorous and exciting.

At the same time if someone is temperamentally suited to a quiet life with a regular routine they should probably not become a war correspondent. Such a dramatic mismatch of occupation and personality is highly unlikely, of course, because people usually know themselves well enough, but there are plenty of people in jobs where they find the level of stress uncomfortably high or uncomfortably low for them.

Apart from anything else, as we saw in the previous chapter, people's needs change over time and so do the requirements of the organizations they work for. What may have been a perfect fit five or ten years ago might now be slipping out of synch, like someone who wanted to work in public service but finds his department turned into a private agency, or someone who enjoyed working for a small publishing company that is taken over by a vast conglomerate run by accountants.

Type A and Type B personality

In the early 1970s a group of medical researchers identified a link between behaviour and heart disease. They argued a link that had first been suggested a century earlier that people who engaged regularly in certain kinds of behaviour were particularly prone to heart disease. These behaviours seemed to fall into such a recognizable pattern that they might be regarded as typical of a personality type – Type A (Friedman and Rosenman, 1974. See KEY STUDY 4). Type A people are workaholics; they work long and hard, are aggressive, competitive and impatient, have a great sense of urgency, are extremely involved with their job and feel that time is passing too quickly (Caplan *et al.*, 1975).

This type of personality is in distinct contrast to that of another identifiable group of people, Type Bs. Type B people are much more easy-going and placid, less aggressive and competitive and less worried about the passage of time than Type As. In terms of stress at work Type A managers are particularly liable to smoke more, have higher levels of blood pressure and cholesterol, and of course to suffer more heart disease. In fact Type As had twice the rate of heart attacks of Type Bs (Rosenman *et al.*, 1975).

But we have already seen that some people enjoy being challenged and put under pressure and seek out high stress occupations, and Type A people are certainly in this category. So if this is the kind of work they are attracted to, and it suits their temperament, why then do they risk getting heart attacks from doing it?

The answer seems to lie mainly in the strong need that Type A people have to *control* any situation they are in. If they feel in control of their work they can manage the stress well. They seem to ride the crest of the wave and be energised by the stress at work. However, if other people or external forces control their work life, or if they are inactive and underutilized for a time, the stress seems to swamp them. By contrast, Type Bs tend to get anxious and feel the effects of stress when there is too *little* external control and they are left more to their own resources (Chesney and Rosenman, 1980).

It is also very important to note that Type A people, by their over-involvement in work, spend less time and effort with family and friends – a crucial source of the support in times of stress which will reduce the likelihood of their suffering ill health. Furthermore, with their aggressive competitiveness Type As would also be likely to deprive themselves of the support of their colleagues at work.

In terms of occupational success or failure Type A managers, as you might expect, do better than Type Bs – up to a point. That is, they seem to have better jobs and be promoted faster, but they are less likely to make it to the very top. Given their reaction to stress this may not be too surprising when you think about it. Type As may simply burn themselves out – or explode with frustration – before they get to the top. Even more important perhaps, their apparent hostility to other people and their self-absorption may lead the decision makers in their organization to decide that they would not be able to take a broad enough view of the organization's goals or engage in the necessary give and take with their colleagues (Baron, 1986).

It is clearly of great importance that Type A people be helped by their organizations to harness their energies as creatively as possible to the organization's goals. Giving such people more control of their work life, if that were possible, would certainly be helpful, but that is not the end of the story. With Type A personalities too much psychological energy is invested in work and too little in personal life. In the long run it would be in the interests of the organization, as well as the individual, to try to balance up the package. But that is something that would require the commitment of a great deal of time, effort and resources by both parties and a readjustment of the psychological contract between them. The first move would have to come from the organization, and how many organizations are willing or able to make it?

Goodness of fit between person and job

We have seen how stress can result from work overload or underload, from too much responsibility or too little responsibility, from work being too complex or too simple and so on. One man's stress can therefore be another man's stimulus, and vice versa. We have tried to isolate factors in the working environment and in the individual personality in our brief survey of mental health in general and stress in particular. But that was to help us understand better the issues involved. In actual work situations we are always dealing with the *interaction* of environmental and personality factors, and it is precisely that interaction which is crucial for we are dealing with dynamic, constantly changing, forces.

The key to good mental health at work, as far as we understand it, lies in the *goodness of fit* between the individual and his or her job. If people feel the job provides them with the right amount of stimulation, reward and challenge they will respond with their best efforts and creativity. The more that individual and job are out of synch with each other the more likelihood will there be of mental health problems occurring (French *et al.*, 1982; Furnham and Schaeffer, 1984).

There are various ways in which this goodness of fit can be achieved and enhanced, starting with better recruitment and selection practices (see Chapter 11). Once in the job better training and development practices are often crucial (see Chapter 12). And finally, and perhaps most importantly, an increased awareness is required at all levels of our own psychological needs, and how they interact with those of other people in the organization.

That is the subject of the next chapter, but before we leave this chapter it might be worth pondering on the research finding that jobs which seem to most people dangerous by their very nature – and therefore stressful – like being a test pilot or a police officer, are perceived differently by the people in those jobs. It is not so much the physical danger that is felt to be stressful; that is usually not dwelt on, or found to be positively attractive. What pilots and police say they find most stressful are the things that everybody else finds stressful; administrative problems at work and domestic problems at home (Kasl, 1978).

CHAPTER 6

The unconscious at work

Introduction

We caught a glimpse of the unconscious at work in the last chapter when we discussed mental health and its physical correlates, the identification of different types of personality, and the importance of interpersonal relationships. In the present chapter we will highlight the unconscious and its workings and trace its effects as they ramify throughout the world of work. But first we have to deal with one of those big issues of definition that bedevil (or enliven, depending on your point of view) the study of psychology: *What is the unconscious?*

The complexity of this term can be gauged from the fact that one dictionary of psychology talks about there being 'no less that 39 distinct meanings of *unconscious*' (English and English, 1958, p. 569). Fortunately most of the fine discriminations involved in these 39 meanings need not detain us. We are interested in only two ways of using the term and of these only one is the subject of this chapter (and indeed this book).

The physiological unconscious

The most general definition is the simple and non-technical one of not being conscious, of lacking awareness of one's situation. This popular usage of the term defines *consciousness* rather than unconsciousness. It coincides with the technical usage of neurophysiologists, who think in terms of a continuum from the full conscious awareness of emotional states like fear or rage to a state of coma where there is a complete loss of consciousness (for example Lindsley, 1952).

It has been found that the electrical activity of the brain changes at different points in this continuum and this can be charted on an electroencephalogram (EEG) as indicated in Figure 6.1.

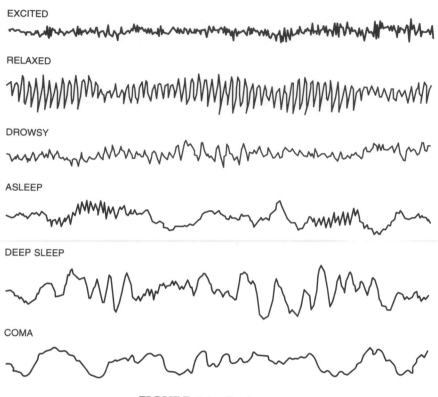

EXCITED

RELAXED

DROWSY

ASLEEP

DEEP SLEEP

COMA

FIGURE 6.1   Brain waves

The brain waves recorded by an EEG have a characteristically different pattern at different states of awareness: they can vary in frequency from less than one cycle per second to about 50 per second. In a state of coma the reading has a long slow wave indicating that the subject is *unconscious*. Even though people who are asleep also lack conscious awareness of their surroundings they are not usually referred to as being unconscious. The distinction is that sleep is a normal state and part of our regular circadian rhythms whereas coma is an abnormal state, caused by injury or disease, that may last for months or years, or from which there may be no awakening.

The dynamic unconscious

The psychological usage of the term 'unconscious' is quite different from the physiological one we have been considering above, and is the one we shall be dealing with in the rest of this chapter. The idea that there are aspects of our psychological life that we are not consciously aware of has a long history in psychology (Klein, 1977). But as we saw in Chapter 1, it was not until Sigmund Freud's work in the late nineteenth and early twentieth centuries that a systematic attempt was made to use the concept as a way of explaining a great deal of human behaviour, originally the 'abnormal' behaviour of clinical patients and then the 'normal' behaviour of people in general.

Freud was primarily interested in what are sometimes called 'the wellsprings of human action'. He was concerned, in other words, with understanding human motivation and the deepest underlying causes of behaviour. From his clinical observations on patients he believed that much of the genesis of their behaviour was unknown to them and indeed to most people in the general course of life, because they did not wish to know about it.

According to Freud, who popularised the use of the term, the *unconscious* is that area of the mind in which we deposit all the things we don't want to be aware of consciously. 'Wicked' thoughts or painful memories and disturbing images of ourselves and close family members, whose powerful emotional content would make us uncomfortable, are either pushed down out of sight ('repressed') or prevented from coming into our heads ('inhibited') in the first place.

These are *dynamic* processes requiring a great deal of psychic energy to be spent on them. There is nothing abnormal or unusual about these processes of repression and inhibition: they go on all the time. And there is nothing passive about them either. Unlike the physiological unconscious there is a lot of activity in the psychological unconscious, both sleeping and waking. This conception of the unconscious lies at the heart of all psychoanalysis, whether Freudian, neo-Freudian or non-Freudian.

We actually have some inkling in our daily lives of what our unconscious can do and of the psychodynamics involved. When we are faced with a difficult decision to make, something that makes us anxious, and we decide to 'sleep on it' what we are really doing is taking the problem away from our conscious mind and trusting it to our unconscious. Often we wake up knowing what decision we should take. We may not accept that decision and we may not act on it – it may simply be too difficult for us or we may not be ready for it – but we know what the right decision is. What has happened is that we have allowed part of our mind to consider the problem without any of the defensive sandbags we normally put up to block out uncomfortable thoughts and feelings. And on waking we allow the answer, however fleetingly, to see the light of day.

Psychologists believe that the more we can allow up from the unconscious, and be fully aware of, the better our psychological health.

There is a lot of evidence (as we will see below and in future chapters) that this may be just as true of the psychological health of the organization. Although Elton Mayo and other prominent management theorists were influenced by the work of Freud and his colleagues it is only since the 1970s that systematic attempts have been made to examine the role of the unconscious in the world of work (De Board, 1978; Kets de Vries and Miller, 1984). Although this orientation is slowly gaining ground it is still regarded as something of a novelty. Yet the unconscious is routinely put to use in the world of work.

Using the unconscious in selecting staff

Work organizations are obviously very concerned to hire people who can do the job, who are competent at performing all the tasks required of them. And for some tasks where the actual performance is all-important – typing or driving for instance – evidence of these skills may be all the organization looks for in selecting its staff.

But much more information than that about job applicants is usually sought by organizations, and even with typing or driving jobs some kind of reference is often required about an applicant's 'character'. In other words work organizations are usually interested in knowing something – and often a great deal – about the kind of person they may be hiring, quite apart from their ability to perform the tasks in question. This kind of information is considered especially important in managerial jobs and is often elicited by *personality tests* designed, and often administered and interpreted, by psychologists.

Personality tests

The aim of a personality test is to get behind the public face that individuals present to the world and obtain a picture of what they are 'really' like; an account of their inner life that is, which they themselves may not be fully aware of. The personality test therefore acts like a probe sent down into the unconscious.

(i) MMPI

The most commonly encountered personality test (often called a paper-and-pencil test) is in the form of a questionnaire that may be administered to a large group of people and has a standardised (often computerised) method of dealing with the responses. There are dozens of these tests, of which the best-known is the *Minnesota Multiphasic Personality Inventory* (MMPI) (Hathaway and McKinley, 1940). The MMPI has 550 statements to which the subject has to answer 'true', 'false', or 'cannot say'. The statements deal with a vast range of thoughts, feelings and behaviour as the following few examples show:

> My way of doing things is apt to be misunderstood by others.
> I am bothered by acid stomach several times a week.
> I have never indulged in unusual sex practices.
> I like to read newspaper articles on crime.
> I never worry about my looks.
> Someone has been trying to poison me.
> I often feel as if things were not real.
> If I were an artist I would like to draw flowers.

This may seem like an odd mixture of innocuous and dramatic statements to use in trying to understand someone's personality, and any one of them by itself would certainly reveal nothing. But responses to a great many statements like these have been shown to reveal patterns of behaviour and attitudes that can give psychologists some clues – and they are no more than that – about deep-lying aspects of personality such as anxiety or depression, or feelings about masculinity/femininity, or even a tendency towards schizophrenia. Taken over the whole range of the MMPI's 550 statements – complete with cross checks on consistency of response – people are considered likely to reveal more of their inner life than if they were asked directly about, say, their masculinity/femininity. The direct approach is thought more likely to elicit the kind of reply the individual considers to be socially acceptable.

(ii) TAT

Considered to be more powerful than the paper-and-pencil test is the kind of personality test that requires the subject to project on to some vaguely defined picture whatever is in his or her mind. These are called projective tests, and perhaps the most widely used of them is the *Thematic Apperception Test* (TAT) (Murray, 1938). The TAT consists of 20 black and white pictures (drawings and photographs) mostly containing one or two people. The emotions portrayed by, and the relationships between, the people in these pictures are made deliberately ambiguous, allowing the subject scope for identifying with the situation being depicted. The subject is asked to make up a story about what is happening in each picture. The picture thus acts like a screen on which parts of the person's inner life may be projected. These stories are then analysed to see what recognisable *themes* may be *perceived* (hence the name of the test) and this again is used to gain some clues about the person's unconscious mind.

(iii) *Rorschach Ink Blot Test*

Named after its inventor, the Swiss psychiatrist Hermann Rorschach, this projective test must be the most famous of all psychological tests (Rorschach, 1942). Ten pictures of actual ink blots are used, five of them in colour. The subject is asked what he sees in the ink blot; what it reminds him of. There are no right or wrong answers, of course, and the theory is that each person will see people or things that are important to *him*. Psychologists experienced in the use of the Rorschach claim that the subject's responses to the shape and colour and detail of the ink blot can reveal a great deal of his unconscious life as it is projected on to the picture (Exner, 1974).

It is important to note that each of these personality tests was developed for use with disturbed people in a clinical setting. Organizations which use them to assess people assumed to be normal are therefore in some danger of abusing them (and the people they are used on) with serious implications that we will consider in Chapter 11: Recruitment and Selection.

The more that organizations wish to know about the personalities of their applicants the more will these kinds of tests be used, normally in conjunction with the interviews and the other standard assessment procedures we will discuss in Chapter 11. But once people have been selected and start work the importance that was accorded to the role of the unconscious seems to be completely disregarded for ever after by the organization. This is not an oversight however; there are very powerful factors at work which prevent the unconscious intruding.

Why you can't hire 'hands'

Unlike, say, the mental processes of learning or thinking or problem solving the unconscious, as we have seen, is concerned with people's emotions and with human relationships. It deals therefore with the most powerful, messiest, most difficult to understand and least rational parts of our psychology. And that is one very good reason why books on the way organizations work usually tip-toe quietly round this whole area. Much more importantly, that is why organizations themselves do so.

Because organizations, and especially work organizations, find the expression of emotions so difficult to handle they usually act as though people didn't have any; a denial of reality with which people themselves collude. So behaviour that expresses things like fear, anger, love, jealousy, joy, hatred or general anxiety is either separated from its underlying emotion and treated as though it suddenly appeared for no good reason, or simply ignored. It is as though there was an unspoken, universal assumption that human behaviour in organizations is entirely conscious, controlled and rational.

There are many everyday examples of this denial of feelings. People whose jobs include physical danger, for instance, will at times be very frightened. But, as many policemen and soldiers have testified over the years, it is virtually impossible for them to say 'I'm scared'. What they may then do instead is meet the danger with increased bravado and take unnecessary risks, just to show how much they're not scared.

Or they may remove themselves from danger in the only honourable way open to them, by becoming sick and incapacitated. Thus soldiers have found their arms paralysed and pilots have gone blind just before combat. These people were not faking it; their afflictions were quite genuine. But they had no physical cause, they were hysterical symptoms similar to the ones Freud had noted, and when the danger had passed the paralysis and the blindness vanished as suddenly as they had appeared (Anderson, 1941).

Whatever way the unconscious chose to manifest itself in the behaviour of these servicemen the underlying cause was the same, fear. Emotions do not go away because we won't consciously admit we have them. They will be expressed somehow. However they may not always be expressed at work. Another common way in which people deal with strong emotions or emotional conflicts that are not being recognised and dealt with at work is simply to leave the job.

A large London teaching hospital had a very serious problem in this area in the late 1950s. They had about 550 student nurses at any one time and something like one-third of them refused to complete their training. (Incidentally this group contained some of the brightest students.) Moreover there was a high absenteeism rate due to sickness. High rates of absenteeism and staff turnover are classic signs of organizational malaise.

The hospital was not sure why there were these problems but assumed that the central difficulty was the administration of the training placements. They called in a consultant to help them, a woman who happened to be a psychoanalyst. She carried out various types of intensive interviews and discussions with 70 of the nurses and with senior nursing staff and came up with some alarming findings (Menzies, 1960: KEY STUDY 5).

The most crucial finding in this pioneering study was that the student nurses were suffering from an enormous amount of anxiety and tension about their role in the hospital. Indeed the psychoanalyst found it very difficult to understand how they could cope with so much anxiety. Many of them of course could not cope, hence the high rates of sickness and failure to complete training. But what was the source of all this anxiety?

The source of the anxiety lay in the job itself. These were young people being called upon to do a job in which some of the tasks are by their very nature highly unpleasant, involving blood, vomit, urine etc, and they may be disgusted by them. Other tasks, with patients who are badly injured or seriously ill, might be very frightening. And of course, in spite of the most dedicated care and attention, patients die – and apart from anything else the experience of death is a rare one for a teenager. This would inevitably trigger feelings of grief, and perhaps anger and guilt and frustration as well.

So these student nurses were experiencing a long list of powerful emotions in a very short time – disgust, fear, grief, anger, frustration, anxiety and guilt. In addition to all this the nurses had to deal with the emotions of the patients and their relatives, and these were by no means straightforward. As well as the gratitude for a nurse's care that you would expect there would be some envy of her youthful health and strength, resentment at being so dependent on her, and perhaps sexual attraction as well. A very complex, messy and highly volatile emotional situation resulted. Clearly the nurses would need a lot of help to cope with these emotions. And what help did the hospital give them? In a word, *denial*.

What the hospital did was to organize itself so that the nurses were 'protected' from feeling anything at all. Partly this was done by reducing the nurse's job to a series of rigidly defined tasks that she had to perform like a ritual, as automatically as possible – like a machine in fact – thereby eliminating not only feeling but questioning, and along with it any individual discretion or creativity in doing the job.

By following this ritual the nurse was relieved of any sense of responsibility for what happened to her patients. She was also moved around from ward to ward constantly to minimise her chances of forming any kind of relationship with the patients. But while the powerful emotions stirred up might be denied by the hospital and therefore battened down into the nurses' unconscious they did not, of course, disappear. By not allowing the nurses even to admit that they had these feelings the hospital greatly increased their emotional turmoil, to the point where for many people it became, literally, unbearable and they fell ill or left the job.

Not much was changed by the hospital as a result of the psycho-analyst's report. Indeed not much has changed generally in the work organization of hospitals since the late 1950s. Emotions are still routinely denied. When multiplied over a whole country the financial costs alone of this denial must be enormous. The human costs are incalculable. And here again it is worth noting that increasing payment for the job will not solve the problem, even though nurses are often disgracefully under-paid.

A recent survey of nurses in Scotland has found that low pay was only fifth on their list of dissatisfactions with the job, well behind concerns about relationships with patients and supervisors (Gilloran *et al.*, 1993). Presumably higher pay, if combined with all the unspoken emotions nurses already have, would simply make them feel more guilty. Yet arguments about nurses' jobs between trade unions, management and government in the United Kingdom are almost entirely concerned with pay. Why?

The idea that people at work could be treated like machines became popular with employers after Henry Ford opened his first car factory in the early years of the twentieth century and put workers on an assembly line. The early success of this method is part of industrial folklore. What is less well known is that Ford almost went bankrupt some years later still using the same method, and indeed the Ford Motor Company has never regained its initial dominance of the market. The lesson has still not been learned by the end of the twentieth century, and it bears a lot of repeating; you cannot just hire hands – or even brains – because people always come as a package deal.

How organizations can split personalities

The denial of emotions in the workplace that we saw with the nursing staff of a hospital is not confined to life or death situations. It may be easier to see in such a dramatic situation but it is the way most work organizations (indeed most organizations) operate and it is for most of us, therefore, a fact of our working lives. It is therefore 'normal' for most people to be asked, implicitly, to bring their hands and brains to work and leave their feelings at home.

To the extent that people are able to do this they are able to split off one part of their personality and separate it from the rest, and psychologically that is not a very healthy direction to go in. If taken far enough that route leads eventually to the condition known as schizophrenia, the most commonly diagnosed form of psychosis or serious mental illness, where people's feelings are typically out of touch with their thoughts and behaviour, often to the point where they may not be able to communicate coherently with anyone else.

There are some organizations which behave differently towards their members. These are organizations which do not encourage their members to split off their feelings but rather to keep them *integrated* within their personality. But what they do encourage their members to do is to behave as if they were different people at work and at home. This is particularly true, for example, in police and military organizations where men are encouraged to be macho or aggressive or highly controlled authority figures at work but to leave this personality behind when they go home, presumably to become loving husbands and fathers.

Just as people in the previous situation cannot simply leave their emotions behind when they come to work, so policemen and servicemen cannot simply switch off when they go home. Indeed to the extent that they *can* do so they are heading down another dangerous psychological route that leads to the mental illness known as multiple – or split – personality, where two or more distinct personalities (like the good Dr Jekyll and the evil Mr Hyde) coexist in the same body.

It might be helpful, for illustration, to think of work organizations as tending *unconsciously* to encourage either a vertical or a horizontal splitting in the individual member, as in Figure 6.2. This is not to say that all work organizations drive people psychotic, but it does suggest that conditions conducive to serious psychological disturbance may routinely be set up and might have harmful effects if the role of the unconscious is ignored.

We will see later that the psychological dangers of splitting – literally *dis*-integration – for the individual member are mirrored in the life of the organization itself.

The most tragic consequence of psychological splitting is the deadening effect on the relationship between members and their

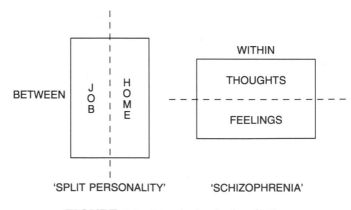

FIGURE 6.2   Psychological splitting

organizations. Most members are eager to give of themselves to their organizations but, as we saw in the case of the nurses, individual creativity becomes the first casualty of not treating them as whole human beings. We will explore this problem further in Chapter 9.

'Self' defence

We should not really be too surprised, however, at the difficulty organizations have in dealing with strong emotions because organizations, as we have seen, are simply made up of people all of whom, to a greater or lesser extent, share that same difficulty as individuals. It is not that we don't want to know what our true feelings are. We do. However we also have a need to be comfortable, psychologically, which is often stronger than our need to know the truth and this need pushes us to defend our self-image, or ego, from the discomfort of experiencing strong emotions. In fact so powerful is this need that to satisfy it we are capable of believing, literally, anything that will make us feel more comfortable.

Freud suggested various stratagems, or defence mechanisms, that we use unconsciously in our everyday life. These stratagems have the effect of allowing us to deceive ourselves by distorting reality to the point where we feel comfortable with it. These forms of 'self' defence are tried and trusted and, as the following examples will show, some of them have even become part of our everyday language.

(a) Projection

We came across the process of projection earlier in the chapter when we saw how projective tests are designed to tap into a person's inner life. Projection is also used regularly in defence of the self.

Sometimes people who feel very uncomfortable having certain thoughts and feelings will assign those same thoughts and feelings to someone else, *projecting* them from within themselves onto others. This is especially clear in the case of the most powerful impulses like sex and aggression. People who are concerned in great detail with the lascivious and violent behaviour of others may be using the cloak of moral righteousness to get close to emotions within themselves that, if faced head on, would be too shocking to accept.

There are also, of course, many everyday examples of projection at work. Lots of industrial disputes, for instance, are between two parties each of whom is quite convinced of its own openness and good faith and the other side's blatantly cynical dishonesty. And we've all met people who fawn on their superiors while looking down on their colleagues as 'crawlers'.

(b) Sublimation

This defence is the one that is most approved of in our society. When we have an impulse or feeling that is too dangerous to express directly we repress it in its raw form and let it emerge in such a way that it will not be upsetting to ourselves or to other people. It is often argued, for instance, that successful businessmen who work long hours in highly competitive fields are, at least partly, *sublimating* their impulses towards unacceptable ways of expressing aggression and competition by channelling their energy in directions that win them material rewards and social approval instead.

Although all defence mechanisms are, psychologically speaking, second-best solutions – the best solution is always to recognize the emotion for what it is and deal with it squarely – this particular defence appears to be a socially creative one. Indeed Freud thought it went a long way towards explaining the artistic and scientific accomplishments of a society.

(c) Rationalization

This is perhaps the most familiar form of 'self' defence which we use in two different kinds of situations, involving frustration in one and guilt in the other.

The first situation may be represented by our reaction to being turned down for a job we applied for. We may relieve our frustration by deciding that we didn't really want the job anyway because the company is not all it's cracked up to be according to what we've heard recently, or because it would have involved too much travelling, or not enough responsibility – or anything else that makes us feel better about what is, after all, a rejection of us.

We find the second form of rationalization when people feel guilty because they do things they know they shouldn't. Rather than admitting the real reason for their behaviour they will often *rationalize* it by inventing plausible reasons for doing what they do. For instance, slave owners in the southern United States kept slaves for economic gain but argued that their slaves were quite happy with their lives, needed firm discipline for their own good and would be completely lost without their masters and the benefits of Christian civilization which they represented.

Scaled down a few notches, white supporters of South African apartheid said similar things.

(d) Reaction formation

Sometimes people who are threatened by an impulse they feel might overwhelm them fight the impulse by going to the other extreme and vigorously denouncing expressions of it in other people. Men who are unsure of their masculinity and afraid of women will often jeer at other men with supposedly feminine or 'sissy' traits like gentleness and kindness. This is particularly true of male-dominated occupations of course.

Such men might unconsciously long to behave in an open and trusting way with a woman but consciously they reject such feelings in themselves as a sign of weakness and vulnerability. They adopt a tough macho disguise instead in a process of *reaction formation* against their true feelings.

(e) Displacement

This form of defence is related to *sublimation* in that the original impulse is diverted from its direct expression. In this case the expression of the emotion does not change form but gets *displaced* away from its original target on to someone else. A loyal worker who gets laid off by his company and feels angry and hostile at the way he has been treated may have some difficulty expressing these feelings directly. Not only is it difficult to turn against an organization in which he had so much psychological capital invested but who exactly should he direct his anger at? At the personnel officer who hands him the redundancy notice? At the personnel manager? At his own supervisor? At the head of the company, whom he never sees? At the owners of the company whose office is in another country?

In this kind of predicament it is very tempting to find a handy *scapegoat* that one can blame and thus give vent to strong feelings that won't simply disappear. This scapegoat is often a minority group, itself struggling to enter the employment market. When times are hard economically, *displacement* is at the root of a great deal of social prejudice. Terrible evidence of this was found in a study of the southern United States between 1882 and 1930 which discovered that when the price of cotton fell in any given year, and with it the income of white farmers, the number of black people they lynched increased (Hovland and Sears, 1940).

How we collude with our organizations

The preceding example is an extreme form of scapegoating in action but there are plenty of other examples of this kind of stratagem woven into the fabric of the organizations in which we live and work. Perhaps the most widespread occurrence of scapegoating is found in the family. Family therapists have found that, rather than face the difficult and sometimes painful task of examining *all* the relationships involved, family members will often collude with each other to give one person the role of scapegoat. 'If only he/she would/wouldn't do x, y or z then we'd have a perfectly happy family', runs the typical fantasy. And often the person in question unconsciously colludes with the scapegoating, acting out their role to the letter time after time. The role of villain in a drama is an important and powerful one after all and, to many people, preferable to having no role at all.

At work, scapegoats perform a similar function, and again there may be a similar kind of collusion by the scapegoat. A study of a residential nursing home, for instance, found a similar emotional situation to that of the nurses' workplace discussed above. Many people relieved their feelings to some extent by blaming their situation on a particular patient or member of staff. 'If only he/she would leave/die this would be a wonderful place to work'. As you can imagine this was a good way of adding a further dollop of guilt to the existing emotional stew (Miller and Gwynne, 1972).

In a different work environment, there is a long tradition on board ship for the crew to regard the Captain as the ultimate father-figure. Thus he may become the embodiment of all the feelings of warm support, encouragement, strength and competence projected onto him by the crew. But if the Captain is regarded, as it were, as the good Dr Jekyll, who plays the nasty Mr Hyde? Apparently it is the First Officer, in a sense the Chief Executive of the ship as opposed to the Captain's more lofty 'Chairman' or 'President'. This process allows the Captain to retain the support of the crew – and the viability of the ship as an organization – even when very unpopular orders have to be given.

A similar splitting process has often been observed in the national life of the United Kingdom between the Queen and the Prime Minister. Guess who plays which role? The splitting process involved in these examples occurs without being questioned as long as everyone involved maintains their psychological contract. If they don't do so the organization is in crisis, as witness the examples of Captain Bligh and King Edward VIII.

It has also been argued that Mrs Thatcher's regal interpretation of her psychological contract when she was Prime Minister might, had it been pushed far enough, have provoked a similar national crisis. It might even be suggested that the dual role of the American Presidency as Head of State and Head of Government is a built-in guarantee of psychological distortion. The attraction of playing the role of Monarch must be very tempting when the Chief Executive role seems to call for hard or unpopular decisions.

The deepest splitting in national life occurs, naturally enough, in time of war – the ultimate crisis for the nation state. Nation states do not usually go to war with each other in a rational, reasoned, sober atmosphere. War is a highly emotional business, and to make sure that the ordinary members (the citizens) support the people who run the organization (the government) a great deal of rhetoric is required to assure them that 'our side' is right, innocent and morally pure while 'their side' is just the opposite. We, in other words, are the Dr Jekylls and they are the Mr Hydes.

The people on the other side are, of course, being given the same treatment. There is no other way you can get national populations to fight or support wars. The psychological contract between government and governed is 'we tell you when the organization is truly threatened and you give us your support and, if necessary, your life'. Of course if this psychological contract is abused by a government it will lose the support of its citizens and any claim to legitimacy, as for example with the military regimes in Greece in the 1970s and Argentina in the 1980s.

Interpersonal relationships at work

In the previous chapter we noted the importance of good personal relations at work for an individual's mental health, especially in times of stress. As we will see in other contexts personal relationships at work are generally of great concern to people, sometimes even more than pay or any other factor. However while most people would want to, and expect to, get on reasonably well with colleagues, things don't always work out. And we have all seen, or even been part of, interpersonal relationships at work where there was a great deal of friction.

Much of the difficulty with this interpersonal friction is that it is seldom analysed and talked through by the people concerned. People are often reluctant to go beyond the most simplistic and superficial judgements of each other – 'she's a different generation', 'he's got a chip on his shoulder', 'we're like chalk and cheese'. It is very difficult for us to realise that someone may respond not to the self we know ourselves to be, but to a perception of our self which is inevitably coloured by the other person's past experiences.

This colouration is, of course, largely unconscious, and therein lies the problem. There is no more point in our saying that working relationships should be entirely professional and impersonal than an employer's intention to hire only hands. Edicts like these extend only as far as our conscious mind will reach. If we are unaware of this we may well be unpleasantly (or even pleasantly!) surprised by the sudden appearance of feelings that have no right to be there, and be disturbed by the interpersonal behaviour that follows.

Transactional analysis

These types of situations have been examined systematically by clinical practitioners of a psychotherapy called Transactional Analysis (TA), a 'transaction' simply being any unit of social intercourse. Eric Berne, a North American psychiatrist, has classified these transactions in a particularly accessible manner (Berne, 1964). Central to Berne's work is the idea 'that at any given moment each individual in a social aggregation will exhibit a Parental, Adult or Child ego state, and that individuals can shift with varying degrees of readiness from one ego state to another' (Berne, 1964, p. 23).

In other words everyone carries around with them not only the adult person they see themselves to be but also their view of their parents and of themselves as a young child.

- The *Parent* aspect represents authority, tradition and the routine knowledge of how things are done.
- The *Adult* aspect mediates between the Parent and Child parts of the personality. It represents the mastery of skills and an objective, rational, data processing kind of approach to a situation.
- The *Child* aspect represents spontaneity, creativity, intuition and pleasure.

The more that people can keep their Adult in control the more mature will they be, but no one can maintain this state all the time. Even mature people act out their Child self occasionally.

Psychologically the healthiest transactions between two people are *complementary transactions* as exhibited in Figure 6.3.

Type I in this figure illustrates the simplest form of transaction, Adult to Adult. Let's imagine an office setting:

Agent: 'Do you know where my file is?'
Respondent: 'It's on your desk.'

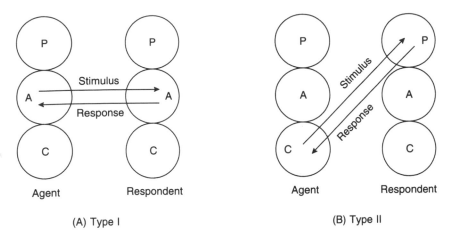

FIGURE 6.3   Complementary transactions

Source: Berne, E. (1964) *Games People Play*, p. 29.

Type II, while also being complementary is not quite so straightforward. In this scenario the Child in one person appeals to the Parent in the other, as for example:

Agent: 'I've lost my file.'
Respondent: 'Well it can't have gone far, let's see if we can find it for you.'

While the transaction here is a complementary one it is not an Adult one and is, presumably, an acting out of an unconscious need by both parties to behave in this way.

Even in the Type II complementary transaction some communication between the parties has been maintained and further transactions continue over time. But in a *crossed transaction* communication breaks down, as illustrated in Figure 6.4.

In Figure 6.4(A) an Adult stimulus is met with a Child response:

Agent: 'Do you know where my file is?'
Respondent: 'How should I know where your file is? You always blame me for everything.'

In Figure 6.4(B) the same Adult stimulus receives a Parent response:

Agent: 'Do you know where my file is?'
Respondent: 'Why can't you keep track of your own files? You're supposed to be a responsible executive.'

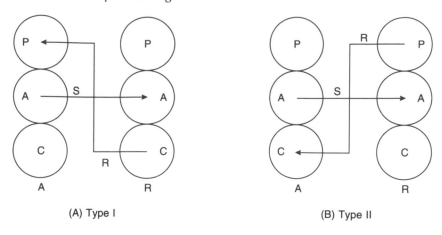

(A) Type I   (B) Type II

FIGURE 6.4   Crossed transactions

Source: Berne, E. (1964) *Games People Play*, p. 30.

In each of these instances the respondent has substituted inappropriate feelings for an appropriate Adult response. Unless this is examined
and acknowledged by the people involved communication between
them will remain blocked.

These little TA diagrams and scenarios are worth thinking through
because they represent the stuff of our daily working lives. As Berne
puts it, 'Simple complementary transactions most commonly occur in
superficial working and social relationships, and these are easily
disturbed by simple crossed transactions' (Berne, 1964, p. 31). What
makes these simple interactions between people so important is the
effect of the unconscious manifesting itself in the relationship – and how
quickly it can appear.

The neurotic organization

In Chapter 2 we noted how much power and what kind of power in
organizations is held by senior managers at the top of the hierarchy. The
way this power is used in practice may be greatly influenced by the
personality of the top manager and in particular the unconscious aspects
of it. If a key individual (or group) in the hierarchy has psychological
problems of which he (or the group) is unaware the organization as a
whole is bound to be adversely affected. Two Canadian psychoanalysts
have identified five commonly found neurotic styles of behaviour and

examined the effects of each style in an organizational setting (Kets de Vries and Miller, 1984).

Kets de Vries and Miller have summarised the characteristic behaviour found in each of these styles, the key fantasy that accompanies it from the unconscious, and the resulting dangers for the organization (see Figure 6.5).

As the key individual's neurosis is expressed within the organization the internal life of that organization comes to mirror the internal life of the individual. What we then have may be called a *neurotic organization* which is, or will shortly become, a failing organization whose identity and sense of purpose has gone off the rails and whose members become increasingly depressed, frustrated and alienated. It has often been argued by psychoanalysts that even whole societies can be damaged in this way, with far more terrible consequences of course than business failure. Hitler's Germany and Stalin's Soviet Union are the examples most usually cited in this context.

The unconscious barriers to change

We have seen how individuals and organizations defend themselves against the anxiety that strong emotions can arouse. We have also seen how these two sets of defences are interrelated and can be mutually supportive. It is important to stress once more that all these manoeuvres are carried out *unconsciously*, without us being aware of them. That is the source of their power, and that is why they are so difficult to change. Their function, indeed, is to preserve the status quo, both individually and collectively, *even where everyone concerned may think consciously that change would be a good thing.*

In large measure, therefore, that is why organizational change is often so difficult and so widely resisted, though the language used is usually that of industrial relations rather than psychology with terms like 'job security', 'pay parity' and 'status differentials' on one side and 'cost effectiveness', 'productivity' and 'market share' on the other. Of course there may be very good *conscious* reasons for people to avoid change. It is not entirely unknown for a proposed organizational change to be in the interests of senior management but not in the interests of staff, or even shareholders. However as the issues involved here are more plainly visible they are of less importance psychologically.

Attempting to change an organization means attacking the system of individual and collective defences that have been built up over time and form the traditional way of doing things in the organization. Added to the basic psychological fear we all have of change because it means

Key Factor	Paranoid	Compulsive	Dramatic	Depressive	Schizoid
Characteristics	Suspiciousness and mistrust of others; hypersensitivity and hyperalertness; readiness to counter perceived threats; overconcern with hidden motives and special meanings; intense attention span; cold, rational, unemotional	Perfectionism; preoccupation with trivial details; insistence that others submit to own way of doing things; relationships seen in terms of dominance and submission; lack of spontaneity; inability to relax; meticulousness, dogmatism, obstinacy	Self-dramatization, excessive expression of emotions; incessant drawing of attention to self; narcissistic preoccupation; a craving for activity and excitement; alternating between idealization and devaluation of others; exploitativeness; incapacity for concentration or sharply focused attention	Feelings of guilt, worthlessness, self-reproach, inadequacy; sense of helplessness and hopelessness – of being at the mercy of events; diminished ability to think clearly; loss of interest and motivation; inability to experience pleasure	Detachment, noninvolvement, withdrawnness; sense of estrangement; lack of excitement or enthusiasm; indifference to praise or criticism; lack of interest in present or future; appearance cold, unemotional
Fantasy	I cannot really trust anybody; a menacing superior force exists that is out to get me; I had better be on my guard	I don't want to be at the mercy of events; I have to master and control all the things affecting me	I want to get attention from and impress people who count in my life	It is hopeless to change the course of events in my life; I am just not good enough	The world of reality does not offer any satisfaction to me; my interactions with others will eventually fail and cause harm, so it is safer to remain distant
Dangers	Distortion of reality due to a preoccupation with confirmation of suspicions; loss of capacity for spontaneous action because of defensive attitudes	Inward orientation; indecisiveness and postponement; avoidance due to the fear of making mistakes; inability to deviate from planned activity; excessive reliance on rules and regulations; difficulties in seeing 'the big picture'	Superficiality, suggestibility; the risk of operating in a non-factual world – action based on 'hunches'; overreaction to minor events; others may feel used and abused	Overly pessimistic outlook; difficulties in concentration and performance; inhibition of action, indecisiveness	Emotional isolation causes frustration of dependency needs of others; bewilderment and aggressiveness may result

Neurotic style

FIGURE 6.5 Neurotic styles

Source: Kets de Vries, M. and D. Miller (1984) *The Neurotic Organisation*, pp. 24–5.

stepping into the unknown, however enticing it may look, we may be left defenceless in the face of emotional anxiety before things have time to settle down and new defences can be erected.

It certainly helps if members of an organization are fully involved in the decision to change and in the way the change is to be accomplished. For people who run the organization, not to do so is simply to produce increased suspicion, distrust, resistance and attachment to the old defences. But this would still be a second-best solution. The best solution is a zillion light years better than that. It is to take a serious and sustained look at what happens to the expression of feelings in the organization at different levels, and see how and why some of them are being repressed and inhibited. But this appears to be an extremely difficult process for organizations to cope with, which is why it so rarely happens.

Kets de Vries and Miller depict the situation crisply and well:

> Sometimes the only way to change the organization's behavior is to change the behavior of its principal actors. And the only way to do that is to convince them *that* they are wrong, to show them *why* they are wrong, and to give them at least some insight into the genesis of their dysfunctional attitudes, beliefs and actions.
>
> This can be done only by gaining insight, not only into organizational problems, but into the people who run the organization. But that is not easy to accomplish . . . Much time and effort are required to make these discoveries, and the process of diagnosis can be disquieting . . . Sensitive issues are raised. Uncomfortable questions are asked. But these travails are necessary to discover the reasons for the organization's problems. Without a sound knowledge of these reasons, no thorough solution will emerge. Only the symptoms will be addressed. The underlying problems will remain, giving rise in the future to similar symptoms. (Kets de Vries and Miller, 1984, pp. 208–9)

CHAPTER 7

Group dynamics and working-group relationships

In previous chapters we have noted in passing some of the effects of group dynamics, including those of working groups. In this chapter we shall focus specifically on these aspects of psychology and the world of work.

The importance of groups

A fairly standard definition of a group would be 'two or more persons who are interacting with one another, who share a set of common goals and norms which direct their activities, and who develop a set of roles and a network of affective relations' (Harré and Lamb, 1986). When social and behavioural scientists talk about 'groups' they are generally referring to small groups of people, also known as 'face-to-face' groups (because members can, for example, all face each other round a table) of about four to eight in number. Most of us belong to about half-a-dozen such groups at any given time in family, school, social and work life.

It is often said that these groups are the building blocks of organizations, but they are much more important than that. Psychologically they are where we live our lives: they are what make us human, a social animal. This is not to say that larger groupings are unimportant, and I will refer to them from time to time, but the psychological forces, or *dynamics*, we are particularly interested in emerge most clearly when a group is small enough for its members to have personal interactions with, and direct information on, each other.

These psychological forces have been intensively studied by psychologists for a long time, resulting in thousands of papers on all aspects of group life. We can do no more than attempt to capture a flavour of this work but because of its importance it is worthwhile to do so as well as looking specifically at work groups and workplace relationships.

There are many ways of categorizing such a vast field but perhaps the most interesting route, for our purposes, into the study of group interactions is to begin by looking at the effects of different kinds of *influences* on groups. In the next section we will differentiate behaviour within groups between that which is the result of conformity to group norms of expected behaviour, that is *intended* effects, and *unintended* effects, which result from the unexpected ways in which people make sense of their social situation.

Unintended influence

Physical proximity and the individual's horizons

Perhaps because they are, on the face of it, so unexpected, examples of people's behaviour being influenced unintentionally are some of the most intriguing in this field. The findings I will cite here are connected by the theme of physical *proximity*.

For instance it was found many years ago that one of the most important ways of predicting whether two people will get married is how far away they live from each other (Katz and Hill, 1958). Thus one study of 5000 couples in Philadelphia found that a third of them had lived within five blocks of each other, and more than half of them had lived within twenty blocks of each other (Bossard, 1932). At least in Western societies people like to feel that their spouse is freely chosen without any arbitrary constraints, but the truth appears to be a little less romantic.

Similarly the development of friendships between people is often based on their physical proximity to each other. A study of friendship patterns between student couples in an apartment block in Boston revealed that next-door neighbours were listed as best friends by 41 per cent of the couples while those living at the far end of their floor were listed only 10 per cent of the time. People living in between were chosen 22 per cent of the time (Festinger, Schachter and Back, 1950).

During the Second World War the United States Army still segregated black and white soldiers, a situation that lasted until rising casualties forced a change in policy. It was then decided to include some all-black platoons within previously all-white infantry companies. Black and white soldiers then found themselves fighting side-by-side *under conditions of equal status*. When a survey was done soon after the war ended it was discovered that the level of prejudice felt by the white soldiers involved towards blacks had dropped dramatically with 7 per cent expressing hostility to the integration as opposed to 62 per cent of whites who had not fought beside black soldiers (Star, Williams and Stouffer, 1965).

Finally in this section it is worth noting that someone's behaviour towards another person may be influenced by the mere presence in his environment of an inanimate object. In a group of college students whose anger was aroused for the purpose of the experiment some were made angry in a room containing a gun and some in a room containing a badminton racket. The students were then given the opportunity to administer what they thought were electric shocks to another person. Students who had been in physical proximity to the gun were willing to give more shocks than those in the badminton racket group (Berkowitz and Le Page, 1967). The mere presence of an object associated with aggression had served to increase their own aggressive behaviour.

Work groups

In 1897 one of the earliest and simplest group studies ever done showed that a person's productivity could be increased by the mere presence of another person (Triplett, 1897). It was found that a subject working on a simple task, like winding a fishing reel, would work harder at the task if there was someone else present, observing the subject's performance but not saying or doing anything.

The effect of another person's sheer presence seems to have a stimulating effect that motivates someone to be on their mettle and show what they can do. This seems to hold true for somewhat larger groups too, as long as the individual's independent effort is clearly visible (Zajonc, 1965). This is part of a phenomenon referred to as *social facilitation*.

On the other hand where an individual's effort is not visible the opposite effect seems to happen. It has been found, for example, that for each new member added to a tug-of-war team the rest of the team put in 10 per cent less effort (Latané *et al.*, 1979). This has been described as *social loafing*. Perhaps this phenomenon operates in reverse when a sports team loses a member and those who are left have to make up the deficit. It has frequently been remarked in soccer, for instance, that a team reduced to ten men will often become more difficult to beat.

As in the case of the student couples noted above, friendship patterns at work can also be directly affected by physical proximity. It has been found, for instance, that small closed offices produce far more friendships than large open-plan offices among clerical workers (Sundstrom, 1986).

Our final example of unintended influence in the workplace brings us to perhaps the most celebrated effect in work psychology, the *Hawthorne effect*. This effect was noticed as part of a huge series of studies at a Western Electric Company plant in Hawthorne, near Chicago that began in 1927 (Roethlisberger and Dickson, 1939: KEY STUDY 6). A group of six young women were studied making telephone equipment in a setting called the Relay Assembly Test Room. The particular focus of the study was on how their productivity was affected by a range of environmental variables such as changes in lighting, rest breaks, hours of work, system of payment and so on.

After every change the result was the same – productivity increased. Even when one of the changes involved a return to the original conditions, productivity still increased. Finally it dawned on the investigators that none of the working conditions made any difference one way or the other. What seemed to matter to the workers was that the organization was interested in them and in observing their performance, and so they did as well as they could in response.

Intended influence

At the heart of group life, and central to the existence of human beings as social animals, is the need we all have to predict other people's behaviour. Unless we are confident about what other people are going to do, group life is simply not possible. Normally we are not even aware of the issue. When we go to an office meeting we don't expect to find people sitting haphazardly round the floor in their pyjamas, and we'd be rather upset if we did. We expected, unconsciously, to find them seated round the table in business clothes, and had we done so we wouldn't have thought about it for a second.

Other people obviously have the same expectations about *our* behaviour and it is therefore very important to us to know how to behave, to know what the *group norms* of expected behaviour are. How we learn these norms is something we will deal with in Chapter 9; here we are concerned with the importance of the norms themselves.

Because so much of our life is lived in groups they provide us with our psychological sustenance, with a sense of belonging, with meaning and even with our very identity, with the content of our self-image.

Maintaining the group norms is thus the paramount objective of any group. Without them the group would cease to exist. There is therefore a constant pressure on members to *conform* to the group norms, a pressure which (like the business clothes) we are only aware of when something unusual happens. People usually conform to group and social norms. Conformity *is* the norm. Several classic studies will help illuminate the psychological mechanism that makes this social engine work and the many different forms it can take.

In the early 1950s, Solomon Asch did a series of studies on the effects of group pressure on the individual which startled other psychologists, and even Asch himself. The typical Asch experiment had seven people seated around a table judging lengths of lines (Asch, 1956). Only one of the seven subjects in Asch's experiment was a real (that is, naïve) subject. The other six were paid confederates of the experimenter, and it was their job to produce the group pressure directed at the naïve subject. The study was billed as an exercise in visual perception and the subjects were supposed to compare the length of a line on one card with three lines on another card, as in Figure 7.1.

The experimenter then asked the subjects whether line X was equal in length to lines A, B or C. Asch deliberately made the task very easy so that subjects when they were alone would always give the right answer. What Asch wanted to find out was this: what would happen if his six confederates all gave the same wrong answer? Would the naïve subject say what he really saw, or would he be influenced by the unanimous judgement of the group to conform and give the same wrong answer as everyone else?

Asch had arranged things so that the naïve subject was always seated in the number six position where he would hear five other judgements before his own turn came. In fully *a third* of the cases the naïve subject succumbed to the group pressure he felt and gave an answer he knew to be wrong. Three quarters of the subjects did so at least once, with only a quarter of the subjects sticking to their own judgements throughout.

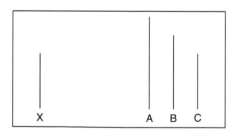

FIGURE 7.1   Asch conformity situation

Asch's experiments have been repeated many times by other psychologists and the findings have usually been the same. A great deal of work has also gone into studying the various factors involved and these are commonly divided into individual factors and group factors.

A study of the people who yielded to group pressure shows that they are much lower in self-esteem and have a poorer image of themselves than the people who did not yield. The most important group factor is whether or not the majority making the wrong judgement is unanimous. If even one other person agrees with the naïve subject, his likelihood of yielding to group pressure is greatly reduced. In this situation there was only 5–10 per cent conformity.

While Solomon Asch was performing his important series of studies on conformity, other psychologists interested in the same phenomena adopted a somewhat different approach. Richard Crutchfield, for instance, developed a technique that dispensed with the need for confederates and gave him a great deal of control over the conformity situation (Crutchfield, 1955).

In Crutchfield's experiments, five people were each making their individual judgements of the stimuli. The subjects were seated side by side, each person seated in his own cubicle facing a switchboard and out of sight of the others. Verbal communication was not allowed, and the only way a subject could communicate with the others, or with the experimenter, was by flicking a switch in front of him that lit up signal lights on everyone else's switchboard.

Each subject was asked to indicate in this way whether he agreed or disagreed with various statements that were presented to the group. The switchboard in front of him registered the answers of the other group members. Unlike the Asch situation, however, each of the people in the group was a naïve subject whose responses to group pressure were being studied. In fact, there was no communication between the subjects in the group. Crutchfield systematically controlled the situation by providing each subject with false information on his switchboard about the judgements of the other four people.

At certain points each subject found himself faced with that looked like a unanimous group choice supporting the wrong answer to a particular statement. Where the statements dealt with the same level of difficulty as in the Asch study – that is, easy perceptual comparisons or arithmetical problems – Crutchfield obtained about the same level of conformity as Asch, about one-third of the subjects,

But when Crutchfield made the arithmetical problem difficult, up to 80 per cent of the subjects were persuaded to conform to the false group consensus and agree with an answer that was clearly wrong. In this situation Crutchfield also induced bright college students to agree with a great number of odd statements: for example, that most Americans are over 65 years old, that the average person only has a life expectancy of 25 years, and that this same average American eats six meals a day – perhaps accounting for the fact that he only sleeps four hours a night.

Most striking of all perhaps was the reaction to the statement 'Free speech being a privilege rather than a right, it is proper for a society to suspend free speech whenever it feels itself threatened'. In the control group free of group pressure, only 19 per cent of the subjects agreed with this statement; in Crutchfield's situation of group pressure, 58 per cent agreed.

A different type of conformity in a group setting was the object of research by Stanley Milgram (1963; 1974). In Milgram's work, the conformity studied was not compliance with a norm set by a group of people in the same room as the subject, but compliance to a general norm of society – obedience to authority. But Milgram's studies were similar to those of Asch in at least one respect: they caused a great stir among psychologists. In fact his dramatic findings have also caused a great stir among non-psychologists.

Like Asch, Milgram was interested in observing the behaviour of one naive subject at a time, in a controlled setting. The subjects thought they were taking part in a learning experiment where they were to play the role of a teacher, while another person (Milgram's confederate) took the part of a learner. The learner was supposed to memorize lists of words which the teacher was supposed to help him learn by giving him an electric shock whenever he made an error. The more errors the learner made, the stronger the voltage he was given – up to 450 volts, at which point the switch was marked 'Danger! Severe Shock XXX'.

In fact no electric shocks were actually given although the subject thought they were. The situation was rigged. Communication between teacher and learner was by means of an intercom, for the supposed learner was supposedly strapped into an impressive-looking electronic apparatus in the next room, out of sight of the teacher. The responses the subject thought he was getting from the learner were actually a tape recording with pre-arranged right and wrong answers. As the errors increased, and the punishment along with it, the subject heard howls of pain, demands to be let out, and finally silence from the room next door. The real purpose of the experiment was to see how far the subject would go in giving someone electric shocks when prompted to do so by an authority, the experimenter.

When people are asked to guess how many subjects continued on up to the 450-volt mark, the usual estimate is about one per cent. In fact some 65 per cent, *almost two-thirds* of the subjects, did so. Milgram is careful to point out that the subjects in his study were not sadists who enjoyed inflicting pain on other people. Far from it; they were extremely uncomfortable about the whole situation and often expressed a desire to terminate the experiment. Yet only a third of the subjects were willing to defy the experimenter's authority and refuse to continue.

As with the subjects in the Asch experiment the people who did not succumb to the conformity pressure tended to be higher in self-esteem than the people who did. The most important situational factor was the amount of personal responsibility the subject had to accept for his or her actions. In one part of the study the subject had to force the learner's hand down on a shockplate in order to deliver the maximum 450 volts. Under these conditions the amount of conformity was more than halved; less than one third of the subjects were willing to go this far.

Another kind of conformity to a general social norm has been suggested by Elliot Aronson in his book *The Social Animal* (1992). The kind of behaviour that Aronson is interested in also involves conformity to a general social norm but in this case the norm is that people do not interact with others – what is sometimes called *bystander apathy*. It is often argued that when someone is attacked or has an accident in a public place, the norm is for other people not to get involved, to walk away from the the scene. Some research studies have also supported the notion of bystanders conforming to a norm of apathy.

At the same time there are instances where people do get involved. But why do people help out in some situations and not in others? A study done in the New York subway system gives us some clues (Piliavin, Rodin and Piliavin, 1969). This experiment was designed to see if people would come to the aid of a man who had collapsed on the floor of a subway car. The man was an accomplice of the experimenters, of course; in some cases he appeared to be ill and in other cases drunk.

The results of this experiment surprised a lot of people. Where the man appeared to be ill, people came to his aid 95 per cent of the time. Even when the man reeked of liquor he was still helped 50 per cent of the time. Aronson suggests that the situation in this experiment provided two conditions that changed the social norm from apathy to intervention. First, everyone in the subway car felt part of the same situation, sharing a common predicament. Second they couldn't walk away. They were part of the scene and had to deal with the fact that someone had collapsed in front of them. In a word they responded as members of a group rather than isolated individuals.

Another classic study of conformity involves the ingenious use of an optical illusion. If you sit in a room that is completely dark except for a tiny pinpoint of light, the light although it is completely stationary will appear to move about. This illusion of movement is called the *autokinetic effect*. Muzafer Sherif (1936) discovered that when he put three people in the room at the same time their individual estimates of how far the light had moved began to converge until a consensus was reached, thereby establishing a group norm.

When each subject then judged how far the light had moved when he was alone in the room, he did not return to his original judgement but opted instead for the group judgement. The subject thus conformed to the group norm, although we should note that he had a hand in setting that norm. This study is about as clear an example of conformity pressure as one can imagine. An outside observer would see nothing happening, no apparent pressure from either the experimenter or the other subjects, merely a group of people sitting in the dark deciding how far a stationary light had moved. What these people were doing was deciding how to make sense of something that had absolutely no meaning by itself.

There is another interpretation we can make of Sherif's findings. It appears that people organized the perceptual cues (tiny light against dark, formless background) in two different ways. By themselves they judged that the light was only moving a little: in a group they judged it as moving further. By themselves they could only rely on their own senses (which were of course being deceived), but in the group situation they had some extra social cues in the form of other people's judgements.

Conformity to group norms may therefore be thought of as a process where people organize social cues to help them understand how one is expected to respond and what the consequences would be if one responded differently. In an ambiguous social situation, with no laws or physical coercion to direct our behaviour, social cues are all-important – even if they are completely misleading.

We will end this section on intended influence with another study from the Hawthorne series that moves us back into the centre of the world of work. This particular study was conducted in what was called the Bank Wiring Observation Room, in which a total of twelve men worked. These workers had formed a strong informal group culture which included a clear norm of production.

A certain number of units of output per day by each man was considered reasonable and fair by the group, no more (despite strenuous management attempts to increase productivity) but also no less. Anyone deviating from this norm in either direction was subject to immediate conformity pressure, which could escalate from a joking remark to a sharp thump on the arm, or ostracism by the rest of the group (Roethlisberger and Dickson, 1939: KEY STUDY 6).

In the next section we will take a closer look at the relationships between members *within* a group and also how these relationships affect the interactions *between* groups.

Intragroup relations

Cohesiveness

We have seen that the mechanism which keeps a group ticking over is the pressure to conform to its norms of behaviour. But the forces that ultimately hold a group together and give it its reason for continued existence are to be found in the *cohesiveness* arising from the mutual regard that group members have for each other and in sharing the same group goals. And the more attracted that members are to a group the harder will they work to uphold the group's norms and achieve its goals.

However cohesiveness is a positive *general* group dynamic and if the group in question is a work group it may or may not lead to increased productivity. If the work group norm is to increase productivity than that is what will happen, but if the norm is to *decrease* productivity than it will be *less* productive than a non-cohesive group (Shaw, 1976).

We should note here that individuals all have their own agenda for being in a particular group. In Chapter 2 we saw that this was true of organizational life in general, but even when we focus down on small close-knit groups people still have their own interests, needs and wants. One person may be in the group because she likes the activity it is concerned with and another because she likes the other group members without being too concerned about their activities. Often the specific motives that people have either coincide or have differences that don't matter very much, but sometimes there are differences that can lead to intragroup conflict.

Communication networks

We also noted in Chapter 2 that the flow of information was crucial to the working of an organization, and this is true in particular ways of small groups. It is possible to see the dynamics involved most clearly when group members are *not* face-to-face. Various kinds of communications networks, as illustrated in Figure 7.2, have been studied in the laboratory (Bavelas, 1968; Shaw, 1976).
The findings from this work include the following:

- for simple tasks centralized networks are usually more efficient (for instance from Circle to Wheel in Figure 7.2);
- for complex tasks less centralized networks are usually more efficient (for instance from Wheel to Circle in Figure 7.2);

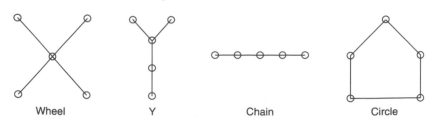

Wheel   Y   Chain   Circle

FIGURE 7.2   Communcation networks in five-person groups

- satisfaction is highest in less centralized networks, particularly in the Circle where everyone was involved in decision making;
- group members can, however, modify a given network if it does not suit their needs by deciding not to communicate along certain paths.

Group decision making

The most important factor underlying relationships between individual members of decisions made by their group is that of *participation*. Individuals are more likely to accept and act on a group decision if they have participated in forming that decision.

An interesting study that throws light on this point was conducted in the United States during the Second World War by Kurt Lewin, widely regarded as the 'father of group dynamics'. Lewin was working on behalf of a government campaign to persuade the civilian population to eat some less popular (though nutritious) cuts of meat than the steaks and so on whose prices had risen sharply. In particular the government was interested in persuading people to eat offal like brains, hearts, lungs and kidneys. Most Americans found offal quite unappealing, and certainly unfamiliar to cook, so the campaign had a difficult task to perform.

Lewin's view was that mass advertising wouldn't be very effective in reaching individuals because people's eating behaviour was largely governed by group norms. So if you wanted to change a person's eating behaviour you would have to change the norms of their group. As the most important group member (of the family) in this instance was the housewife, Lewin designed a study using groups of housewives to see how this might be done (Lewin, 1958).

Six groups were used in the research and they were studied under two different conditions. Half of the women were given a lecture that talked about the influences of nutrition on the health of the family, the war effort and saving money. The lecturer then handed out recipes using offal.

The other condition of the study employed group discussion, based on a group leader's introduction of the same topics, which tried to elicit the specific contributions that the members of the group could make when they went home. In particular the women in this half of the study were encouraged to discuss the reasons for resistance to change in eating behaviour. The recipes were then distributed and the group members were asked who would be willing to try out one of the recipes during the following week.

A week later all the subjects of the study were interviewed at home. The findings were striking. Only three per cent of the lecture group had tried one of the offal recipes but 32 per cent of the discussion group had done so. Lewin's interpretation of these findings was that participation in the group discussions had allowed a new group norm of eating behaviour to develop. This gave the women who were more amenable to change the necessary group support to do so and the confidence that it was their decision.

It should not be too surprising then that when we look at work groups we find evidence that participation by workers in decisions affecting their jobs can lead to increased enthusiasm, commitment and productivity (see for example Coch and French, 1948; Lawler and Hackman, 1969). We should note though that, as in Lewin's study, not all group members respond positively to such opportunities for participation. A certain amount of self-confidence and need for independence is required for behaviour to change under these conditions. More authoritarian types of people tend to be less responsive (see for instance Vroom, 1959).

Group problem solving

A great deal of attention has been focussed on the particular kinds of decision-making processes that groups go through when they have to solve a problem. A high degree of group cohesiveness and participation of all its members is usually regarded as being essential to successful problem-solving. It seems to be taken for granted by some people that groups will come up with better solutions to problems than individuals. This assumption ranges from the common saying 'two heads are better than one', to the common practice in organizations for problems to be tackled by setting up small groups to deal with them. On this view the group product is greater than the sum of its individual parts, a process known as *synergy*.

On the other hand some people are dubious about the effectiveness of the groups, committees, working parties and so on that take up such a large part of organizational life. They would prefer the folk wisdom that 'too many cooks spoil the broth' and suggest that 'a camel is a horse designed by a committee'.

Behavioural scientists can be equally split, even when reviewing the same research evidence. The authors of one textbook conclude that 'in most conditions groups outperform even their best member' (Fincham and Rhodes, 1992, p. 160). But others argue that 'the superiority of individual performance over group brainstorming is an example of how a taken-for-granted assumption can be disproved by social science research' (Buchanan and Huczynski, 1985, p. 197).

Still others have decided that 'it is not possible to generalize about whether individuals or groups are universally better. It depends on the abilities and training of the individuals and groups, and also on the kind of task being tackled' (Arnold, Robertson and Cooper, 1991, p. 213). And I think that would be my own view of yet another complex issue in this field that looks deceptively simple at first glance.

In a similar vein, people have been divided about whether group decisions were more or less likely to be conservative than those taken by individuals. It used to be thought by social psychologists that group decisions were less conservative and that there was a clear tendency for groups to opt for solutions with more risks attached than did individuals. There seemed to be a lot of evidence for a 'risky shift' in attitudes from the individual to the group situation (Kogan and Wallach, 1967).

However later studies showed that groups can also be more conservative in their decisions on some issues than individuals, exhibiting a 'caution shift' rather than a risky one. That is why the term *group polarization* is now used to describe the shift in attitudes between an individual and a group situation, whatever the direction of the shift.

That direction seems to depend on the views first expressed by each of the group members, with the majority view forming the group norm. The shift in attitude by the group as a whole then goes in that direction (Lamm and Myers, 1978). The reasons for the shift appear to be based on the greater weight of argument for one decision or the other together with the need to conform to the now established group norm (Moscovici, 1985).

One celebrated group decision that exhibited a risky shift has been studied in detail to see how the process of group polarization operates. This was the decision of the group chaired by President John F. Kennedy to invade Cuba in 1961 at the Bay of Pigs. The invasion went disastrously wrong for the American government, with serious political consequences. President Kennedy himself later referred to the decision as 'stupid', but he could hardly be described as a stupid person, nor could any other member of his group. The explanation for the bad decision lay in the workings of the group rather than the personalities of its members.

We have seen that cohesiveness between group members and conformity to the group's norms are vital for the proper functioning, and indeed the very existence, of any group. But what the Bay of Pigs decision showed was that there is such a thing as *too much* cohesiveness and *too much* conformity. The group members had such a high regard for each other's ability that as a group they acted as though they were invulnerable to error. It became unthinkable to them that such bright people could get it wrong.

Their cohesiveness meant that they treated outgroups with contempt. Their conformity meant that great pressure was put on people who dissented from the prevailing norm, or even expressed doubts about it. Such views were regarded as disloyal. Information that didn't fit the emerging view made the group uncomfortable and so it was usually discredited or ignored, resulting in a premature closure of the group's options.

Also ignored were the various ethical issues raised by a decision to invade another country. Closed off from other influences and turned in upon itself the group was thus able to decide that about 1500 Cuban exiles could successfully invade the island and defeat a highly motivated and popularly supported army a hundred times stronger. The result was a fiasco that was all over in two days.

This kind of process has been called *groupthink* (Janis, 1982). The Bay of Pigs incident and its analysis has become a case study for foreign service officers and others in avoiding the dangers of groupthink. It is a particularly dramatic example of the process, which therefore lends itself to study. A more recent example in this vein is the suggestion that groupthink by the operators may have been responsible for the terrible nuclear accident at Chernobyl (Reason, 1987).

But every organization in daily life has decision-making groups that are capable of falling into the same traps. One industrial example that has been studied looks at the decisions leading up to the introduction of unsuccessful models of new cars on to the market (Feldman and Arnold, 1983).

Intergroup relations

In discussing groupthink we touched on intergroup relations by noting how the intense build-up of commitment to one's own group (the ingroup) seemed to entail the denigration of other groups (the outgroups). In this section we will focus specifically on the nature of the relations between groups.

There is nothing easier than finding differences between groups of people. Indeed in the way we make sense of the world it seems to be easier for us, cognitively, to discern differences rather than similarities about anything. This can be seen clearly in early childhood. Questions about similarities and differences are a standard feature of the commonly used intelligence test, the Stanford-Binet. On this test six-year-old children, for instance, can usually tell us that summer is hot and winter is cold. But not until they are much older can they tell us that summer and winter are both seasons.

The ability to see similarities as well as differences may therefore require more cognitive complexity than is required to identify differences alone. It is thus easier to learn and to teach differences than similarities, a factor that is reflected in the education curriculum of any school system. Differences of dress, manner, language, customs, behaviour and appearance are very evident and are frequently stressed by all the social institutions (like family, school, religion and play group) that children have to deal with. Similarities have to be sought out, and even when the child is intellectually capable of handling such concepts, there is little reward for doing so.

We therefore grow up with a psychological readiness to seek similarities only with other members of our own group(s) and differences with members of other groups. It is thus a simple and effective and frequently used technique of politicians to tell us how wonderful *we* are and how terrible *they* are in order to gain our support. This is particularly evident in extreme situations like going to war where the differences between our group and theirs must be virtually total; we are all-good and they are all-bad.

In the everyday life of organizations the same process is at work in less dramatic situations. This process is sometimes known as *depersonalization* and it is found in both intragroup and intergroup relations. It involves the members of a group in playing down the personal differences between them, such as values, attitudes, motives and personality characteristics, while emphasizing the group membership they have in common.

This process is even more powerful in intergroup relations where the outgroup is seen as an undifferentiated mass (Park and Rothbart, 1982). Members of each group are also prone to exaggerate the differences between the two groups (Allen and Wilder, 1979). In fact simply being a member of a given group may be enough to produce negative behaviour towards another group, even where the composition of each group is entirely arbitrary and the members were randomly assigned to the groups in an experimenter's lab (Turner, 1975).

In fact it is possible by this random assignment of strangers to groups to get one group of young men to inflict horrifying cruelty on another group of young men. An experiment carried out with student volunteers at Stanford University, California by Philip Zimbardo offers some dramatic evidence of this (Zimbardo *et al.*, 1973). At the toss of a coin the subjects were divided into 'prisoners' and 'guards' and told to role play the appropriate part.

These young men played their parts so well (that is conformity pressures were so powerful) that an experiment scheduled to last two weeks was ended after six days amid real distress on the part of some of the 'prisoners' – and of the psychologists running the study. The 'guards' tended to become aggressive and hostile and the 'prisoners' depressed and angry. One of the 'guards' later told how he forced the prisoners to 'call each other names and clean the toilets out with their bare hands. I practically considered the prisoners cattle, and I kept thinking "I have to watch out for them in case they try something"' (Zimbardo *et al.*, 1973, p. 42).

We have already noted in Chapter 2 that the formation of groups with different interests is endemic to organizational life. The possibilities then for intergroup conflict are always there structurally, and we have now seen that the attractions of group membership and group identity are so important to people psychologically that it doesn't take much to produce the most hostile behaviour against outgroups. So the crucial question for organizations is how to deal with this threatened or actual conflict between the various groups that they are composed of.

This question was dealt with in a famous naturalistic study under the direction of Muzafer Sherif (Sherif, 1966. KEY STUDY 7). The subjects of the study were 11- and 12-year-old boys at a Boy Scout summer camp. The boys were randomly assigned to one of two groups, for example the *Rattlers* or the *Eagles*, and encouraged to compete with each other at various sports. The experimenters arranged things so that ingroup solidarity and intergroup hostility were increased, to the point where name-calling, fighting and other forms of aggression broke out.

The experimenter's task then was to break down the hostile attitudes that had been established and restore harmony all round. Their first attempt involved contact between the Rattlers and the Eagles in pleasant situations, like watching a movie. But this had little effect. Indeed the hostility seemed to increase. Then they presented the two groups with goals that had to be achieved for the camp to function but which required the participation of all the campers at the same time. These are known as *superordinate goals*.

Superordinate goals

The goals, like emergency repairs to the water supply or pulling a truck uphill, were beyond the capacity of either group by itself, and in working together to achieve them the Rattlers and the Eagles began – slowly and with difficulty – to lose their negative stereotypes of each other and their hostile attitudes. Gradually the boys developed new friendships across group lines and cooperated with each other spontaneously.

Earlier in this chapter we discussed the effects of sharing combat situations on the attitudes of white soldiers towards blacks. For these two groups combat was also a superordinate goal. They had fought side-by-side and been dependent on each other while achieving their mutual objective. It is this *mutual interdependence*, as exhibited both by the soldiers and the campers, which seems to be the crucial factor in forming a superordinate group.

Unfortunately the existence of superordinate goals seems to be rare outside of combat or emergency conditions. Perhaps that is why these conditions are often evoked by people in positions of leadership faced by intergroup conflict. They seem to be urging people both to perceive their situation in terms of mutually interdependent goals or other symbols and, by using flags and slogans like 'the Dunkirk spirit' or 'the spirit of '76', are trying to foster a superordinate group *identity*.

Because the reduction of intergroup hostility is so difficult some organizational theorists prefer to concentrate on preventing its occurrence in the first place. Edgar Schein, for example, suggests four *preventive* steps that could be taken in setting up and running the various functional groups of an organization.

1. *Relatively greater emphasis should be given to total organizational effectiveness* and the role of departments in contributing to it . . .
2. *High interaction and frequent communication* should be stimulated between groups to work on problems of intergroup coordination and help . . .
3. *Frequent rotation of members* among groups or departments should be encouraged to stimulate a high degree of mutual understanding and empathy . . .
4. *Win–lose situations should be avoided* and groups should never be put into the position of competing for some scarce organizational reward . . .

(Schein, 1988, pp. 179–80)

Schein appreciates that the fourth point would be particularly difficult for many managers to accept because of the highly competitive ethos that exists (and is encouraged) within most organizations. However he argues, in common with many other theorists and researchers in this field, that cooperation between groups would be, in the long run, a better strategy for organizations and their members (see, for example Aronson, 1992 and Handy, 1985 and, for a review of the data, Johnson *et al.*, 1980).

Working-group relationships

Peers

We have looked, in this chapter, at some of the relationships between group members, colleagues and fellow workers. In previous chapters we saw how important co-workers can be, for example in getting people through the endless routine of a boring job (Chapter 4) or in coping with stress at work (Chapter 5).

In this final section of the present chapter we will focus more on the relationship between the people who run a work organization and those at the bottom of the hierarchy – the managers, with nearly all the decision-making power, and the managed, with little or none. This is a psychological distinction which cuts across the formal hierarchy of shop floor, junior, middle and senior management. As we will see the line between managers and managed may be drawn at different points on the hierarchy in different organizations, but drawn it invariably is.

The managers and the managed

The Hawthorne studies we mentioned earlier in the chapter are associated with one of the first and most celebrated of work psychologists, Elton Mayo. Mayo was particularly excited by his discovery of the informal work group and the influence that it seemed to have on setting rates of productivity. Up to this point Henry Ford's assembly line model had dominated management and consultant thinking about the way work should be organized.

What Mayo suggested to the people who ran the Hawthorne factory was that people regarded work as a social situation. Wherever possible they would try to organise it collectively, and the social relationships involved were more important to them than financial incentives to work harder. It therefore made good managerial sense to go with the grain of the workers' inclinations rather than forcing them constantly into a formal organizational strait-jacket (KEY STUDY 6). After all even though groups restricted output they also maintained a level of productivity that management seemed able to live with, and they also got more satisfaction from their work than Henry Ford's human robots.

Mayo's ideas marked the start of the *Human Relations movement* in work psychology (Mayo, 1946). But although they may have been popular with many social and behavioural scientists they did not – and do not – find such ready acceptance with management. The reason for this opposition then – as now – takes us back, as we shall see, to a central issue of organizational life; *who has the power?*

Following Mayo's lead Human Relations theorists believed that the interests of managers and managed in work organizations were actually identical, if only both sides could be persuaded of this. Any conflict between them was down to bad management and poor administration of the workplace. In fact Mayo believed that conflict was pathological and that, for example, union organisers who saw the interests of their members as different from that of management were downright deviants psychologically.

A generation after the Hawthorne studies a modified view of this approach, know as *neo-Human Relations* was formed by a number of influential theorists including Abraham Maslow and Fred Herzberg, whose work we will deal with in Chapter 13 on motivation (Maslow, 1954; Herzberg, 1966). The key difference between these theorists and their earlier counterparts was that they saw conflict as a normal enough part of organizations and not something that arose only through poor human relations. However they did feel that this conflict was in principle resolvable and not an inevitable product of the way power was distributed in the organization.

Perhaps another difference between the two groups of theorists may have been that some senior managers were a little more ready to apply the newer ideas to the workplace, particularly in the 1970s. There were several interesting attempts at that time to use group working in place of the assembly line model, notably (and appropriately) in the car industry.

Volvo turned an assembly plant on a greenfield site at Kalmar in Sweden over to this form of work organization. In the Kalmar plant each group worked together, largely at its own pace. The group had a space of their own to have coffee breaks at their own discretion. Most importantly perhaps the cycle time of the job – and therefore its complexity – was increased, from a matter of seconds to about twenty minutes, and each group was responsible for its own quality control (Gyllenhammar, 1977).

Similarly Volkswagen experimented with working groups in a new engine plant at Salzgitter in Germany. The experiment involved four seven-man groups each responsible for various tasks including the assembly and testing of the engines. The assembly line was completely done away with and each group was given a quota of seven engines to produce each day. Each team member was trained to perform all the required tasks and each group was allowed to allocate these tasks as it wished. Each group had a spokesman who communicated with management on behalf of his group (Jenkins, 1978).

On the face of it this form of group working looks like an unequivocally good idea. A survey of fifty-three such experiments found that job satisfaction and quality of work had improved in all of them (Pasmore *et al.*, 1984). And productivity apparently either increases or at least doesn't decrease.

It is important to note that the reason for any increase in productivity is not due to the fact that people in autonomous work groups produce more. It is probably due to the companies dispensing with the cost of a whole layer of supervisors who would have exerted close visual control over the production process (Wall *et al.*, 1986). Producing the same number of cars with fewer employees represents greater overall productivity per employee in management accounting. But as we'll see in a moment management may perceive another kind of cost in this type of operation. Neither the Volvo nor the Volkswagen experiments lasted more than a few years. Moreover each remained an experiment and did not go on to become an industry-wide, or even a company-wide, way of organizing work. And this in two companies widely regarded as progressive; and in two nations widely regarded as industrially enlightened.

The problem at Volvo was that the work groups were not fully autonomous – they are usually described as 'semi-autonomous' – and power over their work situation was still centrally controlled by management, who could exert pressure for greater productivity (Berggren, 1989). Workers relaxing after finishing their daily quota, for example, troubled senior management who felt that workers not actually working during work hours represented an under-utilization of resources. So they tried to control this 'unused' time by increasing work quotas, with the inevitable result that any vestige of autonomy felt by the work group disappeared, and with it the job satisfaction and increased commitment that made the system work in the first place (Blackler and Shimmin, 1984).

In the case of Volkswagen the new form of group working upset not only the management but the unions. Management's dealing directly with work group spokesmen undercut the union role in representing the shop floor. Increasing the individual skills of the group members also led to disputes between unions and management about the appropriate rates to be paid for each job (Jenkins, 1985).

The central issue of who controls the workplace and how is particularly evident when the organization of work is changed and when new technology is introduced. We shall therefore return to this topic and consider it in more detail in Chapter 16: 'The effects of new technology'.

CHAPTER 8

Work, non-work and in-between

'The "work ethic" holds that labor is good in itself; that a man or woman becomes a better person by virtue of the act of working.'

President Richard Nixon
Labor Day 1971

'You can't eat for eight hours a day nor drink for eight hours a day nor make love for eight hours a day – all you can do for eight hours is work. Which is the reason why man makes himself and everybody else so miserable and unhappy.'

William Faulkner

'Work? It gets me oot the hoose.'

Unidentified Glaswegian

Introduction

The central issue we will deal with in this chapter is that of unemployment; its psychological meaning and consequences. There are two reasons for dealing with such a topic in some detail as part of a book on the world of work: (1) the threat and the experience of unemployment is becoming part of the life of a worker in the industrialised world with increasing frequency and (2) understanding the nature of that experience can give us a unique and important insight into the place of work in a person's life.

Although the experience of becoming unemployed may occur without much warning, leaving an individual with an abrupt, difficult and indeed shocking transition to cope with, the states of 'working' and 'not working' are not quite as clear-cut and opposed to each other as they might seem at first glance. It is worthwhile to examine these two conditions and what might lie between them as well as focusing specifically on unemployment.

We saw in Chapter 4: 'The time dimension' that our society has certain expectations of us and our relationship to the world of work and that these expectations differ at different stages of our life. The importance of that world and our relationship to it is taken for granted, in small ways and in large, throughout our life. One of the earliest questions a small child is routinely asked is 'What are you going to be when you grow up?'

What this question really means, of course, is 'what job are you going to do for a living?' The expected reply often covers only a limited range: 'doctor', 'pilot', 'engineer' (for a boy) and 'nurse', 'air hostess' and 'secretary' (for a girl) are high on the approved list. The enquirer would be troubled by a more considered and unexpected reply like 'I'm going to be a decent human being, what are you going to be?'

As an adult the question 'What do you do?' is one we are usually faced with when we meet someone for the first time. It is a very important way for people to categorise each other. It offers instant clues to income, social status and lifestyle and some idea of how this person will expect to be treated. For people who are regularly employed to do an identifiable job the question elicits an automatic answer. For people who are not, the answer is much more problematic for both parties.

What if you are a writer who hasn't published a book for some time and are driving a bus to help pay the bills? Are you a writer or a bus driver? Or what about the businessman whose business has just failed? Is he self-employed or unemployed? As we've been socialised practically from birth to regard what we do for a living as a vital part of who we are, psychologically these questions are by no means trivial.

Work and employment: underemployment

We need to be clear about the terms we use in this discussion and how they are commonly applied. The *Concise Oxford Dictionary* (1976) defines *work* as 'expenditure of energy, striving, application of effort or exertion to a purpose'. In contrast it defines *employment* as 'one's regular trade or profession'. These definitions seem clear enough, and at the very least we should be able to declare unequivocally that people in employment work. In fact these terms are often used interchangeably with people talking about being 'in work' or 'out of work', about 'starting work next week', and so on.

But of course it's not quite that straightforward. There are plenty of examples of people in employment where 'expenditure of energy, striving, application of effort or exertion to a purpose' may not be much in evidence. If times are hard and customers scarce shop assistants and salespeople may stand around for hours waiting to serve someone, especially if they're supplying expensive items like cars or financial services.

Or there may not be enough work to do because of a serious mismatch between the work that is supposed to be done and the number of people employed to do it, a criticism often made (rightly or wrongly) of public bureaucracies. In the former Soviet Union (to take an extreme example) where virtually everyone was employed by the state, and unemployment was officially close to zero, there was a popular saying, 'they pretend to pay us and we pretend to work'. People who are in this position will often feel vulnerable, and with good reason, to changing political conditions that might lead to their employment being rationalised out of existence, regardless of how willing they may be to work.

However these are only the most visible signs of *underemployment*. It is in fact a pervasive and insidious feature of the world of work. A 1986 report concluded 'that a large proportion of the workforce report that they are underemployed' (O'Brien, 1986, p. 46). There are two related reasons for this: (1) the application of new technology has resulted in deskilling for many of those workers who kept their jobs and (2) the steady increase in educational standards and qualifications since the 1960s, coupled with rising unemployment, has found more and more people in jobs for which they are over-educated or over-qualified.

The net result is a lot of employed people who feel that their talents, skills and qualifications are being seriously under-utilized. We will return to this issue from different perspectives in later chapters. We have already seen in Chapter 5 how underemployment can be a prime cause of stress at work.

Work outside employment

If 'employment' does not always imply 'work' the converse is even more true. A great deal of work is done outside of employment. Many of the same activities that people work at for a living, in fact, can also be done for other reasons. Driving, painting, gardening, tailoring or teaching are often done by volunteers, for instance to help people who can't do these things for themselves. And many of the leisure activities that people commonly engage in, from model building to music making, from chess playing to disco dancing and dramatics to baseball, can frequently engage them in expending greater energy, discipline and creativity than the work they are employed to do eight hours a day (Csikszentmihalyi, 1975; Stebbins, 1979).

Sometimes when people are employed to do creative work it is even very difficult to tell whether they are 'at work' or 'at leisure', for example in scientific research or the performing arts where few people work solely during 'working hours' even though they may officially be employed (and paid) only during that period of time.

We will return to these issues later in the chapter when we discuss retirement but for the present discussion, and bearing these complexities in mind, we will concentrate on the distinction between being in paid employment and being without paid employment. For our discussion of *unemployment* we will use the term 'work' as being synonymous with 'employment'.

Transitions into and out of employment

During our discussion of the time dimension in Chapter 4 we examined the way in which our attitudes towards the world of work are expected to change at different stages of our life. We noted how there were many exceptions to the ideal model outlined in Table 4.1. In this section we will focus particularly on those periods of transition in a person's life into and out of full-time paid employment, as noted in Table 8.1.

Table 8.1 outlines the key transition points from the educational system into the world of work and out of the world of work into retirement. The model employment career this table is based on is that of someone who enters the world of work sometime between the ages of 16

TABLE 8.1 Transitions into and out of employment

Age	Situation	Exceptions
5–18	School: Non-employment	paper round helping in family business serving hamburgers supermarket assistant
16–18	EMPLOYMENT	training schemes
18–22	Higher education: non-employment	part-time job summer job, helping in family business
22–65	EMPLOYMENT	vocational/professional training courses job training sabbatical maternity leave career change training
50+	Retirement: non-employment	same job part-time same job on contract self-employed same job self-employed different job career change training

and 22 years of age and stays in it until the legal retirement age. The expectation in this model is that there will be two major transition points, one into the world of work and another one out of it again after some 40 to 50 years of unbroken full-time paid employment.

There are two important implications to be drawn from this model. One is that any other employment history is in some way 'abnormal'. The other is that full-time paid employment is supposed to take up most of one's life; in a sense it is what life should mainly be about.

These assumptions underlie not only the educational systems of most industrialised countries but their taxation and benefit systems as well, with the result that people whose career is different from the ideal often suffer for it in terms of reduced opportunities for education and employment, reduced pensions and benefits and so on. As usual, though, real life is much messier than our neat models of it, and Table 8.1 shows how the transitions are rarely as clear-cut as they are supposed to be, with the exceptions listed – which are by no means exhaustive – probably including more people than the general rule.

However the most important exception to the model employment career is not listed in Table 8.1 because we need to concentrate on it separately – unemployment. The effects of unemployment are to be seen throughout the life cycle as well as having a key influence on the nature of the transitions people make into and out of the world of work.

Unemployment

Definitions

The potential workforce of any society is usually taken to be all those people who fall, at any given time, between the two major transition points of Table 8.1; that is people between the ages of about 16 to 65. This potential workforce may be divided into three different orientations to the world of work (for example Warr, 1987a). The largest group are those in paid employment, whether for themselves or an employer. The other two groups consist of people who are 'unemployed' and those who are 'non-employed'.

The 'non-employed' are people who are not in paid employment and who are not looking for paid employment. This group would include people who are retired, people who care for children or elderly relatives at home and people who do not need and/or want paid employment. The definition of who is 'unemployed' is a little more complex, depending partly on who is doing the defining.

The simplest definition of being unemployed is 'someone who doesn't have a job and would like one'. By this definition there were in 1993 in the United Kingdom, for example, about 4 000 000 people unemployed. However the official unemployment figure was around 3 000 000 because the governmental definition required someone to be 'out of work and claiming benefit' before being counted as unemployed.

The 1 000 000 person difference was largely made up of people who were not eligible to claim benefit for one reason or another, who were on youth training schemes instead of in employment, who had reached the age of sixty, or who had simply lost all hope of full-time paid employment and given up searching for it. Even using a conservative estimate almost a quarter of all families in the United Kingdom are directly affected by unemployment *at any one time*. Over a five- or ten-year period we may be talking about most families in the land. And of course everyone else is indirectly affected by the taxation costs of keeping people on the dole and the social costs involved in the waste of human resources.

As people move in and out of paid employment the size and composition of the employed, non-employed and unemployed groups is constantly shifting, of course. The typical rate of unemployment in the industrialised world since the early 1980s is about 7 to 15 per cent of the potential workforce, though this sort of figure can usually be multiplied several times for particularly deprived areas like inner cities, and areas dependent on heavy industry, and for disadvantaged groups like ethnic minorities, the young, the old, the disabled, the unskilled and the untrained (see for example *Social Trends*, 1982–7).

However it is defined, unemployment has been at a generally high level historically since the early 1980s. Unemployment levels for the previous half century were typically less than four per cent. We have to go back to the depression of the early 1930s to find levels of unemployment as high as or higher than recent levels.

More disturbing even perhaps than the experience of the 1930s is the growth of the 'hard core unemployed', usually defined as people who have been out of work for over twelve months. In the United Kingdom in the mid-1980s this figure was 40 per cent of the total unemployed, with about 25 per cent out of work for two years (Smith, 1985–6). The longer a recession continues, inevitably, the larger becomes this segment of the unemployed, many of whom may never work again.

Transitions: into the world of work

The first major transition into full-time employment for most people in industrialised countries is unlikely now to be made directly from secondary education as it traditionally has been. There are two main reasons for this trend: (1) an increase in the numbers of people going on to tertiary education, whether academic, professional, technical or vocational and (2) a decrease in available employment.

The latter reason has the further consequence that the large numbers of young people who leave secondary school and cannot find employment will end up either on welfare or on a government training scheme (often with little prospect of a job at the end of it). For the first time ever there are hundreds of thousands, perhaps millions, of people in the industrialised world, now out of the educational system for several years, who have never had a full-time job.

Even more significant is the fact that for many of them it is difficult to see how they will ever have a full-time job. There is no room here to go into the potentially explosive social and political implications of that prospect, but we will consider the psychological implications for the individuals concerned later in the chapter.

Transitions: out of the world of work

Traditionally most people retired from work at the legal retirement age, usually in their sixties, often having spent their whole working life doing the same kind of work, and sometimes after spending half a century working in the same job for the same organization. (It is worth noting, by the way, that the traditional gift made to these long-serving workers by their organizations was a clock or a watch. A ritual handing back to them of control over their own time?)

But such work careers are now rare and decreasing almost to vanishing point. As we noted in Table 8.1, retirement has now taken on a much more complex significance. The number of workers in industrialised countries taking early retirement has been on the increase for some time. The most common age for early retirement is probably fifty-five, though a general loosening of regulations has resulted in people retiring at any age after fifty.

However in many cases of early retirement it is difficult to discern how planned and how voluntary the decision was on the part of the individual concerned. Whereas traditionally people in industrialised countries knew when they would retire right from the time they entered the world of work (and could prepare for it accordingly) the current practice of early retirement is usually the result of economic change and its effects on organizations. Where organizations are seeking to cut staff and reduce costs 'early retirement' may simply be a euphemism for redundancy (Lee and Harris, 1985).

But the euphemism may be acceptable to people who know they will probably never find another job and prefer the social status of 'retirement' to that of 'unemployment'. This seems to be true especially of older workers who are relatively closer to the official retiring age. There may also be peer pressure on these people to retire early and leave whatever jobs there are to younger people (Walker, 1985). On the other hand given the right social situation and a certain level of personal resources it is becoming increasingly possible for people taking (or being given) early retirement to stay within the world of work. Some possibilities are listed in Table 8.1:

- performing the same job as before but on a part-time basis, for example teaching at various levels;
- performing the same job as before but on a contract basis, for example tradesmen, computer engineers;
- performing the same job as before but on a self-employed basis, for example accountants, management consultants;
- becoming self-employed in a different line of work, for example managers who use their redundancy payout to open a shop or run a franchise;
- training to follow a new career, either while remaining employed or with the aid of redundancy payouts, for example students on part-time or full-time MBA programmes, or New York City policemen retiring on half-pay and studying to be clinical psychologists.

Causes of unemployment

We have seen how the transitions into and out of the world of work have been affected by unemployment. From an organizational viewpoint people might be at particularly vulnerable stages of the life cycle then; younger people because they lack skills and job experience, and older people because they are relatively expensive to keep on the payroll when costs are being cut, as well as being more resistant to proposed changes in the workplace. But with technological and economic changes the threat of unemployment is now a fact of life for most people in work organizations.

As in the 1930s there is once again no such thing as a safe job. Nor is there an industrialised country that has full employment. The public sector has seen huge job cuts and the private sector has gone through tremendous upheavals since the early 1980s. There is now probably no company strong enough to be invulnerable to a takeover bid, with the consequent job losses usually attendant on it. And even the most powerful company has to take account of changing circumstances. Even the largest Japanese companies are having to drop the famous lifetime guarantee of employment for their staff.

If unemployment levels are very low it seems more reasonable to consider personal factors in the search for the causes of unemployment, but when levels are 10 per cent and more of the workforce the overwhelming number of people out of work are unemployed neither by choice nor personal failing but because their jobs have been taken away and nothing else has replaced them.

The causes of unemployment are therefore generally to be found in factors like economic restructuring, such as the decline of heavy industry, or in the invention and application of new technologies (which we will explore in Chapter 16) like the silicon chip, or in a recession that tends to slow down consumer demand. Of course different countries have different levels of unemployment at any given time and this may not be totally unrelated to the policy of the relevant government. Given the particularly high levels of UK unemployment in the early 1990s, for example, it is perhaps not a coincidence that the then Chancellor of the Exchequer, Mr Norman Lamont, considered unemployment 'a price well worth paying' to obtain lower rates of inflation.

From a psychological perspective though it is interesting to note that people's perceptions of what causes unemployment are affected at least in part by their own experience of it. Thus the unemployed tend to cite mainly social and political factors while people in work are more likely to include personal failings as well (Furnham, 1982).

Despite all the evidence that individual failings have very little to do with it, and the huge numbers of people out of work – many of them highly skilled or professional – there does still seem to be some social stigma attached to being unemployed. The norm of full-time paid employment is obviously very powerful and attempts by unemployed people to disguise their situation and protect their self-image are quite understandable.

Unemployment and time

When not engaged in active job hunting unemployed people seem to spend most of their time in what might be described as personal and social maintenance of their lives; housework, shopping, visiting friends and relatives and gardening (*Social Trends*, 1984). In comparison to people in work the unemployed tend to entertain less but smoke and drink more. Perhaps most significantly, and most obviously, the unemployed have more unstructured time in their day where they are just sitting about or watching television, almost by default (Smith, 1985–6).

Of course virtually all the activities of the unemployed are unstructured in the sense that they have little in the way of the kind of set timetable for activities that a job imposes. In this respect they are comparable to the retired, and even the self-employed, though as we shall see later in this chapter their psychological situation may be very different.

Psychological effects of unemployment

The Great Depression

Although there has always been unemployment since the Industrial Revolution (and at times even before that) its effects on the individuals concerned were not systematically studied until the terrible Depression of the 1930s affected the whole of the industrialised world and played an important part in the political extremism which emerged at that time.

One of the first research studies to appear analysed in detail the effects of unemployment on the 1500 people of an Austrian village called *Marienthal* when their major employer – a textile factory – closed down (Jahoda, Lazarsfeld and Zeisel, 1972). This is perhaps the best known study of unemployment in the 1930s partly because one of the authors, Marie Jahoda, has done some comparative work on more recent unemployment (Jahoda, 1979, 1982). But other important research, particularly by E. W. Bakke, was carried out in Britain for example (Bakke, 1933, Israeli, 1935) and in the United States (Bakke, 1940 a,b; Komarovsky, 1940).

There are several useful conclusions we can draw from this early research. Perhaps the most important conclusion is about the orientation of the unemployed to the world of work. It is clear that their psychological and physical health suffered from the lack of a time structure, of social status and of the opportunity to exercise job skills. But it is also clear that a more influential effect of unemployment on the lives of most people affected by it was the sheer loss of income that it entailed.

The brute fact of poverty seems to have been critical for most people for two reasons. In the 1930s welfare benefits in most countries were often either rudimentary or non-existent so that loss of income could be catastrophic, with people sometimes reduced to starvation. And most of the people who lost their jobs were either unskilled or semi-skilled. The jobs themselves were often mindless, hard, dirty, dangerous and exhausting. There were of course skilled, white-collar and professional workers who lost their jobs and missed the world of work very badly. But the evidence is that most people didn't.

The severity and length of the Great Depression, from the late twenties to the mid-thirties, meant that two generations were deeply affected by it (see Figure 4.1 again). A number of longitudinal studies, where people's lives were studied at different times over a period of many years, can give us some clues as to what these effects were. For a start it seems that men who lost their jobs and suffered financial hardship died earlier than people who were more fortunate (Elder, 1974).

The offspring of unemployed men who were of adolescent age at the time were found to strive harder than other people as adults for financial success and job security (Elder, 1981). They were pushed to succeed in this way by their parents, an influence that was particularly strong between mothers and sons. It was also found that the emotional health of young mothers was adversely affected in later life (Elder and Likert, 1982).

Modern times

Half a century after the Great Depression the industrialised world again began to experience historically high levels of unemployment. This experience of unemployment is not (yet) as widespread or (usually) as severe in its immediate effects as the earlier one. However it will probably last for much longer, spanning the whole of the 1980s and perhaps the whole of the 1990s as well.

Marie Jahoda has suggested that there are four differences to be taken into account when considering the implications of unemployment for these two periods of time (Jahoda, 1982):

- the rate of unemployment (though not the absolute numbers of people involved) is lower now;
- there is more welfare provision;
- general levels of health have improved;
- general levels of education have increased.

The net effect of these societal changes should therefore be to make unemployment less catastrophic in its general consequences for both individuals and society because more people remain employed, and people who are unemployed have more personal, social and financial resources to call upon in helping them cope. But this general picture does not, of course, say anything about the effects of unemployment on a given individual, and while few people face starvation many suffer in a number of other ways.

Unemployment has been more extensively studied by psychologists in recent years than in the 1930s. But the effects of unemployment appear to be neither simple nor completely clear. As a recent review of the evidence by Gordon O'Brien says about the central psychological issue involved:

Many studies have concluded that unemployment is a health hazard – the subtle implication being that it is better to be employed than unemployed. But this implication cannot be maintained as a generalization ... The basic question underlying comparisons for the unemployed and employed is rarely asked. This is the question of what is the criterion of mental health, psychological well-being or happiness? To say that employment is preferable to unemployment begs the question of why it is preferable. In what respects or for what aspects of behaviour? (O'Brien, 1986, p. 240)

We have already seen in Chapter 5 on work and mental health how certain kinds of employment, and certain aspects of all employment, can have serious negative effects on a worker's physical and psychological health and wellbeing. Conversely there is evidence that unemployment can sometimes have positive effects for people.

Nearly a thousand men in one study were asked if there had been any change in their health since becoming unemployed. Of the 38 per cent who had noticed some change 27 per cent said it had deteriorated but 11 per cent said it had improved, because they no longer had to worry about stresses at work and they had the time to relax and to take exercise (Warr, 1984).

It has also been found that the effects of unemployment varies with a worker's personal work career and with the general level of unemployment. A third of one sample of unemployed managers in mid-career did not find unemployment stressful because they had not liked their previous job and felt confident about their prospects of finding a better one (Fineman, 1983). Similarly at a time of lower unemployment nearly half of a sample of technical-professional people in mid-career found unemployment more positive than negative for the same reasons (Little, 1976).

Finally it is interesting to note that a comparison of employed and unemployed managers in the United Kingdom, on a management exercise, found the unemployed group higher on imagination, conscientiousness and even assertiveness (Hartley, 1980).

Bearing these important considerations in mind we will now take a closer look at modern findings on the negative effects of unemployment and the ways in which unemployed people respond to them.

Negative effects of unemployment

GENERAL TRENDS

A study of trends between 1910 and 1967 found a strong link between unemployment and mental illness. When the rate of admissions to mental hospitals in New York State was examined for this period it was found that as unemployment levels rose so did the rate of admissions (Brenner, 1973).

This relationship also seemed to hold true for stress-related health problems like cardiovascular disease and cirrhosis of the liver, and even for more social issues like imprisonment and homicide. All these problems increased within two to three years of the unemployment level rising (Brenner, 1979). It has also been found that the longer people are out of work the more likely are these sorts of problems to appear (for example Warr and Jackson, 1984). A similar relationship has been found between rates of divorce and unemployment over time (South, 1984). And this is probably linked to the finding that unemployed men have often tended to lose their status and position of power in their marriage and in their family group (Elder, 1974).

Longitudinal studies have supported the view that people have suffered psychologically after losing their jobs (for example Cobb and Kasl, 1977). Moreover an improvement has been found where people later found new employment (for example Warr and Jackson, 1985). And in the first major transition into the world of work there is evidence that young people who go straight from school to work experience an improvement in their psychological wellbeing while those who go from school to unemployment experience a significant deterioration. This latter finding was observed in samples in the United Kingdom and in Australia (Banks and Jackson, 1982; Feather and O'Brien, 1986).

The situation of adult women is a little more complex and will be considered separately in Chapter 17. But there is ample evidence that the mental health of full-time housewives improves when they enter the world of paid employment (Tavris and Offir, 1977; Brown and Harris, 1978; Haw, 1982).

Unemployed people in these studies whose wellbeing deteriorates typically report a wide range of relatively low-level but continuing psychological problems like increased anxiety, lack of self-confidence, listlessness, feelings of depression and insomnia. There is also an increase in well-known stress-related psychosomatic problems like headaches, stomach ulcers and dermatitis, as well as the more dramatic conditions like heart disease and strokes.

None of these problems is helped by the tendency of unemployed people who are already smokers and drinkers to seek comfort by increasing their tobacco and alcohol consumption (Smith, 1985–6). Nor would these habits do much to help people suffering from medical conditions that might be related to a situation of poverty – like having to live in sub-standard housing. There is evidence from studies done in Britain and Australia that the unemployed suffer more ear, nose and throat problems, and bronchitis, than people in work (Hayes and Nutman, 1981).

Finally in this section we should note that both suicide and parasuicide (attempted suicide) are more common among the unemployed than among people in work. In both the United States and Europe there is generally a strong association between frequency of suicide and rates of unemployment (Platt, 1984). Figures on parasuicide – which is often interpreted as a desperate cry for help – are particularly striking. In Edinburgh, for example, it is eight times more common among the unemployed than among people in work (Platt, 1986).

The importance of job content

We noted earlier in this chapter that some people may dislike their jobs so much that they even find unemployment a preferable option. In this section we will take a closer look at the content of jobs, what people actually do at work that can be compared with the state of being unemployed. Peter Warr has suggested that there are nine factors on which a comparison might be made (Warr, 1987a). They are:

- opportunity for control
- opportunity for skill use
- goals and task demands
- variety
- environmental clarity
- availability of money
- physical security
- opportunity for interpersonal contact
- valued social position.

One of these nine factors, 'availability of money', has come up before.

As we have already seen the loss of income usually entailed in unemployment was the most crucial problem that people faced in the 1930s. Warr accepts that this may still be the case in present-day unemployment, despite the societal changes in the intervening half-century that we noted. And this may be for reasons of psychological as well as material deprivation:

> Studies of unemployed people consistently indicate that shortage of money is viewed as the greatest source of personal and family problems . . . Poverty bears down not only upon basic needs for food and physical protection, but also prevents activity and reduces one's sense of personal control. (Warr, 1987a, p. 345)

Closely related to this factor is that of 'Physical Security'; the need to have a roof over one's head, and with some personal space, that usually requires an income.

The first of Warr's nine factors, 'opportunity for control', is where people tend to feel they have little chance to exert some control over their lives if they are unemployed. The tendency people have to see their lives as internally controlled by themselves or externally controlled by other people is a basic division of personality which we will look at more closely in the next chapter.

For the moment we should note two aspects of this issue. One is the evidence that the longer people are unemployed the more externally controlled do they feel (Patton and Noller, 1984). However this is probably not a fundamental shift in personality as much as a realistic appraisal of their employment prospects and of what they can do about them (O'Brien and Kabanoff, 1981).

The other point to consider here is related to the previously reported evidence that some people preferred unemployment to the job they had. It was shown by E. W. Bakke in the 1930s that what many people learned from doing their jobs was that they were powerless to exert any control over the work they did for a living. So when their jobs were taken away from them this was simply another piece of evidence to reinforce their existing belief that their entire lives were largely controlled by other people and institutions (Bakke, 1933; 1940 a,b).

Two of Warr's nine factors deal directly with job content, 'opportunity for skills use' and 'goal and task demands'. The former refers to lost opportunities both in the exercise of existing job skills and in the possibility of acquiring new ones. The latter really refers to the reduced expectations of other people and the purposeful, busy schedules of activity that these expectations would entail.

Related to this last factor are two more that deal with the organization of daily activities, 'variety' and 'environmental clarity'. 'Variety' refers to the amount of change in someone's routine and the contrast, or lack of it between job and non-job activities. Without a job to go to there may be no need for an unemployed person to leave the house. One day can seem pretty much like another, with little significance to weekends or holidays. The way of structuring the passage of time that people have lived by breaks down and, as we saw in Chapter 4, that can be very disorienting.

'Environmental clarity' is about the ability to plan ahead and make decisions about the future. The uncertainty that unemployment inevitably produces is likely, as we saw in Chapter 5 on Work and Mental Health, to produce anxiety and stress. Some supporting evidence on this point comes from a study of men in Britain who had been unemployed for six to eleven months. Some 60 per cent of them were disturbed by their uncertain future (Payne, Warr and Hartley, 1984).

The last two factors on Warr's list are concerned with relationships to other people *vis-à-vis* work. 'Opportunity for interpersonal contact' is of clear psychological importance given the centrality to our lives of relationships with other people that we have discussed in the past two chapters. In terms of quantity of interpersonal contact the situation is rather complex for the unemployed. Warr points out that married men, for example, tend to spend more time with friends and family, whereas married women tend to spend more time alone, than people in work. But these contacts appear to be less purposeful and restricted to a smaller group of people.

Warr's final factor is 'valued social position', which refers to someone's role in society. In this respect being employed, he suggests, is unequivocally higher in social esteem (and therefore usually in self-esteem) that being unemployed – even when so many people now have experience of being in that position through no fault of their own. Being unemployed is neither an envied nor an enviable state to be in, and even people who prefer it to their last job appear to see it as a temporary situation before their next (and hopefully better) job.

Warr points out that the nine factors he has identified work in combination with each other rather than individually. It is therefore very difficult to take any individual case and try to account for the effects of unemployment. But it is worth trying to view this complex situation from the viewpoint of the individual.

The individual experience of unemployment

We will try now to follow the experience of unemployment from the perspective of the individual. Psychologists have long attempted to discern distinct stages that unemployed people go through over time. In a review of work done in the 1930s it was suggested that a pattern of psychological changes appeared in all the work done on the effects of the Great Depression (Eisenberg and Lazarsfeld, 1938). The stages proposed were *optimism, pessimism* and *fatalism*. A later writer has suggested a prior stage of *shock* resulting in a four-stage model that has achieved a fairly wide currency (Hill, 1978).

There is some question about the timing of these stages and under what conditions someone would move from one to the next (Kelvin and Jarrett, 1985). None the less the model is quite a useful description of the typical experience of unemployment, though the term *phases* might have a more appropriately flexible connotation. We can use it as a framework for examining the effects of unemployment from the individual's perspective as well as noting the range of individual differences in the experience of unemployment.

Phase 1: Shock

In discussing stress in Chapter 5 we noted how high on a scale of stressful life events was the experience of losing your job (Figure 5.1). It is in fact the most stressful experience that you can have in the world of work. The more unexpected the loss the more shocked you are likely to be of course. But even when you can see it coming from a long way off the actual event may trigger a lot of anger and distress and incomprehension: 'Why this organization?' 'Why me?' 'Why now?' However this may also be tinged with relief at knowing the worst: there is some evidence that depression may increase with the anticipation of unemployment but decrease when it actually occurs (Cobb and Kasl, 1977).

Phase 2: Optimism

After the initial shock has worn off there may be a period of time where people feel that they are just between jobs – 'resting' as they say in the acting profession – and are quite optimistic about the future. We saw earlier in the chapter that it is quite possible for people to feel reasonably positive about a period of unemployment if they disliked their previous job and are confident of getting another, better one. Such optimism will be rarer for everyone in a time of recession and high unemployment though because there are simply fewer opportunities of employment available.

Phase 3: Pessimism

If unemployment continues for longer than about six months the optimistic phase will inevitably be left behind. As people head for the twelve-month mark of unsuccessfully searching for a job, and official membership in the group of long-term unemployed, it becomes extremely difficult for even the most self-confident and resilient souls to persuade themselves that they're still just taking time out between jobs. People in this phase are seriously concerned about their employment future and how they will manage financially. However their mental health seems to stabilise at this stage after deteriorating for three to six months (Warr, 1987a). Given their situation the feeling of pessimism may be entirely rational, justified and healthy.

Phase 4: Fatalism

By the fourth phase people have been unemployed for so long that they have become fatalistic and effectively given up any hope of ever being employed again. They may become apathetic and hopeless about the prospects of employment to the point where they simply stop looking for a job and are lost to the labour market altogether.

In this phase people seem to draw in upon themselves to protect themselves from the continual disappointments and rejections of the job market. They seek satisfactions from other areas of their lives instead, though by comparison with employed people these tend to be more restricted and impoverished (Warr, 1987a).

Individual differences in experience of unemployment

(I) AGE

As we have already seen people who are close to the usual retirement age may opt to redefine their unemployment as 'retirement' and avoid the four phases outlined above. Under favourable circumstances, like good health and a decent pension, this can be a more desirable alternative than returning to the world of work. Young people just making the transition into the world of work may also redefine their unemployment quite successfully as 'not yet employed'.

But people in their 20s, 30s and 40s face a particularly difficult situation, which cannot be redefined, and they are the group most badly hit psychologically according to evidence from both the 1930s and the 1980s (Eisenberg and Lazarsfeld 1938; Warr and Jackson, 1985). And these mid-life years, in any event, are often a time of questioning values and identity.

(II) SEX

For people on the official unemployment rolls the effect on their emotional wellbeing seems to be equally harmful for men and women (Banks and Jackson, 1982). If we look at the differences between groups of women, unemployment does not seem to be harmful for married women. It does however for unmarried women, whose emotional wellbeing seems to improve with paid employment (Warr and Parry, 1982).

(III) WORK VALUES

People who are highly committed to the world of work and place a lot of value on their jobs suffer the most psychologically when they lose them (Warr and Jackson, 1985). Conversely people who place less value on paid employment, like young people and married women who tend to have poorly-paid, low-status jobs, suffer least. The first shock of unemployment will hit the most committed people hardest and their self-esteem suffers (Warr, 1984). We might expect them to stay longer in both optimistic and pessimistic phases but perhaps never to enter the fatalistic phase at all.

(IV) LEVEL OF ACTIVITY

One general behavioural characteristic on which individuals vary is simply their level of activity. The extent to which people have an active – or *proactive* – orientation to their situation seems to have an influence on how well people cope with unemployment. People who have a reactive, passive orientation to unemployment tend to sit around the house a lot, watch television and so on and deteriorate physically and psychologically.

On the other hand proactive people seem able to create a richer environment for themselves and suffer much less damage. An in-depth study of eleven such people found that they were able to organise their time in a creative and fulfilling way by working as a community project leader, for example, or participating seriously in religious or political organizations (Fryer and Payne, 1984).

These were mainly people who had found the hierarchical organization of their previous jobs irksome and constricting and actually found what they did in unemployment to be more satisfying, giving them more opportunities to use their skills and abilities, than their experience of employment had been. After dealing with the initial shock of unemployment these people seem to have embraced their situation and side-stepped the phases of optimism, pessimism and fatalism in relation to paid work.

(V) SOCIAL SUPPORT

Social support can affect individual responses to unemployment in two ways, via the family and the community in which people live. We have already noted in Chapter 5 how the emotional support of a man's family can reduce the stress he feels and the subsequent illness he suffers, during the initial phase of shock at losing his job. In one study it was found, for example, that among men with a low level of family support 41 per cent became arthritic while in the group with a high level of support from their wives this figure was reduced to 4 per cent (Cobb and Kasl, 1977). Another study found that people with low support had raised cholesterol levels and a higher incidence of depression (Fineman, 1983).

Support from the community is more indirect. There is some evidence that unemployed men from areas of high unemployment are in better shape psychologically than men from areas of low unemployment (Trew and Kilpatrick, 1983). The process of social comparison, that we all engage in, would reveal many other people in the same situation and lessen any stigma or sense of failure. Moreover there did seem to be more and closer social interactions between men in high unemployment areas than in areas of relatively low unemployment, perhaps allowing them to share their problems in a way that would not be possible in areas where unemployment was rare (Kilpatrick and Trew, 1985).

Retirement

On the face of it retirement has a lot in common with unemployment: retired people are also excluded from full-time paid employment and they usually experience a fairly sharp drop in income as a result. A comparison between the two provides a useful additional perspective on the world of work and we will find that the picture is a little more complex, of course, than it appears at first glance.

As we noted in Table 8.1 retirement is not a monolithic condition where everyone does the same things at the same age. With the increasing prominence of early retirement, either voluntary or involuntary, age of retirement is no longer automatic for people in work. And there still are, as there always have been, people in professional jobs, or self-employed, who retire later than the usual age, or gradually, or never.

Most people probably still retire at a fixed age though, when the state or sometimes occupational pension may be drawn. As we saw in Table 5.1 retirement is a stressful event in life, perhaps almost as stressful as unemployment. Unlike most unemployment full retirement usually means a one-way ticket out of the world of work and into something unknown. But retired people seem to cope with this stress better than unemployed people and nothing like the four-phase model of unemployment has been observed. And it is a situation that more people look forward to happily – 35 per cent in one study (Parker, 1987).

Other than searching for jobs retired people spend their time in a similar fashion to unemployed people, and for similar reasons. People with relatively high levels of personal activity, education, income and good health tend to enjoy a creative and satisfying retirement. As well as domestic and family activities they pursue hobbies like music, golf or fishing, travel, join clubs and committees, do voluntary work or take up further education (McGoldrick, 1982). People who lack these advantages, and who often had hard or stressful blue-collar jobs, tend to be much more passive, and sometimes bored and lonely in their retirement (Kasl, 1980).

If retirement is voluntary, rather than reluctant, and planned rather than enforced by circumstances, then it will probably be a relatively happy period in a person's life (Beehr, 1986). Having a high sense of self-esteem and a continuing interest in one's own life has been found to be particularly important for retired managers, who have to cope with giving up a position of responsibility and power within an organization (Beveridge, 1980).

In general terms retired people tend not to suffer the kind of physical or psychological damage that occurs to many of the unemployed. A British survey found that 36 per cent of retired men and 35 per cent of retired women were very pleased with their lives. The figures for those in work were only 23 per cent and 17 per cent, and for the unemployed 21 per cent and 19 per cent (Warr and Payne, 1982). These differences in general wellbeing can probably be attributed to the different status of the two situations. Retirement is still widely seen as the appropriate culmination of a working life; unemployment is still seen as at best an aberration in the world of work, at worst a personal defect and a source of shame.

PART III

THE INDIVIDUAL'S WORKING LIFE

This part of the book adopts the perspective of the individual within the work organization. It analyses individual psychological processes and also the way people are treated as 'human resources'.

Chapters 9 and 10 examine the formation and expression of individual personality characteristics and abilities. Chapters 11 and 12 are concerned with the use and misuse of human resources by organizations, from the initial recruitment onwards. Chapter 13 on motivation deals with the basic questions of why people work, and why they work as hard as they do. These questions are linked to the issue of job satisfaction, which is taken up in Chapter 14. Finally, Chapter 15 is devoted to the topic of leadership and its relevance to people in organizations, particularly managers.

CHAPTER 9

Personality factors

What is meant by personality?

The term 'personality' is commonly used both in psychology and in everyday speech and like most terms that have this dual usage it does not mean quite the same thing in each context. Psychologists interested in this subject want to know what makes someone a unique person. What are the *characteristic* ways in which she behaves? What is the overall *pattern* of how she relates to other people and how they react to her?

In everyday speech we talk about someone as being 'tough and aggressive' or having 'an attractive personality', showing that we are trying to discern characteristic patterns in their behaviour. These patterns are categories of behaviour, as defined by our society, that we have learned to recognise from our previous experience with people. Where the difference lies is that unlike the psychologist other people do not normally try to assess the uniqueness of an individual at the same time as they place him in categories that emphasize his 'sameness'.

It is interesting to note that one of the attributes of a great novelist or playwright is the ability to create characters of some psychological complexity and subtlety. But we don't always have the time in living our lives to be as reflective as novelists or playwrights. In fact our way of life usually encourages us not to be considered and reflective in relating to others.

We know little or nothing about many of the people we come across in the day-to-day business of life, and very often we have nothing to go on but appearance – someone's colour, size, clothing, gestures and so on. When you get on a bus, for instance, how much uniqueness does the driver have for you as opposed to his sameness to all the other bus drivers you've seen? If you stopped to appreciate the uniqueness of this individual the people standing behind you in the rain might not appreciate *your* uniqueness. But there is also a balance between the two to be observed. A bus driver I once heard of resigned after his wife got on his bus one day and walked right past without recognising him.

Both the psychologist and the layman use the term 'personality' to make sense of an individual's behaviour. It is only an individual's *behaviour* after all that we have to go on. We can never know for sure why somebody has acted in a certain way: all we can do is observe their behaviour and infer what inner processes motivated them to do it. And this is just as true of psychologists as it is of anyone else.

It is important to realise therefore that both psychologist and layman carry out this procedure by referring to a set of ideas – a theory if you like – about what personality is, how it came into being and how it operates. The difference is that the psychologist makes his theory of personality explicit while that of the layman usually remains implicit and not consciously thought about. In this chapter we shall examine both explicit, or *formal*, theories of personality as well as implicit, or *informal*, theories.

Because they are such an important way of understanding human behaviour these theories are of obvious general relevance to the world of work, but in the remainder of the chapter we shall consider some aspects of personality with a more specific relevance.

Formal theories of personality

Introduction

There are many formal theories of personality. There always have been. They go back to Aristotle, Plato and beyond. The history of psychology is dominated by attempts to understand and explain the human personality. From the time of the earliest thinkers to the present day it is this aspect of psychology that has excited the greatest interest. Indeed it is a subject of intrinsic fascination to most people.

The authoritative work on the subject by Hall and Lindzey (1978) lists fifteen contemporary theories. We may reasonably divide the list into a few broad groups, however, based in turn on their general philosophical approaches to the human condition. We met two of these approaches in Chapter 1, Psychoanalysis and Behaviourism. A third approach, *Humanism*, has emerged over the course of this century as has the *Trait* approach based on statistical techniques.

We will look at a theory of personality based on each of these approaches, but before that it might be helpful for us to have a definition of the term personality to bite on, though we should note that any definition given will inevitably be influenced by a particular orientation to understanding the human condition. However I don't think this is something that textbook writers should duck so let me declare an interest here – if you haven't already discerned it. I am persuaded more by the psychoanalytic approach than that of the others. This does not mean though that I reject the behaviourist or humanist views as being of no value. I have learned a lot from each. But they place little or no significance on the unconscious which I, and a large and growing number of other psychologists, believe to be the most powerful explanatory concept we have in psychology.

My favourite dictionary of psychology defines the term personality thus:

> The sum total of all the factors that make an individual human being both individual and human; the thinking, feeling and behaving that all human beings have in common, and the particular characteristic pattern of these elements that makes every human being unique. Theorists in this field often stress the integrated and dynamic nature of an individual's personality and the important role of unconscious processes that may be hidden from the individual but are at least partly perceptible to other people. (Statt, 1990)

The key words in this definition are *characteristic pattern* and *unconscious processes*. Wherever I use the term 'personality' in this book, that is the definition of it I have in mind. When we look at behaviourist and humanist theories of personality below we will observe some important differences there in the way the term is used.

All formal theories of personality attempt to do something *extremely* difficult: they attempt to explain *why* people are the way they are and *why* they do what they do. They are general theories of human behaviour, in other words, which are centrally concerned with *motivation*, and integrated around the concept of a *complete person*. The workings of motivation is itself so complex that it is usually abstracted for closer study as a separate process, and we will do that in Chapter 13.

As we have already seen in Chapters 5 and 6 the integrated structure of an individual's personality is crucial to his psychological wellbeing. This is something that all theories of personality agree about. Anxiety, conflict, physical and psychological stress, can sometimes lead to the *dis*-integration – or even the destruction of a personality's structure. That is not an automatic result of course and most formal theories of personality are also interested in how people cope with the inevitable vicissitudes of life.

Finally in this section we should note that no formal theory of personality comes even close to fulfilling its ambitions. Human lives are much too complex and multi-variate (or, if you prefer, rich and interesting) to be subsumed under, explained with, or predicted by any one existing theory. The best we can hope for, therefore, are useful guidelines or helpful clues leading towards a partial understanding.

The psychoanalytic approach

Freudian theory of personality

The psychoanalytic approach is most intimately related to the work of Sigmund Freud, of course, and Freud's theory will be our representative of this approach (Freud, 1953–74). Personality theories have their roots either in the psychological laboratory or, more often, in the consulting room. Freud's theory, like most theories of personality, emerged from his clinical experiences as a psychotherapist.

Freud thought of the human personality as being in three parts, the *id*, the *ego*, and the *superego*.

(A) ID

The id is composed of powerful drives, raw impulses of sex and aggression that demand to be satisfied immediately. We are not usually aware of the id; it is unconscious.

(B) EGO

We are aware of the ego. It is the rational, conscious, thinking part of our personality. Our self-image would be contained within Freud's description of the ego. The ego gets its working energy from the id, but when the id impulses are too strong and threaten to take over the ego, it represses them and defends itself from knowing about them.

(C) SUPEREGO

The superego, like the id, is usually unconscious so that we are unaware of its workings. It is the part of our personality that deals with right and wrong, with morality, with the correct and proper way to behave, feel and think. The superego can be just as powerful as the id in its demands on the ego that we behave the way we should – or take the consequences of feeling guilty.

This way of conceiving of personality has often been depicted as an iceberg, and Freud himself was very fond of using hydraulic metaphors to illustrate his theory (see Figure 9.1).

These three aspects of the personality are constantly interacting with each other as we move through life. Frequently they are in conflict. This conflict appears in the ego as the conscious feeling of anxiety, whose source we are unaware of because both the id and the superego, with their conflicting demands, remain unconscious. The id growls 'Do it,' the superego cries 'No, no,' and the poor old ego is caught in between, doing its best to separate them and keep the peace.

To the extent that the ego succeeds, the personality is well-adjusted, balanced, content and happy, allowing the individual, as Freud emphasized, to *love* sexually and to *work* productively. To the extent that the id and superego influence someone's personality, he or she suffers conflict, feels anxious and therefore behaves in a disturbed, neurotic fashion.

Freud believed that the first few years of a person's life were absolutely crucial in shaping the adult personality. Conflicts that inevitably arise in early childhood between id, ego and superego are at the root of neurotic behaviour in adulthood. These conflicts are repressed into the unconscious and the job of the psychoanalyst is to help the patient become conscious of these problems and to strengthen his ego so that he may bring them squarely within the image he has of himself and face them unflinchingly.

Repression is not simply a passive business of not wanting to know certain things. On the contrary it is an active process that takes up a huge amount of psychic energy to hold things down in the unconscious. For

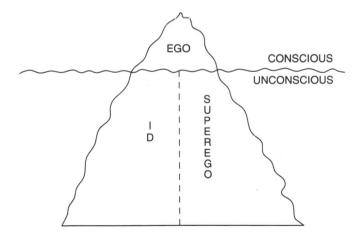

FIGURE 9.1   The Freudian structure of personality

this reason Freud referred to the 'dynamic' unconscious and the psychological processes involved in it are often referred to as *psychodynamics*.

The psychoanalytic or psychodynamic view of the human condition, that the most powerful causes of human behaviour are unconscious, and therefore unavailable to external observation, was a powerful one that attracted an important following around the world, first in a clinical or psychiatric setting and later in virtually every area of life. We looked specifically at the role of the unconscious in the workplace in Chapter 6 but we will also trace the influence of the unconscious on many other aspects of psychology and the world of work including motivation, leadership, unemployment, mental health, work-group relationships and even learning and personnel selection.

Freud's developmental stages

Freud's theory of personality is a developmental one. He believed that from birth to psychological maturity the individual would normally pass through a series of developmental stages in a particular order and at a particular time. Successful negotiation of all these stages resulted in a healthy personality; unsuccessful negotiation inevitably led to psychological problems in later life. He related these psychological stages to biological stages of development and called them the *oral, anal* and *phallic* stages. Unresolved conflicts at any stage led to a *fixation* with the particular features of that stage which found later expression in certain corresponding adult personality characteristics.

(I) ORAL STAGE

The mouth is the most important source of gratification and physical stimulation for the first couple of years of life. It is the medium through which infants first learn about the world. A lack of sufficient gratification at this stage can produce a hostile sarcastic kind of personality much given to making 'biting' remarks about other people. On the other hand too much gratification can also lead to fixation of a different kind leading to someone being too dependent on others or gullible and liable to 'swallow' anything.

(II) ANAL STAGE

At around the age of two the child realises he has some control over the muscles of the anus and therefore the elimination or retention of faeces.

This control produces its own gratification, a source of gratification which meets external authority for the first time in the form of parental toilet training. A child may be fixated at this stage by toilet training that is too strict or too lax. Strictness leads to an anal personality that is obsessively clean, controlled and ordered – and this concept is supported by some contemporary research (Kline, 1983). Laxity leads to disorder and messiness.

(III) PHALLIC STAGE

At about four years of age the child should be entering the phallic stage of development where gratification is associated with sensuous pleasure from the genitals including masturbation and fantasy. This is the stage at which the famous *Oedipus complex* appears. Oedipus was a king, in ancient Greek mythology, who inadvertently killed his father and later unknowingly married his mother.

Freud used the story as a metaphor for the attraction the child has to the parent of the opposite sex, accompanied by the unconscious wish to remove the parent of the same sex. The anxiety about retribution from the rival parent leads the child to identify with that parent instead, and thus obtain at least vicarious satisfaction. The guilt the child experiences for having these feelings in the first place is the basis for the primitive superego.

Though the Oedipus complex is repressed after the age of five it remains a crucial part of the personality for life and plays a large part in determining someone's attitudes, not only towards the opposite sex but also towards people in positions of authority. Freud considered his discovery of the Oedipus complex (which came to him while watching a performance of *Oedipus Rex* in Paris) to be one of his most important contributions to psychology. It is also one of his most contentious, of course, though there is some research evidence to support it (Kline, 1981).

The behaviourist approach

J. B. Watson

We encountered Behaviourism in Chapter 1 where we considered the work of J. B. Watson and his incorporation of Pavlov's discoveries on conditioning. The contrast between Watson's approach to personality and that of Freud could hardly have been greater. Observable human behaviour was all that mattered to Watson and in his emphasis on studying the links between a given stimulus and a given response he exemplified all that was typical of the Behaviourist, or *behavioural*, approach.

The behavioural view of personality is concerned with the objective, empirical testing of hypotheses in a controlled laboratory setting. The key to understanding (and predicting) human behaviour is to be found in the process of *learning*. People learn a particular response to a particular stimulus. The association of the one with the other – the essential link – is what we normally refer to as a *habit*.

Thus the stimulus of stress at work may be associated with the response of lighting up a cigarette, or receiving a rejection slip from a job application with a raid on the refrigerator. People engage in this kind of behaviour because they find it rewarding in some way. It fulfills a need for them. However if they should come to believe that smoking and over-eating are irrational, and even self-destructive, habits to have they can be reversed, as they were acquired, by the process of learning. They can be unlearned in other words. To Watson and the other S-R theorists it's simply a matter of specifying what response you want to see and designing an appropriate system of rewards, called a *schedule of reinforcement* (both positive and negative) to produce it, similar to the way Pavlov did with his dogs.

We will return to this topic when we discuss the process of learning in Chapter 12. Here we just need to note its overriding importance to the behavioural view of personality. We should also note that behaviourists, unlike psychoanalysts and most other theorists of personality, used animals extensively in their experiments, especially laboratory-bred white rats. This gave them the ability to control the genetic inheritance, the experience and the environment of their subjects, but at the (considerable) cost of having to extrapolate their findings from rats to humans.

One other point about Watson's career might be worth considering. Like most behaviourists then and now his work was carried out in an academic setting, and in 1920 his academic career ended when he was asked to leave Johns Hopkins University following the publicity given to a messy divorce he was involved in. Watson then went into the world of business where he did well in advertising, becoming a Vice-President of the J. Walter Thompson company. We noted in Chapter 1 the intrinsic attraction that the behaviourist approach to human behaviour had for the American business world so perhaps Watson's subsequent career was not so surprising.

Later behaviourists and their relationship with psychoanalysis

Although behaviourism is largely an academically-based approach there have been behaviourists who were concerned with mental health and psychological abnormality. Typically the behaviourist believes that, as virtually all human behaviour is learned, neurotic behaviour is also learned (for example Eysenck, 1952). What a behavioural therapist would therefore do is to concentrate on the unlearning of that behaviour. Where a psychoanalyst would regard neurotic behaviour as being simply a symptom and direct his efforts at finding the underlying causes of that symptom the behaviourist believes that there are no underlying causes; the 'symptom' is all there is, and *that* is what needs to be changed (Eysenck, 1976).

At the same time a few behaviourists have come much closer to the psychoanalytic view by accepting the importance of unconscious conflicts on human behaviour (Dollard and Miller, 1950). What to a psychoanalyst would be the active repression of threatening material into the Id is however interpreted quite differently by these behaviourists. They would see it as a learned technique of 'not-thinking' which is reinforced as a response to the stimulus of potential conflict because it allows the individual to avoid the experience of fear and anxiety that would otherwise ensue.

Behaviourists would generally agree with the psychoanalysts in two other respects. Even though they would not accept anything like Freud's theory of developmental stages they do tend to agree with the importance of early childhood experience and the habits learned there, for the adult personality. Indeed Watson wrote a book on the subject entitled *Psychological Care of the Infant and Child* (Watson, 1928). In addition neither behaviourists nor psychoanalysts believe that any human behaviour is randomly caused but that all our present behaviour is determined by past events.

B. F. Skinner

B. F. Skinner is generally considered the most influential behaviourist since Watson, both inside and outside Academia. Like Watson he believed in the importance of an undiluted Stimulus-Response view of human behaviour that did not require any reference to internal psychological processes, which he called 'explanatory fictions' (Skinner, 1938). Like Watson, Skinner was also attracted to the process of conditioning as the key mechanism of learning, and this is where his major contribution was made.

Skinner developed a form of conditioning known as *operant conditioning* which carried Pavlov's work a stage further. We have seen that Pavlovian or *classical conditioning* is a very basic form of learning that depends on a stimulus being given to an animal that results in a particular response. The animal's behaviour in this S-R pattern is said to be *elicited* from it. The animal does not initiate the conditioning process by its own behaviour. However, much of animal behaviour is not elicited by outside stimuli but is *emitted* by the animal's own spontaneous actions. Without waiting for a push from outside an animal will often begin to explore its surroundings, to 'operate' on its environment.

When an animal engages in this kind of activity it is said to exhibit 'operant' behaviour, which Skinner defined as a response which *operates* on the environment and *changes* it. Using operant conditioning techniques Skinner showed that it was possible to *shape* an animal's behaviour in some very ingenious ways. We will return to operant conditioning when we discuss learning in Chapter 12, but we might note here that a lot of the behaviour that seems to give trained animals a kind of 'personality' is the result of this process. By using such means animal trainers can get horses to dance and dolphins to perform acrobatics. Skinner himself taught pigeons to play ping pong and demonstrated it to his students.

Skinner believed that reward, or *positive reinforcement*, was a more powerful way of shaping desired behaviour than punishment, or *negative reinforcement*. Where punishment merely told the subject what behaviour to abstain from, reward indicated the behaviour he should actively perform. And in dealing with humans punishment can often lead to undesirable side effects, of course, like anxiety or hostility. Skinner felt that authority figures like parents and teachers had, on the whole, tended to give up the use of punishment in favour of reward in the shaping of young personalities (Skinner, 1971).

Humanism

Humanistic psychology is not to be confused with the Human Relations Movement in work psychology which began with the Hawthorne studies and included some of the other research on group dynamics which we considered in Chapter 7. There is, however, some overlap between the two. *The Dictionary of Personality and Social Psychology* (Harré and Lamb, 1986) lists ten sources of humanistic psychology, one of which is group dynamics. Moreover the stress on the importance of relationships between people and work, which is central to the Human Relations Movement, is also one of the key elements of humanistic psychology.

The other sources that go to make up humanistic psychology lead it much further afield, however. They include Zen Buddhism, Taoism and psychedelic drugs for instance. They also include the psychoanalytic Existentialism of R. D. Laing (1967), the self-actualization ideas of Abraham Maslow (which we shall consider in Chapter 13 on Motivation) and the person-centred work of Carl Rogers, to which we now turn.

Carl Rogers

Carl Rogers is often taken to be the primary personality theorist in humanistic psychology, which 'opposes what it regards as the bleak pessimism and despair inherent in the psychoanalytic view of humans on the one hand, and the robot conception of humans portrayed in Behaviourism on the other hand' (Hall and Lindzey, 1978, p. 279). Humanistic psychology takes an optimistic view of the existence of creativity and potential for growth within every human being.

The fact that this potential so often remains unfulfilled, Rogers and others would argue, is due to the oppressive effects of family, school and all the other social institutions that shape the lives of individuals. The key to overcoming these influences, and so unlocking the human potential hidden underneath, is for everyone to take responsibility for his or her own life. If people can take this first, crucial step they can then start to explore and then enrich their 'inner life' – their unique experiences and their deepest feelings – and eventually free themselves from what Rogers called 'the conformity of institutions and the dogma of authority' (Rogers, 1974).

Like Freud, but unlike Skinner, Carl Rogers' theory of personality grew out of his clinical experience as a therapist. However Freud was a physician while Rogers was trained as a psychologist and their differing professional backgrounds are reflected in their different approaches, both to an understanding of personality and to the practice of psychotherapy. Freud's underlying view of human nature was that people are driven largely by irrational forces which only a well-ordered society can hold in check. Rogers on the other hand believed that people are basically rational and are motivated to fulfill themselves and become the best human beings that they can be.

Freud as a medical man regarded the therapeutic relationship as one between doctor and patient, where the patient comes to the doctor because of some sickness which the doctor identifies and tries to cure. In Rogers' system a 'client' (not a 'patient') comes to a therapist (not a physician) for help with a problem. The Rogerian therapist does not try to interpret what the client says or try to guide him along certain lines of thought; nor does he offer praise or blame. In this sense Rogers' system is non-directive and *client-centred* (Rogers, 1961).

Finally Rogers stresses the importance of the *conscious self-image* in his therapy; he is not very interested in the workings of the unconscious. To the extent that a client is maladjusted in his behaviour his self-image is out of touch with reality, like the academic who considers himself a stimulating teacher despite the glaring fact that people tend to fall asleep in his classes. Such a client may have a rigid self-image which he tries to guard from any negative perception of himself that might threaten it.

If the client can relax his defences and free his self-image he can come to integrate within it what he really feels and thinks and does – and still like himself even if he is no longer perfect. Rogers encouraged this process by treating his clients with *unconditional positive regard* and maintaining an empathy with their inner self.

Trait theory

There is one other kind of formal personality theory we need to consider. Unlike the three we have already looked at it is not based on a particular approach to understanding the human condition. It is, on the contrary, empirically-based; that is it sets out to identify and measure all of the relatively stable characteristics of someone's personality at any given time using the methods of experimental psychology and statistics. Each of these characteristics is known as a *trait*, either physical (like height and weight) or psychological (like imagination, assertiveness, or even intelligence). While traits are therefore shared by everyone people may differ from each other on each trait.

We will take up this topic again from a different viewpoint in Chapter 10 on Measuring Human Abilities and again in Chapter 11 on Recruitment and Selection. We are concerned here with the use of the trait concept in the attempt to build up a general theory of personality. The leading theorist in this field is Raymond Cattell, whom we shall consider below. The fundamental technique used by trait theorists like Cattell is a sophisticated one known as *factor analysis*, which we shall only describe very briefly. For a full technical explanation you should consult authorities like Gorsuch (1983) or Child (1990).

R. B. Cattell

Factor analysis is a statistical procedure for identifying a small number of underlying dimensions, patterns of factors contained within a much larger set of data. It is a way of both reducing and summarising the original data set. Given that the English language contains an estimated 4500 adjectives that describe behavioural traits, for instance, the first task of a trait theorist must be to reduce these to a manageable number. However as many terms are virtually synonymous (for example reserved, detached, cool, reticent, taciturn, aloof, restrained, laconic, remote and distant) the task is not quite as difficult as it might look. Cattell eventually came up with sixteen different factors, each forming a continuum, as follows in Table 9.1 (Cattell, Eber and Tatsuoka, 1970).

The identification of these sixteen factors allowed Cattell to score people on each one and so obtain a 'personality profile' for any given individual. This personality test is now widely-used as the *16PF* in selection and in vocational guidance (Cattell, Eber and Tatsuoka, 1970). Later exponents of factor analysis have carried the narrowing down process of Cattell even further and come up with only five factors, as shown in Table 9.2 (Rust, Sinclair and Barrow, 1992). However this classification has not yet been as widely accepted as Cattell's.

Cattell suggested that there were three important sources of data about any given individual personality, life data, self-report questionnaire data and objective data from personality tests (Cattell, 1965). The life data would consist of ratings on various factors by people who knew the person being studied and the objective data would come from the kind of personality tests that we encountered when discussing the unconscious in Chapter 6. It is interesting to note therefore that despite his rigorously empirical and statistical approach Cattell was happy to accept the influence of unconscious forces and, indeed, the psychoanalytic concepts of ego and superego.

TABLE 9.1   Cattell's 16 personality factors

Outgoing	Reserved
More intelligent	Less intelligent
Emotionally stable	Affected by feelings
Assertive	Humble
Happy go lucky	Sober
Conscientious	Expedient
Venturesome	Shy
Tender-minded	Tough-minded
Suspicious	Trusting
Imaginative	Practical
Shrewd	Forthright
Apprehensive	Placid
Experimenting	Conservative
Self-sufficient	Group-dependent
Controlled	Casual
Tense	Relaxed

TABLE 9.2 Reduction to five personality factors

Extroversion	for example:
Talkative	Silent
Agreeableness	for example:
Good natured	Irritable
Conscientiousness	for example:
Fussy..	Careless
Emotional Stability	for example:
Calm	Anxious
Culture	for example:
Intellectual	Unreflective

Summary

The four major kinds of formal personality theory are now regarded by psychologists in a somewhat less definitive way than they used to be. They are no longer regarded as being utterly different from each other in every way. We have seen, in particular, that only a radical behaviourist would deny the existence of the unconscious which was quite acceptable to behaviourists like Dollard and Miller, as well as trait theorists like Cattell. The issue for many non-psychoanalysts is therefore more a matter of emphasis; not so much does the unconscious exist, but how and when can you see it in operation?

This point should be borne in mind when looking at the comparative summary of formal personality theories in Figure 9.2.

As we see in the right-hand column the least appealing theory for managers is still probably psychoanalysis, though as we noted in Chapter 6 there may be some evidence that this is slowly changing. People who run organizations in the world of work can sometimes come to realise that neither organizations nor the people in them are entirely influenced by factors that are rational and clearly observable. But this of course is a very difficult realisation to deal with. Slightly easier is the humanist orientation that often appears in counselling practices and in the recipes for 'progressive' management espoused by business gurus.

But the most appealing theories to most managers are trait theory and behaviourism. They are simpler and more straightforward in practice, they deal largely with observable and localised units of behaviour, and they are *quantifiable*. These features are perfectly valid and useful as a way of grasping the *mechanics* of human behaviour in action. What they lack is the potential power of Freudian concepts to *understand* people as a

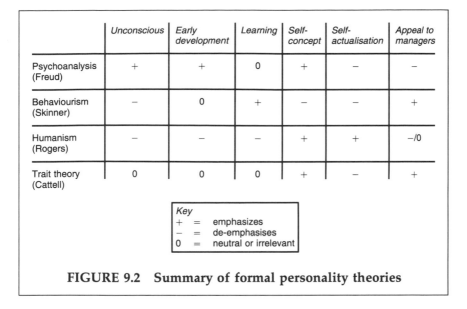

	Unconscious	Early development	Learning	Self-concept	Self-actualisation	Appeal to managers
Psychoanalysis (Freud)	+	+	0	+	−	−
Behaviourism (Skinner)	−	0	+	−	−	+
Humanism (Rogers)	−	−	−	+	+	−/0
Trait theory (Cattell)	0	0	0	+	−	+

Key
+ = emphasizes
− = de-emphasises
0 = neutral or irrelevant

FIGURE 9.2   Summary of formal personality theories

whole and *why* they do what they do. Hall and Lindzey put the case for Freud very well:

> Over and above all the other virtues of his theory stands this one – it tries to envisage a full-bodied individual living partly in a world of reality and partly in a world of make-believe, beset by conflicts and inner contradictions, yet capable of rational thought and action, moved by forces of which he has little knowledge and by aspirations which are beyond his reach, in turn confused and clear headed, frustrated and satisfied, hopeful and despairing, selfish and altruistic; in short, a complex human being. For many people, this picture has an essential validity. (Hall and Lindzey, 1978, p. 70)

Informal theories of personality

We noted at the beginning of this chapter that psychologists and non-psychologists alike have a need to make sense of the individual personalities they encounter. We have examined major ways in which psychologists explicitly and (usually) consciously attempt to do so. In this section we will look at the ways in which non-psychologists implicitly, and often unconsciously, try to do the same thing.

Implicit personality theory is based on the process of *impression formation*, or *person perception* as it is also known; that is, the way in which we construct our understanding of an individual and his behaviour, how we perceive him, the impressions we form of him.

A major pioneer in this field was someone we encountered in Chapter 7 on Group Dynamics, Solomon Asch. Asch systematically studied the ways in which we go about forming our views of someone's personality (Asch, 1946). Perhaps his most important finding was that varying only one item in a list of seven characteristics or traits seemed to lead to a substantial difference in the overall impression that people formed of someone's personality.

The traits are listed in Table 9.3.

Subjects who received a description of someone that included the description 'warm' formed a much more favourable impression of him and his generosity, humour, popularity, irritability, ruthlessness and so on than those whose imaginary person included the term 'cold' among the seven descriptive traits.

The effect of this central trait has also been demonstrated in a real-life setting. A class of students was given a written description of a visiting instructor who was due to lead a class discussion. The whole class was given the information that the visitor was 'industrious, critical, practical and determined'. But while one half of the class was told that the instructor was 'very warm', the other half learned that he was 'rather cold'.

All the students then had the chance to interact with the instructor for twenty minutes, after which they were asked to rate him on the usual list of personality characteristics. Despite the personal interaction involved the judgements made differed between the two halves of the class along the same lines as in Asch's 'warm/cold' laboratory experiment (Kelley, 1950). It is interesting to note that negative information about an individual seems to have more influence on people's judgements than positive information (Warr, 1974).

Later research has supported Asch's ideas and elaborated on them (Higgins, King and Mavin, 1982). We tend to categorise other people on the basis of how well they fit our existing images or prototypes of different personalities. A key trait like the warm/cold dimension seems to act as a kind of 'halo effect' where it spreads out and influences our overall impression of an individual.

TABLE 9.3   Asch 'Warm-Cold' Study

Intelligent		Intelligent
Skilful		Skilful
Industrious		Industrious
Warm	OR	Cold
Determined		Determined
Practical		Practical
Cautious		Cautious

Social perception

As well as verbal information we rely heavily on the *non-verbal information* that our eyes provide us with about people in our environment, in particular their appearance, their bodily posture and movement and their facial expressions.

Appearance is particularly important where other sources of information are lacking, and in first impressions. Sex and skin colour are the most obvious forms of data for use in our personality prototypes. But these are very broad categories and people are capable of making much more subtle distinctions from clothing, for instance, or hair style. Because we make a personal statement by the way we present ourselves in public it is often possible to infer someone's political attitudes or sexual preferences in this way. Indeed English soccer fans form even more detailed images of each other from tiny details like the way a scarf is tied or the kind of footwear being displayed (Marsh, 1982).

Bodily posture and *movement* offer us other clues about personality. Tension, aggressiveness or shyness are all reflected in this way in forms that we learn to perceive very early in life. Skilled managers, interviewers and salesmen have developed a particular sensitivity to this kind of information in interacting with people at work (Argyle, 1983).

Facial expression is probably the most important source of non-verbal information we have in interacting with other people. A few facial expressions are almost universally recognisable and convey a clear and strong message (Ekman, 1982). As might be expected these include the expression of powerful underlying emotions such as anger, fear and happiness. We can also receive mixed messages in this way, of course, like a warm smile accompanied by a cold gaze, or as President Mitterrand said of Mrs Thatcher, 'she has the mouth of Marilyn Monroe and the eyes of Caligula'.

In this case (as we saw earlier) the negative information would have more influence. Indeed *gaze* itself can contain some complex information, in its frequency, intensity and content, and decoding it is a social skill in its own right (Argyle and Cook, 1976).

Kelly's personal construct theory

We have noted more than once in this chapter how psychologists and non-psychologists alike try to make sense out of someone's personality. We will close this section by looking at the work of a personality theorist, George Kelly, who made this point an integral part of his approach (Kelly, 1955).

Kelly believed that what people actually do, without realising it, is to act *as if* they were scientists studying human behaviour. Where psychological scientists consciously develop concepts about why people do what they do which they then test out in dealing with actual behaviour and then change as necessary, so do non-psychologists. They do it by developing what Kelly called a *construct system*, that is a method of 'construing' or trying to explain the behaviour of others to their own satisfaction.

If we construe a colleague at work as being 'conscientious', for example, we are predicting that he will act in a certain way rather than another and we shape our behaviour in relation to him accordingly. If he acts in a different way from our expectations we will have to revise our concept of him. Predictability is at the very heart of all social interaction, of course, and having to change our constructs because something unpredictable has happened can therefore be a psychologically uncomfortable experience.

Personal constructs seem to be made up of 'bipolar adjectives', like rejecting-accepting or stable-unstable. People seem to use the same sets of constructs over time to describe other people (and themselves). The more complex and differentiated someone's construct system the more successful will they be in relationships with other people (Neimeyer and Hudson, 1985).

For our purposes a particularly important aspect of Kelly's theory is what he referred to as *sociality*. Sociality occurs where someone 'construes the construction processes of another'. Personal constructs are part of a reciprocal process, in other words, and effectiveness in social situations depends on our ability to put ourself in the other person's place and understand how they are making sense of *our* behaviour. There are obvious implications here for relations between people at work and between providers of services and their customers (Singleton, 1983).

Socialization

Introduction

So far in this chapter we have considered theories, whether formal or informal, that have tried to account for personality *as a whole* and across the entire range of humanity. In this final section we will focus on some individual aspects of personality which are generally regarded as being particularly important and which have been widely studied. We have already encountered some of this work in Chapter 5 when we discussed stress and Type A personality for instance.

Before looking at these aspects of personality in detail however we need to be aware of the importance in this context of another social psychological process, *socialization*, the way in which an individual child becomes an adult person and that person a functioning member of his or her society.

The term 'socialization' is sometimes used as though it described something that was done to people, without their consent or participation. We talk of people 'being socialized' into society but never of people 'socializing themselves' into society. In fact however socialization is very much a two-way process. People influence their social world and are influenced by it from birth on. We separate the two forms of influence artificially, to enable us to study each more closely, but in real life they are closely interwoven.

Psychologists have observed for example that some newborn infants are more active than others. This simple difference means that people will react to them differently, and have different expectations of their future behaviour. The infant will in turn react to their reactions and the process of socialization – and the construction of personality – will have begun. In a very real sense children can socialize their parents, for example, just as parents socialize children. Each can influence and even manipulate the other's behaviour (Danziger, 1973).

The effect of institutions

As we saw in Chapter 7 we all live our lives among groups of other people. Some of these groups are more important to us than others in our socialization. A few groups are important to everybody and are officially recognised as such by our society. What happens in these groups is crucial to the working and the future of our society, so it watches over them carefully, passes laws and creates regulations dealing with them, and thus turns them into *institutions*.

The institutions that have the most powerful influence in our socialization are the *family*, the *school* and the *nation-state*. Figure 9.3 illustrates the individual's progress towards being recognised as a fully adult member of her society.

(I) FAMILY

Most children in our society, until they go to school, live their lives mainly within their family. Freud was not the first to argue that the

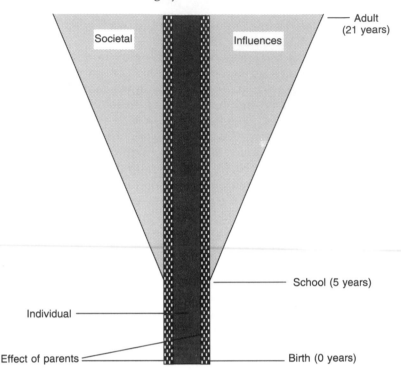

FIGURE 9.3   Socialization as illustrated by the Statt Cone

Source: Statt, D. (1990) *The Concise Dictionary of Psychology*, p. 121.

child's family experiences are crucial in determining his adult personality, but he was certainly the most influential. Probably the great majority of modern psychologists would agree with him on this point, especially with regard to the influence of parents.

That is why in Figure 9.3 I have represented parental influence as two parallel lines that accompany the individual from birth on. In the first few years of life the behaviour of his parents is of paramount importance to a child. They are all-powerful (no matter how benign). They always know the answers. They know what to do in every situation.

As the child grows up and increases his contacts outside the home he can begin to put his parents and family within a wider social framework. He acquires a perspective on his family as he comes into contact with other families and other models of behaviour. As he widens his social horizons his parents become less and less of an immediate, daily, physical presence, and their influence is diluted by other social influences.

But in a psychological sense the child's parents will be with him in some form for the rest of his life, for he will have internalised what he learned from them. And one of the things he will have learned is an image, a model (a construct) of what being a parent means. So it should come as no surprise to us that parents who abuse their children, were usually abused by their parents when they were children.

(II) SCHOOL

The next important institution the child meets links him to the educational system. Our society requires certain levels of academic skills of its members – at least the ability to read, write and count – and we tend to regard this as being the function of school. This is obviously an essential part of the socialization process and nobody can be a fully accepted member of our society unless he has acquired these skills. But to a psychologist the school has a much more important task: it prepares the child for his adult role in society.

In his family setting the child was probably used to having someone around to whom he could turn for information or explanation about the world as it filtered through to him; for example in the form of comic books or television. But in school he actually becomes part of the world and he must deal with it alone. Play gradually gives way to work, and even play must be performed in a certain way at a certain time with other people.

This is the child's first non-academic lesson in socialization; how to behave in an extremely complex mass society where everyone's life is ruled by the clock. As we saw in Chapter 4 this socialization is crucial for the world of work. So are the accompanying lessons that are learned about cooperation and competition with others, relationships to authority, the rewards for achievement and the punishments for non-achievement. And these lessons are learned within a highly structured context of values, meanings and *feelings* associated with working (Neff, 1985).

Schools therefore reflect the values of the society around them and instruct their members in those values. As we are dealing here with the psychological processes of learning, these processes will operate regardless of the social desirability of the outcome. What some children may learn, if they have difficulties at school in either learning or relating, is that they are failures who are not expected to achieve anything in life.

As the child goes through school the other children who accompany him from grade to grade (his peer group) will assume an ever-increasing importance to him, and eventually their opinions will influence him more than those of his parents.

(III) NATION-STATE

At a certain point in his life, society recognises that the individual has become a fully adult human being – socially. Psychologically, as we saw in Chapter 4, individuals of adult age may be at various stages of maturity in their development as persons. The official age of becoming an adult varies with time and place, as with the particular social behaviour we choose to look at, but certainly by the age of twenty-one people in our society are regarded as adult. They can now fulfill all aspects of citizenship, they may have entered the world of work, and they will certainly come into contact with the third key socializing institution, the nation-state.

The most important single fact about the way people on this planet are divided up socially is that virtually everyone is the citizen of some national government. The few people who are not really have no social existence; they cannot travel (having no passport) nor do they have the right to live and work in any country. National governments are the only legitimate sources of power in a given country (controlling the army) with the ability to raise taxes and pass laws.

The individual in his role of citizen comes into contact with these social influences as a taxpayer, voter, soldier and signer of all kinds of legal documents. These are all signs that the socialization process has achieved its purpose and produced an adult social being who can behave in the ways expected of him. Different nation-states may produce different kinds of adult social beings. People are taxed, vote and fight under similar but different systems of values. These values in turn are reflected in different educational systems and family patterns.

There is some evidence that even nations with such similar institutions as the United States and Canada can produce people who regard the world, and their own place in it, in very different ways (Statt, 1972). To a psychologist such differences are neither good nor bad, merely interesting. But whatever the effects that socializing institutions have on people, whatever kind of people they are meant to produce, they form the boundaries within which the psychological development of the person takes place, and they select from the vast range of psychological possibilities those aspects of behaviour that they consider most valuable.

The institutions of family, school and nation-state are all linked together, of course, and normally share the same social values and reinforce the same kinds of behaviour. Typically the basic ways of relating to the world which are laid down in the family are expanded upon and applied in school to actual forms of behaviour, behaviour which the individual then engages in as an adult.

The young child in our culture, for instance, learns certain attitudes in his home about the rightness (or inevitability) of obeying authorities. The schools offer examples (both in school life and in history and civics lessons) of what this means in terms of appropriate behaviour. As an adult our individual will be likely to pay his taxes. In societies that value this kind of authority less highly, fewer people may pay their taxes.

Occupational socialization

(I) ANTICIPATORY SOCIALIZATION

We have seen how socialization for the world of work begins at school in the earliest years of a child's education. This is a form of very general *anticipatory socialization*. A more specific form begins to occur as the transition from full-time education into the world of work is approached. Different social groups may be affected in different ways by their family experiences where parents and other relatives act as *role models* for particular occupations or types of work.

Thus working-class school children will start to adopt the norms and values of people who work in unskilled manual jobs (Willis, 1977). Middle-class college students on the other hand will begin to anticipate life in the professional/managerial kinds of jobs they have seen modelled in their rather different family backgrounds (Goodale and Hall, 1976).

These experiences will usually influence young people in one general direction or another rather than into a particular occupation. None the less there are some striking examples of just this kind of effect. It has often been remarked that an unusually high proportion of children of general medical practitioners become doctors themselves, presumably because with a surgery in the home of many GPs the role model can be closely observed. It has also been noted that the children of prominent actors often become actors too, though here the role modelling may be augmented by an important social factor, influence.

For most people specific occupational socialization begins when they start the period of training or apprenticeship that all but totally unskilled jobs require. It has been found for instance that even in the first year of medical school as many as three-quarters of a group of medical students thought of themselves as doctors if they had occasion to interact with patients (Merton, Reader and Kendall, 1957).

(II) INITIAL ENTRY TO OCCUPATION

The process of occupational socialization is a continuous one from the time someone first anticipates entering an occupation until the time he leaves it. But there are certain points in this process that are more salient than others and perhaps the most important of these is the point of entry into the occupation. Whether or not an organization has a formal period of induction newcomers will usually be singled out for special attention.

In a formal induction the organization will present the newcomer with its (carefully-scrubbed) public face. It will attempt to give him or her the most positive image possible of the organization; the kind of picture one would get from its brochures or annual report. As always the part played by one's immediate supervisor is strongly influential here. At the same time the new recruit will be informally inducted into the organization by his or her colleagues.

Inevitably, as we saw in Chapter 7, the informal groups that the newcomer comes into contact with will present quite a different picture of the organization. 'This is the way things *really* are' they will say. 'This is what *actually* happens here'. It is at this point that new recruits may experience their first reservations about the job. In any event they will be left with a more complex view of the organization they have joined.

In terms of job content occupational socialization means actually experiencing what the job is like rather than anticipating it or training for it, however long and thoroughly this may be done. Medical students may see themselves as doctors but actually working as a qualified physician (or lawyer or accountant or teacher or plumber) is quite another matter.

People are often psychologically unprepared for the reality and may require to make some serious adjustments to their psychological contract with the organization if they are to stay in the job (Richards, 1984). The 'reality shock' that most people seem to experience leaves them with an urgent need to make sense of their new surroundings. Surprise at the unexpected and the contrast with previous experience in work or training may thus lead people to make hasty and erroneous interpretations of their new environment (Louis, 1980).

(III) ADAPTATION

Another important point in the process of occupational socialization really involves the resocialization of people who have been in the organization for some time and who are promoted and/or moved to another job (Katz, 1977). We will look specifically at the issue of promotion and its implications in Chapter 12. However any move involves change and change, as we saw in Chapter 5, can result in stress. Even if it doesn't there will always be some psychological adaptation to be done by the individual together with a renegotiation of his psychological contract with the organization.

People seem to be moving to new jobs with increasing frequency. A United Kingdom survey in the late 1980s found that the average time spent in a job was three years (Nicholson and West, 1988). Moreover these can be quite radical job changes. One-quarter of the subjects interviewed were changing their employer, their status and their function at the same time. Needless to say most organizations fail to take account of the effects of these changes and usually deal with them badly.

Occupational choice

As we saw in Chapter 8, and as we have already noted in this chapter, choice of occupation is often dictated more by situation than by personality. People with few, or unsaleable, skills and qualifications are often dependent on whatever employment happens to be available, if any. Choice is therefore largely a middle-class phenomenon, and even here parental role models may influence personal choice of occupation.

For those people who have some choice of occupation the most influential aspects of their personality involved are their abilities and their intelligence. In Chapter 10 we will examine how abilities and intelligence are defined, identified, measured and compared. The important point for us to note here is that people have a pretty clear idea as early as their teens what kind of abilities and intelligence they possess, as well as how these register in the job market (Furnham, 1984).

However this self assessment can often be different from that of other people, or even objective tests (Farh and Dobbins, 1989). Part of the process of both general and occupational socialization therefore is that people modify their assessment of their abilities and their intelligence in the light of feedback from other sources and the opportunity to compare themselves with other people (Mabe and West, 1982).

While many occupations can be followed equally well by people of vastly different personality there are some kinds of occupation that do emphasize particular personality characteristics and there is usually a clear match between the two. As we noted in Chapter 5 people who are quiet and reflective would probably choose to work in a museum or library rather than a newsroom. The most outgoing, extroverted managers in an organization are likely to be found in sales, with the least extroverted in research and development (Eysenck, 1967).

The self concept

The self concept, as we saw earlier in Table 9.3, is widely used by personality theorists as the basic building block of personality. As such it underlies all the work we will consider below on particular aspects of personality.

We are not born with a sense of self, of who and what we are; it develops throughout our childhood and youth and continues to change, however slowly, for as long as we live. As the newborn infant develops into a person, his concept of himself is the most important concept he will ever form. It is of crucial importance to how he perceives the world and everyone in it.

The self concept is formed in the process of interacting with other people. From the moment of birth people respond, as we noted above, to an infant's behaviour and the infant reacts in turn. From the very beginning of life he receives feedback from other people about himself; how he is regarded by them, the effects of his behaviour on them (see for example Livesley and Bromley, 1973; Suls, 1982).

At first the infant has difficulty knowing where he ends and the environment begins. Gradually he begins to be aware of his own body and, at about the age of ten to twelve months, starts to distinguish 'me' from 'not me'. During the first few years of life the infant is closely concerned with exploring his own body, seeing what's there and finding out what it can do. As various groups of muscles mature he takes delight in using them, gaining more and more mastery over himself, and exploring the environment.

By about the third year of life the child begins to be aware of himself. He can think of himself as a separate object but still has only the crudest idea of himself as a person. He has trouble, for example, in distinguishing processes internal to himself from his environment. Dreams may be located 'in the room' or 'beside the bed'.

Children also have great difficulty, as they acquire language, in using personal pronouns. A child will start to use the word 'I' to refer to himself when he is two or three years old, but he won't use it consistently. He hears people talking about objects called 'table', 'dog', and 'ball', and he very quickly learns to use these terms correctly. But he hears people refer to *him* both as 'you' and as 'George', and so he may also refer to himself in both these ways. At the same time he is learning that people announce their wants and intentions with the word 'I', so he tries that one out too.

All of this early exploratory activity normally takes place, of course, within the social context provided by the child's family and in particular by his mother, with whom much of the activity takes place. The feelings other people have about him and the way these feelings are expressed can exert the most crucial influence on his development. If the child feels secure and loved and encouraged in his earliest explorations of himself and his world, he is off to a good start in his development as a person. If not both his intellectual and emotional development may suffer.

With the broadening of the child's horizons that comes with the development of language there also appears a more detailed self image. As at every other stage of life the self image is a product of the interaction between the child and the people around him. But whereas later in life it is possible to reinterpret the judgements of these others or to seek out different judgements, the young child has no alternative but to believe that he is what his parents tell him he is. If the message from his parents is that he is unlovable then that is the judgement he will make of himself. We should not be surprised to find that he may then start to behave in an unlovable fashion.

By the end of adolescence the outlines of our self concept have been set and the crucial question of our self image, whether or not we like ourself and have high or low *self-esteem*, has been answered. In one sense though our self concept is never completely formed or finally finished, and our self-esteem can be raised or lowered to some extent by social factors. Thus it has long been known that if someone is deliberately treated by her group as popular and attractive she will come to *feel* popular and attractive and behave in the way that popular and attractive people behave – to the point where the group begin to believe that she really *is* popular and attractive (Guthrie, 1938).

It has been found more recently that if someone applying for a job is sitting in a waiting room prior to being interviewed, and there are other candidates present his self-esteem may be affected by his perception of these other candidates. Candidates who seem more likely than him to get the job will lower his self-esteem while those who seem less likely to get the job will raise it, with obvious implications for his own interview performance (Gergen and Morse, 1967).

Internals and externals

In Chapter 8 we touched on a personality difference with regard to someone's experience of unemployment and their perception of its causes. We saw there how people in manual, mindless jobs came to feel that they were powerless to influence their work lives which were externally controlled by others. Losing these jobs then tended to reinforce this view of their own position and extend it to the rest of their lives.

Essentially they learned that they were helpless in the face of external forces; the *locus of control* of their lives was external rather than internal. We also noted in Chapter 5 how the feeling of not being in control of situations in one's life was the major cause of anxiety, which could lead to stress and stress-related illnesses.

While it is always difficult, looking at any given individual in any given situation, to tease out the effects of social or personality factors in his feelings and behaviour, a number of personality researchers are convinced that there is a basic personality dimension here that holds across all social situations. This dimension involves a person's expectations of whether or not they can control their own lives and is known as the Internal-External locus of control (Rotter, 1966; Ashkenasy, 1985).

A questionnaire has been developed that differentiates between people on an Internal-External scale (Rotter, 1966). People who are high Internals on this scale believe that they have a great deal of influence on the things that happen in their lives and will have high self-esteem. People who are high Externals on the I-E scale believe that events in their lives are down to chance, or luck, or the power of other people, or forces beyond their understanding. They will have low self-esteem.

The authoritarian personality

The description of the 'authoritarian personality' type arose from a large, pioneering study that attempted to link social and political issues with particular aspects of individual personality (Adorno *et al.*, 1950: KEY STUDY 8). This study was firmly rooted in psychoanalytic theory, suggesting that people who were raised in an authoritarian home (that is with strict, harsh, critical, inconsistent and emotionally repressed parents) were left with a weak ego and low self-esteem.

A child of such a home environment will be totally dependent on pleasing and obeying his parents in order to obtain their approval of him. Placing such conditions on the granting or withdrawing of approval and love will leave the child in a constant state of insecurity. He is bound to feel resentful, afraid and hostile about such treatment. But he knows very well what will happen to him if he expresses those feelings, so he bottles them up by repressing them into his unconscious where he no longer has to be aware of them all the time.

Such a child might conceive of the world as a place where relations between people are based on power, status and authority rather than on trust, affection and fellow feeling. Outwardly such a child may well grow up to be a conventional, rather rigid adult with a great respect for his parents and all other authorities. Inwardly he may be very angry and filled with hate that he dare not express directly.

The authoritarian personality is often a willing participant in the sentiments of group prejudice that can always be found in a large and complex society. In such cases the anger and hatred within is often directed outwards on to a convenient social scapegoat (Cherry and Byrne, 1977).

From the time the child first thinks of himself as 'I' he does everything he can to support his self image and to protect it from negative experiences and interpretations. In an authoritarian environment he inevitably comes to feel, and to see himself as being, weak, insecure and powerless. Because it is painful to think of himself in that way he uses a variety of devices to defend his self image.

Such a person may try to identify himself with the strong and despise the weak; he may cling to ideals of order, continuity and tradition and be very threatened by the prospect of change; he may blame others for all the problems he has and find no fault with himself; he may have learned to fear and distrust his own impulses, particularly sexual ones, and come to attribute these feelings to other people, seeing *them* rather than himself as licentious and immoral and finding obscenity where none exists.

Deeply prejudiced people, it seems, are prejudiced against anybody and everybody as long as it helps them feel better about themselves. If an authoritarian white man can bolster his self image by hating, or feeling superior to, or being angry at, a black, brown, or yellow man, then he will probably do so. The prejudice of the authoritarian personality is thus a necessary part of his life. It is an integral part of the way he sees himself and the world around him. If you took away his prejudices he would have to look himself squarely in the self image – and that can be a painful experience for even the least prejudiced among us.

Machiavellianism

A variant of the authoritarian personality is the personality type named after the sixteenth century Italian courtier and political philosopher Nicolo Machiavelli (Christie and Geis, 1971). The key characteristic of *Machiavellianism* is the desire to manipulate other people for one's own gain by using whatever forms of deviousness and deception may be necessary. The scale devised to measure this personality type uses many statements taken from Machiavelli's own writings.

Apparently these characteristics can be recognised in childhood and, as in the authoritarian personality, Machiavellian children have similar parents. In adulthood there is some evidence that Machiavellian personalities tend to be found working successfully in professional occupations, particularly those dealing with people, and to be particularly good at bargaining!

The entrepreneurial personality

We will end this chapter by examining the research on entrepreneurial behaviour and the personality factors that are thought to affect it. The importance of a strong achievement motivation in producing entrepreneurs was first highlighted by David McClelland (McClelland *et al.*, 1953). McClelland referred to the need for achievement, or *n Ach*, and considered this need to be largely unconscious. N Ach therefore had to be identified and measured by projective techniques, and the one McClelland used most was the *Thematic Apperception Test* (TAT), which was described in Chapter 6.

Although n Ach could be found wherever there was a strong drive to accomplish a certain goal successfully, McClelland was particularly concerned about its appearance in an entrepreneurial setting, though not necessarily in the private sphere. Its most obvious occurrence was in people who started their own businesses. People high in n Ach also tend to be high Internals (O'Brien, 1986). They will seek out personal responsibility, distrust authority and have an optimistic future-oriented approach to their work.

The psychological source of high n Ach, McClelland argued, lay in a home background that expected mastery of oneself and the environment from an early age and actively encouraged the child to be independent in taking care of himself and in learning and competing. This is especially true of the relationship between mothers and sons. Indeed it should be pointed out that the n Ach concept has only been concerned with male children and male entrepreneurs.

McClelland attempted to test his ideas more widely than the American setting in which they were born. In an ambitious and imaginative series of studies he tried to show that the appearance of widespread n Ach in the child-rearing practices of a given time and place led to a critical mass of adult entrepreneurs who sparked off the upsurges of commercial and cultural activity that come to be described as 'golden ages' of civilization, like ancient Athens or sixteenth century Spain (McClelland, 1961: KEY STUDY 9).

Later work on n Ach has suggested that in the business world it may be most relevant to entrepreneurial success in small companies or in sales departments, where there is an immediate link and feedback between personal efforts and results. However for managers in large organizations, whose success is less directly linked to individual effort, what may be more important than high n Ach is the ability to influence the efforts of other people. And this might require instead a high need for power coupled with a low need for affiliation, that is close relationships with other people (McClelland and Boyatzis, 1982).

Self-fulfilling prophecy

Throughout this chapter we have been dealing with examples of the way we organize cues about other people's behaviour into a picture of their overall personality. We have seen how people will distort the evidence of their senses to make what they actually perceive fit what they expect to perceive. In this final section we will follow this process one step further and look at how people make their expectations happen.

Gustav Jahoda made a very interesting discovery about the Ashanti people of West Africa (Jahoda, 1954). Apparently they believe that people born on different days of the week have different personalities. To accompany this belief they tend to name their children according to the day of the week on which they were born: thus Kwadwo was born on a Monday and Kwakwu on a Wednesday. Kwadwos are supposed to be quiet and even-tempered, Kwakwus aggressive and quarrelsome.

The Ashanti seem to have had their expectations fulfilled for when Jahoda checked the police records he found that the Kwadwos born on Monday had a very low rate of criminal offences while the Kwakwus born on Wednesday had a very high rate. This study suggests not only that people tend to behave the way they are expected to but that if the expected behaviour becomes part of their self image this is also the kind of behaviour they will tend to choose for themselves. Both the individuals and their society were involved in the process of *self fulfilling prophecy*. Making our images of ourselves and of other people come true is a process that affects all areas of our behaviour and we will come across it again before the end of this book.

CHAPTER 10

Measuring human abilities

The identification and measurement of human abilities is closely bound up with the study of *individual differences*, something that seems to be terribly important to us. The use of tests in pursuit of this study has grown enormously over the course of the twentieth century and was busier than ever during the 1980s (Anastasi, 1990). But like so many of the issues dealt with in this book it is not a new concern. The Chinese civil service made extensive use of testing over three thousand years ago, and it was used by the ancient Greeks as part of their educational system.

Psychologically we seem to feel more secure when we can pigeonhole people in the 'right' boxes and then compare ourselves with them; it is an essential aspect of our need to make sense (Statt, 1977). Socially it makes the lives of people who run organizations easier if they can have a quick, and preferably quantifiable, way of summarising a large number of people and their various abilities (Hollway, 1991). An impression of social order is thus created, and with that of course come the feelings of predictability and control.

Testing

The great interest in individual differences has led to the creation of a sizeable industry devoted to the construction and application of psychological tests and measurements. There are many hundreds of tests in use in educational, clinical and occupational settings. In this chapter we will consider tests of abilities which are found mainly in occupational settings, though the tests themselves may have been designed with other environments in mind. In the following two chapters we will see how these tests are used in practice.

In the world of work there are a large number of psychological tests which attempt to provide an *objective* and *standardised* measure of someone's behaviour in any given area. These tests are often called *psychometrics*. But first we need to consider how these tests are devised. There are some technical aspects of any test that we need to examine, in particular its *reliability* and its *validity*.

Reliability

As the term implies, a test exhibits its reliability by measuring something in a *consistent* fashion, so that you know you can always depend on it. Like a tape measure, for instance. We can measure our waist size with it today, just as we did last week or last year. We may not like what it tells us but we know we can rely on the information to be accurate every time we use it. And every time anyone else uses it. When a psychological test is reliable it provides the same results when it is given at different times, so that the scores of a group of managers who took the test yesterday will have the same order that they had when the test was given six months ago.

There are different kinds of reliability that apply to different kinds of test. Three of these are particularly important for our concerns, *internal* reliability, *test-retest* reliability and *inter-judge* reliability.

(I) INTERNAL RELIABILITY

This form of reliability deals with the internal consistency of the test. To what extent do the different items that make up the test each come up with the same kind of result? The usual way of testing the extent of internal reliability is *randomly* to split the number of test items in half and compare the scores that people produce on one half with their scores on the other. The higher the *correlation* between the scores on the two halves the greater the reliability of the test.

Correlations in testing are measured by a statistical technique called a *correlation coefficient* (denoted by the letter r) of the extent to which the two variables go together. Correlation can range from zero to a perfect positive correlation ($r = 1.00$) where the variables are always associated in the same way, or a perfect negative correlation ($r = -1.00$) where the variables are always associated but in different ways.

(II) TEST-RETEST RELIABILITY

This measures the extent to which the administration of the same test two or more times to the same group of people produces the same result each time. If test-retest reliability is high it means that the test in question is not affected by extraneous and temporary factors, like the nervousness of the people being tested.

(III) INTER-JUDGE RELIABILITY

This is used in tests which require a series of observers' judgements to be made on someone's verbal or written behaviour. Obviously each observer's judgement is quite subjective and so any two people might score the same behaviour very differently, like judges at a boxing match, sometimes. So for such a test to be accepted as reliable all (properly trained) observers must produce very similar scores or interpretations.

Validity

Test validity deals with the question 'to what extent does this test measure what it's supposed to measure?' In a sense, therefore, there are as many forms of validity as there are tests. However we will consider four main forms, *content* validity, *predictive* validity, *concurrent* validity and *construct* validity.

(I) CONTENT VALIDITY

To what extent is the content of the test a representative sample of the ability being measured? This is sometimes confused with what is called *face validity*; that is does the test *look* valid to the people taking it? For instance a driving test that did not involve someone actually getting into a vehicle would probably lack face validity though, theoretically at least, it might have high content validity through the use of simulators and so on.

(II) PREDICTIVE VALIDITY

To what extent does the test predict to some criterion of future behaviour, like job performance for example? If a group of widget designers can design widgets equally well even though they had widely different scores on the Widget Design Test then the test is low on predictive validity.

(III) CONCURRENT VALIDITY

To what extent does the test correlate with other tests or measures of the same behaviour? In a sense this is like predictive validity except that it's concerned with 'postdictive' behaviour. Thus a new and cheaper test of widget designing ability might be correlated with an existing test known to be high on predictive validity, like the Schnell and Schmutzick.

(IV) CONSTRUCT VALIDITY

To what extent does the test measure the *construct* it is supposed to measure? This is the key form of validity when a test is first being put together. A construct is a complex idea derived theoretically from a number of simpler ones. Intelligence is one widely used theoretical construct. Tests that claim to measure intelligence need to identify the particular aspects of behaviour that go to make up intelligence (like verbal reasoning for instance) and then see whether their test is able to measure it successfully. Unlike other forms of validity there is no measure of correlation available. It depends on the accumulation of evidence about the factors that go to make up the construct.

Standardisation

We noted earlier that a psychological test was an objective and standardised measure of behaviour. In discussing reliability and validity we saw what was involved in making a test objective. We will now consider how a test is *standardised*; how it is devised, how it is scored, what the scores mean and how the test is administered. We will illustrate these aspects of standardisation with an example that nearly everyone in the industrialised world has some experience of, *intelligence* testing.

Individual differences: Alfred Binet

While the Victorian scientist Francis Galton, as we saw in Chapter 1, was the first person to attempt the measurement of mental abilities, or what we would call intelligence, it was not until a generation later, at the beginning of the twentieth century, that the first generally accepted intelligence test was developed by the French psychologist Alfred Binet. Galton had opened a small laboratory in London in 1882 where members of the public could have themselves tested for various abilities. These tests dealt with aspects of sensation and perception such as reaction time and visual acuity, Galton assuming that sensory discrimination was an intellectual ability in which eminent men would make much finer discriminations than men with mental deficiencies.

While Binet admired Galton's work he felt (in a kind of parallel to the development of psychophysics) that the measurement of intellectual ability required a study of the higher mental processes of learning, memory, thinking and imagination. Throughout the 1890s Binet studied these processes in schoolchildren. Around 1900 he began a close study of the thinking processes of his own two school-age daughters. Finally, in 1904, he was appointed to a commission that was set up to find ways of identifying subnormal children in the Paris school system who could then be removed and placed in special schools.

Binet was stimulated to produce a large range of mental tests, each of which were tried out on a great number of schoolchildren with the object of seeing which tests discriminated the bright from the dull. The ones that did so most successfully were incorporated into a battery, making up the first intelligence test, published in 1905. It is crucial to note that the judgements of who was bright and who was dull, *against which the test results were compared*, came from other sources, usually teacher's ratings of classroom performance.

In other words this is an operational definition of intelligence only, and it involves huge assumptions about what intelligence is. Indeed nearly a century after Binet's work we are not much further on. The nearest that psychologists can get to an agreed definition is that 'intelligence is what intelligence tests measure'.

In using his intelligence test battery Binet had computed a Mental Age (in years and months) for each child tested. This was then compared with the child's chronological age to see whether he or she was abnormally retarded. After Binet's death in 1911 other psychologists decided that it was more useful to use the ratio of the two ages instead of dealing with the Mental Age as an absolute figure. The ratio was formed by dividing the Mental Age by the chronological age. Multiplying the quotient by 100 yielded a single figure, thus:

$$\frac{\text{MA}}{\text{CA}} = \frac{4 \text{ years } 2 \text{ months}}{8 \text{ years } 4 \text{ months}} = \frac{50 \text{ months}}{100 \text{ months}} \times 100 = 50$$

So the above child has an intelligence quotient, or IQ, of 50.

We should also note that an IQ score is meaningless in itself. It is not like height, for instance, which tells you something definite about someone. We compare our height to that of other people because of our need to know how we compare with others. But we don't need to compare our height with other people *in order to know how tall we are*. For that we simply use a tape measure. There is no tape measure of intelligence.

An IQ score simply tells you how you compare with other people who have taken the same test. *It does not tell you how intelligent you are*. But then, an intelligence test is not meant to tell the subject anything; it is meant to discriminate, to differentiate *between* people for the purpose of assigning them to various educational, occupational and social categories.

In 1916 psychologists at Stanford University in the United States produced an English-language version of Binet's test battery, known as the Stanford-Binet. This version incorporated IQ scales and used a revised edition of Binet's work that extended the range of the tests up to the age of fifteen. With the publication, and subsequent revision, of the Stanford-Binet the field of mental testing in general and intelligence testing in particular, assumed a high public profile and an ever-increasing importance in psychology and the life of industrialised societies.

There is now a fourth edition of the Stanford-Binet (Delaney and Hopkins, 1987). This edition extends the range of tests up to age twenty-three. It was standardised on a sample of 5000 people from all over the United States and contains fifteen items grouped into four areas, Verbal Reasoning (including Vocabulary), Quantitative Reasoning, Abstract/ Visual Reasoning and Short-Term Memory.

Individual intelligence tests specifically for adults have also been devised (notably the *Wechsler Adult Intelligence Scale* or WAIS), and during the First World War the American military authorities introduced the first mass, group-administered tests of intelligence, the Army Alpha and Army Beta Tests, to screen the million and a half new recruits that had flooded into the armed forces.

One test of general intelligence that has been developed for use with both individuals and groups, and is widely used by a variety of organizations, is the *Wonderlic Personnel Test* (Schmidt, 1985). It consists of 50 items dealing with verbal, numerical and spatial abilities. It is particularly simple to administer and score and takes only 12 minutes to complete, which may have something to do with its popularity. The Wonderlic does have norms on a range of occupational groups.

Norms

In studying the nature of individual differences Francis Galton had noticed that physical attributes like height and weight were normally distributed throughout the population. The term 'normally' in this context has no moral, ethical, social or psychological connotation. It is a purely statistical description of the way the numbers concerned fall out. This description is usually illustrated by the *normal distribution curve* as in Figure 10.1.

A normal distribution is therefore the distribution of data taken from a random sample of the population. When these data are plotted on a graph they will form a symmetrical bell-shaped curve with scores clustering around the *mean* or arthmetical average and declining towards either extreme. In Figure 10.1 the curve illustrates the distribution of height in American men.

Galton then suggested, crucially, that not only were physical attributes randomly distributed in the population but so too were psychological attributes, like intelligence. This suggestion was quickly accepted by makers of intelligence tests such as the ones outlined above and the mean score was set at 100. Ninety-five per cent of the population scores an IQ between 70 and 130 and this allows the testers to talk about the normal range of intelligence between these two figures and abnormally low or high intelligence outside this range, as illustrated in Figure 10.2.

Intelligence and the world of work

There is strong evidence that an IQ score is a good predictor of future school performance (for example McCall, Appelbaum and Hogarty, 1973). Given the original purposes of intelligence tests and the way they were conceived and constructed this is hardly surprising. However IQ is

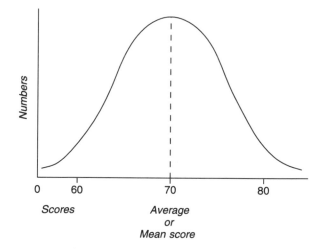

FIGURE 10.1   **Normal distribution curve (height in inches of male adults)**

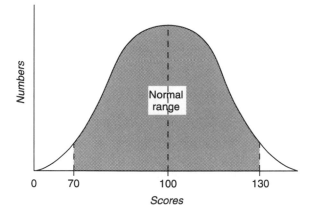

FIGURE 10.2   IQ distribution

less predictive of success in higher education. In the United Kingdom, for example, access to higher education can be predicted more accurately by knowing an individual's social class and the type of school he or she attended (Halsey, Heath and Ridge, 1980).

When it comes to predicting where an individual will be placed in the world of work an IQ score is of even less predictive value. It has been known since the Second World War that people in middle class groups will usually produce much higher average IQs than those in working class jobs (Himmelweit and Whitfield, 1944). Yet the *range* of IQs may show a huge overlap, as in the study that found a range for accountants of 94–154 while that for labourers was 46–145 (Harrell and Harrell, 1945). It could also be argued that the differences between the two groups might be largely accounted for by the origins of intelligence tests that we noted in the previous paragraph, especially the emphasis on verbal ability.

The relationship between an IQ score and someone's performance in a particular job seems therefore to be fairly tenuous. Moreover the kinds of abilities represented by general intelligence tests may not be the only ones (or even the most important ones) required for the successful performance of a particular job. Numerical or mechanical abilities might be more relevant for example (Thorndike and Hagen, 1959). However as we will see in Chapter 11 the assumption that IQ is directly related to job performance is still a widely-held assumption.

Social implications of IQ testing

There is another important set of issues related to psychological tests that has acquired particular prominence in intelligence testing, the social, political, cultural and ethical factors involved which we have only glanced at so far. These issues are of daily relevance but the constant debate about them came to a head most recently in the 1970s with a renewal of the politically-charged 'heredity versus environment' debate, centring not on individual differences but on racial differences. I use the word 'renewal' deliberately because, as we will see later, this is a debate that has occurred before, and for similar reasons.

In discussing the effects of genetic inheritance on human behaviour we quickly encounter the age-old question of how much behaviour is accounted for by heredity and how much by the environment a person is born into. How much is due to what *nature* provides someone and how much to the kind of *nurture* he or she receives?

The issue is usually phrased as nature *versus* nurture; heredity *versus* environment, and when put in this either/or fashion the controversy is just plain silly. No human being could exist without having a genetic heredity *and* a social environment, and both play an indispensable and completely interwoven part in an individual's behaviour. Any example of human behaviour is the result of an *interaction* between someone's inherited predisposition to act in a certain way and the environment he finds himself in.

The nature-nurture debate becomes a little less simplistic when we deal with it in terms of *genotypes* and *phenotypes*. An individual's genetic endowment is seen in terms of potentialities, known as genotypes. There is no way of observing someone's genotype, for genetic potential can only appear in actual behaviour. All the behaviour that we can observe from birth right throughout life is thus the result of the interaction between the genotype of inherited tendencies and the social environment. The result is known as the phenotype. For example we know that physical size is a genotype. So how is it that children can grow up to be taller and heavier than their parents? If environment (nutrition and so on) played no part then, other things being equal, parents and children would be exactly the same size.

One of the most important phenotypes that psychologists have studied is the behaviour resulting from the set of mental processes we call intelligence. For comparison purposes this is usually boiled down to an IQ score. It has been known since the Second World War that black people as a group tend to score about 10–15 points lower on IQ than white people as a group (Klineberg, 1944). It is important to note that the scores referred to here are *average group scores* that say nothing about the IQ of a specific individual. Thus some blacks have always scored higher IQs than most whites.

What this finding means has been the subject of frequent and heated debate, both among psychologists and the general public. It does *not* mean that blacks are less intelligent than whites; it means they score lower on IQ tests. Nativists put the difference down to heredity, with blacks less able to score well on IQ tests. Nurturists attribute the gap to cultural differences and the material poverty that most black children have to grow up in.

Certainly the scoring of intelligence tests seems to reveal some bias. Thus in answer to the question 'What would you do if another child grabbed your hat and ran away with it?' most white middle-class children say they would report it to an adult. This is considered the correct answer. However black kids tend to say that they would chase the offender and fight to get their hat back, which is considered the wrong answer (Albee, 1978).

Psychologists who worry about these things have generally estimated that heredity is probably more important than environment in determining IQ by setting broad limits to achievement (for example Shields, 1962). Arthur Jensen carried this estimate one step further (Jensen, 1969). He calculated that individual IQ is 80 per cent determined by heredity and 20 per cent by environment, and that average racial differences in IQ are also largely determined by heredity. Thus social programmes of compensatory education for blacks and other minority groups cannot succeed, Jensen argued, because these children do not have the genetic potential that would endow them with the IQ to profit from such education.

Jensen has since been subject both to hysterical charges of racism and to reasoned and comprehensive professional criticism of the soundness of his research and thinking. It is difficult to understand why he would attempt to argue about differences between large *groups* of people on the basis of *individual* test scores. Perhaps he was seduced by the attraction of finding neat and relatively simple genetic causes for behaviour that is extremely complex, difficult to disentangle and of wide social interest.

When the dust from this controversy settled we found ourselves back in the same place. Whatever intelligence is it is not entirely captured in an IQ score; it remains a phenotype whose genetic component sets limits but which can be greatly affected by environment – thus even identical twins can have a 25-point difference in IQ if reared in different environments (Shields, 1962; Scarr-Salapatek, 1971).

The attempt to measure the relative importance of heredity and environment continues, with a definitive test remaining as elusive as ever. And while there is no hard evidence that there are genetic racial differences in IQ there is plenty of evidence that the IQ tests currently in use are biased in favour of urban white middle-class children (Loehlin, Lindzey and Spuhler, 1975; Scarr, 1981).

But there is nothing new about this kind of controversy; it took place both in the 1930s and in the early years of the twentieth century.

Immigrant groups to the United States from Eastern and Southern Europe in the 1930s were found to have relatively low average IQ scores. This prompted one 'expert' to declare that 79 per cent of Italians, 80 per cent of Hungarians, 83 per cent of Jews and 87 per cent of Russians were feeble-minded (Kamin, 1976). Yet within a generation these groups were achieving IQ scores equal to or greater than the national American average.

Even more blatantly racist was the father of intelligence testing himself, Francis Galton. Here is what he had to say about Jewish immigration to Britain around the turn of the twentieth century:

> It strikes me that the Jews are specialised for a parasitical existence upon other nations, and that there is need of evidence that they are capable of fulfilling the varied duties of a civilised nation by themselves. (Pearson, 1924, p. 209)

Galton's disciple, Karl Pearson, who is well-known in the history of psychology and intelligence testing for developing techniques of statistical correlation, actually carried out a campaign in the 1920s against the immigration of East European Jews into Britain on the grounds of their genetic inferiority as illustrated by intelligence testing (Pearson and Moul, 1925).

In Chapter 11 we will consider in more detail the relationship between the organization giving (and using) the test and the individual who is subject to it, but we will end the present section with a cautionary tale. A four-year-old child in New York City was classified as one point below normal on an IQ test and on that basis was put into a special class for the mentally retarded. He was re-tested at the age of eighteen and was found to be in the normal range. He then proceeded to sue the city's Board of Education for denying him a proper education during all the years in between the two tests. A jury awarded him $750 000 damages (Fiske, 1977).

Measurement of interests

Our interests in anything are of course directly related to that same amalgam of personality and environment that produces our intelligence and our intellectual abilities. We have already seen in previous chapters some of the effects that our environment has on deciding the jobs we end up doing. Here we will consider the attempts to assess and measure the individual personality aspect of our vocational interests.

Holland's vocational typology

John Holland has proposed a very influential typology of six distinct vocational personalities based on his work as a careers counsellor (Holland, 1985). This typology seeks to match each type with its appropriate work environment, thus:

TABLE 10.1   Vocational personality types

1. *Realistic*   Physical, outdoor type. Tends to enjoy activities involving strength and coordination (for example farming and forestry).

2. *Investigative*   Cerebral type. Interested in conceptual abstract thought (for example physics and mathematics).

3. *Artistic*   Imaginative type. Interested in ideas and expressing emotions (for example arts and education).

4. *Social*   Sociable type. Primarily concerned with interpersonal relations and working with other people (for example psychology and social work).

5. *Enterprising*   Sociably active type. Needs to influence other people to gain power or status (for example law and management).

6. *Conventional*   Well-organized, orderly type. Needs a structured environment (for example accounting and banking).

From what we have already seen of formal personality theory in Chapter 9 we are aware, of course, that these are ideal types and that actual people do not fit exactly into any given type. Holland has indeed proposed that individuals be described by the three types that are most appropriate to them, ranked first, second and third in order of closeness.

The essence of Holland's approach is that people will be happiest and most productive in situations where there is a close fit between their occupation and their personality. As we saw in Chapter 5 this matching of personality and occupation is considered crucial to good mental health and work.

Strong-Campbell Interest Inventory (SCII)

The SCII is the fourth edition of the best-known of all interest inventories (Hansen and Campbell, 1985). This measure began life in 1927 as the *Strong Vocational Interest Blank* (SVIB). E. K. Strong asked his respondents about their liking or disliking for a large number of situations and activities and different kinds of people. These responses were then compared with the responses of people in different occupations, as

Strong had found that people in a particular occupation had a common pattern of interests that differed from those of other occupations (Campbell, 1971). These differences went far beyond job activities and included sports, hobbies and cultural interests.

The SCII represents a considerable revision of the original SVIB. The world of work had changed greatly in the intervening sixty years. The SCII's classification of occupational interests was based on the work of Holland described above, and the list of (over one hundred) occupations included was much longer, and in some instances different from, that of the SVIB. But the aim of matching individual interests with occupations remains, and the SCII is probably still the most widely used measure of its kind.

Tests of specific aptitudes and abilities

Of the many hundreds of tests in existence most are much less ambitious than the few relatively well-known ones we have considered so far. Most tests are concerned with very limited aspects of human behaviour and in this final section we shall consider a range of the ones most relevant to the world of work.

Physical and psychomotor abilities tests

These tests deal with the wide range of physical and mental efforts and coordination required in the use of machines and controls. They assess

TABLE 10.2   Catalogue of physical and psychomotor abilities

Physical abilities	Psychomotor abilities
Dynamic strength	Choice reaction time
Trunk strength	Reaction time
Explosive strength	Speed of limb movement
Static strength	Wrist-finger speed
Extent flexibility	Multilimb coordination
Dynamic flexibility	Finger dexterity
Gross body coordination	Manual dexterity
Gross body equilibrium	Arm-hand steadiness
Stamina	Rate control
	Control precision
	Aiming

the ergonomic factors that we discussed in Chapter 2 on the work environment. The abilities required have been categorised by E. A. Fleishman and his colleagues as shown in Table 10.2 (Fleishman, 1975, Fleishman and Hogan, 1978, Fleishman and Quaintance, 1984).

Tests of these abilities are usually related to a particular piece of apparatus that provides a direct and easily calibrated measure of performance. In the case of psychomotor abilities particularly, the tests are usually related to the requirements of a specific job. Driving tests and typing tests are common examples. They will, of course, show high reliability and validity. Indeed the closer any test is to the actual work situation the more confidence can we have in it. This is an issue we will explore further when we look at the process of selection in Chapter 11.

Mechanical abilities

As might be expected there are a number of tests of mechanical abilities that deal with an understanding of the way machines work, both in principle and in practice. Stripping down an engine and putting it back in working order would be one obvious example of such a test, as would the assembly or construction of a machine from a set of plans. These abilities would be required in the building and maintenance of moving vehicles, for instance.

But tests of mechanical abilities also cover a wider range of functions than that. There are cognitive aspects like speed of perception or the ability to visualise a relationship between the different parts of a machine. And there are also psychomotor aspects like manual dexterity or rapid coordination between eyes, hands and feet that would be of obvious use to drivers and pilots, for instance.

Because mechanical abilities can cover such a wide range there is room for wide variation between individuals with some people showing an aptitude for some kinds of abilities and not for others. Indeed there are also sometimes group differences involved. Women are particularly good at tests involving manual dexterity and perceptual discrimination, for instance, while men are typically much better at tests of mechanical information or mechanical reasoning (Anastasi, 1990).

An example of a paper-and-pencil test for spatial aptitude is shown in Figure 10.3, *The Revised Minnesota Paper Form Board Test*, which is considered one of the best of its type (Anastasi, 1990).

Each item in this test is a figure that has been cut into two or more pieces. The person being tested is asked to choose which of A, B, C, D or E represents the complete figure in the upper left-hand box. As well as being of obvious use in engineering this test also has some predictive validity for dentists and art students (Anastasi, 1990).

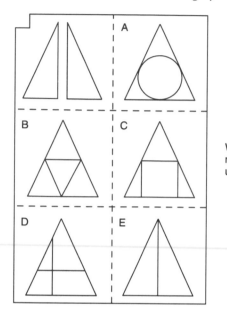

Which of the lettered parts (A, B, C, D, or E) may be formed by the parts shown in the upper-left square?

FIGURE 10.3   Sample item from the Minnesota Paper Form Board Test

Source: The Psychological Corporation, USA.

Another paper-and-pencil test is often used to test mechanical understanding. This is the *Bennett Mechanical Comprehension Test*, two items from which are shown in Figure 10.4. The Bennett draws on a wide range of situations commonly found in everyday life. As a paper-and-pencil test it has both a wider mechanical application than a hands-on mechanical test and can be administered to a large group simultaneously, of course (Anastasi, 1990). Incidentally this test seems to have been a good predictor of successful pilots during the Second World War (Guilford and Lacey, 1947).

Clerical abilities

Speed of perception is the typical aptitude measured by tests of clerical abilities. In the *Minnesota Clerical Test* illustrated in Figure 10.5 the subject is asked to check lists of names or numbers for errors as quickly as possible. A combination of speed and accuracy is required in most clerical jobs (and in other jobs too of course) and this last has been found to be quite a good predictor of performance (Anastasi, 1990). Females, of all ages, are typically better at this test than males, though why this should be so is open to interpretation.

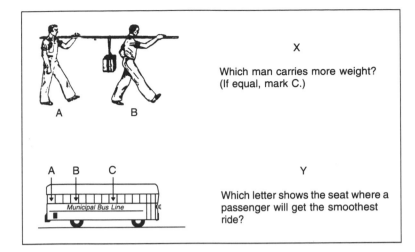

FIGURE 10.4   Sample items from the Bennett Mechanical Comprehension Test

Source: The Psychological Corporation, USA.

Professional testing

The particular occupational tests we have considered so far have been designed for use in either blue-collar manual jobs or white-collar clerical jobs. There is also another range of tests that is concerned with professional jobs in law, medicine, engineering, architecture and so on. Most of these tests aim to predict the performance of future students in professional training, however, rather than in the performance of the profession itself, though there are some tests which do try to assess the competence of trained professionals.

> When the two numbers or names in a pair are <u>exactly the same,</u>
> make a check mark on the line between them.
>
> 66273894_____66273984
> 527384578_____527384578
> New York World_____New York World
> Cargill Grain Co._____Cargil Grain Co.

FIGURE 10.5   Sample items from the Minnesota Clerical Test

Source: The Psychological Corporation, USA.

The most commonly encountered professional tests, particularly in the United States, are those required for entry to professional training, such as the *Law School Admission Test* (LSAT) or the *Medical College Admission Test* (MCAT). Rather than being entirely original these professional tests tend to be a selected amalgam of existing tests of intelligence, personality, interests, aptitudes and so on. Obviously the particular content used will be oriented towards the professional field in question, though without requiring any specialist knowledge on the part of the candidates.

The LSAT for example is a highly verbal test which emphasizes reading comprehension of very complex passages as well as the analysis of conclusions and the evaluation of arguments, all of which abilities would be appropriate for law students and the test seems to be a fairly good predictor of success in law school. Despite its high verbal content the test does not appear to discriminate against ethnic minorities. Nor is there evidence of any bias against women. Though the LSAT does not claim any predictive validity beyond law school there is some evidence that it may predict performance at least as far as the bar examination (Anastasi, 1990).

Anne Anastasi examined the merits of one test used in the United States that does claim to assess the post-training competence of professionals – in the field of psychology (Anastasi, 1990). This test is called the *Examination for Professional Practice in Psychology* (EPPP). The EPPP is designed to test basic psychological knowledge across the various specializations and deals with information, methodology and ethics.

The test is used particularly in the licensing of clinical, counselling, industrial/organizational and school psychologists, who will be providing professional services, in order to safeguard the potential users of these services and maintain a minimum level of assured competence. What the EPPP cannot do is predict who will be more or less skilled in any given specialization because of the great practical difficulties involved in obtaining comparative data on a psychologist's actual job performance.

The limits to measuring human abilities

We have seen throughout this chapter that some human abilities are easier than others to identify and measure and therefore compare people on. We have also seen that if an organization wants to predict how someone will do in a particular job it has to match the abilities being sampled with the required job performance. The closer the match the more confident the prediction of future job performance. In the next chapter we will examine what organizations actually do in practice and how tests of abilities (and of personality) can be misused.

The National Research Council in the United States has suggested three ways in which tests of human abilities may be rather limited (Garner and Wigdor, 1982):

(i) the popular and economical group tests may measure comprehension but they give candidates no opportunity to show how well they can express themselves;

(ii) group tests allow only for people's reactions to certain materials thus denying them the opportunity to display initiative or imagination;

(iii) group tests do not allow scope for demonstrating either insightful forms of thought or perseverance over time.

CHAPTER 11

Recruitment and selection

The use of human resources

The topics dealt with in this chapter and in the next chapter are concerned with the way organizations treat the people who work for them; the way they go about recruiting a pool of potential staff members, selecting specific individuals for employment and then training and developing these individuals (or not, as the case may be). These topics are often referred to collectively as 'the use of human resources', though we will also examine the *misuse* of human resources.

Ideally these topics, as we shall see, should all form a coherent package as an organization's human resource or personnel policy, running all the way from recruitment to retirement. The ideal is very rarely attained in practice and usually recruitment and selection decisions are treated in isolation from decisions about training and staff development. These human resource issues are spread over *two* chapters of this book largely for reasons of space, but it might be helpful conceptually if you treated them as one long chapter.

The process of recruitment and selection

I would suggest an ideal model for the process of recruitment and selection is as outlined in Figure 11.1.

Organizations will typically enter the recruitment and selection process at one of two stages in this model, stage 2 or stage 6.

Stage 2: Why is this job needed?

This question may be asked either when a job falls vacant or as part of a staff review process. The question as put deals with the part this

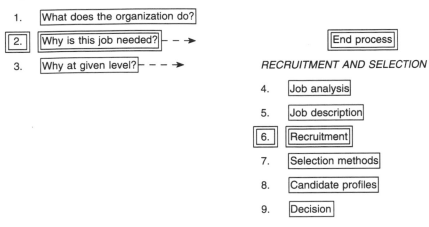

FIGURE 11.1   Stages in the recruitment and selection process

particular job plays in the life of the organization, and should therefore be preceded by the answer to the question at stage 1 on what the organization does and what the point of its existence is. But in reality this rarely happens. To the (great and apparently ever-increasing) extent that organizations are cost driven the question becomes more like 'can we cut this job?' And with staff costs being anywhere up to 90 per cent or more of total costs that is a powerful question for any organization to deal with. The recruitment and selection process may well end right here.

Stage 6: Recruitment

If the job still exists after Stage 2 most organizations will go straight to Stage 6. The answer to the recruitment question 'how do we find applicants?' is usually to advertise in the relevant newspapers and journals and/or whatever other methods are habitually used. The advertisement used might even be the same one that was used to recruit the previous incumbent of the job. If not it will probably be something similar but updated. It should not come as a great shock therefore to find that the new incumbent is very similar to the old one. Of course this may be just the outcome the organization needs, but it will never know because nobody has actually thought about it.

For the rest of this chapter we will consider the ideal model, based on best practice, for the recruitment and selection process. We will examine the difficulties involved for organizations in following this model and how these might be dealt with.

Pre-recruitment questions

1. What does the organization do?

This is the most fundamental and often the most difficult question that any organization has to face. As the celebrated management guru Peter Drucker puts it:

> Nothing may seem simpler or more obvious than to know what a company's business is. A steel mill makes steel, a railroad runs trains to carry freight and passengers, an insurance company underwrites fire risks, a bank lends money. Actually, 'What is our business' was almost always a difficult question and the right answer is usually anything but obvious. (Drucker, 1988, p. 70)

Asking about an organization's reason for existing, argues Drucker, is the job of senior management and is always a painful experience because it involves a choice of alternative values, attitudes and opinions and, I would add, a set of unquestioned assumptions that have to be examined, often for the first time. The obvious and plausible kinds of answers given above are part of these unquestioned assumptions.

Drucker suggests that the starting point for answering the question 'What is our business?' should be the *customer*. This has now become a very fashionable viewpoint, which does not, of course, mean that organizations which embrace it have thought through all of its consequences. There are several important questions that Drucker would like to see addressed.

(a) *Who* is the customer?
(b) Who *should* the customer be?
(c) *Where* is the customer?
(d) What does the customer consider *value*?

Often there is more than one customer for the goods and services an organization produces. Banks for example lend money to individuals, organizations and also governments, and, even in the public sector, welfare agencies have to be aware of the client at the sharp end but also of the taxpayer who provides their income and the government that allocates it.

Drucker points out how the American carpet industry revived dramatically after the Second World War when it switched its emphasis from the customer as homeowner to the customer as building contractor. Asking individuals to buy what they considered luxury items – especially when they were moving house and short of cash – was a losing proposition. Persuading builders to incorporate wall-to-wall carpeting in their new buildings was a much more profitable approach because it was cheaper for them to do so than laying expensive finished floors.

Asking *where* the customer is can also be important. The mail order pioneers Sears, who sent off their first catalogue to mid-western American farmers in the late nineteenth century, found by the 1920s that their customers now had cars and were coming into town more often. This led them to examine the issue of store location before anybody else and became an important part of the answer to the question 'What is our business?'

Finally the question of what the customer *values* needs to be addressed. As Drucker points out this is often assumed by the organization to be 'quality', often wrongly. To a teenager buying clothes, for example, value is probably high fashion, even if the article falls apart in a month. To her mother, though fashion is not unimportant, durability and fit have higher value. And to her grandmother price and comfort may be the most important values or interpretations.

So already, in a very short space, we have come a long way from the obvious answers to the question 'What is our business?' Whatever the answer an organization comes up with two things are quite clear; this is not a question that should go unasked for very long, and the answer must be intimately related to satisfying the wants of the organization's customers.

In terms of recruitment and selection therefore it is obviously helpful, to put it mildly, that an organization be clear about what it is supposed to be doing before it hires people to do it. This has to be the task of the people who run the organization, the senior management usually, and if they don't do it they have abdicated one of their most important responsibilities. One practical solution might be to hire an external consultant, who could at least air the alternatives and perhaps think the unthinkable, without having a personal stake in any of them.

2. Why is this job needed?

We saw earlier how this is often the entry point into the recruitment and selection process for the organization, at which time it may well be driven to justify retaining the position in question firstly on grounds of cost-benefit alone. This seems to be particularly true at middle management levels and below.

If the hurdle of cost is overcome, the question about why the job is needed may still not be asked. The thrill of being *able*, financially, to hire someone, especially in time of recession, seems to override that potentially awkward question. If the question 'why does the organization need this job?' is actually put the answer is usually 'because the person who did it has left'. It may be in the interests of the head of department, or even the head of the organization, to have the post filled before the purse-holders change their minds, but the question of the organization's interests as a whole are rarely pursued.

If this question *was* pursued it would inevitably lead back to the prior question about what the organization exists to do, which for many senior managers is a good reason not to ask it. But unless someone asks the question there is no way of knowing how essential or valuable the job (as opposed to the person occupying it) is to the organization. Or even whether there is actually a job there at all.

3. Why is this job needed at this level/position?

This question is a corollary of the previous one, and is often answered in the same way. 'The job is needed at this level because it's the level the last person was at'. There is thus no attempt made to see how the particular position of this job on the organizational chart relates to its goals and its functioning. Sometimes a compromise is reached between the accountants and the appropriate managers where the job is retained but at a cheaper level, thereby allowing both parties to feel that their interests have been satisfied, and without asking any hard questions too.

The ideal model: recruitment and selection

Given that the three pre-recruitment questions have been successfully negotiated we are ready to consider how the organization should tackle the remaining stages of recruitment and selection.

4. Job analysis

The purpose of a job analysis is to uncover, or discover, all the qualities (including psychological qualities) that are necessary to perform the job successfully. Several sources of information may be used to analyse a job; documents, respondents and observation.

(A) DOCUMENTS

Unless a job is being newly created there will be documents already in existence within the organization that will provide information about it.

There may well be an existing job description, for instance. It will probably not be totally accurate however. Job descriptions inevitably start to slip as soon as they are put into practice. In a sense the sell-by date of a job description is the date it was written. Moreover the production of this document might not itself have been the result of a rigorous job analysis but, more probably, the fruit of negotiation between organizational interests.

Organizational charts, staff audits, work flow records and so forth might also be useful sources of information, and would become especially valuable if no job description existed or a new job was being created. Even more general indicators like the goals and objectives set by the organization within its public documents, together with the distribution of staff employed to achieve them – and how these have evolved over time – may also provide useful clues.

(B) RESPONDENTS

Easily the most common and most important source of information is the response of the people who actually do the job to interviews and questionnaires about what they do. In particular job analysts would look for a *priority* listing of all the various tasks and duties that go to make up the job and an indication of how *frequently* each is performed (Landy, 1989).

Although personal interviews provide a rich and detailed source of material the information they provide cannot always and entirely be taken at face value (in this or any other field) because of their necessarily subjective nature and the accompanying problems of defective – or selective – memory. Attempts have therefore been made to provide a standardised written questionnaire or similar technique that will overcome this difficulty.

One of these techniques is to ask people to keep a diary of what they *actually* do at work, as opposed to what they're supposed to do or what they think they do. Done properly this is a very time-consuming procedure, of course, but it can also be very revealing. It is how we know, for instance, that 'most managers spend their time in brief, fragmented activities, switching every few minutes from one person or problem to another. They talk or listen for three-quarters or more of the day' (Stewart, 1986, p. 20).

The most widely used written technique is the *Position Analysis Questionnaire* (PAQ), developed in the United States, which consists of 187 job elements organized into six divisions (McCormick, Jeanneret and Mecham, 1972):

- information input
- mental processes
- work output
- relationships with others
- job context
- other job characteristics.

The PAQ is a worker-oriented rather than a task-oriented question-naire. As such it is not linked to any particular job or type of job but, by focussing on the behaviour of the person doing the job, can be applied very widely throughout the world of work. A British job analysis questionnaire also exists now, known as the *Job Components Inventory* (JCI), that was developed in the field of education and training (Banks, 1988). These and other instruments have also been used with the colleagues who surround a particular job on the organizational chart whether peers, superiors or subordinates, and this can offer another useful perspective on the job being studied.

(C) OBSERVATION

Another very helpful source of information in job analysis is simply direct observation; watching carefully to see how someone actually carries out a job. This is especially true where people have been performing the same job for a long time and can do it almost automatically. As we shall see when we discuss training in the next chapter people who perform a job at this level of expertise often have great difficulty in telling you how they do it. Moreover there is often slippage between what people believe they do and what they actually do.

Of course as we saw in Chapter 7: 'Group dynamics', the very presence of an observer can alter someone's work performance, and job analysts may decide instead on participant observation in which they will perform the job themselves. There are obviously many jobs where participant observation is not possible – performing surgery springs immediately to mind – but where it is it can be a very valuable source of insight about what a job entails. Insight is a particularly valuable quality in performing a job analysis because understanding the essence of what a job is about is at the heart of the enterprise and that is not accomplished by simply accumulating more and more bits of information.

It should now be abundantly clear how important a job analysis is to the recruitment and selection process (and to other aspects of organizational life, as we will see in the next chapter). Yet depressingly often a job analysis is simply not done (see for example Herriot, 1987).

5. Job description

One of the major products of a job analysis should be a *job description* for a particular position. Such a description should include not only the work content of the job itself but the key characteristics of the person who will occupy the position – what is often called a *personnel specification*. For some jobs this specification is not difficult; labourers need physical strength and stamina, accountants should be numerate, politicians require a flexible approach to the truth. Others are less clear; machine operators or van drivers, or managers, may have a wide range of characteristics and still work successfully at their jobs.

In such cases where there are few obvious characteristics to be discerned, and tested for, the usual fallback position of the organization is to specify experience (often without looking at the quality of that experience):

> WIDGET PRODUCTION
> DEPUTY ASSISTANT DIRECTOR
> Must have at least
> five years
> experience in the
> management of widget
> production for a
> major company.

This is particularly true where an organization is offering career advancement or there is a buyer's market in staff. In conditions of recession and high unemployment, where there is a large pool of available labour, arbitrary specifications are often imposed either to cut down the number of applicants or in a misguided attempt to find the widget world's answer to Superman:

> WIDGET PRODUCTION
> DEPUTY ASSISTANT DIRECTOR
> Must have three
> doctorates, speak
> eight languages, ten
> years relevant
> experience and a black belt in
> flower arrangement.

This example is intended to highlight the inconvenient point that for many jobs there isn't a hair's breadth of difference between most of the obviously qualified applicants and it really doesn't matter who the organization chooses. What does matter is what the organization does with the person it hires, a topic we will explore at some length in the next chapter. Why an organization should spend a huge amount of time and resources in hunting for a mythical 'best applicant' is an issue we will return to later.

6. Recruitment

Having done a thorough job analysis and produced an accurate job description, including a realistic personnel specification, the ideal organization is now ready to start recruiting potential applicants. Before we look at this process we need to put the whole issue of recruitment to work organizations in its *social context*.

The most common method used by organizations for external recruitment is the job *advertisement*, usually placed in appropriate newspapers, trade journals and so on. But even though these advertisements may attract a large number of replies there is no guarantee either that these replies include all possible qualified applicants or, indeed, that the successful candidates will even have replied to the advertisement in the first place.

A study of the London Fire Brigade has noted that:

> . . . even as late as mid-1985, over 70 per cent of applicants did not respond to particular job advertisements, but simply applied for jobs on the basis of their knowledge of the Brigade and the job, knowledge that was available within a relatively limited social area of London. (Salaman, 1986, p. 45: KEY STUDY 10)

The social area in this case was white and working-class, as was the overwhelming composition of the organization. The organization was also overwhelmingly male, and with a distinctly macho set of attitudes about the job of being a fire fighter. We will examine the sexual issues involved in Chapter 17: 'Women at work'.

The point to be made here is that the members of the organization thought this state of affairs was perfectly natural and saw nothing amiss with the method of recruitment into it. After all a rigorous selection procedure then took place in which over 90 per cent of applicants were rejected. And nobody had any complaints with the quality of the fire service the successful applicants provided, so what was the problem?

It was only after government legislation on equal opportunity in the late 1970s that these issues were even raised in the London Fire Brigade, and elsewhere. Only then did it become widely apparent that some jobs, whatever was done officially, in practice recruited applicants from particular social groups and excluded potential applicants from other groups. This was not usually made explicit, or if it was it was rationalised on grounds of harmony and the need to maintain a homogeneous work force.

Members of the 'wrong' group rarely got to the stage of applying. They already knew that blacks (or Jews or Irish or whoever) were not wanted. This is something that excluded groups have always known. Thus a form of *self-recruitment* (or self non-recruitment) reinforces the social networking that commonly surrounds the decisions about suitable applicants for certain jobs – from police officer to stockbroker – in many societies. Advertising is thus a necessary but not nearly a sufficient condition for fair and efficient recruitment to an organization.

The long-term problem with informal recruitment from the organization's viewpoint is that it will never know how much talent, creativity, freshness and enthusiasm it is rejecting. Of course in times of recession long-term views are rarely taken. Indeed long-term views are rarely taken at any time so changes in recruitment practices, especially where these may disturb existing members of the organization, are very difficult to accomplish.

It is now the custom for organizations to state that they are 'equal opportunity employers', or something similar, as a result of legislation but this, of course, is meaningless without some indication of how recruitment patterns have actually changed over time. If change is truly desired it may take a little more active recruiting effort than a job advertisement.

The ideal job advertisement is one which comes to the attention of all *suitable* potential applicants. If this happens then, unless the job is obviously a highly specialised one, the organization can often expect to be swamped with applications. Attempting to cut down the number of applications by increasing the requirements tends to be self-defeating. As we have already seen in our discussion on stress in Chapter 5, and as we will see again in later chapters, people who are greatly over-qualified for a job don't do it better, they tend to get disgruntled and may end up doing it worse.

Of course organizations tend to regard the receipt of hundreds of applications for one job as a successful recruitment process and *if* the job description is accurate and *if* the applicants really are suitable then it may well be. The organization can then, after paying careful attention to equal opportunities issues, put the names into a hat and draw out the short list for further selection – if not the lucky winner herself.

These are big 'ifs' however and what is much more likely is that the organization doesn't know or can't decide on what qualities it really wants and the job advertisement is written sufficiently ambiguously to attract applications from the world and his sister, thus:

WIDGET PRODUCTION
DEPUTY ASSISTANT DIRECTOR
Dynamic, enterprising, go-ahead
executive required for leading
widget producer. Must be
energetic self-starter able to
communicate effectively and
contribute enthusiastically to
the work of the management team.

All these words are commonly used in job advertisements for managers. Strung together like this they mean absolutely nothing. As well as a failure of nerve by the organization it also represents a failure of imagination; the imagination to look at the advertisement from the viewpoint of the potential applicant who wants to know 'What exactly will I be doing?' and 'What is the organization like to work in?' The answers given by an organization using the advertisement above are 'we don't know' and 'difficult'.

The second of these two questions refers to an organization's sense of itself, its identity or, as some writers prefer, its personality (see for example Landy, 1989). When potential applicants see job advertisements for McDonalds or Marks and Spencer, or the US Marine Corps, they have a fairly clear image of what these organizations would be like to work for and, if they feel they have a choice of job, they will then recruit themselves into or out of the applicant pool.

It is probably no coincidence that organizations with a strong and immediately recognisable personality tend to pay a lot of attention to the first of our pre-recruitment questions, 'What does our organization do?' Again we can see that if an organization declines to ask the difficult questions before it begins the recruitment and selection process the problems involved don't simply disappear. They will almost certainly reappear in some other form.

7. Selection methods

The point of any selection method is to assess how well someone is likely to do in a given job. It is but a means to that end and has no other function. I realise that this is a simple and obvious point but it bears spelling out – and keeping in mind – because organizations typically ignore it and will frequently employ their favourite methods of selection as ends in themselves rather than means.

It follows from this point that there is no single correct or even best method of selection. It depends on the job in question. In fact, as we shall see, the most frequently used methods of selection are often *not* the best methods to use in a given situation. There are half-a-dozen major methods of selection and we will examine them in descending order of usage. Organizations almost always use more than one method and generally use all of the three most common methods, biodata, references and interviews.

Before we consider specific methods though there is one useful distinction that can be made amongst the different ways of trying to predict someone's future work behaviour. This is the difference between a *sign* approach and a *sample* approach (Wernimont and Campbell, 1968). The sign approach involves the attempt to link future work behaviour to particular psychological characteristics such as intelligence or the other personality traits we have discussed in the last two chapters. The sample approach is just that; the individual is given a typical sample task to perform that the job entails, such as driving or typing. The sign approach is the traditional one in job selection, the sample approach being a more recent one.

(I) BIODATA

As the name suggests 'biodata' makes use of biographical information about an applicant. The simplest source of biodata is the applicant's curriculum vitae (c.v.) or the application form the organization uses. I would suggest that the curriculum vitae is a much more informative document than a standard application form.

A standard application form, where specific information is requested in a particular format, tends to produce standard applications. But an application in the form of a c.v. gives the applicant the scope to order the information he considers relevant in any way he wants. The applicant is being asked to present himself (his 'self') to the organization and so he will, consciously and unconsciously, include some useful clues about this personality along with the basic information.

In a sense the c.v. can be viewed as a kind of projective test and as such the problem, as we have seen in earlier chapters, is being able to interpret the clues. What does it mean if the applicant gets a date wrong, for instance, or misspells a name, or misses something out? At the very least these are items that should be followed up if an interview is given.

The c.v. is thus a richer document than an application form (even where it is professionally prepared) and although it takes a little more time to extract the relevant biographical facts from comparison with other applicants it can represent a quick first step to understanding what the person in question is 'really like'.

But the use of biodata can be much more elaborate than this. Inventories consisting of hundreds of items have been constructed that require great detail not only on objective aspects of someone's life, like their age and qualifications but also subjective features like their attitudes or opinions and their preferences about different aspects of the job. The individual items of the inventory are correlated with job performance and those that are most predictive of successful job performance are highlighted. For example a 484-item inventory was found to have five key factors. When compared with the criterion of the number of patents applied for (which is often thought of as an indicator of success) by a group of research scientists being studied, two of these factors tended to indicate that success was likely. One factor, as might be expected, was 'inquisitive, professional orientation'. A less obvious factor was 'tolerance for ambiguity' (Morrison *et al.*, 1962).

Finally in this section it should go without saying that the information an applicant gives on qualifications, experience and so on should be verified as far as possible, and *before* she or he is hired. In some organizations this is standard practice: in many it is not. The reason for verification is only partly to check that the individual has been truthful.

Although there are periodic shock-horror headlines of the FAKE DOCTOR CARRIED OUT 300 OPERATIONS! variety these cases are comparatively rare – though they do raise the interesting question of how an unqualified person could get away with it for any length of time, which we shall come back to in our discussion of training in Chapter 12. But we all have a selective memory about our past, however, and it is possible that candidates may misremember things in ways which offer useful clues about what they are 'really like'.

(II) REFERENCES

Organizations generally insist on receiving references from applicants, though it's hard to know why. As far as one can gather they are usually taken with a large pinch of salt, unless they are unusual in some way – in which case they are regarded with suspicion. References are invariably glowing (so much so that candidates might fail to recognise themselves), and it is therefore difficult to differentiate between them, especially if the organization has no knowledge of the referees.

(III) INTERVIEWS

Along with references and some biodata, interviews are standard practice in the process of selection. They are also widely regarded by organizations as the most crucial selection method and are usually the final hurdles that applicants have to clear after surviving the application stage and perhaps some psychometrics. Important and popular they may be, but I can assure you from having been on both sides of the table many times that the typical organizational conduct of interviews has a fairly narrow range, from generally inadequate to absolutely awful. This is also the view of everyone I've ever spoken to on the subject. As a way of predicting future successful job performance, interviews generally have low validity (Hunter and Hunter, 1984).

There are many, many pitfalls to be avoided in job interviewing. I will group the major ones under three headings, *first impressions*, *procedure* and *interpretation*.

(a) First impressions

The very first impression interviewers have of a candidate is his or her *appearance*. And this provides an immediate opportunity for an interviewer's bias – unconsciously (or not as the case may be) – to influence his judgement, on grounds of sex, colour or physical attractiveness (Arvey and Campion, 1982). There is some evidence, for example, that recruiters may be more inclined to hire people they find attractive (of either sex) than those they find unattractive (Dipboye, Fromkin and Wilback, 1975). Our reactions to people who are trying to persuade us of something can be influenced, at least to some extent, by how attractive we find them (Eagly and Chaiken, 1975).

A *halo effect* seems to operate and we may attribute all sorts of positive personal characteristics to people merely because we find them attractive (Dion, Berscheid and Walster, 1972). The opposite effect (sometimes known as the 'horn effect') also seems to apply, and they are both aspects of the implicit theories of personality that we considered in Chapter 9. Moreover this seems to be a deeply rooted aspect of our social existence that has even been found as early as nursery school (Dion and Berscheid, 1992). Of course agreed definitions of what is attractive vary over time and between different societies. Western recruiters discriminate strongly against people considered fat and in favour of men who are tall – though not too tall! (Argyle, 1988).

These are the most immediate impressions that interviewers are subject to. They are followed by a set of both verbal and non-verbal behaviours by the candidate that we might call 'second impressions'. As soon as the candidate sits down there are factors like eye contact, posture and positioning of hands and feet that may denote to the interviewer (whether the candidate intends them or not) aspects like confidence and assertiveness, or the lack of them (Argyle, Alkema and Gilmour, 1971). Moderately assertive candidates seem to be regarded most favourably by interviewers (Dipboye and Wiley, 1977).

As soon as the candidate opens his or her mouth, verbal factors come into play. The pitch, intonation, timbre and loudness of voice, and of course the accent used, are cues the interviewer may respond to even before he has registered what is being said. If candidates are lively and expressive in their non-verbal behaviour and speak fluently they increase their chances of being hired (Forbes and Jackson, 1980). Of course the question of whether there is anything of substance behind the expressive fluency may not arise until they have joined the organization and sometimes, as we shall see in the next chapter, not even then.

Other things being equal interviewers will tend to like people who are most like them in age and background, and indeed will probably conduct more insightful interviews with such candidates (Ulrich and Trumbo, 1965). Perhaps related to this is the finding that interviewers generally have some image of the ideal candidate in mind (whether consciously or not) against whom they compare the people they see (Schmitt, 1976). Finally in this section, it is worth noting the disturbing evidence that an interviewer's *mood* can affect how favourably he views a candidate (see for example Baron, 1987).

(b) Interview procedure

I was once marched (literally) into a job interview at a university by a uniformed flunkey who paused at the door to bark out my name before marching off again leaving me staring at the interview panel, some 13 men in suits, seated round the most enormous D-shaped table I have ever seen in my life. This is a very good way not to conduct an interview. But it did tell me a lot about the organization.

Not much attention has been paid in research on interview procedure to the effects of the sheer number of interviewers present but the general assumption seems to be that two or three people is usually the optimum number, depending on the skills of the interviewers as interviewers and their specialised knowledge as line or function colleagues and supervisors. Certainly the presence of 13 interviewers would be universally condemned as ludicrous. Apart from anything else, that many participants in the usual 30 to 40 minute interview would restrict each one to about two or three minutes, long enough to ask one standard question and receive one standard reply. What could the organization hope to learn from candidates like that?

The reason for the silly number of interviewers lay in organizational politics of course. Every department with an interest in the appointment demanded to be represented, so we ended up with the Dean of this and the Chairman of that, but nobody who knew anything about interviewing. And this, we should note, in an organization that had such expertise at its fingertips.

The point of the interview, as with any other method of selection, should be to get as accurate an idea as possible of how someone is likely to do in the job. There are two related difficulties with this; very few jobs consist of being interviewed, and someone's behaviour in an interview is not necessarily representative of their behaviour in any other situation. If one cannot obtain much of a 'sample' of job-related behaviour it would therefore seem to make sense to look for a 'sign' of the desired qualities. A job interview for most people is a fraught situation and it is difficult to see what an organization gains by making it more tense and intimidating than it has to.

I realise there is a school of thought which argues that since candidates are presenting themselves in the best possible light, interviewers have to put them under stress to see if they can get the mask to slip. This argument may *sound* quite plausible but stems, I would argue, from the defensiveness of people who are unsure of their interviewing abilities.

However it is only an extreme case of what is probably a very common practice; looking for reasons to reject a candidate (Webster, 1982). And this is a decision which is made very quickly; within the first few minutes of the interview (Springbett, 1958). The rest of the interview can then be spent gathering material to back up the rejection. The successful candidate may then emerge by a process of elimination, if not by default, thereby saving the interviewer from the much more difficult task of positively choosing a candidate because he or she possesses particular qualities.

One major reason for the almost universal use of the job interview is the desire of people representing organizations to meet and assess a possible new colleague. That is a reasonable and a human desire and of course an interview is (however fleetingly) a situation in which human relationships occur. It is important that this is perceived within the organization because the way the organization conducts the interview is both a sign and a sample of *its* behaviour. An incompetent or intimidating interview is unlikely to impress even the successful candidate with the worth of her new organization.

So rather than being seen as a test of the interviewer's manhood the interview should encourage the candidate to be as relaxed and open as possible. It is true, of course, that candidates will try to present the most favourable picture of themselves they can and engage in *impression management*. This often takes the form of pandering to expected interviewer prejudice. For example women who wear masculine-approved business suits tend to be more successful in managerial appointments than women who don't (Forsythe, Drake and Cox, 1985).

That kind of behaviour sounds like understandable self-defence to me, and it should not be difficult to arrange an interview situation that removed the need for it. As far as the physical setting goes two or three interviewers comfortably seated round a coffee table (containing coffee) with the candidate doesn't seem too much to ask.

A friendly welcome and a genuine interest in hearing what the candidate has to say would also help – though that might be more difficult to arrange – and will quickly communicate itself to the candidate. It should go without saying that nobody should be interviewed unless they have a genuine chance of being hired. But whether for reasons of organizational politics or simply to make up the numbers this does happen, and it is deadly. People know when they are dealing with interviewers who are just going through the motions, and the organization's reputation will suffer.

Having come this far successfully we arrive at the heart of the interview, the questions that are asked. Asking interview questions is a much more difficult affair than it looks and it is the basis of an interviewer's skill. I have met very few people who can do it well. However there are some common elephant traps that everybody should be trained to avoid before they ever do any interviewing. These are three in number: *leading* questions, *multiple* questions and *hypothetical* questions. A *leading* question begins something like, 'wouldn't you agree that . . . ?' This is self-indulgence by the interviewers, sometimes disguised as intellectual weight. Even where it is honestly intended it pushes the interview down a side street and focusses attention on the interviewer rather than the candidate.

A *multiple* question might be intended as a single question but actually contains two or more questions within it, so that the candidate may be confused about what is being asked or may deal with only one part of what is being asked. An example might be 'what do you think of the trend towards digitizing widget blockers in Japan; is it something we should get into now or should we try to develop a new spilding process instead?'

Hypothetical questions are perhaps the most common elephant traps. They usually begin 'what would you do if. . .' and indicate a lazy interviewer who hasn't thought about the implications of his question. What you get when you ask a hypothetical question is, inevitably, a hypothetical answer. This doesn't mean that candidates will lie to you (though they might) but, as we will see in Chapter 14, nobody knows for sure what they would do in a hypothetical situation. As an indication of what someone's behaviour is likely to be it is useless. Indeed worse than useless, because it can give the illusion of having gleaned some useful information.

Apart from not asking leading, multiple or hypothetical questions there are some well-established ways of putting questions fruitfully that all interviewers should be aware of. For more detail on this topic see for example, the work of Goodworth (1979), Ingleton (1988) and Webster (1982). In general terms it is important, given the artificiality of the interview situation, for interviewers to concentrate on previous samples rather than signs of the candidate's behaviour (and accompanying emotions) even in this second-hand way (Wernimont and Campbell, 1968).

Concentrating on samples of behaviour would involve asking the candidate specific questions about what he or she had actually done in various situations. For example instead of the inevitable 'Why do you want to work for the Wizard Widget Corporation?' a whole range of specific questions might be put to obtain less guarded (that is, less monitored) and more interesting replies:

● How did you first come into contact with widgets?
● What do you enjoy most/least in doing your present job?
● Describe the interview situation for your present job.
● What surprised you most about the organization after you were hired?
● Did you discuss your application for the present job with anyone?

By asking these behaviour sample questions the interviewer begins to probe beyond the 'signs' on the c.v. with its descriptive labels of qualifications and job titles, to what the candidate has actually done and how she felt when doing it. This has the added advantage that the candidate's monitoring system, which would go to red alert with a why-do-you-want-to-work-for-us type of question, must be switched off to allow her brain to access the relevant set of memories (Lindsay and Norman, 1977).

Apparently the candidate's eyes flick downwards when the monitor is in place and considering how to present a reply with the most favourable reflection on her, and flick up again when the brain is asked to scan the memory for actual episodes of behaviour.

(c) Interpreting the interview

As with all instruments of selection, whatever the information that may be gathered about candidates by interviewing it does not simply speak for itself; it usually has to be interpreted. The interpretation of interviews has its own difficulties and we will highlight two of them here, the effects of *primacy* or *recency* and the interviewer's *striving for coherence*.

The primacy and recency effects refer to the advantages of candidates going first or last in a series of interviews. We noted earlier the generally important influence of first impressions on interviewers. Other things being equal we would expect the first candidate interviewed to stick in the interviewer's mind more than the others. That would be the *primacy* effect.

On the other hand the last person to be interviewed would have the advantage of presenting the most recent impression to the interviewer: the *recency* effect. But do these effects cancel each other out, or is one more dominant? The key variable seems to be time (Aronson, 1992). If the decision is to be made right after the last candidate is seen the recency effect would predominate. If there is a gap of a day or two between the last interview and the decision the primacy effect would be more influential.

Either way, of course, the candidates in the middle of the interview order would appear to be disadvantaged. This is obviously something that could easily be brought to an interviewer's attention so that he could bear the possibility of order effects in mind when making a judgement. However a sense of proportion needs to be maintained and it is possible to over-emphasize what is a relatively minor technical point in the training of interviewers (Bernardin and Pence, 1980).

Of greater general importance is the problem of interviewers *striving for coherence* in their attempt to make sense of a candidate, especially when asked to do so in summary form. We seem to have a deep-seated need to find consistency in the personal characteristics we attribute to an individual. We find it difficult to hold in our minds a picture of someone with both positive and negative characteristics, like warmth and laziness, for instance, or openness and cruelty (Argyle, 1989). It is the same pull as the halo effect really, this need to simplify and stereotype and round off rough edges or pieces of the jigsaw puzzle that don't quite fit. As everybody is a mixture of positive and negative characteristics it is obviously a tendency one would like interviewers to be aware of.

There is another important aspect to the striving for coherence in assessing candidates. We seem to have a general tendency in considering someone's behaviour to overestimate the contribution of personal factors and underestimate that of situational factors. We typically attribute to people more control over what happens in their lives than is reasonably justified (Ross, 1977).

This is known as the '*fundamental attribution error*', and it allows us the psychologically comforting belief that people's motives and behaviours are clearer and more consistent than the messy reality. In an interview the interviewers would thus be prone to attributing the candidate's behaviour more to her personal characteristics than the fact that she was in an interview, with all the situational implications that we have just examined.

(IV) PSYCHOMETRICS

The term 'psychometrics' refers to psychological testing and measurement in all its forms. We have already encountered the major forms of psychometrics that are used in the world of work. In Chapter 6: 'The unconscious at work' we looked at personality tests. In Chapter 10: 'Measuring human abilities' we dealt with intelligence tests and tests of particular abilities, both sometimes called cognitive tests, and measures of interests.

Any specific personality test, such as the 16PF, the MMPI, TAT or Rorschach, used by itself has had low predictive validity for assessing job performance, which is – and it bears repetition – the only point of using it (Guion and Gottier, 1965). Paper-and-pencil tests of general intelligence have been widely used in selection. They are after all fairly cheap and easy to administer, especially now that they are usually computerised. How justified their use might be is another matter.

We saw in Chapter 10 that there is still no agreement on what general intelligence is and that intelligence tests are usually biased in favour of white, middle-class urban people who understand and use language well. Of course the fluency skills and attitudes that people in this group would typically possess may be just what an organization is looking for and intelligence tests have been found to have a relatively high predictive validity to job success across a wide range of managerial and administrative jobs (Hunter and Hunter, 1984).

However other selective procedures, like the biodata we considered earlier and the work samples we will look at in a moment, have a predictive validity at least as high as general intelligence tests (Schmitt *et al.*, 1984). And these procedures don't have the built-in social biases of the general intelligence tests.

This is a point worth considering because the potential applicants disadvantaged by these tests are often the same people who are disadvantaged by the kind of recruitment practices we discussed earlier. They thus have two gates to get through that other applicants don't, while the organization continues to renew itself largely in its own image and is unaware of what it might have lost.

The tests of specific aptitudes and abilities that we examined in the last chapter are freer from social bias than general intelligence tests and with at least as much predictive validity (Schmitt *et al.*, 1984). Tests of mechanical aptitude or clerical ability, in jobs where such specific skills are required, would have face validity as well. That is they would be seen to be appropriate and fair to all potential applicants.

There is a growing feeling among researchers in psychometrics for job selection that personality testing is potentially much more useful in predicting job performance than its typically low validity scores would suggest (Hough *et al.*, 1990). The richness and diversity of the data resulting from traditional individual personality tests like the TAT or the Rorschach is not fully captured by the statistical procedures used in predictive validation.

The well-established personality tests we examined in Chapter 6 were originally devised for use in a clinical setting with emotionally disturbed people. Their use in job selection would obviously require the sensitivity, knowledge and insight of a well-trained and experienced psychologist. The services of such an individual would cost money, of course, and the organization has to weigh this cost against the potential advantages.

Some organizations cut corners by administering a paper-and-pencil test, like the MMPI or 16PF, themselves and then try to interpret the results themselves. As interpretation of test data is the greater part of psychological skill this is a dangerous form of penny-pinching.

Even under optimum conditions though, it is not always clear what the links between a detailed personality profile and the job in question might be. One might want as much information as possible about the future head of a children's home, but how is an applicant's unresolved oedipal complex relevant to the job of sales manager or production director, for instance?

While not quite as widely used in selection as the job interview, psychometrics – particularly personality questionnaires – are now big business. Half of all companies in the United Kingdom now use personality tests, for instance (Blinkhorn and Johnson, 1990). There are hundreds of tests in existence and new ones are being devised all the time. Publishing, marketing, using and training people in the use of these tests is now a multi-billion dollar industry, active throughout the world. And like any other such industry it has an internal dynamic that pushes it to promote its own product. So I think a few countervailing views are in order.

A recent review of three leading personality questionnaires (including the 16PF) took a careful look at the way correlation coefficients were analysed and interpreted in arriving at the predictive validity claimed for these tests. The authors concluded:

> . . . we see precious little evidence that even the best personality tests predict job performance, and a good deal of evidence of poorly understood statistical methods being pressed into service to buttress shaky claims. If this is so for the most reputable tests in the hands of specialists, one may imagine what travesties are committed further down-market. (Blinkhorn and Johnson, 1990, p. 672)

An example of what can happen 'further down market' is the case of a new selection instrument marketed in a classic aggressive fashion:

One common marketing strategy in this area is to publish related articles in magazines and soft trade journals that are read by organizational decision makers. These outlets often lack the expertise to critically assess the veracity of claims regarding the instrument. Airline magazines are a great target for this strategy. For example, three articles appeared in airline magazines in 1983 extolling the virtues of handwriting analysis for predicting sales and managerial success. All were by the same author who happens to have a consulting firm specialising in graphology. In fact, there is virtually no evidence to support the use of handwriting analysis to predict work performance. (Bernardin and Bownas, 1985, p. vi)

Incidentally it is interesting that graphology, despite the lack of any evidence for its predictive validity, is apparently becoming ever more popular as a method of selection. It is now used quite widely in several European countries, particularly France where the method was pioneered (Shackleton and Newell, 1991).

On the face of it there seems to be no inherent reason why a method which uses a valid, unique and permanent sample of someone's behaviour like their handwriting should not be at least as useful as any other personality test. The problem, as ever, is in the interpretation of the data and its relation to the job in question. Whereas the Rorschach Ink Blot test, with all the criticisms levelled at it, has a vast database linking responses to behaviour, and experienced psychologists to do the linking, graphology does not. It remains at the level of a seductive idea. What could be easier than to send a shoal of applicants' handwritten letters to a graphologist who would then send back the winner. No expensive psychometrics; no time-consuming messy and difficult interviews. The ultimate *quick fix*. And the ultimate abdication of managerial responsibility.

This brings me to my final countervailing opinion, from the management guru, Tom Peters:

> . . . I strongly oppose the use of a company psychologist to interview candidates, and the use of psychological testing in general. These devices impart precisely the wrong message about the company's value system. They suggest you are looking for flaws rather than strengths, and for pat 'personality profiles' rather than interesting human beings. Further, it is an unequivocal indicator to the candidate that you value staff experts over line input. It also makes it darned tough for line managers, no matter how highly they esteem a candidate to overrule a negative evaluation by the highly paid, jargon-spouting psychologist.
>
> Finally, the use of such techniques suggests that there *are* pat answers, and evades the hard work of really figuring out what you (line person) want and how to discern whether it's present. (That is, the judgements that you are making are much more subtle – and thoughtful – than anything that could be provided by a given profile on the *Minnesota Multiphasic Personality Inventory* test.) (Peters, 1989, p. 318)

(V) WORK SAMPLE TESTS

Work sample tests are the desirable alternative method of selection to the 'sign' methods like psychometrics. They sample job behaviour under job-like conditions. We have already mentioned the obvious examples like typing tests or driving tests. These deal with actual attainments rather than the ability or aptitude tests we have already discussed. There are also 'in-tray' tests where an applicant would be given the typical contents of an in-tray for a given white-collar job to see how they handled the material. These tests are generally among the best predictors to future job performance (Muchinsky, 1986).

One difficulty with work sample tests is that their validity weakens over time spent in the job (Robertson and Downs, 1989). The reason for this seems to be that these tests by their nature are highly task-specific whereas, as we saw in Chapter 4 on the time dimension at work, other factors, both individual and situational, assume a greater importance over time in the way someone performs their job.

(VI) ASSESSMENT CENTRES

The final method of selection we will mention is the use of an assessment centre where a combination of procedures may be used, usually including interviews, psychometric testing and work sampling. The use of these centres is usually limited to selection for relatively senior jobs because of the expense involved. Their origin lies in the selection of military officers, pioneered in Germany in the 1930s (Thornton and Byham, 1982). An important part of the assessment centre approach was to see how people reacted in groups where they were involved in decision-making, problem-solving and role playing.

Assessment centres have been extensively used by major American companies including AT&T, IBM and Standard Oil. The predictive validity of this method has been fairly good, though better at predicting future promotion than actual performance. It has thus been argued that the people doing the assessing have simply formed in their minds a stereotype of a successful member of that organization and give people high ratings if they conform to the stereotype (Klimoski and Strickland, 1977). This raises a very important issue of staff development within organizations that we will look at in some detail in the next chapter.

CHAPTER 12

Learning, training and development

In the last chapter we considered the first stages of what should really be an integrated organizational policy for dealing with human resources; recruitment and selection. In this chapter we will be concerned with the stages that occur after someone is hired, particularly *training* and *career development*. Before we deal with these stages however, we need to survey the major psychological issues underlying them, especially training which has grown out of a vast reservoir of research on the basic processes of *learning*, including *memory* and *thinking*.

Learning

Learning, according to E. R. Hilgard (Hilgard *et al.*, 1975), a leading authority on the subject, is 'a relatively permanent change in behaviour that occurs as the result of prior experience'. Most psychologists would probably define learning in a similar fashion, so let us accept Hilgard's definition and examine it a little more closely.

By *relatively permanent* we mean behaviour that is not due to the effects of temporary situations like taking alcohol or drugs or being very tired, any of which can dramatically affect the way we behave for a limited period of time. When we say that learning is the result of *prior experience*, we exclude the changes in behaviour that accompany the process of growing up and maturing in both animals and people. And we also exclude, of course, the behavioural changes that may follow brain damage or any other disability.

These exclusions seem to add up to a lot of behaviour, and we may begin to wonder how much of our behaviour is actually changed by learning. But in fact a truly enormous amount of behaviour change is due to learning. Some psychologists would argue that learning is the most important process in human behaviour, ramifying through every area of our lives. Even those popular old pastimes, sex and aggression, are largely learned behaviours. We have to *learn* how to mate.

The effects of learning on behaviour are easiest to see in young children, for whom the world is new and waiting to be discovered. As they become increasing aware of their environment, their society *socializes* them, instructs them in how they should behave. In the process of being socialized, children must learn the approved ways of walking, talking, eating, excreting and thinking, to name just a few of the more obvious kinds of behaviour. They must also learn how to make sense of life in the fashion approved by society; whom to like and whom to dislike; who is friendly and who is dangerous.

In place of the term *prior experience* in the definition of learning, the word *practice* has been used by learning theorists.

We tend to associate practice with repeated attempts at the same behaviour, like piano exercises. But in the more precise way the term is used by psychologists it would also refer to staying out of the rain, putting your left sock on before your right, or leaving half your salary at the race-track every week. All of these behaviours are learned, and learned from experience by *repetition*. Like all psychological processes, practice is quite neutral in its social implications, and bad habits seem to be distressingly well-learned.

Conditioning: Pavlov and Skinner

In the first chapter of this book we saw how Behaviourism became one of the two most influential approaches to the modern study of human behaviour. We also examined the most crucial concept of Behaviourism, that of *conditioning*, as discovered and developed by Ivan Pavlov. Because of the demonstrable control of an animal's behaviour achieved by Pavlov, conditioning was regarded in the early twentieth century almost as the Holy Grail in the attempt to understand how behaviour arose and how it could be changed. And the belief was that if learning behaviour could be understood in animals it could also be understood in people.

We have seen that classical (or Pavlovian) conditioning is a very basic form of learning that depends on a stimulus (S) being given to an animal which results in a particular response (R). The animal's behaviour in this pattern of stimulus-response is said to be *elicited* from it. The animal does not initiate the conditioning process by its own behaviour. However, much of the animal's behaviour is not elicited by outside stimuli but is *emitted* by the animal's own spontaneous actions. Without waiting for a push from outside an animal will often begin to explore its surroundings, to 'operate' on its environment. An animal engaging in such activity is said to exhibit *operant behaviour* and this brings us back to the work of another famous psychologist, B. F. Skinner, whom we met in our discussion of personality theory in Chapter 9.

Skinner carried Pavlov's work on conditioning a step further and showed that it was possible to *shape* an animal's behaviour in some every ingenious ways by using conditioning techniques (Skinner, 1938). This process is known as *operant conditioning* or sometimes *instrumental conditioning*. He designed a cage for a laboratory rat that completely controlled the animal's environment. With this cage (now known as a 'Skinner box') he could control the amount of light, heat and sound that the animal was exposed to. But the crucial feature of the Skinner box was a small bar set low down on one wall. When this bar was pressed a food pellet automatically dropped down into a tray below it.

As the rat explored the Skinner box it accidentally pressed the bar, winning itself some food. It ate the food but didn't make the connection. In the course of moving about it pressed the bar again and this time the idea clicked. The rat now made the connection and associated the bar pressing with the appearance of food. It then proceeded to press the bar as often as it could. As with classical conditioning as long as the rat's operant behaviour of bar pressing was reinforced by the appearance of food it continued with the behaviour. When Skinner withdrew the food and the rat was no longer rewarded for this particular operant behaviour, it stopped doing it.

Skinner also neatly demonstrated that the avoidance of pain is at least as important in reinforcing operant behaviour as the gaining of a reward. Through the floor of the box he produced a mild electric shock which could be turned off by pressing the same bar that had produced food in the previous experiment. The rat went through the same random movements before pressing the bar accidentally and turning off the current. As before it quickly learned to press the bar as soon as the current came on, thereby avoiding further shocks. Skinner called this *aversive conditioning*.

When discussing Pavlov's work we saw that animals could learn to generalise from one conditioned stimulus to others and conversely to discriminate between one particular stimulus and any other stimuli. Skinner has shown that these principles also apply to operant conditioning. In fact by building up the animal's learning step-by-step he has shown that animals can learn some very complex tasks. Animal trainers in zoos and circuses are actually applying operant conditioning by reinforcing the animal with food when it exhibits the desired behaviour. It is by this means that they can get horses to dance and dolphins to perform acrobatics. Skinner himself, as we have noted before, actually taught pigeons to play ping pong and demonstrated it to his students, a feat that he later regretted and got fed up talking about!

Kohler's Insightful Apes

In our discussion of conditioning we were looking at a very simple and basic form of learning behaviour. Even in an operant conditioning situation, where the animal took some initiative, the learning involved was accomplished by trying out the behaviour many times until it was satisfactory to the trainer. Circus tricks performed by animals require a great deal of patient step-by-step training, a lot of tries and a lot of errors corrected, before the animals have learned the trick. *Trial and error* learning is thus a slow and laborious process. People, as well as animals, learn by this means but a lot of human learning is due to *insight*, where the understanding of a situation or the solution to a problem seems to occur quite suddenly and without any careful step-by-step process of learning.

The phenomenon, where everything seems to click all at once (an 'aha' reaction), also occurs among the most intelligent animals. Wolfgang Kohler for instance has described some striking examples of insight in the behaviour of the apes he studied (Kohler, 1925). In a typical experiment, a banana is placed outside a chimpanzee's cage but well out of his reach, even with the aid of the short stick that Kohler has provided for him. Just outside the cage is another stick, long enough to reach the banana from the cage. The animal reaches for the fruit, first with his hand, then with the short stick lying inside the cage. He is unable to reach the banana of course and gibbers about in frustration. After a time he calms down, backs off and surveys the whole situation once more, taking in all the elements of the problem. Suddenly the answer comes to him. He uses the short stick to pull in the longer stick then successfully hauls in the banana with the new tool at his disposal.

By such a process of *insightful learning* Kohler's apes have solved much more complex problems than this. They have made tools and used them and they have combined various elements in their environment (like ropes and sticks) to reach distant objects. But there is a limit of course to animal insight, and even the brightest chimps cannot learn beyond the level of a three- or four-year old child.

The greatest advantage of an insightful solution is that, unlike trial and error learning, it can be applied to new situations. No specific skill or set of movements is learned, but an understanding of a relationship between a means and an end is gained.

A theory of learning

Because the learning process is so important to human behaviour, learning theory based on animal research has given rise to a long series of controversies within psychology. Generally speaking there are two main schools of thought. One of these schools emphasizes the *associations* that link a stimulus to a response to form a new connection, a new way of behaving. The classical conditioning of Pavlov is the prime example of this type of new behaviour. Learning, to the psychologists of this school, is thus the formation of new *habits*, like the habit of associating the word *ball* with a round object, or the habit of laughing and crying in particular ways. The organism must go through a process of trial and error before learning is accomplished in this way.

The other school of thought emphasizes the importance of under-standing and insight; some higher mental processes like the 'aha' reaction of Kohler's apes as opposed to the conditioned responses of Pavlov's dogs. Psychologists of the insight or *cognitive* school feel that the sheer formation of habits, no matter how complex, cannot entirely account for the ability of people and animals to cope successfully with problems they have never experienced before. Some other process, they argue, takes place inside the learner's head that allows him to use the habits already learned and then go a step further into unknown territory.

Harry Harlow (1949) has done some research that suggests a way in which these two schools of thought might be reconciled. He presented his monkeys with a series of problems where they had to choose between two objects, under one of which some food was hidden. The two objects were either different colours or different shapes and their position was alternated randomly from trial to trial, with the food always under the same object.

Over 300 such problems were presented to the animals and in the course of the experiment Harlow noticed an interesting phenomenon. On the first trial of each problem the monkeys had to guess the answer, and so they chose the correct object about 50 per cent of the time. For the first few problems, the monkeys didn't do much better than by chance. On the tenth problem they could manage about 75 per cent correct choices by the sixth trial. But by the three hundredth problem they had correct solutions 98 per cent of the time by the second trial.

At the beginning of the study the monkeys had approached the problem in a trial and error fashion, making no systematic use of what they discovered on the first trial. By the end of the study they understood that if the food wasn't under the first object they chose it had to be under the other one and they correctly chose this object on all subsequent trials regardless of its position.

The animals had acquired what Harlow called a *learning set* for the series of problems they were given which enabled them to transcend the original trial and error approach and use their insight to make sense of, and master, the situation. The animals were in fact 'learning to learn.'

Studying the learning process

It may be as well to mention at this point that we have a fundamental difficulty in trying to study the learning process – we can't see it even in animals, let alone humans. What we can see is the *performance* of some behaviour and it is this performance we study in trying to understand the learning process. We have to infer from someone's performance whether any learning has taken place inside his head.

Making such inferences from performance to previous learning would be very difficult in humans unless the process were simplified for study. How do we know whether the subject learned the task he was given entirely during the course of the experiment or was aided by some earlier learning he'd had elsewhere?

Psychologists therefore try to devise tasks that will be completely new to the subject so that old learning will not interfere with the new. Thus, instead of giving people lists of words and measuring how well they can learn them in a certain order, psychologists devise lists of nonsense syllables like MYV, ZOJ and PEM for the same purpose. Their reasoning is that people are not able to associate these nonsense syllables with anything they have previously seen (at least in English!) and thus everybody has to learn them from scratch, making it possible to measure individual learning abilities and to compare them with others.

Readiness to learn

There are two major factors which govern the likelihood of people learning something, *arousal* and *motivation*. The wider awake and the more aware we are of the moment the more aroused is our mental apparatus and the better are we likely to learn.

While a state of arousal is probably necessary for a person or an animal to learn, it is not by itself a sufficient condition for learning to take place. Something more is required – the will, drive, urge, need or desire to learn. The organism in other words must have the right *motivation* for learning. We will consider motivation in detail in the next chapter and I simply mention the topic at this point.

Motives represent a kind of energy within us that push us in a certain direction toward the fulfilment of a certain goal. Some of these motives, such as hunger and thirst, are very evident. If we are hungry we are in a high state of arousal and are very motivated to look for food. When we have eaten our fill the arousal level drops and the food-seeking motivation disappears. This is a biological motive that animals as well as people are born with.

However, you will remember from our discussion of genotypes and phenotypes in the last chapter that whatever we are born with (genotype) has to be expressed in behaviour (phenotype) that can be observed. So it is with biological drives or motives. A person's need for food, drink and sex can be satisfied in many different ways, resulting in many and varied behaviours; and each of these behaviours is learned. Oriental and Arabic food and ways of eating may seem strange to Westerners and vice versa but all these customs represent different ways people have learned to deal with the same unlearned motivation of hunger.

There is some evidence that people, and many animals, have a biological motivation towards exploring their environment – curiosity, perhaps. In exploring the environment a certain amount of learning may happen incidentally without there being a deliberate attempt to learn something specific. For human infants such *incidental learning* might be that mother is soft and warm and the source of food.

Adults are also capable of incidental learning. You learn the location of certain landmarks on your way home not because you deliberately set out to do so but simply because you see those landmarks every day when you walk past them and your brain registers that information for you. You needn't learn how to do it, as it were.

However, any other kind of learning must be learned. It is a far cry from curiosity about the environment to studying accounting in college for instance, and people have to learn that this kind of learning is rewarding. An accounting student has already learned the rewards society gives for going to school, for studying, for passing exams. These rewards are *extrinsic*; they are awarded because a task has been performed though the task in itself may not be rewarding enough to motivate anyone.

On the other hand our accounting student may have learned that he likes working with figures and learning how to use them. This would be an *intrinsic* reward, where the person would be motivated to perform the task for its own sake. In everyday life of course the learning we do is extremely complex and we are usually motivated by a combination of intrinsic and extrinsic rewards.

We noted earlier that a high degree of arousal is necessary to motivate learning successfully. We should now note in passing that there is such a thing as too much arousal, and this is often detrimental to learning. If a person in a learning situation is so aroused about it as to be anxious, the anxiety can interfere with learning. There appear to be three factors involved – motivation, emotion and performance. Any performance of any kind of behaviour is affected by motivation and by emotional arousal, but not always in the same way.

When motivation and arousal regarding a given task are low, it will be poorly performed. Increasing motivation and arousal result in increasingly good performance – up to a point. Beyond this optimum point, any increase in motivation and arousal will lead to a poorer performance. This finding is known as the Yerkes-Dodson Law, after the two psychologists who first proposed it at the beginning of the twentieth century (Yerkes and Dodson, 1908).

It has also been found that different kinds of tasks have different optimum levels of motivation and arousal. Simple tasks have a higher optimum level than complex tasks before you begin 'freezing' under pressure. So if you are mowing the lawn you can be very anxious about your performance and still perform well. But if you are taking the Graduate Record Exam and feel the same level of anxiety, your performance will suffer accordingly (Spence, Farber and McFann, 1956).

Conditioning in humans

Earlier in this chapter we discussed some basic forms of learning that were discovered from research on animals. We will take a look here at some of the implications this research has for humans and then discuss some forms of learning that have been discovered by research on humans.

Both classical (Pavlovian) conditioning and operant (Skinnerian) conditioning exist in human as well as animal learning. Psychologists have long realised the frequency with which conditioned responses appear in everyday human behaviour. In the early years of this century J. B. Watson provided a convincing demonstration of how children can learn to fear something they have previously liked (Watson and Rayner, 1920).

Watson took an eleven-month-old child named Albert and showed him a rat. Albert was quite unafraid of the rat and wanted to play with it. Then Watson showed Albert the rat again and this time he accompanied the appearance of the rat (CS) with a loud noise (US). Very young children are automatically frightened of unexpected loud noises (UR) and Albert was no exception. After the appearance of the rat had been paired with the noise a few times, Albert showed signs of fear when the rat appeared (CR), even if the noise was not sounded. He had now learned to fear rats.

Indeed the child now showed fear when he was presented with other furry objects, like a rabbit or a man with a beard. In a sense he had learned more than he had been taught via the process known as *stimulus generalization*. History does not record whether Albert was left with his new fear but we can presume he wasn't, for it should have been a simple enough matter to re-condition him by associating the appearance of the rat with something pleasant.

There is a case on record of a woman who had an irrational fear, a *phobia*, of running water and the splashing sound it made (Bagby, 1923). She had no idea how she came to have this phobia. Eventually under treatment for her phobia the woman remembered an important incident from her childhood. Despite her parents' instructions to the contrary she had gone wading in a stream with a fast current and found herself trapped beneath a waterfall with the water splashing over her. She was found by an aunt, and being very much more anxious about having disobeyed her parents than about her physical safety, she begged her aunt not to say anything. The aunt agreed and the child quickly forgot the whole incident. Shortly thereafter her phobia appeared. She had been conditioned to fear waterfalls and had generalized the stimulus to include any kind of running, splashing water.

In everyday life the way we react to company brand names may exhibit a kind of stimulus generalization. For example an early liking for Heinz baked beans may be generalized to the rest of Heinz' 57 varieties. Or a happy experience with Marks and Spencer's underwear might be transferred to the rest of their clothing lines.

In fact the basic link in classical conditioning between the conditional stimulus and the unconditional stimulus is at the heart of all consumer advertising. The attempt here is to associate a product (US) with a particular image (CS) that is thought to be attractive to the potential punter. Thus cars aimed at young people emphasise speed, power and style; those aimed at older people go for comfort and safety, and all of them have a magic carpet ideal of mobility. And think of all the products – from booze to life insurance – associated with sun-filled leisure, far from the world of work, usually on a golden beach empty of all but a handful of beautiful people. You can see why J. B. Watson did well in advertising.

Operant conditioning, where the subject must deliberately emit some kind of behaviour in learning a new response, can likewise be seen in many common forms of human experience. In the laboratory the effects of operant conditioning can be demonstrated quite simply. In conversation with a subject, an experimenter can get him to increase the number of opinions he gives by reinforcing all such statements. Thus, whenever the subject begins a sentence with 'I think', or 'In my opinion', the experimenter responds with 'Right, I agree', or 'M'hmmm'. Conversely, statements of opinion can be decreased by disagreeing with such statements or just being silent when they are made. There is an obvious relevance here for the skills of interviewing (Argyle, 1983).

This deliberate shaping of behaviour has become complex and sophisticated and is now known as the technique of *behaviour modification*. It has been widely applied – usually in the form of aversive conditioning – in situations where someone's existing behaviour is considered undesirable, whether in school, prison or mental institutions (Rimm and Masters, 1979).

Rewarding or reinforcing desirable behaviour at work, such as having good sales figures or keeping to timetables, can range from subsidised lunches to stock options, from a pat on the back to the use of a company swimming pool, and negative reinforcers for undesirable behaviour include the denial of these rewards as well as demotion, pay cuts and so on (Luthans and Kreitner, 1985).

The skills we learn in doing things are a result of operant conditioning and these skills include writing, driving, typing, riding a bicycle and even answering the telephone. But perhaps the most important skill we learn via operant conditioning is the ability to speak our native language.

Language and verbal learning

Babies are born with the capacity to speak any language on earth and when they discover they can produce sounds they start to babble. This babbling contains all the sounds the human voice is capable of making, and the language that this babbling will grow into depends entirely on which language his parents happen to speak. Out of their child's babbles, parents will pick up what seems to them recognisable sounds – like 'Dada'.

The emission of these sounds will quickly be reinforced by cries of parental delight and the child will thus be encouraged to continue. When he learns 'Dada', he will probably generalize from this stimulus and affix the label to any male he sees. By appropriate reinforcement and extinction, he will gradually learn to discriminate and apply the word 'Dad' to his father alone. In this way by trying to make sense of their child's babbling, parents teach their children what language to speak.

Verbal learning may be unique to human beings (because of the way our brains are constructed) and is probably the most important kind of learning we do. Learning the use of words is the essential basis for practically all of the formal learning we do in school, in higher education and in job training, and also for a great deal of the informal learning we do throughout our lives. In the last chapter we saw how important verbal ability is both in taking intelligence tests and in being interviewed. Verbal learning is necessary for the acquisition of language, and language is closely bound up with thought. We put problems and concepts into words, communicate them, think about them, and reason our way towards future behaviour.

Remembering and the need to forget

Whatever we learned would be of no use to us unless we had some way of storing it, ready to be retrieved when needed. This procedure is often referred to as *information processing*. Whenever we learn something, the brain engages in various activities that probably result in some kind of physical traces. We then store this information and experience in our *memory*. Exactly how this happens or what these physical traces are like, psychologists can only speculate about. It is quite conceivable, however, that some trace of past learning will always remain. The problem is to retrieve it. Whatever can be retrieved is *remembered*; whatever cannot be retrieved is *forgotten*.

There are several ways in which you can try to retrieve previous learning from your memory. If you have been given a set of figures to learn and you are then asked to recite them from memory, you are being urged to *recall* what you learned. Similarly, if you have essay questions on an exam, you have to recall previous learning in order to answer the questions.

If the exam was composed of multiple choice questions instead of essays, then only *recognition* of previous learning would be called for. You would normally be able to recognise more of the material learned than you could recall.

The most reliable and sensitive measure of remembering the material you had learned would be obtained if you were asked to *relearn* it. In fact if you ever have to relearn something you will probably find that things you thought were long forgotten can be remembered quite clearly.

A celebrated study of relearning concerns a fifteen-month-old boy who was read passages of ancient Greek every day until he was three years old (Burtt, 1941). The poor child had absolutely no understanding of this material, of course. When he was eight years old (and still knew no Greek), he was asked to memorize these same passages, together with similar passages that had not been read to him in his earlier experience. The difference was striking. He required 30 per cent less effort to memorize the old passages than the new.

These three processes of recall, recognition and relearning are three different kinds of response to the same stimulus; to the same jogging of the memory. In discussing how much learning has been retrieved or remembered by these means and how much forgotten, it must be understood, as we mentioned earlier in this chapter, that we have no direct access to learning processes. When we look at test results and see that Joe learned more than Moe but less than Flo, we are talking about *performance*. And, as we noted before, various factors other than what is learned and what is remembered can affect performance.

The actual process of committing something to memory seems to involve three distinct stages. When the sense organs react to environmental stimuli by sending information to the brain a fleeting trace of the stimulus remains after the message is sent. For example, if you just glance at a telephone number you will have a very brief memory of it as it registers in your brain. This *sensory memory* lasts for less than a second and if you want to use the information from your senses it has to be transferred on to the next stage of memory.

This second stage lasts for a slightly longer period of time (up to 30 seconds), long enough to work through the task in hand and to decide whether or not the incoming information is worth keeping (Baddeley, 1986). As most of the information is not worth keeping, it gets tossed out or, in other words, forgotten. If you call half a dozen local stores to see if they have a certain make of computer you will not remember their telephone numbers for very long. Nor would you want to remember this kind of information; it would be a waste of time and effort and confusing to boot. But some of the information that we have to consider in this *short-term memory* stage is important enough to be kept in a permanent record, and it must then be transferred to the third and final stage in the process.

This third stage is called *long-term memory*, and in order to get there the information has to be processed while being held in short-term memory. New information is constantly passing from sensory memory into short-term memory, and as it does so it pushes out the information already there. Information that is earmarked for long-term retention is therefore repeated or *rehearsed* (for example, by saying it aloud or writing it down) so that it sticks. It is then coded in such a way that what we consider essential about it is retained and the rest is discarded. The information is then ready to be placed alongside similar information in long-term memory storage, where it will probably remain forever.

Contrary to widely held belief, memories that are filed away in long-term storage do not fade with time, although they may change somewhat. Our memories of school, for instance, may become distorted as we add things that didn't occur or subtract things that did, in an attempt to make better sense out of what actually happened and the way we experienced it at the time. If our memories are permanently stored and do not fade away, why then do we forget things that have happened and information we have learned? The answer depends on *why* we cannot remember. It may be that the stimulus we are given is not sufficient for us to *retrieve* the memory, or it may be that we don't *want* to retrieve the memory.

As we saw in our discussion of recall, recognition and relearning, the form in which the stimulus is presented can determine how much is remembered and how much is forgotten at any given time. Another sign that the stimulus given may not be sufficient to retrieve the desired information from memory lies in the feeling, familiar to everyone at some time, that the answer is on 'the tip of the tongue' but can't quite be produced.

It seems that verbal information which is stored away in long-term memory is filed under several different systems – the way it sounds, the way it looks and what it means, for example (Baddeley, 1986). Thus, if the word you want is the navigational instrument *sextant* but you can't get it past the tip of your tongue, you may actually produce the word *sextet* which looks and sounds similar, or the word *compass* which has a similar meaning.

A failure to retrieve information because we don't want to is a different matter altogether. Our earlier example of the woman who was conditioned to avoid running water is a good example of this kind of forgetting. The woman's childhood fear had been so great that the only way she could cope with it was to blot out the entire incident from her memory as if it had never happened. She had a need to forget it. This is sometimes called *motivated forgetting*.

Of course the memory was not really blotted out, it just went underground where she was not conscious of it. When she acquired her phobia, the psychological effects of the memory surfaced in her behaviour. It was only when she went for help with her phobia that she was able to remember her childhood fear and deal with it. Such a need to forget is by no means rare or bizarre. Repressed memories, though usually less dramatic in their effects, are a central concern of the methods for treating emotional disturbance employed by many clinical psychologists.

The most striking instance of the need to forget is the case of *amnesia*. Amnesia can occur as the result of brain injury or disease of the brain or in severe alcoholism. But the type of amnesia that has captured the popular imagination is where someone is found wandering around unable to remember who he is or where he lives. This kind of amnesia does indeed happen, but probably occurs more often in fiction than in real life.

Such amnesia is the result of extreme repression of painful personal memories dealing with severe emotional conflict. It can last for days or years and is often accompanied by a physical move to get away from the agonizing conflict, which is why amnesiacs frequently turn up in strange surroundings far from home. As with other instances of the need to forget, amnesiacs can remember everything unconnected with their conflict – in this case, everything that would not remind them of their identity – and if they can deal with their problems in therapy, their memories are usually restored.

Making learning meaningful

The desire to make human learning as efficient as possible has promoted an enormous amount of research for many years. A lot of this research has been devoted to the study of competing methods of learning (see for example Anderson, 1981; Bower and Hilgard, 1981; Gagné, 1977).

1. MASSED VERSUS DISTRIBUTED PRACTICE

There is a lot of evidence that learning something a little at a time is usually more efficient than trying to learn it all at once. For instance, if you have a week in which to learn a list of French vocabulary and you can only spare three hours to study it, you would be much better advised to divide that time into half an hour a day for six days than to spend three straight hours on it.

Apparently our brain needs some time after each learning period to *consolidate* the changes that have occurred and thus allow the information to be permanently recorded in our long-term memory bank. For this reason it is useful to have a learning period shortly before going to sleep.

2. WHOLE VERSUS PART METHOD OF LEARNING

Another basic problem in learning is whether it is more efficient to study something as a whole or broken up into a number of parts. Is it easier, for example, to learn a ten-line poem as a poem consisting of ten lines or as ten separate lines of poetry? In this case, as in most human learning (especially verbal learning), the whole method is definitely superior to the part method. Occasionally, if the task falls naturally into separate parts, the part method may be quite effective. This is true of some sporting skills like those required in golf or tennis – but not in swimming or cycling, where the skill is best learned as a whole.

3. READING VERSUS READING AND RECITATION

It is well established that some people learn better by reading and others by hearing the same material. It has also been found that, even for people who learn best by reading, simply reading over some material is a much less efficient way of learning it than reading combined with recitation. The recitation of the material, whether out loud or to oneself, has the effect of fixing it in the memory.

4. RULE VERSUS ROTE LEARNING

Learning by rote requires simply the repetition of material until it is learned. Learning by rule involves finding some pattern, meaning or logic in the material and learning that rather than the material itself. Many of us learned arithmetic in school using both methods. We learned by rote that three times five is fifteen, but we also learned by rule that if you divide fifteen by five you get three. We learned multiplication tables, but we learned *how to* divide.

Most formal learning is a combination of rote and rule. If it is possible to learn something by rule, then it is certainly preferable to do so as it makes both learning and remembering much easier. But some learning simply requires the grind of sheer repetition. To make this grind easier we have to take our time and go over the material frequently and attentively, attempting to learn only one set of materials at a time.

5. FEEDBACK

No matter what you are learning or how you are trying to learn it, it is extremely helpful to know how you are doing – one reason students may welcome mid-term exams. Any feedback you receive on your learning performance enables you to pick out problems that have come up and generally makes the learning more interesting. This principle is the basis for teaching machines and programmed learning units where the learner receives feedback at every step of the way.

6. MNEMONICS

In ancient Greece, public speaking was practically a spectator sport and orators were highly skilled at making long and elaborate speeches without notes. They were able to do this in the same way modern entertainers perform amazing feats of memory for a living, they developed their own system of *coding* the information they wanted to remember into 'chunks' that could easily be retrieved from their long-term memory bank.

Thus the Greek orators would break up their speech into paragraphs and associate each paragraph with a statue in their favourite temple. As they were making their speech they would take an imaginary walk through the temple, and each succeeding statue they came to would be the stimulus to trigger the retrieval of the paragraph associated with it. Such devices are called *mnemonics*, from the Greek word for remembering.

We sometimes use mnemonics ourselves. Many of us learned the number of days in each month by reciting the jingle, 'Thirty days hath September . . .'. Spelling was made a little easier by putting 'i before e except after c'. Even in the absence of mnemonics we like to group and cluster things together as if we were making keys that would unlock doors where more information is stored away. As long as we remember where we put the keys, we're in business.

For instance, if I'm sitting in an office in Manhattan and I want to call someone in Westchester County whose number I don't have I may have to dial eleven digits to get the information I need: 99145551212. Now, if that's how the number was presented to me I would have a hard time remembering it. The normal memory span is able to cope with about seven digits (Miller, 1956). However, all the memorizing I have to do is in three or four chunks, thus: 9-(914) 555-1212. I know you have to dial 9 to get off the internal system, and I know the area code for Westchester County is 914. So all I really have to learn is the directory assistance number, 555-1212.

Meaningfulness

The thread running through these methods of learning is the search for meaning, for understanding, for ways of making sense. In making sense of our learning processes we are learning how to make sense of our whole world. We search for patterns, codes, keys and rules that will make our learning easier, and we *must* do this because there is so much to learn. We learn new things by linking them with things we already know. We interpret the unfamiliar new information in terms of what is familiar to us. We strive constantly for logic and order and have difficulty learning if we don't find it.

In a word we *organize* our memories. The organized packages that we form are sometimes called *schemas* (Kolodner, 1983). These schemas normally serve us very well but like all of our attempts to make sense of the world they round off the edges of things that don't quite fit – and this can lead to a distortion of our memory in some particular instance. A nice example of this process was provided by a famous experiment, shown in Figure 12.1, done many years ago (Carmichael, Hogan and Walter, 1932).

The subjects in this experiment were all shown the drawings of stimulus objects in the centre column. Then half of them were given the description of the object in Word List I and half in Word List II. When the subjects were later asked to reproduce the drawings from memory they were clearly influenced by the different descriptions they had been given. Their eyes had all received the same sensory stimulation but their brains had encoded the information differently, the codes being distorted in the direction suggested by the description.

Transfer of learning

The final aspect of learning we will consider, the transfer of learning, is of particular relevance to the field of training. Indeed some psychologists would classify training as another way of describing the transfer of learning (McKenna, 1987).

If we had to learn a new response to every new situation we found ourselves in, we would have to lead very restricted lives indeed. But fortunately for us much of the learning done in one situation can often be transferred to other situations. If you learn to drive a car in one particular model you can probably drive other models too. If you've already learned Spanish, it will help you in learning Italian. The *transfer of learning* involved in these examples is *positive* : your present performance or learning is helped by learning you did in the past.

But if you learn how to drive a car, then how to steer a boat with a tiller, your learning will be made *more* difficult. In a car you turn the wheel the way you want to go; in a boat you push the tiller in the direction opposite to the way you want to go. Your experience in driving a car is thus a *negative* transfer of learning because it hinders your new learning. Similarity of stimuli (similar cars) and similarity of responses (similar ways of driving them) result in a positive transfer of learning. Dissimilarity of responses (steering systems of cars and boats) result in negative transfer of learning.

The previous learning that we transfer to a new situation is not just a matter of particular skills or specific information that may be relevant. We also transfer *ways* of learning. Like Harlow's problem-solving monkeys we learn how to learn. However, research on both animals and children has always shown that learning to learn is only possible when the original learning is thoroughly mastered. If simple things are

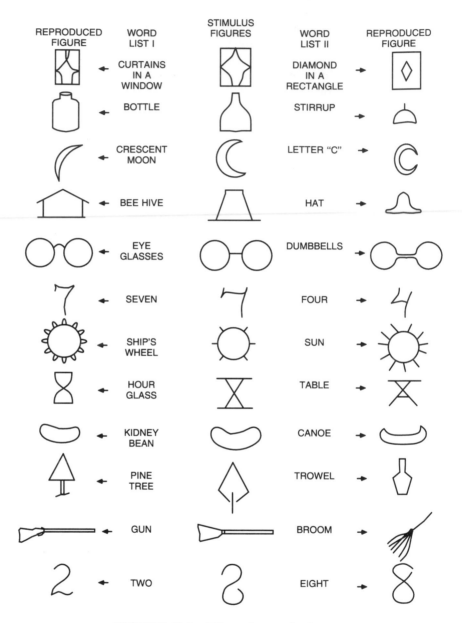

FIGURE 12.1   Distortions of schemas

Source: Carmichael, L., H.P. Hogan and A.A. Walter (1932).

not properly learned, there can be little positive transfer to more complex learning. It is quite useless to introduce a sixth-grade child to Shakespeare if he has not yet mastered a first-grade reader. If a child has not learned how to learn, putting him into increasingly complex learning situations, simply because of his age, can only pile frustration upon frustration.

Training

As in the case of the recruitment and selection process, which we examined in the last chapter (Figure 11.1), we are able to use the relevant research in training to suggest a model of best practice for organizations to follow. This model includes the five stages in the training process outlined in Figure 12.2. As with Figure 11.1 it should be stressed that this is an ideal model and what happens in real life will differ from it to a greater or lesser extent. Before looking at each of these five stages in turn we should examine the question of definition.

Training and education

Sometimes the terms 'education' and 'training' are used interchangeably to refer to the same activity. At other times a distinction is made. In the latter case education (from the Latin word 'educere' meaning 'to draw out') is regarded as dealing with more fundamental concepts while training is more narrowly focussed and concrete in its concerns, like the

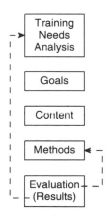

FIGURE 12.2   Stages in the training process

difference between mathematics and applied statistics perhaps, or logic and computer programming. One emphasizes *understanding*, in other words, and the other emphasizes *techniques*.

Even where this distinction is made it can never be regarded as watertight. Both education and training are firmly rooted in the psychology of learning, which we have just considered, and there will be times, for example, when education requires a narrow and concrete application (such as memorising lines of poetry or a historical sequence of events). Similarly management training may deal with abstract and general principles of psychology or economics.

In the world of work, however, it is probably reasonable to expect that most of the learning that people will be required to do is concrete, specific, narrowly focussed and, indeed, often task-based. So for the sake of brevity we shall refer to all the workplace learning we will now consider as training. One important implication of this is that, unlike education which ideally aims to maximise the potential of each individual and therefore the differences *between* individuals, we shall be dealing with a process whose objective is to minimise individual differences to the (ideal) point where anyone who has done the training can perform the task in question equally well, regardless of their particular background or abilities.

Before we consider the process of training in organizations it is worth pointing out that we are not dealing with those occupations which, have, or had, standard training programmes leading to formal qualifications, like doctors or printers. The social anthropologist Erving Goffman has pointed out how the period of training for these occupations is often grossly inflated beyond what is needed to perform them successfully. This is done to show how important the occupation is or to maintain a monopoly of practice (see for example Cockburn, 1991a). He calls this the *rhetoric of training* (Goffman, 1971).

Stage 1: Training Needs analysis

As in the case of recruitment and selection the first stage of the training process *should be* an analysis of what needs to be done. But here again this is often more ideal than actual. As one training expert has put it:

> Any systematic approach to training must begin with an analysis of the task in question. This is an obvious statement, but nevertheless it remains the case that this essential first stage in training is one that is often poorly carried out, or in some cases not carried out at all. It is all too easy to assume that what is to be trained is 'obvious', or that experts in the area are best able to decide what the content of training should be. (Stammers, 1987, p. 58)

We saw in the last chapter that an organization's entry into the recruitment and selection process was typically because of someone leaving their job and a vacancy therefore appearing. With regard to training the stimulus is usually just as mechanical and perfunctory:

> To most managers, needs assessment means telling the personnel department that there are production problems and maybe some people 'need' training. (Landy, 1989, pp. 309–10)

Or perhaps there is still some money left in the training budget that needs to be spent by the end of the financial year.

Three aspects of a proper *training needs* analysis (TNA) have been identified. These deal with the *organization*, the *job* in question and the *person* to be trained (Goldstein and Buxton, 1982).

(A) THE ORGANIZATION

A TNA focusing on the organization should deal with its goals, its resources and its environment and the balance between these facts. It should tackle the questions: '*Where* is training and development needed and *where* is it likely to be successful within an organization?' (Wexley and Latham, 1981). Where an organization's goals outstrip its resources, for example, it might need to train people in making priorities – or in saying 'no' to unreasonable demands from superiors. If the organizational environment is very macho then training men in safety procedures and the use of protective equipment will be a waste of resources unless their attitude changes first (Landy, 1989). If only 'wimps' use machine guards in the widget making industry there is little point in providing them for everyone.

(B) THE JOB

The essential requirement for a TNA of any given job is the *job analysis* with which the recruitment and selection process should have started, as we discussed in the last chapter. This is one more instance of the need for an integrated human resources policy and one further example of how ignoring essential organizational issues simply piles up problems for the future. When people are hired and already identified with a job it is much more difficult to go back to square one and consider what abilities or attributes are necessary for successful job performance, or even what the most important tasks are in that performance.

(C) THE PERSON

The final aspect of a TNA concerns the people who are to be trained. Here again something that seems obvious requires unpacking. How should they be chosen? What should they be trained in? And how should the training of new staff members differ from that of experienced people? Poor job performance is not in itself a reason to think of training. Is it a constant level of poor performance or just on Monday mornings? Is it just one person, or one team, or is it the whole sales force? Is the poor performance really due to human factors at all or might it result from clapped-out equipment or a job that needs re-thinking after twenty years?

If training is to be successful even after all these questions have been dealt with, the needs and wishes as well as the abilities of the potential trainees must also be taken into account. One study that looked at this issue in a public service agency found that:

- people aged 40–49 wanted training in management skills
- people aged 50–59 wanted training in technology
- people aged 60 and over didn't want any training at all

(Tucker, 1985)

A review of management training courses looked at both the personality and organizational factors which contributed to the effectiveness of these courses. The application of training ideas in practice was taken as an indicator of effectiveness. It was found that managers with a high need for achievement and internal locus of control, working in an organization which favoured training and the application of new knowledge, were the most effective (Baumgartel, Reynolds and Pathan, 1984).

With the benefit of hindsight these findings may seem like common sense, but we have already seen many times in this book that unless the right questions are asked, and the results treated with respect, what everyone already 'knows' can be spectacularly wrong.

Stage 2: Goals

The end point of any training at work is to change the way someone does their job in a desired direction so that he or she will then perform the job better. Getting him or her to that point is what the training is about. And deciding how that end point will be recognised is crucial to the process, both in focussing thought on the nature of the training and in measuring outcome.

A distinction may be made between general long-term goals like 'understanding how the unconscious operates between colleagues in an organization' and more specific short-term goals like 'being able to run a widget production line single-handed for a whole shift if the other operator is taken ill'. Obviously the more specific and short-term the training goal the easier will it be to assess the outcome. But an attempt should still be made to assess the outcome of much more general and long-term goals. The fact that this is much more difficult is not a good reason for not doing this kind of training, though it is an oft-heard excuse.

Stage 3: Content

As we saw in our brief survey of research on learning, people will learn something new much more easily if it can be hooked on to *existing* knowledge and understanding. This is a particularly important principle in devising training courses (Mayer, 1977). It also emphasizes the need to match the training with the trainee. This aspect of training content has been labelled the *instructional* phase.

In the learning of practical skills a *practice* phase is entered where particular procedures have to be learned and the crucial requirement is for *feedback* (Annett, 1969). It is probably impossible to learn any practical skills without getting regular feedback about one's progress and the correction of (inevitable) mistakes – from an instructor, whether human or mechanical. Just think back to any such skill you have acquired, like swimming or riding a bicycle, like learning a keyboard or a musical instrument, or driving a car.

However, while the need for feedback may be quite obvious in training for practical skills it is just as important in social or human relations skills (Argyle, 1989). Like assessing the outcome of more general goals it may be harder to organise, but again that should not be an excuse for avoiding this kind of training. That way we may end up with fewer organizations which think they've trained their staff in customer relations because they can make eye contact, use the customer's name and tell him to have a nice day.

The knowledge required by trainees has been divided into three categories; *general*, *functional* and *task* knowledge (Stammers, 1987). Task knowledge focusses on the rules governing the way the task is actually performed. Functional knowledge is about *why* the task is being done rather than how it is done. General knowledge sets the task in the context of the system it is part of. An example might be:

Knowledge level	Training
general	business diploma
functional	accountancy course
task	management accounting workshop

Stage 4: Methods

No fewer than 22 different methods have been identified in management training alone (Campbell *et al.*, 1970). Some of these methods, as we shall see, are often used in combination. They have been divided into three major types; *information presentational techniques, simulation methods* and *on-the-job training*.

(A) INFORMATION PRESENTATIONAL TECHNIQUES

These techniques include lectures, conferences or seminars, sensitivity training, laboratory education, systematic observation, closed-circuit television, programmed instruction, correspondence, films and reading. These techniques cover a huge range, from the traditional lecture to the largely self-taught programmed instruction. We have room here to comment on only a few of the more important ones.

The *lecture* is perhaps the most widely used of all training techniques. The traditional 'chalk-and-talk' situation, in which an expert presents a body of knowledge to a group of varying size, actually can be an efficient way of communicating information. It can also be extremely tedious of course. Apart from the personal qualities of the lecturer and the receptiveness of the audience there are a number of ways in which any lecture can be made more effective.

The use of *visual aids*, if appropriate, is often helpful, probably because vision is usually our most important and trusted sensory medium. Blackboard diagrams, slides, overhead transparencies and, especially, videotapes are all useful. Hand-outs that summarise or complement the lecture can also be helpful, as can well-written textbooks (such as, to take a case entirely at random, the one you're now reading).

Perhaps the most important way of improving a lecture is to arrange the format so that feedback for the lecturer is built in. Discussion between audience and lecturer, or between members of the audience, provides for a two-way rather than a one-way flow of information. With audiences over a certain size this is, of course, much more difficult to arrange, and in those cases the lecturer may be left wondering what, if anything, the audience is receiving.

Programmed instruction was introduced in the late 1950s and 'teaching machines' became very popular in the 1960s. But the use of a particular kind of machine is not what distinguishes this type of training so much as the process of learning which, in contrast to the one-way lecture, is based on *self-instruction*.

The material to be learned is arranged in sequence, in order of complexity and difficulty, together with questions to test the trainee's understanding and feedback on her answers. Each trainee thus drives the system, and at her own pace. Programmed instruction need not be arranged in machine form at all. Printed booklets have been widely used and, indeed, any 'teach yourself' book on any subject makes use of this method.

The 1970s and 1980s saw the development of *computer-assisted instruction* (CAI) which was a more sophisticated electronic form of the old teaching machine. However there is little evidence that CAI is any more successful than non-CAI, and it is usually more expensive, time-consuming and difficult to set up (Boettcher, Alderson and Saccucci, 1981).

Sensitivity training groups, or T (for 'training') – groups as they are often called, were first used for management training in 1946. They were developed by the National Training Laboratories in Maine and were very fashionable in the 1960s and 1970s. They owe their existence to 'the father of group dynamics', whom we met in Chapter 7, Kurt Lewin (Aronson, 1992).

Lewin had been running a series of small groups, composed of people from public service, education and social science, discussing social problems. The dynamics of these groups were observed by Lewin's assistants who met to discuss what they had seen each night. One night they were joined by a few of the participants and there was some serious disagreement between observers and participants about what had actually happened.

When all fifty of the participants joined in on subsequent nights there was frequent disagreement and Lewin quickly realised the significance of what was happening. He saw that people engaged in a work group activity, in this case a problem-solving discussion, could benefit by leaving the objective of the group aside for a time and focussing on the way the members of the group related to each other – the group dynamics or 'group process' – because each participant knew what his intentions were better than any observer could.

What evolved from these early sessions was the practice of a group that met with no formal agenda and no objective other than the exploration of its own dynamics. The role of the trainer in each group is to help people give others feedback about the effects of their behaviour and to receive feedback in turn.

For this to work the group members are encouraged to be as open, straightforward and non-judgemental as possible in their communications with each other. The ideal is to heighten participants' awareness and self-awareness of things they had not been conscious of. Evidence of T-group effectiveness in management training is mixed. Where some managers found it a positive, liberating experience others found it negative, oppressive and manipulative (Back, 1973).

Although sensitivity training is used much less often now 'the practices and principles of communication that evolved from T-groups have filtered into the larger culture, where their influence is felt in a variety of institutions, including large corporations and public education' (Aronson, 1992, p. 388).

(B) SIMULATION METHODS

Simulation methods include case studies, critical incidents, role playing, business games, task models and the in-tray technique. The equipment designed for use with simulation methods range from an explanatory diagram to a full-scale model of an aeroplane flight deck.

We have seen that learning specific skills involves making errors and correcting them. The effects of these errors in work learning situations varies enormously; in many situations they may be fairly harmless, but in learning how to pilot an aircraft, for example, they could be catastrophic. Such training therefore needs a medium which is both *forgiving* and *safe* (Stammers, 1987).

Cost would also be an important factor in pilot training; few airlines could afford to risk even an empty plane every time a trainee pilot made a serious mistake. And a simulated model could even provide a more effective learning experience than the real thing if it allowed the trainee to isolate and practice specific parts of the task at varying speeds.

Not all simulation techniques need to be as *physically* realistic as in pilot training in order to be useful. Situations of low physical reality need not matter as long as they have high *psychological* reality (Weitz and Adler, 1973). That is, where the thinking and feeling involved in responding to the training stimuli are close to those experienced in the job itself, and where the trainees are engaged by the training situation as though it were the real thing.

In a sense this applies to the *case study* method too. The case study may be the most widely-used of all simulation techniques. It was pioneered by the Harvard Business School and is now used almost universally in business and management schools. The essence of this method is the representation of an organizational problem (actual or hypothetical) to a group of trainees who are asked to analyse the situation and produce a solution. The case may deal with technical issues or human relations issues. It may be presented in writing or on videotape, or it may be combined with *role playing*, which we will consider in a moment. The method has obvious face validity and trainees are usually committed to it.

Needless to say discussion groups for case studies will be subject to the same forces of group dynamics that we examined earlier in Chapter 7. It is therefore very important for the trainer(s) to provide an open and encouraging atmosphere for all participants to contribute as and how they wish. One possible problem with the case study method might be the impression left on trainees that all organizational problems have solutions or, even more worrying, that they can learn techniques for dealing with every problem they are likely to face – yet another example of that seductive old Quick Fix.

Role-playing is a relative of the case study method. They share the same technique of asking trainees to analyse a problem and find a solution to it. Where they differ is in acting out the roles of the individuals portrayed in the case study. It is therefore used to depict interpersonal relationships, particularly between two people, and the situation most frequently simulated is that of an interview, for example in selection (as we saw in the last chapter), or in counselling or sales.

Usually the roles are unscripted, with one trainee playing the part of the interviewer and the other the interviewee. What often happens is that the trainees get really involved in playing their roles and a genuine interaction takes place between them. This is not only useful for them but for the rest of the trainees who are observing them. Learning takes place through both role playing and observing and, perhaps most importantly, from the discussion and analysis that follows (Lawshe, Bolda and Brune, 1959).

Role playing can be combined with the clinically based Transactional Analysis that we looked at in Chapter 6: 'The unconscious at work'. This seems to be especially useful where a supervisor and a subordinate have a crossed transaction and are relating to each other at different levels of personality (Rush and McGrath, 1973; Makin, Cooper and Cox, 1989). Role playing seems to be a particularly useful training method in the attempt to change attitudes and behaviour, a subject we will examine in some detail in Chapter 14.

(C) ON-THE-JOB TRAINING

This training method includes job rotation, committee assignments, executive boards, coaching and performance review. However what often passes for 'on-the-job training' is the practice of throwing new staff members in at the deep end to see if they sink or swim. If the trainee swims it's a cheap training method; if she sinks it's extremely expensive. Either way the organization will not really know what happened. The temptation is, of course, to ascribe failure or success to individual personality factors – the *fundamental attribution error* we met in the last chapter.

However many people do learn how to do the job by their own efforts at it, especially in manual work. But at the same time learning the job in this fashion doesn't imply that it will be done well. It has been found that job effectiveness may actually decrease with experience (Fiedler, 1970). Moreover people can learn bad habits at work just as thoroughly as in their private life (Argyle, Gardner and Cioffi, 1958). And we saw in Chapter 1 how badly the basic task of shovelling was done routinely until Frederick Taylor decided to study it.

The best form of on-the-job training is apparently *coaching*. If it is done well it can combine the invaluable feedback of programmed instruction with the personalised attention of the trainer, or coach, who acts as a role model for the trainee (Bass, 1981). It is obviously important for the coach to be an expert in the skill being imparted, but this is only a beginning because experts are often unable to tell you how they did something. Think about great sports stars (or even actors) being interviewed about *their* skills for instance. 'I just closed my eyes and went for it' seems to be about the average level of explanation.

Indeed you can see this phenomenon in your everyday life. By the time you go to school as a young child you can speak your own language fluently. Before you've had a single grammar lesson you have mastered the rules of grammar. Yet you may never be able to describe what the rules are to someone else. Even experts have great trouble in doing so.

In blue-collar work situations it is apparently not unusual for a highly experienced work operator to obtain a greater output from a machine than the person who designed it, yet be unable to tell anyone else what it is he does that is so successful (Broadbent, 1987). Similarly a trainee taking part in a business game may be able to take the correct decisions needed to achieve certain goals about, say, prices or use of resources, yet not do nearly as well when questioned about the same task verbally (Broadbent, Fitzgerald and Broadbent, 1986).

For coaching to be successful, therefore, the trainer needs a great deal more than the appropriate expertise. He or she must also be a good teacher – a rare natural ability, and a rarely-taught skill outside of the primary and secondary educational systems. The trainer and the trainee also need a good personal relationship – it apparently helps if they come from similar backgrounds – and there should be some reward or recognition for the trainer's work (Wexley and Latham, 1981).

Stage 5: Evaluation

The evaluation of training effectiveness is an extremely difficult and complex matter, so of course it is usually not done, or done badly. However there are a few good models of evaluation available (Latham and Saari, 1979). Ideally the evaluation of training should not be a one-shot activity but a process that continues throughout the life of a training programme. Neither should it be an all-or-nothing activity that defines success only in terms of finding the best conceivable training programme.

One particularly influential set of guidelines for evaluating how far training does what it is supposed to do has four different criteria, which make use of data at four different levels. In ascending order of validity these are *reaction, learning, behavioural* and *results* criteria (Kirkpatrick, 1967).

(A) REACTION CRITERIA

This criterion is concerned with the trainees' own views. While this is a valuable and a necessary source of data about training effectiveness it has to be treated with some caution. Most people enjoy a break from the workaday routine and this might colour their impression of what they have learned and how valuable it might be.

There might also be a kind of Hawthorne effect operating (such as we discussed in Chapter 7) where people respond favourably when their organization pays particular attention to them. And this effect alone could lead, as in the original Hawthorne effect, to employees changing their behaviour in the direction desired by their employers.

(B) LEARNING CRITERIA

This criterion uses data of higher validity in evaluating training effectiveness. It poses the question 'What have the trainees learned?' Data collected to answer this question usually involve some kind of written test or assessment given to the trainees immediately after the training course. However as with any written test people might give convincing evidence of their learning but be unable to transfer it to their behaviour at work, for whatever reason.

(C) BEHAVIOURAL CRITERIA

At this level what is being assessed is the effect which the training has had on the trainees' behaviour. The measures of effectiveness used are usually three-fold: *productivity* (quality of output, quality of performance and so on), *personal* (absenteeism, sickness, time-keeping and so on), and *observational* (ratings of job performance by superiors, colleagues, customers and so on).

(D) RESULTS CRITERIA

This level has the most rigorous criteria of evaluation. The feedback at this level refers, like the three previous criteria, to the Methods stage as represented in Figure 12.2. But unlike these other three criteria this set also refers back to the effect of the training on the organization as a whole, with implications for any future Training Needs Analysis. How the organization has changed, as well as being the most demanding level of validity is also perhaps the most difficult to isolate as organizations often exist in a very complex and volatile world.

Even within the organization there may well be differences of opinion in the way results are interpreted, mirroring the built-in conflicts of interests we discussed in Chapter 2. A striking example is that of the government-sponsored programme in the United States which had the objective of raising the self-esteem of a group of female trainees. At the end of the programme the trainees walked out of their boring, badly-paid jobs (O'Leary, 1972). Was the training a success or a failure? This could be seen as a Hawthorne effect in reverse, perhaps.

This last study does raise an important and frequently-heard objection to providing training for employees that employers make in general terms: 'Why should we provide training for people if it makes them more employable elsewhere?' and its corollary: 'Why should we spend money training people when we can hire people who've already been trained elsewhere?' As we will see in the next section this gets us to the heart not only of training policy but of an organization's overall policy on using its human resources.

Staff development

Staff development is the term often applied to the total set of functions that deal with the use of human resources in organizations; training, placement and promotion. This chapter has been devoted largely to the first of these functions, which is by far the most important. In the remainder of this chapter we will deal, very briefly, with placement and promotion and then consider some general issues of staff development.

Placement

For most organizations the considered placement of people in jobs that best serve the interests and abilities of the individual and the interests and needs of the organization is a non-issue. If someone is recruited and selected for a certain job at a certain place in the organization then that is where she is likely to stay until she leaves or the job disappears – unless she is promoted.

This is partly because of the effort expended in the recruitment and selection process where so much emphasis is placed on finding exactly the right person for each job. And it is partly because a serious attempt to match individual and organizational needs and interests inevitably entails, as we saw in the last chapter, the posing of such difficult and fundamental questions as 'what is the point of our existence?'

The concept of having a rationally planned career within an organization, where someone progresses in experience, knowledge, skill, responsibility and so forth, exists more in theory than in real life and is usually left entirely to the mechanism of promotion. This produces several kinds of problem for both organization and staff which may be summarised as follows (Nicholson and Arnold, 1989):

1. *Restrictions*
Organizations often create unnecessary restrictions in the movement of staff within the organization, for example between different functions, so that the only movement allowed is via promotion.

2. *Political*
As we saw in Chapter 2 both individuals and groups in an organization have their own interests and these may not be the same as the organization.

3. *Mechanistic*
The movement of staff in organizations, especially large organizations (whether in the public or private sector), is often hedged around with detailed rules and regulations, designed perhaps for objectivity and fairness but which can't handle exceptions, and are in any case usually outdated.

4. *Neglect*
If the organization does not consciously identify career paths that progress over time then they will not be visible to ambitious or idealistic individuals whose energies may be frustrated rather than harnessed to the organization's benefit.

Some observers claim to see an increasing awareness of these problems by organizations (Gutteridge, 1986). For organizations which want to tackle the problems outlined above there are a number of things they can do. The most obvious of these is to let people know what vacancies exist or will exist within the organization, what the requirements for each position are and how they can be met.

Most organizations, however unenlightened, have some kind of *appraisal* system, usually annual, for monitoring staff performance and dealing with issues of salary increases and promotion. These sessions could first of all be held more frequently, but also extended to consider the individual's present needs and future hopes, and how they related to the organization. They could then be linked to the whole array of training methods we discussed earlier in the chapter.

But they could also include individual counselling and/or psycho-metrics *if* the person involved thought that might be helpful in increasing his self-knowledge and flexibility in future career planning. Whatever the organization decides to do about the placement of its staff along these lines it must, as I have stressed throughout this chapter and the last, be integrated within a coherent staff development policy beginning with recruitment and ending with retirement (Gerstein and Amos, 1986). Adding bits of psychometrics or training or whatever onto the existing systems because they're fashionable, or a senior manager's pet enthusiasm, or in hopes of a quick fix to quell staff unrest, is worse than useless.

Promotion

Career movement in organizations usually takes the form of *promotion*. In many organizations promotion is dependent on seniority, given adequate performance and adequate adherence to the cultural norms of the organization. Promotion usually entails increased responsibilities and increased pay and benefits. However the criteria of performance and cultural conformity may not always be appropriate or easy to assess or deal with.

When people are hired their competence is naturally assumed. The greater the effort that has gone into their selection the greater the organization's psychological investment, as well as financial investment, and the greater the need to justify the selection decision. (This is an example of cognitive dissonance reduction at work that we will discuss in Chapter 14.)

As we saw in the last chapter, the most important part of the selection process is the interview. The interesting suggestion has been made that people who do *particularly* well on interviews, because they are confident, assertive, charming and physically attractive for example, may be hired for this reason, and do well at future appraisal or promotion interviews for similar reasons. But they may be so self-absorbed that they have *only* their own interests in mind, or may even mask incompetence behind their interview skills. Thus it may be that, in some cases at least, 'Superior self-presentational skills drive careers, not competence' (Hogan, 1990, p. 42).

We don't have room here to develop this theme further but it's worth re-reading the appropriate part of the last chapter considering the artificial nature of most interview situations and reflecting on the personality characteristics required to impress interviewers, and why.

Another difficulty that promotion may cause for the organization is highlighted by the celebrated *Peter Principle* (Peter, 1969). Peter's suggestion is that people rise in an organization to their level of incompetence, and stick there. Peter's work was intended as a humorous view of organizational failings based, initially, on his own experiences in education but it struck a heartfelt chord with many people who suffered from incompetent managers in their own organizations.

The core of Peter's approach is that since people are promoted as a reward for doing a particular job well they find themselves in an unknown situation for which they have neither experience nor training nor any known aptitude. If they do this job well they will find the process repeated until they come to a job that they cannot do well – their 'final placement' within the organization. Organizations are thus full of incompetent people in their final placement, says Peter, but neither they as individuals, nor the organization collectively, can admit this.

There is little empirical research that would bear directly on these ideas, though on the basis of what we have discussed in this chapter about skills training, and in previous chapters about personality factors and abilities, it is certainly reasonable to suppose that people who are promoted into a different kind of job may well have serious difficulties without a lot of conscious help and support from their organization. Salesmen who become sales managers, scientists who become laboratory directors, or teachers who become principals may well include the clearest examples of the Peter Principle at work.

Selection OR Training?

We conclude these two chapters on the use and misuse of human resources by considering some general issues and attempting some tentative conclusions.

While reliable figures are patchy and difficult to come by, there is little doubt that organizations generally spend far more money on the recruitment and selection of their staff than they do on their subsequent training and development. The situation varies from one organization to another, of course, and from one country to another (Handy, 1987). It has been found that in the United Kingdom, which is particularly poor at investing in training, the larger the organization the more likely is it to train its staff (Silver, 1991). Almost 75 per cent of the smallest companies (less than 50 employees) have no training as opposed to 20 per cent of the largest (over 1000 employees). But the pattern is clear; selection is much more important to organizations than training. Earlier in this chapter we noted the commonly-heard argument *against* expenditure and training that it would simply make staff more marketable and likely to leave for more money elsewhere.

At the same time, however, it is also common to find in the public literature of organizations statements such as the following:

> In today's world, our challenge must be to energise and empower the talents and commitment of our people and build our success from the bottom up.
>   Ralph Larsen, Chairman and CEO,
>   Johnson and Johnson, 1993

It is difficult to see how these goals can be put into practice *without* spending a great deal of money on the training and development of staff. Perhaps that is what is intended and perhaps such widespread sentiments are indicative of recent organizational changes. Perhaps not. After all we have been here before:

> The chief problem of big business today is to shape its policies so that each worker will feel that he is a vital part of his company with a personal responsibility for its success and a chance to share in that success.
>   Cooper Procter, President,
>   Procter and Gamble, 1887

My own feeling is that there is a rather profound psychological cause for the emphasis on the critical selection of staff as opposed to their later development. It is psychologically much more comfortable to believe that if we get it right at the very beginning then nothing more needs to be done. To take training and development seriously requires openness to criticism and change on the part of *everyone*, from the chairman down, and the higher up the hierarchy you are the more you will have invested psychologically in the status quo. And we saw in Chapter 6 the enormous *unconscious* resistance to change that always exists in organizations.

It's a bit like marriage. The Western romantic myth has it that the goal is to find *the* boy or girl of your dreams, get married, and . . . live happily ever after of course. This idea that marriage is the *end* of the process rather than the beginning may have something to do with the fact that getting on for a half of all Western marriages end in divorce. The need for give-and-take, for trying to understand, for being open to change – all of which may be psychologically rewarding but none of which are easy – is rarely quoted after the stages of 'selection' and 'induction' have been passed.

Above all what is needed in any relationship is *trust* between the parties involved. Without it the relationship will founder whether it's a psychological contract between two people or between staff and organization. Which brings us back to the issue of training staff only to lose them. If the senior management of an organization looks upon any training or development scheme in a manipulative fashion, designed to serve only its own ends (for example more profitable output for the same pay, or staving off staff discontent), this will inevitably be perceived as a breach of psychological contract by the people at the receiving end, who will draw their own conclusions and look after *their* own interests as far as they can.

Training people in these circumstances might well result in them going elsewhere to be more appreciated. But *if* the terms of the psychological contract are honoured *and* staff are treated honestly and with respect then, given what we have already learned in this book about people's needs in the world of work, it is difficult to see why they in turn would not want to honour their side of the deal. The psychological needs that would be satisfied thereby are, as we have already seen and will see again, much more important to people than simply making more money.

CHAPTER 13

Motivation

What is meant by motivation?

The *Penguin Dictionary of Psychology* describes motivation as an 'extremely important but definitionally elusive term' (Reber, 1985). Having attempted a definition of the term myself I can assure you that this is no cop-out. What I finally decided on was the following (Statt, 1990).

> A general term for any part of the hypothetical psychological process which involves the experiencing of needs and drives and the behaviour that leads to the goal which satisfies them.

You can see what they mean by 'definitionally elusive', can't you?

The key words in this definition are 'needs', 'drives', 'goal' and 'satisfies', and we will return to them as we surround the topic and close in on it. We can say here though that any behaviour whose object is to reach a particular goal is motivated behaviour. And that's an awful lot of behaviour.

Motivation is one of those terms which is used in a variety of ways both by psychologists and by non-psychologists, and has been applied to a truly vast amount of human behaviour. In fact we have encountered it several times already in this book:

1. F. W. Taylor (KEY STUDY 1)

The inventor of 'scientific management', who we first met in Chapter 1, was an early student of motivation at work. In particular he advocated the use of money as a motivator in getting workers to achieve their own individual goals, allied to the objectives of the organization. The use of money in this way, and the limits to that use, will form an important aspect of this chapter.

2. Hawthorne Studies (KEY STUDY 6)

In Chapter 7: 'Group dynamics and working-group relationships' we explored the relationships between people in work groups which seemed to provide an important non-monetary form of motivation for a worker's behaviour, and one that might even be more powerful at times.

3. Personality factors

After considering various key theories of personality in Chapter 9 we looked at some identifiable types of personality that seemed to be organized around the satisfaction of particular needs. Thus the 'authoritarian' personality *needed* to be prejudiced against other people to bolster his own weak ego and his self-esteem; the 'Machiavellian' personality *needed* to be devious and deceitful in his relations with other people' and the 'entrepreneurial' personality had a particularly high *need* for achievement.

4. Learning and forgetting

In the last chapter we noted how before we can learn anything we must have a *need* (will, drive, urge, desire) to learn it. If we really don't want to learn a foreign language then it doesn't matter how good the teaching is that we receive, or even how much time we spend in the country where it is spoken; we won't learn it. Refugees who have not come to terms with their enforced exile will never really learn – be at home in – their new language. Conversely we may forget things because we have a *need* to do so, if remembering them is too painful for us.

We should now try to draw together all the threads represented by these examples in a systematic way, noting as we do so that motivation is intimately bound up with *emotion*. As we did in our discussion on personality in Chapter 9, we will consider both formal (academic) and informal ('common sense') theories of motivation. We will also examine the specific links between motivation and the world of work, particularly the practice of management.

Informal theories of motivation

Just as we have a need to make sense very quickly of the individual personalities we encounter, to come to some decision about what they're really like, so likewise do we need to make sense of the motivations for their behaviour – why they did what they did. Three different types of informal theory have been discovered, each one based on a particular view of human nature. Two of these theories, Theory X and Theory Y, have been suggested to describe the different assumptions of managers, by a psychologist of the neo-Human Relations school, Douglas McGregor (McGregor, 1960), using the work of Abraham Maslow among others. The third, the theory of Social Assumptions, has been put forward by organizational theorist Edgar Schein based on the Hawthorne Studies and later human relations-oriented work by Elton Mayo and others (Schein, 1988).

Theory X

- people are inherently lazy so they must be motivated by external incentives
- they will pursue their own goals, which run counter to those of the organization, so they need external controls to keep them in line
- they are quite irrational and incapable of self-discipline or self-control
- the rare individuals who *are* rational, controlled, and self-motivated will therefore have to manage all the others.

Theory Y

- people seek meaning and a sense of accomplishment and to exercise autonomy and be independent in their work
- as they are basically controlled and self-motivated they will find external incentives and controls demeaning
- if they are only given the chance to do so they will come to regard the organization's goals as their own.

Social assumptions

- human behaviour is primarily motivated by social needs
- a sense of individual identity comes from interpersonal relationships

- much of the intrinsic meaning of work is lost through industrialization so meaning is sought in social relationships at work and the forming of peer groups
- people are often more responsive to peer group forces than external financial incentives or attempts to control their behaviour by management.

In Chapter 9 we examined the construction of informal theories of personality and in Chapters 11 and 12 we noted how these theories have an impact on the way managers conduct the recruitment and selection of new staff and the training and development of existing staff. This was particularly clear in the way interviewing was done.

The same is true of motivation. The particular theory of human nature that a manager favours will have immediate implications for the way he relates to the people he manages; for how he interprets *his* psychological contract with the organization, and theirs. This is especially important, of course, in the case of senior management and people in positions of influence in an organization. We noted in Chapter 6 how the individual psychology of influential people might set the culture, the expectations, beliefs and unspoken assumptions of an organization.

Organizational implications

A proponent of Theory X's rather cynical view of human nature would therefore adopt a 'hired hands' approach to motivation and be a follower of Frederick Taylor and Henry Ford. Authority and control are firmly vested in management. The employee's task is therefore to perform the work efficiently and do what she's told without question in return for wages. If production is poor or the workers' morale is low the remedy is sought in standard techniques such as re-designing the job, or even the organizational structure, changing the financial incentives, and tightening up the system of control.

Someone who believed in Theory Y's idealistic view of human nature would want, above all, to make work meaningful for people so their self-esteem would be raised and they could take a pride in what they did for a living. They will also be keen to delegate authority and responsibility for the work to the people actually doing it. Thus management will give up some of their control of the worker and the workplace to allow the worker the opportunity to marry her individual goals to those of the organization.

The implications of the Social Assumptions theory of motivation are different again. As well as being concerned about the job in hand it is important for the manager to be aware of the psychological needs of the people he manages, who need to feel that they belong and to be part of a peer group. These peer groups should be accepted and respected by the organization, with junior managers representing their interests to senior management where necessary. In return for caring about the non-material needs of its workers the organization will expect a high degree of loyalty and commitment. This kind of organizational system is often called 'paternalistic' (Schein, 1988).

In chronological order Theory X appeared first (in Frederick Taylor's day and earlier) followed by the Social Assumptions theory between the two World Wars, and finally by Theory Y. There is thus a tendency on the part of some writers on management and organizations to see them as *progressing* from one to the other, with managers becoming more enlightened and sophisticated over the course of the twentieth century.

But we saw in Chapter 4: 'The time dimension' that progress cannot be assumed simply by charting changes over time, and that is certainly true in this case. Theory X is as alive and robust as it was in Taylor's day, if not so universally assumed and unquestioned. Moreover organizations, and individual managers, are rarely unilateral or totally clear-cut in their views of motivation. Motivation is an extremely complex affair and we inevitably try to simplify it for our practical concerns. We will return to management and motivation at the end of the chapter but let us now consider more formal theories of motivation.

Formal theories of motivation

Like formal theories of personality, theories of motivation are at best partial explanations. The factors that motivate people to behave in particular ways are numerous, ever-changing, often unconscious and sometimes contradictory. They vary from one individual to another and within the same individual over time because although formal theories of motivation are more systematic and more consciously considered than informal theories – and therefore essential for serious study – they may not be very much more useful in practical terms.

It is widely accepted that a theory of work motivation need not be different in any important way from a general theory of motivation. There are many such theories and more than one way of classifying them, but perhaps the most common is to make a distinction between four types; *need* theory, *expectancy* theory, *equity* theory and *goal-setting* theory.

I NEED THEORIES

The group of theories usually gathered under this heading contain the most numerous and probably the best known theories of motivation. These theories support the notion that people have a series of psychological needs arising out of, though going far beyond, basic biological drives like hunger, thirst, sex or the avoidance of pain. Satisfying these needs is therefore the *content* of what we refer to as motivation, and needs theories are sometimes called 'content theories'.

1. MASLOW'S HIERARCHY OF NEEDS

Abraham Maslow's is probably the best known of general need theories, if not the best known theory of motivation (Maslow, 1943). He was a leading advocate of Humanism in psychology as a 'third force' between Behaviourism and Psychoanalysis. It might be useful at this point, therefore, to re-read the brief section on Humanism in Chapter 9: 'Personality factors', before continuing.

Maslow talked about five levels of need, that formed a loose hierarchy, as illustrated in Figure 13.1.

FIGURE 13.1   Maslow's hierarchy of needs

People strive to fulfill their needs, first at the most basic physiological level. When these needs are fulfilled they are no longer motivated by them but other needs will always take their place which *are* motivating. These will be more psychological needs for social acceptance and personal achievement. As people continue striving to have their needs fulfilled they arrive finally at the level of *self-actualization*. At this level they would seek to express personality characteristics like independence and autonomy, to strengthen and deepen personal relationships, and to maintain a sense of humour and a balanced view of life.

Maslow did not coin the term 'self-actualization' (that was done by a Gestalt theorist called Kurt Goldstein), but he did a great deal to popularise it. What Maslow meant by the term, in brief, was the need to actualize, or realise, all of one's unique potential; to be all that one could be. In a sense this need can never be fulfilled, so that even people who reached this level – and Maslow thought they were a small minority of the population – would have no shortage of motivation. The more self-actualized people become, the more they want to become. This is a motivation with its own inner dynamic.

Maslow did not intend these five levels to form a totally rigid hierarchy. Although lower level needs are usually more widely satisfied, or satisfiable than higher level ones, more than one level of need could be experienced at the same time by someone, people could have different priorities of needs, and there are always people who are willing to make sacrifices for others and give up the chance to fulfill their own needs (Maslow, 1970).

As a psychotherapist Maslow's theory of motivation was based on his clinical observation, and he was not specifically concerned with management or the world of work. But we have already seen in Chapter 6 and Chapter 9 how clinical ideas and findings have been pressed into active service in the workplace and Maslow's ideas soon found an appreciative audience among management writers. We shall examine the implications this had for the world of work later in the chapter.

ALDERFER'S ERG THEORY

Alderfer based his work on that of Maslow but made one or two new suggestions (Alderfer, 1972). Instead of Maslow's five levels of need Alderfer has proposed three basic groups of needs for Existence (E), Relatedness (R) and Growth (G). A comparison with Maslow is illustrated in Figure 13.2.

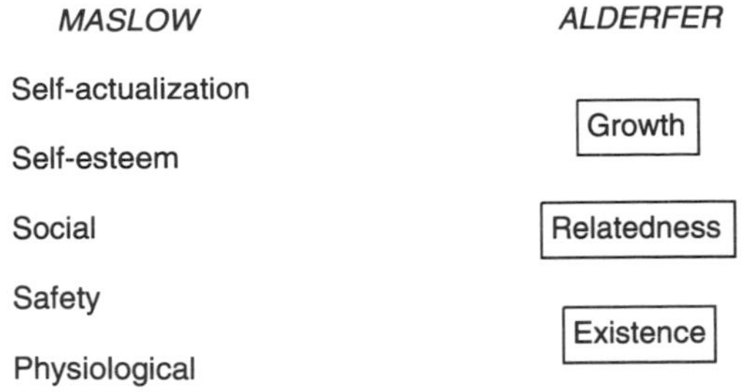

MASLOW	ALDERFER
Self-actualization	
	Growth
Self-esteem	
Social	Relatedness
Safety	
	Existence
Physiological	

FIGURE 13.2   Comparision of Maslow and Alderfer models on needs

Existence needs are material and include food, drink and pay.

Relatedness needs are psychological and fulfilled through personal relationships with family, friends and colleagues.

Growth needs are psychological and fulfilled by personal development.

Alderfer places less emphasis on the hierarchical order of needs than Maslow. Satisfaction of needs at one level may or may not lead on to experiencing needs at the next level, and more than one set of needs may be operating at the same time in any given individual. Moreover the frustration of a higher level of needs may lead the individual to regress to a lower level, Alderfer suggests, as opposed to Maslow's idea that frustration of a higher level need produces continuing efforts at satisfaction.

Perhaps the biggest difference between the two is in what happens once a need is satisfied. Maslow proposed that needs decrease in strength as they are satisfied, but research based on Alderfer's work has found that – at least for Relatedness and Growth – needs become *more* important to the individual as they are satisfied (Wanous and Zwany, 1977). This clearly has implications for the workplace which we will return to later.

HERZBERG'S TWO-FACTOR THEORY

One of the most influential theories of motivation since the Second World War, for both theorists and (to some extent) practitioners of management, has been that of Frederick Herzberg (Herzberg, 1966). Where Maslow had five factors in his categorisation and Alderfer three, Herzberg had two; *Hygiene* needs and *Motivator* needs. Unlike the other two theorists Herzberg's ideas on motivation were specifically work-oriented and grew out of his empirical research on job satisfaction where he interviewed people about their attitudes towards their work. (Herzberg, Mausner and Snyderman, 1959. KEY STUDY 11). Herzberg asked groups of engineers and accountants what made them feel strongly satisfied or dissatisfied.

Hygiene needs in Herzberg's theory are those that are usually satisfied by regular care and maintenance – pay, working conditions, job security, company policy, relations with colleagues and supervisors. Hygiene needs must be met for an organization to function properly. If they are not then people will be *dissatisfied* with their jobs. But however well hygiene needs are met they do not, by themselves, produce job *satisfaction*; for that to happen motivators are required, and these are intrinsic to the work itself. Achievement, independence, recognition, responsibility, challenge and so on, are examples of motivators. Where hygiene needs represent the avoidance of pain, the lower part of Maslow's hierarchy, motivators represent the need for self-actualization. We will return to Herzberg's work when we discuss job satisfaction in the next chapter.

Frank Landy has pointed out that a very similar two-factor theory had been suggested thirty years before Herzberg by a Belgian psychologist Henri De Man (Landy, 1989). This work also consisted of extensive interviews with workers about their attitudes towards their jobs, and the fact that both Herzberg and De Man arrived at the same interpretation of their data, despite their different circumstances, is certainly worth noting (De Man, 1929).

NEED ACHIEVEMENT THEORY

Several specific needs have been singled out for attention by various theorists, largely because of their importance to motivation at work. The need for *achievement* is probably the best known of these, and we have already encountered it when discussing 'the entrepreneurial personality' in Chapter 9.

The need for achievement was one of twenty needs motivating behaviour suggested by Henry Murray (Murray, 1938). Murray developed the *Thematic Apperception Test* (TAT), which we discussed in Chapter 6, as a way of gauging the strength of these needs. As we noted in Chapter 9, David McClelland then used the TAT to concentrate on the need for achievement, which he labelled n Ach, and tried to find both historical and cross-cultural evidence for its collective importance to societies (McClelland 1961: KEY STUDY 9).

People high on n Ach, McClelland maintained, have a preference for particular situations, where:

- the degree of risk involved is neither high nor low but moderate
- feedback on their performance is provided
- individual responsibility is acknowledged.

Moderately risky tasks would provide a reasonable probability of success for people high on n Ach whereas low risk situations would be unchallenging and unlikely to engage their interest. However tasks that look too daunting would also be avoided for *fear of failing* at them. Thus it is not making the attempt that counts but the outcome. Failure would apparently be too damaging to self-esteem, regardless of the worth and importance of the goal.

McClelland also investigated two other, and related, specific needs, the *need for affiliation* (n Aff) and the *need for power* (n Pow). These other two suggested needs have not been investigated to anything like the same extent as n Ach but they are interesting ideas and we will consider them in Chapter 15: 'Leadership'. The need for achievement is generally considered to be a higher-order psychological need than the other two, corresponding to Maslow's Self-esteem or Self-actualization levels, with n Aff at the Social level and n Pow at the Safety level.

SUMMARY

The four theories we have just considered may all now be summarised and compared, as in Figure 13.3.

Needs theories have attracted a good deal of attention in psychology, and with that, of course, a good deal of criticism. Indeed some people

Maslow	Alderfer	Herzberg	McClelland
Physiological	Existence	Hygiene	
Safety			Power
Social	Relatedness		Affiliation
Self-esteem	Growth	Motivators	Achievement
Self-actualization			

FIGURE 13.3 Classification of needs theorists

have grave doubts that needs even exist (Mischel, 1973). Most psychologists would probably agree that 'needs' as a concept, and attempts to classify needs and link them to behaviour, are thought-provoking and interesting but generally of limited usefulness.

Empirical research carried out to test needs theories has often failed to support them and where empirical work has been carried out by needs theorists themselves this has produced some heavy criticism – particularly in Herzberg's case – of the way the research was done (Salancik and Pfeffer, 1977). Needs theories have not been able to deal adequately with individual differences in motivation – like what does 'satisfaction' mean to different people – and deviations from the theoretical hierarchy of needs.

It has also failed to deal with what is admittedly one of the most difficult issues in psychology, the relationship between needs and behaviour. Thus a given need could be satisfied by different kinds of behaviour while the same behaviour in two people could be aimed at satisfying different needs. However, many people in psychology, and in management, intuitively feel that needs theories are tapping something very important about motivation and more recent evaluations have been somewhat kinder about them, believing for instance that only long-itudinal research could evaluate them fairly (Weiss and Adler, 1984).

IMPLICATIONS FOR THE WORKPLACE

Because of their high level of generality most needs theories have found their practical expression in the workplace through the informal theories we discussed earlier. With their stress on self-actualization, growth, achievement, autonomy and so forth, the needs theorists would be committed supporters of Theory Y assumptions. They would favour human relations training in organizations and a careful attention to individual development. And organizations that have considered themselves progressive, since the mid-1960s, have often adopted this approach. This is something we will explore in more detail in the next chapter.

The work of McClelland has, however, been open to a more detailed application to the workplace. A review of the theory, and research based on it, is contained in Beck (1983). McClelland himself has found that the need for achievement is not limited to childhood experience but can be learned by adults (McClelland and Winter, 1969). He has also found that high n Ach is not limited to business activity. Thus college students have been trained to create their own fantasies of achievement which have actually resulted in improved grades and academic attainments, and, one might reasonably predict, to future achievement in the world of work.

McClelland has always been interested in comparative tests of his theory over both time and place; of looking at developing societies in both a historical and a modern economic sense. He therefore devised a training programme to raise the n Ach levels of businessmen in a village in India (McClelland and Winter, 1969). Again this involved fantasies of achievement, this time of classic entrepreneurial activity, together with concrete plans for realising (or actualizing) these fantasies, and the discussion with others on the programme of the best methods for attaining their objectives.

In a follow-up study of this programme and its effectiveness McClelland compared it with a more conventional aid project carried out in a similar Indian village by the American Friends Service Committee, an agency noted for its international sensitivity (McClelland, 1978). The AFSC project was intended to raise living standards in the short-term – in water supply, sewage, education, health, farming and so on – and to teach the villages how to help themselves in the long-term.

An assessment of the AFSC project ten years later found that there was no long-term improvement at all in the villagers' lives. All the procedures and techniques they had been shown by the aid workers were largely abandoned when they left. The project itself had lasted for ten years and cost $1 000 000 and there was virtually nothing to show for it.

McClelland's work had very different results. The businessmen on his training programme became much more entrepreneurial, increasing the scope of existing enterprises and founding several new ones. They ended up providing jobs for over 5000 local people. And the whole programme lasted only six months and cost only $25 000.

What was the difference between the two projects? Small but crucial. The AFSC project was run on the assumption that people will do things that change their life if they only know *how* to do them. McClelland's grew out of his psychological concept of motivation that, unless people have a *need* to change their behaviour, knowledge by itself is irrelevant.

II EXPECTANCY THEORY

We have seen how needs theories were concerned mainly with the content of motivation. Expectancy theory by contrast is concerned mainly with the *process* of motivation; it deals with the question of *how* people decide on what behaviour to engage in. There is one major expectancy theory and it is usually associated with the work of Vroom (1964).

The theory Vroom proposed is known also sometimes as 'instrumentality' theory but more often as *VIE* theory, standing for *Valence, Instrumentality* and *Expectancy*. The term 'valence' is borrowed from chemistry and refers to how attractive or unattractive a particular outcome or psychological objective is to us. It is based entirely on our anticipation of the desired outcome rather than what happens afterwards. Obvious examples like gaining promotion or a particular life partner may not actually coincide completely with anticipation.

The 'instrumentality' of a given outcome is the extent to which it is instrumental in securing for us a further outcome that we desire, for example a promotion being instrumental in providing more money or a partner enabling us to experience emotional closeness.

Finally the element of 'expectancy' links behaviour to outcome. It is the point where, according to Vroom, we estimate the probability that a particular behaviour will achieve the desired outcome, that is the odds for or against gaining the promotion or the partner.

Expectancy theory proposes therefore that we ask ourselves three kinds of questions before any action that we consider taking. Working backwards from the event these questions are:

● if I attempt this action how likely am I to succeed? (Expectancy)
● would successful action lead to the desired outcome? (Instrumentality)
● how much do I value these outcomes? (Valence)

The theory argues that the answers to these questions are combined in determining our motivation. As these factors are multiplicative in their effect negative Instrumentality, or zero Valence or Expectancy, means that that behavioural choice would not be pursued.

Expectancy theory has an intuitive appeal to management because of its rational and quantifying approach (Porter and Lawler, 1968). The theory has stimulated a lot of discussion and research among psychologists, resulting in some support and a lot of criticism, pretty much along the lines of their reaction to Behaviourism in fact, from which it is not a million miles removed. That is, while the VIE theory can explain a lot of the immediate motivation behind the workplace behaviour that has been studied there is also a lot that it can't explain (Schwab, Olian-Gottlieb and Heneman, 1979).

A consciously calculating, rational decision-making theory simply ignores a large part of our lives. We have already seen throughout this book that there are many non-rational, irrational, unconscious or uncalculating aspects to our behaviour, in the workplace and out of it. Moreover the multiplicative aspect of the theory often seems to be much too complicated for the cognitive capacities of many people to deal with

(Slovic, Fischoff and Lichtenstein, 1977). We have also seen several times already how we have a tendency to simplify our psychological processes wherever we can. In one study of VIE nearly two-thirds of the subjects just added V + E to reach their decision (Stahl and Harrell, 1981).

Finally the *intrinsic* motivation to be found in achieving something because it is enjoyable to do so for its own sake is not usually found in expectancy theory. It is much more concerned with *extrinsic* outcomes, like promotion, money or status (Bandura, 1987).

III   EQUITY THEORY

Equity theory is another example of a theory concerned with the process of motivation, and in particular the cognitive factors involved in the way an individual deals with motivational forces. The cognitive factors emphasized in this case are those that we use, it is suggested, in making *social comparisons* between the situations of other people and our own.

Comparing our personal situation with that of other individuals and groups is fundamental to the way we make sense of our lives (Statt, 1977). Our behaviour in the world of work is one aspect of that process. Equity theory is specifically concerned with our sense of fairness and justice about the way we and others are treated at work in terms of the ratios of *inputs* (like experience, qualifications and effort) to *outcomes* (like pay, promotion and status). The theory holds that we are pushed psychologically to *equalise* the two, however we perceive equality.

The earliest research related to this issue was conducted during the Second World War. A series of interviews with a diverse group of people by Herbert Hyman produced the concept of a *reference group* by which people seemed to measure their own social situation (Hyman, 1942). In judging their status, whether financial, intellectual or in terms of prestige, people did not do so by comparing themselves with the population as a whole but with particular groups within it. And it is these reference groups, chosen because they are of particular importance to the lives of the people concerned, that are used as the standard of comparison. Thus a salesman will compare his salary and lifestyle to those of other salesmen rather than pop stars – or the chief executive of his own company.

An early example of reference group comparison in operation was reported by American social scientists in the course of their regular monitoring of military morale during the Second World War (Merton and Rossi, 1949). At one point the troops were asked about their chances of promotion within their branch of the military and it was discovered that their subjective assessment was inversely related to the objective reality. Thus although members of the Army Air Corps had a much greater chance of promotion than those in the Military Police, for example, they were much more pessimistic about their chances.

The explanation given for this finding was that the members of each unit used that unit as a reference group rather than the military as a whole. Those in the Army Air Corps were therefore comparing themselves to a group in which they could see other people being promoted while they were not, and they therefore felt deprived. But as promotion was relatively rare in the Military Police there was little occasion for feeling deprived or pessimistic about one's own chances.

Our perception of deprivation therefore appears to be a *relative* rather than an absolute matter. In terms of the relationship between inputs and outcomes, so does our perception of equity (Adams, 1965). When we perceive that other people in our reference group have a similar ratio of inputs to outputs as we do we experience that as an equitable state of affairs. If the ratio favours other people, so that we feel underpaid or under-promoted by comparison, we experience that as inequitable and are motivated to do something about it because of our uncomfortable feelings of injustice or unfairness.

Equity theory also holds that we should feel similarly motivated if we perceive the ratio to be inequitable in the other direction, so that we see ourselves as *over-paid* or *over-promoted*. But you will be astonished to learn that we seem to cope with this kind of inequity much more comfortably. People may accept that the situation is unfair but still feel, bravely, that they can live with it (Austin, McGinn and Susmilch, 1980). Or if they do feel uncomfortable it doesn't last long (Carrell and Dittrich, 1978). Or they might *say* they feel guilty and uncomfortable but actually feel no such thing (Rivera and Tedeschi, 1976).

Clearly the theory doesn't work too well in a situation of over-reward so for the moment we'll consider the effects of perceived under-reward only. However we will return to this issue when we consider attitude change and job satisfaction in the next chapter. But the issue of equity is not quite as straightforward (naturally) as it first appeared.

It has been argued that people appear to have more than one definition of equity in mind. At least three have been suggested (Birnbaum, 1983):

- *relative* equity is the definition we've been using here, where people with the same relative input receive the same relative outcome (for example a five percent increase in salary).
- *absolute* equity is where people with the same input get exactly the same outcome (for example a $5000 increase in salary).
- *adjustment* equity is intended to equalise outcomes over the long run where people have the same inputs but started off with a different level of reward (for example the person on the lower

salary level receives an increase that is more in both dollar terms and percentage terms, until the gap is closed).

It has also been pointed out that there seem to be individual differences in how important any concept of equity is to people (Huseman, Hatfield and Miles, 1987). And there is evidence that men are more concerned than women about inequity (Brockner and Adsit, 1986). So equity theory has to be classed as another interesting but limited account of human motivation.

IV GOAL-SETTING THEORY

Goal-setting theory was first formulated by E. A. Locke (Locke, 1968: KEY STUDY 12). Locke argued that having a (conscious) specific goal or purpose in mind that one was trying to accomplish was the most important factor in explaining motivation. The research based on this simple proposition has been enormous – more than all the other motivation research put together – and goal-setting theory has been rivalled only by Herzberg's two-factor theory in its impact on both academic and managerial approaches to work motivation over the past 25 years.

Locke drew on two primary sources for his own work, one academic and the other managerial. The academic source was T. A. Ryan who argued for the role of an individual's *intention* in understanding her motivated behaviour (Ryan, 1970). The managerial source was Peter Drucker's celebrated formulation of Management By Objectives (MBO) which highlighted the importance of setting specific objectives for – and by – each member of an organization, as well as the various branches of the organization. Drucker emphasized particularly the element of self-control and taking responsibility for one's own work (Drucker, 1954).

Reviews of research on the effects of goal-setting on performance, whether by Locke and his colleagues or by others, have found a lot of support for the theory, which has been applied to groups as diverse as professors and lumberjacks (Locke and Latham, 1990; Tubbs, 1986; Mento, Steel and Karren, 1987). The theory seems to work best where three conditions are present:

1. Feedback

We noted more than once in the last chapter how crucially important feedback is to the learning process. This is a particular example of that process in which having *knowledge of results* provides someone with the information necessary to judge how she is doing in the pursuit of her goal. Moreover having that information may in itself help to strengthen her motivation to make further progress (Locke *et al.*, 1981). Adding feedback like this to the setting of goals has been found to be most effective in improving performance; more than either factor by itself and much more than using neither factor (Nemeroff and Cosentino, 1979).

2. Setting specific goals

Setting specific goals for people is a more effective way of improving their performance than simply asking them to do their best. Having a target to aim at seems to be psychologically helpful for people.

3. Setting difficult goals

Provided that people *accept* difficult goals for themselves they will lead to better performance than easy goals. (In psychology that kind of proviso, however, is always a crucial one.)

There are other findings from this huge body of research that have achieved widespread support:

- people must have the necessary ability first before goal-setting can affect their performance. This is not quite as obvious as it sounds. In a 'can-do' environment where the social norm is that you can do anything if you only want to badly enough it is a salutory reminder that there are some things you may not be able to do no matter how clear your intention or how steely your resolve, or how great the reward. If you have trouble distinguishing your left hand from your right you are not going to become a concert pianist no matter how motivated you may be.
- material incentives, like money, *may* improve performance by increasing commitment to a particular goal. (But see the above point!)
- participation in decision making about setting goals does not appear to have any more effect on performance than assigned goals which have been justified to, and accepted by, the people in question. But the justification is apparently necessary. Simply assigning goals to people is less effective (Latham, Erez and Locke, 1988).
- people who are confident of their ability to perform a particular task are more likely to be successful at it, other things being equal, than people who are not. This dimension of individual difference is

often referred to as *self-efficacy* (Bandura, 1986). This concept should be distinguished from two we have already encountered, 'self-esteem' (a sense of one's own worth) and 'locus of control' (a belief about the nature of causality in one's life).

CRITIQUE OF GOAL-SETTING THEORY

It would appear that goal-setting theory is the best account of motivation we've had yet. Not only do the vast majority of laboratory studies support it but it seems to work just as well in workplace studies. The oft-quoted lumberjack research is a good case in point (Latham and Locke, 1979).

Before the lumberjacks were set a specific goal they were asked just to do their best in a job that required them to fell trees and load them on to trucks for delivery to the sawmill. They loaded the trucks to 60 per cent of their legal capacity. They were then asked to load the truck to 94 per cent capacity, a goal the men considered difficult but do-able. No rewards or punishments were given in connection with this goal yet the lumberjacks achieved it within a few weeks. What's more they sustained this level of performance for at least the next seven years. Apparently the group norm had been changed and a new work practice established (see Chapter 7). The accountants were, of course, delighted. They calculated that in the first nine months alone the company had saved some $250 000. So does goal-setting theory win the motivational jackpot? Well, you will already have observed that no invention of a better psychological mousetrap, from Frederick Taylor on, has ever been *that* straightforward, so why should goal-setting be any different? And your astute observation would be correct. There are indeed some unanswered questions.

In the first place there is nothing new about goal-setting in the workplace, or at least in the use of knowledge of results feedback which is at the heart of it. A field study in an American power station gave each operative an indication of the efficiency of his boiler, which resulted in an annual saving for the power station on coal consumption of $330 000, the same rate as in the lumberjack experiment. But as this study was done nearly half a century earlier the relative saving was many times greater (Bingham, 1932). If knowledge of results had such a striking practical effect then, why did it disappear for fifty years?

A few other questions have been raised about the theory (Austin and Bobko, 1985). One of the most important of these deals with the issue of *quality* of work as opposed to quantity. Studies of goal-setting have invariably dealt with quantifiable aspects of work performance, like percentages achieved or money saved, which is fair enough as the most obvious test of the theory. But for many people, especially in managerial and professional jobs, the essence of the job is its quality. Quantifying what they do might be experienced as inappropriate, or misleading, or even a violation of their self-image. Consider the uproar caused by attempts to impose a performance related pay system on teachers, doctors and police officers, for example.

Another important difficulty with the theory is the inconvenient fact that many jobs have conflicting, if not mutually exclusive, goals. The most familiar of these is perhaps the pursuit of quality or quantity under a condition of time constraint. How should goals be set in a highly competitive service industry where both quality and quantity are considered essential for the viability of the business? Or what if an individual's goals include the desire for both the camaraderie of the work group and the lonely responsibility of the chief executive?

It is also far from clear, in those field studies where goal-setting has such a dramatic impact on performance, just *why* it did so, as opposed to the particular technique used. The authors of both the lumberjack study and the earlier power station study reported that there was a lot of competition among the workers concerned who treated the situation almost like a game. Was this the motivational engine involved? We don't know and the theory doesn't help us there.

There is some evidence that goal-setting may not work if the levels, or norms, of expected performance in a situation are different from those of the goal. In other words if there are already strong work group norms in existence about what constitutes acceptable performance, as in the Hawthorne studies, the goals set may not be accepted by the group members (Meyer and Gellatly, 1988).

This is but one example of the many situational factors that can influence the setting of goals in a real-life workplace. As we also noted in Chapter 7: 'Group dynamics and working-group relationships', this is particularly true of interpersonal relationships with supervisors and colleagues and the way these relationships interact with the personal agenda that everyone brings to the workplace (Hollenbeck and Klein, 1987).

Part of anyone's work situation, as we saw in Chapter 4, is the length of their time horizon. Hard as it was for people like Donald Roy (KEY STUDY 2) and other academic researchers to work at a mind-numbing job, they knew they would be returning to a slightly more stimulating workplace in a matter of months. But what about the people they studied who knew they were there *for the foreseeable future*. How are they likely to feel about being encouraged to set high goals for themselves?

Finally it appears that in a new task situation, where the generation of different ways of accomplishing the task are particularly important, the setting of specific, difficult goals results in a *less* effective outcome than simply asking people to do their best. People seemed to be directing their resources so much towards the goal that had been set that they had too little left for dealing with the task itself (Earley, Connolly and Ekegren, 1989). In sum then it looks as if goal-setting theory also has to be classified as interesting and useful, but limited.

Motivation theories in general

Just as in our review of formal personality theories in Chapter 9 we have seen how each of the major formal theories of motivation is capable of explaining some aspects of an extremely complex issue very well, though none comes close to being a universal theory. However there have been a few signs of a convergence, and even an integration, between various theories.

On the face of it goal-setting theory and expectancy theory would appear to be in direct conflict with each other. Expectancy theory predicts that people are more likely to be motivated by relatively easy tasks they feel confident about accomplishing, whereas goal-setting theory would have them aim for relatively difficult tasks at which they might fail.

This apparent contradiction has been resolved by the Japanese researcher Matsui and his colleagues who examined the V and the E (valences and expectancies) of VIE expectancy theory to see what their influence might be on goal-setting. In an attempt to explain why (rather than how) people accept certain goals they concluded that the value (or Valence) that succeeding at a difficult task has for people is more powerful than a low expectation of success. So a greater effort would then be produced which would increase chances of successful performance (Matsui, Okada and Mizuguchi, 1981; Matsui, Okada and Inoshita, 1983).

It has also been suggested that some aspects of needs theory and goal-setting theory might be more closely related than had been thought originally (Hollenbeck and Brief, 1987). In particular the need for achievement has been suggested as a possible influence on the difficulty of a particular goal set, the amount of commitment involved in achieving it and the ultimate value that it had for the individual. And you will recall the importance of feedback to the development of n Ach. In fact it could be argued that at certain points on the hierarchy of needs people have a need for goal-setting, and indeed for equity of treatment.

Motivation and management

Throughout this chapter we have seen illustrations of motivated behaviour in the world of work. Most of the theorists we have considered and most of the research based on their theories is concerned, implicitly or explicitly, with the factors that motivate people to work, and to perform well at work. It is a short, though crucial, step from there to adopting the full-frontal managerial position, represented by bookstall titles like *How to Motivate People: A Guide for Managers* (Dell, 1989). Before we deal with the implications of that position, though, we need to examine the prior question, 'Why do people work?'

Why do people work?

Only the needs theorists of motivation have addressed this fundamental question in any way, and that in general terms only. Work satisfies certain needs they argue. But what needs for what people, why, when and how are another matter. For most of us, of course, there is no choice; we work because we have to. Our physiological/existence/hygiene needs take care of that. But what if we didn't have to? What if we won millions on a lottery and never had to go out to work again: would we still do so?

Well for most of us the answer appears to be 'yes we would'. About two-thirds of the people surveyed on this question say that they would continue to work – and about half of these would even stay in the same job (Warr, 1982). If (like me) you find this hard to believe, you may not be surprised to discover that, in the event, people do not always do what they say they would do, as we shall see in the next chapter. Nevertheless even the sceptics among us have to admit that for most people there is a lot more to work than simply making a living.

We have also seen other instances in this book of the limits that material factors can have on motivation. You will recall the disgruntled nurses in Chapter 6 for whom pay was *not* the problem, despite being poorly paid. And the Hawthorne studies, and others, of Chapter 7 showed that being part of a group could be more important for people than financial incentives.

Right away there seems to be a conflict here with the Theory X assumption of work motivation that people work purely for the money. You get them to work by paying them a wage; you keep them there by threatening to remove it; and you get them to work harder by increasing it. This crude version of Behaviourist reward and punishment theory has been greatly modified in psychology but apparently it is still commonly assumed to be true by many economists, who even have a Latin term for the person it describes – 'Homo Economicus' (Economic Man). It also seems to retain a certain attraction for many politicians and Treasury officials, in setting tax and welfare policies for instance. And it is depressingly familiar, of course, in employers.

The kind of psychological contracts and industrial relations that flow from this approach are also depressingly familiar. The managerial stance on motivation that follows it is thus openly and completely authoritarian. As we saw when we discussed Henry Ford's assembly line in Chapter 1 this approach must be able to afford a plentiful supply of labour because of high turnover, plus absenteeism and sabotage. There is not much room here for any subtle managerial thinking about motivation.

Motivating people at work

In striking contrast to this view of motivation is the Theory Y type of approach which would emphasise making work meaningful for people through growth, achievement, autonomy and, ultimately, self-actualization. We will look at the practical implications that would arise out of Theory Y – and the paternalistic Social Assumptions model – when we consider job satisfaction in the next chapter. What I would like to do in this final section of the present chapter is to examine the assumptions that Theory Y makes about motivation a little more critically.

Any organization that considers itself progressive usually flies some version of the Theory Y flag proudly from its masthead. Yet no work organization that I know of is set up for the express purpose of helping its members to self-actualize. Whether profit-making, governmental, statutory or voluntary, organizations have a set of objectives that exist irrespective of the people who work in them. A very obvious point once made, I realise, but it does need making none the less.

The most important implication of this starting point is that the people responsible for attaining the organization's objectives, the management, are also responsible for seeing that the people they manage fit themselves and their motivation into this pre-existing world – or leave the organization if they cannot do so. Under a Theory X regime the rules are clear and methods of management quite straightforward. Managers 'manage' – that is they tell people what to do all the time – and those who are 'managed' do what they're told. To paraphrase Stalin, a great believer in Theory X, 'the function of the worker is to obey'.

But managers cannot operate that way under an explicit Theory Y system. They have to consult the people they manage about the job; they have to accept their autonomy to do the job as they see fit; they have to give up their close supervisory role of the people for whom they are, still, responsible. That organizational management collectively, and many managers individually, find this changed conception of managing very difficult to deal with we have already seen in Chapter 7 with the collapse of the Volkswagen and Volvo experiments based on Theory Y-type values.

However even if all managers could be persuaded to alter their conceptions of what it meant to be a manager to fit in with Theory Y values they would still be responsible for mediating between individual and organization, and they would still have to accord organizational needs – as defined by the people in control of the organization – paramount importance. If the people being managed found their needs in conflict with those of the organization managers would then have the responsibility for reconciling the two and reconciling them, inevitably, in favour of the organization. Theory Y values would preclude the use of coercion, so what could managers do?

Critics of the use of motivation techniques in management have argued that what happens in this case is that managers have to persuade (that is manipulate) their staff into believing that the organization's needs and objectives are really identical to their own. They do this, runs the argument, by narrowing down and focussing the psychologist's conceptions of motivation to fit the particular organizational situation (Thompson and McHugh, 1990):

> Information about the social and material rewards available, or perhaps the danger of redundancy, can be manipulated to reinforce control practices by getting the worker to internalise the rationale for increasing productivity. What is effectively happening here is that extrinsic factors, those largely outside the control of the individual such as pay and conditions, are being translated into intrinsic factors. These include those processes assumed to be under individual control, for instance, satisfaction and motivation, thus making employees personally responsible for their own objective situation. . . .
>
> That management has become such a great consumer of theories and techniques of motivation is in itself an indication that there is little in much work which can in itself act as a source of meaning . . . The 'motivations' served are the managerial aims of greater 'unit' productivity, the drive for more work and less waste operating under the cover story of a *consensus-based* participation provided by motivational techniques. (pp. 278–9; original italics and quotation marks)

The unquestioning and unquestioned assumption that an important part of a manager's job is to motivate her staff would certainly lend support to this critique. Would anyone seriously suggest that surgeons or psychologists need to be motivated in this way? Or vets or vicars? Or actors, artists and astronomers? There is a serious danger, therefore, that the unquestioned assumptions of management and motivation may result in ever-more sophisticated, though ultimately self-defeating, attempts to persuade people that a job they know is pretty worthless, but are resigned to doing because they need the money, has real value for them.

As we will see in the next chapter, when we discuss job satisfaction, people are not easily conned by these means. But what is the poor manager to do then? This is a classic bind of middle management and very hard to deal with, especially as they themselves are usually the prime objects of motivational techniques.

At the risk of getting too prescriptive I would like to address this question because it has important implications for the study of motivation in organizations. Taking as cool and objective a look as possible at what they are being asked to do would certainly seem to be the first step. If the objective situation is that the people they manage have mindless jobs, or the employer is exploitative, or the working conditions are poor it would be difficult, though not impossible, for them to suggest to senior management that perhaps these conditions might be dealt with first.

If such conditions did exist, without any sign of improvement, managers would not, of course, need to inform their staff about them. They would already know. It might be possible for managers to agree on the objective situation, implicitly if necessary, with their staff and then to concentrate on the problem of satisfying those particular needs where they could have some effect. In other words they might be able to deal with *real* as opposed to manufactured motivation.

We have noted in several contexts in this book how important the relationship with his or her supervisor is to everyone in a work organization. This is one need that a manager is always in a position to do something about. In Chapter 6 we traced some of the basic interactions between two individuals, that make up so much of one's working life in organizations, through the concepts of Transactional Analysis. There is another TA concept that we might usefully consider at this point. It is known as *stroking*.

The term derives from the way people physically handle infants. As Eric Berne puts it (Berne, 1964):

> By an extension of meaning, 'stroking' may be employed colloquially to denote any act implying recognition of another's presence. Hence a *stroke* may be used as the fundamental unit of social action. An exchange of strokes constitutes a *transaction*, which is the unit of social intercourse.(p 15; original italics and quotation marks)

Recognition in this context implies respect, and there is no more powerful motivator than that. Even in the biggest multi-national business of them all, organized crime, respect is (so one gathers) the deepest need around. Far more important than mere money – which may well be used to try to buy respect. Strokes may vary in intensity, from a cheery 'good morning' to a bunch of flowers to an extended enquiry about someone's health when they come back from sick leave.

But strokes should be distinguished from rewards in that they are given unconditionally, not for *doing* something but for *being* someone. And this stroking invariably sets up a reciprocity that has a dynamic of its own. Thus if negative feedback is given by a manager to a subordinate it will be within the context of this stroking relationship and received accordingly, with a minimum of defended ego in what should be an Adult-Adult interaction.

This seems to me the only framework in which the issue of 'difficult' employees or 'mavericks' can be understood. As we have seen in various ways throughout this book people will defend their sense of self from organizational attack. In some people at some times this will take the form of 'acting out' in ways that are officially disapproved of.

While there may be some people whose own personality difficulties require them to be members of the awkward squad no matter what situation they find themselves in, it is much more likely that 'mavericks' are people whose need to give to the organization creatively is being frustrated, and that 'difficult' employees feel unrespected. A stroking relationship with people in these situations will not lead to rapid self-actualization but it will allow manager and managed to deal with real, ongoing and important needs and form a sound basis for the difficult task of helping individual and organization live together as fruitfully as possible.

CHAPTER 14

Attitudes, attitude change and job satisfaction

In our discussion of motivation in the last chapter we touched, at several points, on the issue of job satisfaction. In the latter part of this chapter we will consider job satisfaction, and its implications for both individual and organization, in the context of the forming and changing of *attitudes*. Like motivations attitudes have an important emotional component to them and are very complex areas of psychology. So before we can turn our attention to a specific set of attitudes like job satisfaction we need to examine the attitudinal framework that contains it.

Attitudes and opinions

Most people would use the words *attitudes* and *opinions* interchangeably in many situations, along with 'values' and 'beliefs'. Psychologists have found it useful, however, to make a distinction between these terms. *Opinions* (and beliefs) are mainly *cognitive* and would be offered in answer to the question 'What do you *think* about X?' *Attitudes* (and values) are mainly *affective*, with a high emotional content, and would be given in answer to the question 'What do you *feel* about X?'

The difference is between saying 'New York City is big' and 'New York City is terrible/wonderful'. An attitude, while it includes a cognitive, evaluative component, is (crucially) emotionally charged, making it more powerful (and dynamic and difficult to deal with) than a relatively emotionless opinion.

There is a third component to an attitude, usually described as a *behavioural predisposition* or 'tendency' to act in a certain way towards a particular object, whether abstract or concrete, alive or inanimate. It is important to notice that this predisposition is an *intention* to act, for as we'll see later in the chapter there is a great deal of slippage between expressing an attitude about something, however strongly felt, and acting on it. You may tell your friends how much you hate your job and intend to leave it but if you need the money and there's nothing else available it may not be possible for you to carry out your intention.

Attitude change

Attitudes are entirely learned, and they are learned the way most other human behaviour is learned. Through our socialization process, as we noted in Chapter 9, we imitate our parents and are rewarded for it; we respond to the influence of our peers and other social groups; we discover what attitudes are appropriate to our social situation and what attitudes we find most compatible with our self-image.

The important point in dealing with changes in attitudes is not what attitude is being expressed but how deep the emotional roots behind it are. For example most people would regard the shape of the Planet Earth and its relationship to its Sun as cognitive matters, matters of factual information to be decided by scientific research. Their belief that the Earth is more or less round and part of a heliocentric system orbiting the Sun has no emotional content whatsoever.

But despite the scientific evidence there have been many people who believed (and some who still do) that the Earth was flat and that we lived in a geocentric universe where everything orbited around a stationary Earth. Indeed the great astronomer Galileo was threatened with death for suggesting otherwise. His persecutors and their supporters could not be convinced by rational argument to change their belief or opinion because it was actually a deeply-rooted, emotionally-held attitude which they *needed* to believe. And if psychologists have discovered anything about the human condition it is, as we have seen repeatedly throughout this book, that when it comes to Reason versus Emotion there's no contest. Beliefs about issues that people regard as matters of fact are easy to change; attitudes that are social expressions of powerful individual emotions are very difficult to change.

It's easy to laugh at the flat earthers and to feel superior to Galileo's persecutors but what about people who believe, despite scientific evidence to the contrary, that men are physically and intellectually superior to women? These attitudes – which may be held by both men and women – are probably learned from parents in early childhood. They are part of the emotionally charged package that comes with learning the difference between male and female. And even where people are convinced *intellectually* that these attitudes are factually untrue, it may be very difficult for them to change their *feelings*, and therefore their behaviour.

Trying to change people's attitudes, in order to change their behaviour, is an integral part of the world of work. Selling is the most obvious example of this but it is not just relevant to people in sales, advertising or public relations. Or even to people who make a living by selling religion as evangelists, or themselves as politicians. It applies to anyone who ever wants, for whatever reason, to persuade his or her colleagues to act in one way rather than another. Although we are rarely conscious of it we are constantly being bombarded by attempts to change our attitudes, both at home and at work, and we ourselves will often try to change the attitudes of other people.

As with all the other psychological processes we have studied we will examine the constituent parts of the process of attitude change individually. But in real life of course they interact with each other all the time. We will consider then the *source* of the communication, the *communication* itself and the *audience* for that communication.

I   The source

There are two important factors that determine the persuasion of the communicator who is the source of a communication aimed at changing people's attitudes; *credibility* and *attractiveness*.

(A) CREDIBILITY

What makes a communicator credible is to be perceived by the target of the communication as being *expert* and *trustworthy*. The more a communicator seems to know what he or she is talking about and seems to be trustworthy the more effective will her/his communication be (McGuire, 1985).

Arguing against one's own apparent interests is a particularly effective way of gaining the target's trust, as when a gangster argues for a tougher criminal justice system (Walster, Aronson and Abrahams, 1966). Thus it has been suggested that the heir to the R.J. Reynolds tobacco fortune, who urged sufferers from smoking-related illnesses to sue the tobacco companies, will be the most persuasive advocate for the anti-smoking lobby (Aronson, 1992).

Historically there are powerful examples of this effect when the source is arguing the opposite of what his position is popularly supposed to be. In a 1955 broadcast Winston Churchill, the aristocratic, Conservative Prime Minister, declared that 'Trade unionism in Britain has done a good job for our people and our nation'. Similarly in 1960, at his farewell address, President Eisenhower warned of the growing power of the 'military-industrial complex' in the United States. This would have been a striking enough statement for any Republican President to make. From one of America's most celebrated generals it was positively startling.

In Chapter 11 we noted that confident, articulate interview candidates were likely to be the most successful. This factor seems to carry over into the field of communication as well. It has been found that smooth, fast-talking communicators tend to be more credible than slow, hesitant ones (Miller *et al.*, 1976). In an era of public discussion by television soundbites this seems a particularly depressing finding.

However it has also been found that under certain conditions communicators low on credibility can be just as effective as those with high credibility, not at the time of the communication but a few weeks later. What seems to happen in this *sleeper effect* is that the message is important enough for people to remember, while they forget who gave it to them (Cook *et al.*, 1979).

(B) ATTRACTIVENESS

But why then are sports stars paid a lot of money to advertise razor blades on television, or showbiz stars to advertise washing-up liquid? Do they really know all that more than the rest of us about shaving or washing-up? And it's not as if we thought they were touting the stuff for free, out of a sense of great conviction. On American television it is quite common for actors to advertise products on the basis of the fictitious parts they play in a series. Thus Karl Malden, who played a detective, has reassured punters worried about theft on holiday of the advantage of using a particular brand of traveller's cheque, and Robert Young, who played a doctor, has given them valuable advice on health care.

In the case of the sports and showbiz stars trustworthiness and expertise would not come into it. Their *attractiveness* as popular celebrities is their selling point. In the case of the actors it's the attractiveness of a fictitious character. We also saw in Chapter 11, when we discussed the unconscious influences on interviewers, how we are inclined to favour attractive people and to try to please them. And the way to please the celebrities in the television ads is, of course, to buy whatever it is they're trying to flog to us.

The accepted wisdom in social psychology is that this ploy works, but only up to a point. That is, it only applies to *trivial* issues like choosing an aspirin or a detergent, but not for really important issues like choosing a President (Aronson, 1992). Well, I suppose it depends what you mean by 'trivial'. After all our whole consumer economy rests on the assumption that people will continually make these – essentially trivial and irrational – kinds of decisions. And why are Presidential, and other, candidates so keen to have celebrity endorsement if they don't affect voter behaviour? (I suppose you could argue that the choice of candidate people are usually faced with *is* pretty trivial and this is good evidence for it.)

II The communication

The nature of the communication itself, and the manner of its presentation, are also influential factors in its effectiveness. Several key questions are often considered here (Aronson, 1992):

- should the appeal be to reason or emotion?
- are images or statistics more persuasive?
- should the message be one-sided or two-sided?
- the primacy or recency effect
- the size of discrepancy in attitude being addressed.

(I) REASON OR EMOTION

This is a particularly difficult distinction to draw. We have seen throughout this book how pervasive emotional influence is on what appear to be rational mental processes. Modern research in this area no longer tries to make the distinction of reason versus emotion but looks rather at the effects of different levels of emotional arousal, and particularly the arousal of *fear*. Is it more persuasive to present a mild threat to the target audience or should you really try to scare people?

Such a question is of interest to insurance companies or people running public health and safety campaigns for instance. Do you persuade people more effectively not to drink and drive by hitting them with pictures of broken bodies and machines in gory detail or do you soften the impact with less explicit images and more reasoned argument perhaps?

The answer seems to be that the more fear you arouse in people the more likely they are to be influenced by the communication, *provided* that you give people clear and practical ways of dealing with the fear you have aroused (Leventhal, 1970; Leventhal, Meyer and Nerenz, 1980). It is the *combination* of high emotional arousal plus specific instructions for dealing with it that produces the effect. Either factor on its own is ineffective.

However it also looks as though this effect is context-specific. It can be used to increase the take-up of inoculation against a particular disease, for instance, but it doesn't seem to work if the problem and the solution are more diffuse and related to a change in lifestyle. In particular it doesn't seem to work in the fight against AIDS (Leishman, 1987). But then there is no inoculation at present, or any other medical procedure, that can prevent AIDS, or the acquisition of the AIDS virus HIV. It is a matter of changing sexual and social behaviour and not a medical matter at all.

(II) ARE IMAGES OR STATISTICS MORE PERSUASIVE?

The old Chinese proverb about one little picture being worth a thousand words seems to make intuitive sense and is widely quoted in many contexts. Can we extend 'picture' to include mental picture and 'words' to include numbers? When we face a buying decision about a stereo system or a car do we consult the appropriate Consumer's Reports and make a rational decision based solely on the statistical findings from painstaking tests and surveys?

Well we might like to think so but it does appear as if we find personal anecdotes about a particular brand or model somewhat more persuasive, even if it's (say) just one negative instance of a car falling apart as opposed to many hundreds of positive instances to the contrary. Apparently the vividness of the individual image is more persuasive than a list of statistics (Nisbett and Ross, 1980). The psychological hook is more powerful.

Elliot Aronson and his colleagues have applied this effect to energy conservation in the home. They trained representatives of local power companies to use vivid images rather than facts and figures when recommending energy saving measures to homeowners. Thus they did not recommend weatherproofing by pointing out gaps around door-frames and measures of heat loss but by suggesting that these gaps added up to the size of a basketball, 'and if you had a hole that size in your wall, wouldn't you want to patch it up?' Before this image was introduced into the communication only 15 per cent of homeowners had accepted the recommendations; afterwards the figure rose to 61 per cent (Gonzales, Aronson and Costanzo, 1988).

(III) ONE-SIDED OR TWO-SIDED ARGUMENTS

Is it more persuasive to present only one side of an argument in your communication or to mention the opposing side (before demolishing it of course)? Like so many simple-sounding questions in psychology the answer is 'it all depends'. This issue was first studied by social psychologists interested in the indoctrination of American servicemen during the Second World War (Hovland, Lumsdaine and Sheffield, 1949).

There were two major findings from this research:

- for people who held the same opinion as the communicator the one-sided approach was more effective; for people who held the opposing opinion the two-sided approach was more effective
- if people were uninformed they responded best to a one-sided argument; if they were well-informed a two-sided argument was more persuasive.

These findings were replicated in the 1960s and are still generally accepted as valid (Tesser and Shaffer, 1990).

(IV) THE PRIMACY OR RECENCY EFFECT

When we discussed the unconscious factors involved in interviews in Chapter 11 we noted that interviewers might be influenced by the order in which candidates presented themselves, with the first candidate possibly benefiting from the *primacy* effect and the last from the *recency* effect, depending on the circumstances. These order effects were first teased out in an experiment which simulated a jury trial where the subjects (the 'jurors') received the arguments of both the prosecution and the defence (Miller and Campbell, 1959).

The key factor is time. The recency effect is found when there is a relatively large gap between the two arguments and a small gap between the second presentation and the jury's verdict. The primacy effect is found when there is a small gap between the two presentations and a large gap between the second one and the verdict.

(V) SIZE OF ATTITUDE DISCREPANCY

The final aspect of the persuasiveness of a communication we will consider is the size of the discrepancy between it and the attitude of the target audience. Generally speaking people are more inclined to change their attitudes if there is only a relatively small discrepancy between them and the message. However if the source of the communication is a particularly credible one the *greater* the discrepancy between the message and the attitude of the audience, the *more* likely will they be to change their attitude (Aronson, Turner and Carlsmith, 1963; McGuire, 1985).

III   The audience

The final set of factors we will deal with concerns the characteristics of the audience for a communication. We have already seen how the pre-existing attitudes of an audience and the extent to which they are informed about the relevant issues can affect the persuasiveness of a given message. We will take a quick look here at some other factors, *self-esteem*, the need for *social approval*, the *prior experience* of the audience just before the communication is made and whether the audience is asked to make a *public commitment*.

(I) SELF-ESTEEM

Though there are differences of interpretation here there is some evidence to suggest that people of low self-esteem may be more persuasible by a given communication than people of high self-esteem (Zellner, 1970). Certainly there is a lot of evidence from the conformity studies of Asch and Milgram, which we discussed in Chapter 7, that people of low self-esteem are more susceptible to the *implicit* influence attempts encountered in those situations. It should make at least as much sense in situations of explicit influence attempts.

(II) SOCIAL APPROVAL

Allied to the issue of self-esteem is the finding that people who have a deeply felt need for social approval tend to be more affected by social influence than other people (Marlowe and Gergen, 1969).

(III) PRIOR EXPERIENCE

This is the most important audience factor in attitude change. There are two aspects to it. Generally speaking we may be persuasible when a belief we take for granted is questioned, like the value of democracy, for instance. The reason for this is apparently that we are unused to defending this belief and lack the time to marshall the arguments in its favour.

One way of defending against such an attempt at persuasion is to be 'inoculated' against it by prior exposure to a mild form of the argument. In medical terms an inoculation consists of imparting a weak form of the disease in question which stimulates the body's natural defences to deal with it. So if the full-blown disease attacks the body at a later time the defences that have already been stimulated provide it with immunity.

Something analogous to this process of *inoculation* may take place in resistance to attitude change. In an experiment by William McGuire a group of people were faced with arguments against their previously unchallenged assumption that regular brushing of teeth prevents decay. This was followed by a refutation of these arguments that supported their original beliefs. A week later this group, and a control group who had not received the 'inoculation', were presented with another challenge to their belief about tooth brushing. The 'inoculated' group in this situation were not nearly as susceptible to persuasion as the control group (McGuire and Papageorgis, 1961).

Even where counter-arguments cannot be mustered simply *forewarning* people of a communication that will challenge their beliefs can have some effect. Where people are strongly committed to a particular belief they find the communication less persuasive (Freedman and Sears, 1965). However if people are not strongly committed in their belief they seem to become *more* persuasible (Kiesler, 1971).

(IV) PUBLIC COMMITMENT

In Chapter 7 we discussed group decision making and I described a study by Kurt Lewin that was part of a wartime campaign to persuade more Americans to eat cheaper cuts of meat (Lewin, 1958). You will recall that nearly a third of the women who took part in group discussions on the subject were actually persuaded to try out the recipes for the cheaper meat as opposed to only three per cent of the women who simply heard a lecture.

The aspect of this study that I emphasized was of course the opportunity to participate in making the group's decision. But there is another, if related, aspect which is important for us to consider at this point, and this is that the people involved were making a *public commitment* to try out the new recipes – that is to change their attitudes and their behaviour towards eating cheaper cuts of meat. The people who were not in the discussion groups could only make a private commitment to do so in response to the communication they received. Since Lewin's initial work this effect has been widely used by change agents in organizations (Kiesler, 1971).

Attitudes and behaviour

In a sense we are not really interested in someone's attitudes. What really interests us is knowing how they will *behave* in a particular situation and we use the attitudes they express as a way of predicting what that behaviour will be. Attitudes are therefore a *sign* of someone's future behaviour, rather like the projective tests we discussed in Chapter 11 on selection were signs of someone's likely future behaviour in a particular job.

The more we know about the three components of an attitude the more accurate will be our prediction of the behaviour that could result from it. Knowing someone's *opinions* on an issue, like an election, for instance, will tell us something about the way she will behave. Knowing her *feelings* about the candidates as well will tell us more. And if we can find out whether she *intends* to act on her opinions and feelings by actually voting, we should have a very accurate prediction of which candidate will receive her vote on election day.

Modern polling organizations are aware of these factors and, partly by phrasing their questions precisely so as to get at them, they can make very accurate predictions about election results. External factors can also be important. The shorter the time gap between finding out someone's intentions and the actual event taking place the more accurate will the prediction be of course. Polls typically increase in accuracy as the election draws near, and those taken on the eve of an election will be the closest to the final results.

So why was it then that in the British general election of April 1992 the final polls taken predicted a victory for the Labour party yet the Conservatives won with a clear majority? Well this question encapsulates the central difficulty we have in predicting behaviour from attitudes; we can only go on the information that people give us.

Does this mean that the people questioned about their voting intentions deliberately lied to the opinion pollsters? We can but guess. To start with it would only have been a small, though significant, minority of people whose behaviour would have run counter to their stated intention by telling their questioner that they would not vote Conservative when in the event they did. The vast majority of people apparently did what they said they'd do. And there is evidence from other sources to suggest that the misleading information given to the polls may have been deliberate.

An American study of the gap between attitudes and behaviour examined this issue. Asking someone if he would cheat on an examination usually produced the answer 'no'. When that person actually took the exam and did cheat did that mean he had deliberately lied to the questioner? In this case probably not. When the subject stated his intention of not cheating he was not faced with the actual exam situation. He may quite honestly have considered himself beyond the temptation of cheating, even in the kind of stressful situation which the study had devised for him. But when he was actually in that situation he learned that he was not (Wicker, 1969).

In Chapter 7 we came across an even more striking illustration of the discrepancies between attitudes and behaviour. When we discussed Stanley Milgram's research on obedience to authority we noted that people found it hard to believe that anyone (including presumably themselves) could administer a 450-volt shock to another human being as part of a 'learning' experiment. This applied to both first-year psychology students and psychiatrists at Yale Medical School. They predicted that less than one per cent of subjects would obey the experimenter while the actual figure was as high as 65 per cent.

We can be quite confident that many of the people making these confident predictions would themselves have administered the shocks if they were put in the same position. In fact quite a few of Milgram's subjects who had not believed themselves capable of such behaviour were shaken up by what they had discovered about themselves (Milgram, 1974). The gap between opinions and beliefs about oneself and one's actual behaviour are at their greatest in this type of situation. The subject after all had to deal publicly with the stress of either causing pain to another human being or disobeying an authority figure, a situation whose pressures he could not have anticipated.

In situations we have never been in before we simply don't know how we will behave, especially if we are put under pressure. But in the familiar privacy of a voting booth a person is not usually subject to pressure and simply has to pull a lever or mark an X beside a name. Behaviour would normally be very close to expressed attitudes in this situation and to the extent that there is a discrepancy I'm afraid we have to question the veracity of the information given to the opinion pollsters.

Attitude change, behaviour and cognitive dissonance

We have seen how difficult it is trying to predict someone's behaviour from their attitudes and how attempts to change deeply held attitudes *in order to* change the behaviour associated with them are often fruitless. In this section we will see that in fact it's often more effective to reverse the process; that changing behaviour is more likely to lead to changing attitudes.

Self-justification

Central to this process is the powerful need we all have for *self-justification*. The need to justify, to make public sense of, our actions is one of the many ways in which we aspire to a rational explanation of human behaviour, even when we don't have one. There are many examples of this need in psychological research (see Aronson, 1992, Chapter 5 for example). But one classic example will serve our purposes here, a study by Stanley Schachter and Jerome Singer on the links between cognition and feelings (Schachter and Singer, 1962).

Schachter and Singer wanted to duplicate in the laboratory the physiological state of excitement that accompanies strong feelings, but without the kind of environment in which these feelings are normally found. They did so by giving their subjects an injection of adrenalin, a stimulant that causes a strong physical reaction (as we saw in discussing stress in Chapter 5), with symptoms like trembling hands and a pounding heart. Some of the subjects were told about the physiological effects of the injection and some were not. The subjects who were not told of the effects were then divided into two groups. In the first group when each subject came to the lab he was asked to sit in a waiting room, where he was soon joined by someone else who had supposedly received the same injection. The second person was not a subject in the study, however. He was the experimenters' assistant and he had a carefully written role to perform.

The assistant began to behave in a carefree, happy manner, telling jokes, flying paper aeroplanes round the room, playing basketball with the wastepaper basket and so on. In the course of his act the assistant invited the subject to join in – and sure enough he did and they both had a great time. The second group of subjects met the same person in the same waiting room but this time be behaved in an angry and aggressive manner, and once again each subject shared the assistant's emotions and behaviour as he too became angry and aggressive.

All of these subjects, you will recall, were experiencing the effects of the adrenalin injection, effects which they had not been told about. In the control condition the subjects who *had* been told what effects to expect also encountered either a 'happy' or an 'angry' assistant. But this time his behaviour had no effect on the subjects. They refused to join in either his happy or his angry behaviour. What caused the difference?

Where the subjects knew what symptoms to expect from the injection they attributed their feelings of physiological excitement quite simply to the adrenalin. To them the assistant was just some guy acting strangely, whose behaviour was irrelevant to their feelings. But the people who didn't know what symptoms to expect had no way of knowing why they were starting to feel physiologically excited. However they couldn't leave it at that, they needed some way of explaining their feelings – and that's exactly what the assistant gave them. Those who encountered the happy assistant interpreted their feelings as 'happiness' those who met the angry one interpreted *the same feelings* as 'anger'.

The subjects in this experiment were illustrating one aspect of the universal need we all have to justify our beliefs, attitudes, feelings and values so that we can convince ourselves and everyone else that our behaviour really does make sense. We need to believe that our thoughts, feelings and actions are in harmony. And indeed a lack of such harmony, as you may recall from Chapter 6, is a prime characteristic of psychological abnormality.

Popular catch phrases like 'the devil made me do that', 'it's in the blood' or 'it must be the weather' are quite revealing in this context. Behaviour that is left unexplained is very disturbing – especially our own behaviour. It upsets our sense of order and predictability. We find it more comfortable, psychologically, to provide a superficial or even a silly justification than to have no justification at all.

Cognitive dissonance

A few years before the experiment outlined above, in 1957, Leon Festinger had proposed a simple but far-reaching theory to account for the process of self-justification. Noting the powerful drive towards consistency, or *consonance*, Festinger suggested that if an individual holds two psychologically inconsistent cognitions (beliefs, attitudes, values, ideas) at the same time, he will be in a state of *cognitive dissonance* (Festinger, 1957).

Because cognitive dissonance is a state of psychological tension it is inherently unpleasant, Festinger argued, and we are strongly motivated to reduce it. It is important to note here that dissonance theory does not deal with *logical* inconsistency but *psychological* inconsistency. In other words people are not so much concerned with actually *being* consistent as *feeling* consistent; not so much with being rational as with *rationalizing*.

Suppose you've moved to New York to work, and in thinking things over one day you decide that the city is a horrible place to live. Presumably you regard yourself as a sensible person. If so you're now in a state of cognitive dissonance. Your cognition 'I am a sensible person' is inconsistent with your other cognition 'I'm living in a horrible place when I don't have to'. Now logically there's only one thing you can do – leave – but psychologically you have a choice.

To reduce dissonance you could follow the logical route and argue 'I am sensible; sensible people don't choose to live in horrible places. I'll move'. Your cognitions would then be consonant, but of course your attitudes towards New York would not have changed. Or you could work on the other cognition (that New York is horrible) which would give you two choices. It is the different consequences of making these choices that interests psychologists most. You could say 'Yes it is horrible but I stay here because I have a great job', thereby reducing dissonance with an external justification for your behaviour. But your attitude towards New York would remain the same. Suppose, however, that you couldn't find any such justification in your situation yet you continued to live in New York. Perhaps you would become defensive and argue 'Well actually, if you think about it, the city is not too bad; in fact parts of it are rather attractive and it has exciting people and opportunities that exist nowhere else'.

Once more your dissonance would be reduced and your cognitions would be consonant; you would be a sensible person who chose to live in an attractive place. But notice what else has happened – you've changed your attitudes about New York. In fact you have *convinced yourself* that New York is an attractive place. And you should underline that conclusion three times in red, because that kind of *internal* justification underlies the most powerful kind of attitude change.

Festinger tested this theory experimentally in the key study of what has become an enormous body of research on cognitive dissonance theory and its ramifications (Festinger and Carlsmith, 1959: KEY STUDY 13). His student subjects worked at some very boring and repetitive tasks for a long period of time. They were then placed in a situation of cognitive dissonance. They were asked to tell other students waiting to participate in the study that the tasks were very interesting and enjoyable. Some of the subjects were paid twenty dollars (a sizeable sum in the late 1950s) for telling this lie and some were paid only one dollar.

The subjects were then asked to report how they themselves felt about the tasks. The group which had been paid twenty dollars found it boring and dull, just as it was. But the group that was paid one dollar claimed the task was interesting and enjoyable. The first group had reduced dissonance by an external justification – it was worth twenty bucks to tell someone that a boring task was enjoyable. But they didn't believe it themselves, of course, and so their attitude towards the task didn't change.

The other group had no such external justification for their behaviour so they had to look internally to make sense of what they had done. Their cognition 'I told someone a boring task was enjoyable' was dissonant with their cognition 'I am an honest person'. One of these cognitions had to give, and as their self-image was deeply felt and strongly implanted it was easier to change the other attitude. So these people *persuaded themselves* that the task had been really enjoyable, just as they had told the other students it was.

There are a couple of points of particular interest to us here. One is that these findings run contrary to common sense, which would presumably argue that if you want somebody to adopt a certain attitude the more you pay him the more likely he is to do so. In this study the *less* people were paid the more readily did they change their attitudes.

The second point concerns the relationship between attitudes and behaviour again. We've already seen that a person holding certain attitudes doesn't necessarily act on them; there are many other factors involved. Similarly a change in behaviour will not necessarily follow from a change in attitude. However the cognitive dissonance studies have shown that if the appropriate *behaviour comes first* then it's more likely that a change in *attitude will follow*. Behaviour is usually a lot more resistant to change than attitude, as any heavy smoker who's decided to give it up can tell you.

Post-decision dissonance and the world of work

One of the earliest findings of the cognitive dissonance studies is also of particular importance for the world of work. It deals with the dissonance that arises as a result of making a decision. A decision costs us time and effort and it leads to a choice. By definition we then have to forgo whatever it was we didn't choose. But choice usually implies that each alternative has at least something positive in its favour, and the closer the alternatives are in attractiveness the harder will be the decision to make and the greater will be the dissonance experienced afterwards. What do you do about the negative points of the alternative you chose and the positive aspects of the one you didn't?

It is particularly clear how we cope with this dissonance when consumer choices are involved, like buying a new car for instance. The evidence is that as soon as we've made the decision and bought the car we'll be especially attentive to advertisements that extol the virtues of that particular model – and we'll carefully avoid the ads for competing models (Ehrlich *et al.*, 1957). In fact even when people were offered a reward, for taking part in a study, of one out of two electrical appliances they previously considered equally attractive, a few minutes after making their choice they rated the one they had chosen more highly and the one they rejected less highly (Brehm, 1956).

Difficult choices in the world of work can encompass the whole of an individual's career, from choosing an occupation and preparing for it, through taking a particular job, deciding whether to relocate and, eventually, deciding whether to take early retirement. Within an organization the decisions would include the selection of new staff, investment issues, which system of computerization to go for, and so on. Every one of these decisions will usually involve some personal as well as organizational investment, thus making the need to reduce dissonance all the stronger (Aronson *et al.*, 1974).

It becomes extremely difficult for people to admit that they may have made the wrong choice in any of these situations. So individuals and their organizations can find themselves locked into a spiral of justification which guarantees that the more uncertain they were at the time of the decision the more energy and ingenuity will they exert to prove themselves right. If the decision *was* a bad one this can only end in tears.

Attempts to change such psychologically strengthened attitudes directly will probably fail. In fact attacking these attitudes, as we have seen, is a good way to strengthen them further. Only the intervention of external factors is likely to lead to attitude change – if they are serious enough to cause a change in behaviour. So if the shiny new computer system collapses, or the market for the product dries up, or the brilliant new finance director is arrested for fraud a year later, the spiral of justification for prior decisions can go into reverse and behaviour – and the accompanying attitudes – will be loosened up.

Attitudes to work: job satisfaction

Not anybody can be a gravedigger. You can dig a hole any way they come. A gravedigger, you have to make a neat job. I had a fella once, he wanted to see a grave. He was a fella that digged sewers. He was impressed when he seen me diggin' this grave – how square and how perfect it was. A human body is goin' into this grave. That's why you need skill when you're gonna dig a grave . . . I start early, about seven o'clock in the morning, and I have the park cleaned before the funeral. We have two funerals for tomorrow, eleven and one o'clock. That's my life . . . I enjoy it very much, especially in summer. I don't think any job inside a factory or an office is so nice. You have the air all day and it's just beautiful. The smell of the grass when it's cut, it's just fantastic. Winter goes so fast sometimes you just don't feel it.

Elmer Ruiz, gravedigger

The above quotation comes originally from a book by the American writer and broadcaster Studs Terkel (1974). Terkel's book contains verbatim transcripts of interviews he had with hundreds of people, from an enormous diversity of backgrounds, about their working lives. Mr Ruiz was one of the people he interviewed, and the brief extract from the interview quoted above is reproduced from a leading American textbook of work psychology by McCormick and Ilgen (1987, p. 267).

'I find this work truly fulfilling in many ways – there's exercise, the sense of accomplishment, and, most important, the opportunity to make lots of noise.'
From *The Wall Street Journal*, with permission of the Cartoonists and Writers Syndicate.

McCormick and Ilgen use this quotation to counter what they consider the widespread assumption ' . . . for instance, that college professors work because they love their work and that grave diggers work only because they need the money' (p. 268). Certainly the quotation from Mr Ruiz appears to be striking evidence against such an assumption. Here is a man doing a hard, semi-skilled manual job who seems to love his work.

Yet if we look a little further at Mr Ruiz's testimony we find that he also says:

When I finish my work here, I just don't remember my work. I like music so much that I have lots more time listenin' to music or playin'. That's where I spend my time. I don't drink, I don't smoke. I play Spanish bass and guitar. I play accordion. I would like to be a musician. (Terkel, p. 510)

Does this other quotation not give us a somewhat different picture of Mr Ruiz's attitude towards his job? Of a good-natured and thoughtful man perhaps, whose employment horizons are surely constrained by his lack of formal education; who is doing the best he can with what he has but would actually prefer to be doing something a little more creative?

When people are asked by survey researchers how satisfied they are with their jobs, the great majority of them do claim to be fairly satisfied or very satisfied. Only a small minority (around 12 per cent) tend to express dissatisfaction and say they dislike their jobs (Weaver, 1980). It would appear from this evidence, therefore, that the psychological contract most workers have with their organizations is quite acceptable to them.

At the same time it is important to note that this is an *overall* measure of job satisfaction and it therefore disguises how people feel about different kind of jobs. For example it has also been found that given the choice of doing the same kind of work or something different eight or nine out of ten professional workers would keep their existing jobs but less than two out of ten unskilled factory workers would do so (Blauner, 1960). And level of occupational status does seem to be closely associated with job satisfaction (Weaver, 1980). As well as the professional groups studied, managers and technicians (and the self-employed) also seem to consider themselves more satisfied with their jobs than do blue collar workers.

It is thus the underlying story behind the aggregate figures that we have to probe to achieve a fuller understanding of what 'job satisfaction' means to people. The qualitative work of writers like Terkel helps to add flesh to the dry statistical bones. It has to be said that Terkel's general conclusions are rather bleak and pessimistic. He does not deny that some people do love their work and are fulfilled by it and satisfied with it. And he has some moving testimony from such people: musicians, a bookbinder, a stonemason and a fireman, for example.

But these workers are striking exceptions to the general rule. Here is how Terkel introduces his book:

> This book, being about work, is, by its very nature, about violence – to the spirit as well as to the body . . . It is, above all (or beneath all) about daily humiliations. To survive the day is triumph enough for the walking wounded among the great many of us. (p. xi)

That doesn't sound like too high a level of job satisfaction to me. So how can we reconcile this kind of evidence with the survey finding that about 88 per cent of workers express satisfaction with their jobs? Well it all depends, of course, on what you mean by job satisfaction.

E. A. Locke, the motivation theorist we met in the previous chapter, has proposed a widely-accepted definition of job satisfaction as 'a pleasurable positive emotional state resulting from the appraisal of one's job or job experiences' (Locke, 1976). But what researchers understand by job satisfaction may not be quite the same as their subjects. A celebrated study of semi-skilled car assembly workers in England came up with the usual high levels of expressed satisfaction with the work on the initial survey. However, follow up interviews suggested that job satisfaction did not mean they found the job pleasurable so much as 'practical'. In other words what they were satisfied with was the (relatively high) wages that went with it (Goldthorpe *et al.*, 1968). There was nothing intrinsic to the job itself that gave them much satisfaction, just the most basic extrinsic, or external, reward of them all.

Dissonance theory would predict that paying people high wages for a boring job is a good way to ensure that their negative attitudes towards it will not change. Indeed if they were *only* doing it for the money they would be forced to deal with the unpleasant aspects of the job head-on, without the psychological comfort of persuading themselves that things were not really so bad. What that implies is that if they believe there is a slightly better alternative, or if the job is so awful that even the money can't compensate, then people will simply quit. And that is what research seems to find (Jackofsky and Peters, 1983). You will recall that something like this happened to Henry Ford when he had a 400 per cent turnover of staff after the first year's operation of his assembly line.

Cognitive dissonance theory would also predict that the longer people stay in a job the more pressure will they feel to justify their personal investment of time and energy. We would therefore expect to find older, senior people expressing more job satisfaction than younger, junior people and that is what the research seems to bear out (Weaver, 1980). But again there is some question as to what it is they are satisfied with.

You may recall that when we discussed the time dimension of the world of work in Chapter 4 we found some evidence that attitudes towards a job changed over time (Katz, 1978: KEY STUDY 3). After five years in the same job the *context* of the job seemed to become more important to people than its *content*. Pay and benefits and relations with colleagues and supervisors seem to provide the basis for job satisfaction at that point.

Theories of job satisfaction

There are many theories that try to explain the causes and sources of job satisfaction. Each of the theories of work motivation considered in the previous chapter would have something to say on the issue, for example. But simply enumerating them once again would not do much for our understanding of this topic. *Herzberg's Two-Factor* theory is so widely known and quoted, and so specifically concerned with this issue, that we do need to consider it again.

We should also consider two other, specific theories of job satisfaction. The first of these is known as the *Job Characteristics* model of Hackman and Oldham (1975; 1976). The second is one we have come across already in a different context. It is the *Job Content* model of Peter Warr which we considered in Chapter 8 when we discussed the psychological effects of unemployment.

(I) HERZBERG'S TWO-FACTOR THEORY

In the last chapter we noted how Herzberg talked about people having two sets of needs, which he called *hygiene* needs and *motivation* needs. Hygiene needs, you will recall, are satisfied by regular care and maintenance in an organization, such as pay, working conditions, job security and relations with colleagues and supervisors. If these needs are not met then people will be *dissatisfied* with their jobs.

But however well these hygiene needs are met they do not, by themselves, produce job *satisfaction*; for that to happen motivators are required, and these are *intrinsic* to the work itself. Achievement, independence, recognition, responsibility, challenge and so on, are examples of motivators. Thus in Herzberg's thought the sources of job satisfaction are quite separate from the sources of job dissatisfaction and reducing dissatisfaction does not lead to increased satisfaction.

Attempts to test Herzberg's theory have largely been unsupportive. There have been studies which did support the theory though. A study conducted in Zambia, for instance, found negative attitudes linked to hygiene factors and positive attitudes linked to motivators (Machunga-wa and Schmitt, 1983). But the balance of the evidence goes the other way. However as Frank Landy has pointed out:

> In spite of the absence of empirical support, Herzberg's theory is probably a reasonable one at the descriptive level. It does a good job of describing what a manager might expect to find – *on the average* . . . One valuable research line that continues to maintain the interest of investigators is the difference between 'intrinsic', or job content (motivator), and 'extrinsic' or job context (hygiene) factors . . . On the whole, Herzberg has had a positive effect on the research in job satisfaction. As a result of his theory, variables are more clearly understood, the operations involved in measuring important variables are more reasonable, and people are thinking more flexibly about the meaning of job satisfaction than they did before his theory appeared. (Landy, 1989, p. 455)

(II) JOB CHARACTERISTICS MODEL

As its name suggests this theory adopts the straightforward approach of looking for the causes of job satisfaction in the characteristics of the job itself. Hackman and Oldham identified five major dimensions of a job that determine its level of job satisfaction for people (1975; 1976). These dimensions are as follows.

1. *Skill variety* (the extent to which a variety of skills are called upon).

2. *Task identity* (the extent to which one can complete a whole piece of work and not just a part of it).

3. *Task significance* (the extent to which the worker has an impact on other people inside or outside the organization).

4. *Autonomy* (the extent to which the worker can exercise responsibility and discretion).

5. *Feedback* (the extent to which the job provides the worker with knowledge of results about his effectiveness).

This theory has also met with mixed results when put to the test of empirical research. Some studies have found a link between job characteristics and attitudes expressing job satisfaction. One study looked at clerks in the South African civil service (Orpen, 1978). Another looked at shift workers on a greenfield factory site in the United Kingdom (Kemp *et al.*, 1983). However when research focusses on behavioural measures like productivity or job performance there is little support for the theory (Umstot, Bell and Mitchell, 1976).

(III) JOB CONTENT MODEL

You may recall that in Chapter 8 we compared the states of being employed and being unemployed in some detail. As part of that process we considered the suggestion by Peter Warr that there are nine factors on which a comparison can most usefully be made. These are:

● opportunity for control
● opportunity for skill use
● goal and task demands
● variety

- environmental clarity
- availability of money
- physical security
- opportunity for interpersonal contact
- valued social position.

As well as the issue of mental health and unemployment this model can also be used to evaluate job satisfaction. Warr thinks of these factors as psychological 'vitamins' and suggests that they may operate in a manner analogous to that of vitamins in physical health (Warr, 1987b). We therefore require a minimum daily amount of these nine vitamins for healthy job satisfaction. Some of these vitamins, like C and E, will cause no harm in large amounts. But just as we can suffer from vitamin deficiency if any are missing from our diet we can also suffer from an overdose of vitamins. Too much vitamin A and D, for instance, can be harmful to our health. In a similar way, argues Warr, the equivalent of vitamins C and E in his list (money, security and social position) won't do us any harm in large doses. However the vitamin A and D equivalents (the other six factors) can cause us psychological harm if the dosage is too high. Thus externally generated goals and task demands or even the opportunities for control and use of skills can lead to overload and stress. Warr's theory is too recent for it to be fully tested in empirical research but it is an interesting and unusual contribution.

Job satisfaction and justifying feelings

We have seen that job satisfaction/dissatisfaction is a set of attitudes with a strong emotional component to them. It has been suggested that our need to make sense of these emotions in the manner outlined earlier in the Schachter-Singer experiment may be operating here (Landy, 1989). This might explain why some of the job enrichment measures introduced by organizational followers of Herzberg's theory don't work.

Any serious change in the workplace, like job enrichment, will arouse strong feeling. The suggestion is that this feeling still needs to be interpreted by the workers affected. We saw how a single individual in the Schachter-Singer experiment could provide cues powerful enough to influence a subject's interpretation of their feelings, and their subsequent behaviour, in radically different directions. How much more persuasive would a work group be? As we saw in Chapter 7, group pressure on individuals to conform to the norm of a certain belief or practice is extremely difficult to resist. If the group norm is to be satisfied or dissatisfied with the job it is highly likely that any given individual will go along with it and interpret his or her feelings accordingly.

Personality and job satisfaction

Quite a lot of research in this field has concluded that job satisfaction is related to general satisfaction with one's life (Locke, 1976). And it has also been widely suggested that there are individual differences in general life satisfaction (Bandura, 1987). There does appear to be some evidence for the idea that, at least to some extent, job satisfaction or dissatisfaction may be a relatively stable personality characteristic, or *disposition*, that people take with them from one job to another (Staw and Ross, 1985).

The authors of this latter study go on to consider the implication that prospective employers, if they could, might therefore select *only* people who are generally satisfied with life (like Mr Ruiz perhaps) rather than trying to satisfy 'difficult' employees. As if they didn't do so already.

If there was a 'scientific' way of making this selection however it could, as we saw in the case of intelligence testing, acquire a spurious legitimacy, and leave the onus for change entirely on the individual. But very little is known about the links between personal disposition and actual work performance, as the authors also point out. So, apart from the ethical implications, employers could well be the losers in practical terms. There is some evidence, for example, that depressives, though they may not be so much fun to work with, are more realistic in their judgements than other people.

There is also some evidence though that extrovert people are generally happier than introverts and this is probably a personality characteristic that seems to affect the workplace, though its effect on performance is unclear (Argyle, 1987). Extroverts seek out social interaction more than introverts and are presumably more popular because of that, leading to greater satisfaction with their *experience* of work – though not necessarily with the content of a particular job. People who are relatively more neurotic than others also tend to be less happy and express more dissatisfaction. They are more given to anxiety and stress. People who are low in charm, intelligence, attractiveness or other desirable characteristics are also thought to be less happy and more dissatisfied with life, including work (Argyle, 1987).

Job satisfaction and behaviour

In the final section of this chapter we will take a brief look at the major effects of job satisfaction or dissatisfaction to see how far the attitudes expressed can be related to particular behaviour, like *productivity*, *absenteeism*, or *rate of turnover* of staff. Common sense would suggest that satisfied workers are more productive than dissatisfied workers and less likely to leave a job or be absent from it without good cause. These beliefs seem to be widespread among managers and for a long time they seemed to be solidly supported by psychological research (for example Vroom, 1964; Bhagat, 1982). Moreover high job satisfaction was correlated with other desirable work activities like not deliberately doing poor work – or even sabotage – or spreading malicious gossip (Mangoine and Quinn, 1975).

More recently the picture has become, inevitably, a little more complex. While job satisfaction probably *can* lead to high productivity, it has been shown that the causal relationship can also work the other way round: being highly productive can be a source of job satisfaction (Bateman and Organ, 1983). Moreover some third factor might increase both, like giving people a fair reward for their efforts (Schermerhorn, Hunt and Osborn, 1985). And how do you account for the workaholic who spends all his time at work because he can't bear to go home?

The assumption that low job satisfaction always means high absenteeism has also been challenged. While low job satisfaction probably *can* lead to higher absenteeism the relationship is not a strong one (Porter and Steers, 1973). There are simply too many factors in a person's life that can influence whether he or she will go to work on a particular day.

In fact there is a suggestion that absenteeism is part of a social process where individual behaviour might be related, not to individual differences in job satisfaction, so much as the particular set of group norms prevailing in a given workplace about what is expected and acceptable behaviour (Chadwick-Jones, Nicholson, and Brown, 1982). Under what conditions is it 'reasonable' to take a day off work and how often can this happen?

There is a similar story with regard to turnover of staff. Even in times of high unemployment, a lot of turnover is probably bad news for an organization if the people who leave do so voluntarily, because they are likely to be the ones who perform best (Hunter and Hirsch, 1987). Generally speaking the lower the level of job satisfaction the more likely are people to leave, but the link is not a strong one (Mowday, Koberg and McArthur, 1984). Leaving a job voluntarily is, of course, a very big decision to make, and there are many other factors that can influence someone's decision – not least the prospect of finding anything better.

Lastly we have seen yet again in this chapter that, regardless of the implicit view of what motivates people held by the people who run (or think they run) an organization, they must at some point come to terms with their employees' construction of workplace reality. In the last chapter we considered Theory X, Theory Y and the Social Assumptions model, and the great differences between them. But we can now see that what is even more crucial in determining job satisfaction, and the behaviour that might result from it, is the *interpretation* the workforce makes of what its management does. The way they make sense of that may, in the end, be more important to both individual and organization than any particular theory that management hold, whether explicit in their official literature or implicit in their attitudes towards their workers.

Part of this need to make sense is a heartfelt desire to believe that what one does for a living matters. We saw this with the story of Mr Ruiz. But often it is simply not possible for people to feel this way about their job. I'll end this chapter as Studs Terkel ends his book, with the last paragraph of an interview with Tom Patrick, a Brooklyn fireman:

> I worked in a bank. You know, it's just paper. It's not real. Nine to five and it's shit. You're lookin' at numbers. But I can look back and say, 'I helped put out a fire. I helped save somebody.' It shows something I did on this earth. (Terkel, 1974, p. 589)

CHAPTER 15

Leadership

Then all the elders of Israel . . . came to Samuel . . . and they said unto him . . . 'make us a king to judge us like all the nations'. But the thing displeased Samuel . . . And he said 'this will be the manner of the king that shall reign over you; he will take your sons, and appoint them unto him, for his chariots, and to be his horsemen . . . and to plow his ground, and to reap his harvests, and to make his instruments of war . . . and he will take your daughters to be perfumers and to be cooks, and to be bakers. And he will take your fields, and your vineyards, and your olive groves . . . and give them to his servants . . . He will take the tenth of your flocks; and ye shall be his servants. And ye shall cry out in that day because of your king whom ye shall have chosen . . . and the Lord will not answer you . . .' But the people refused to harken unto the voice of Samuel; and they said 'Nay; but there shall be a king over us . . .' (Samuel I, VIII, 4–19, Soncino Books of the Bible)

As they said to Schubert, 'take me to your lieder' (Tom Lehrer).

Introduction

Leadership is generally regarded as a crucial factor in the success of any kind of social activity, and especially competitive activity, from team sports to world wars. As far as we know, it has been ever thus. Indeed from the beginning of recorded history it was widely believed that what moved people and events, in both large and small ways, were individual leaders.

In a world of absolute monarchs and autocratic owners of land and factories it is not difficult to see why the 'Great Man' theory of history was simply assumed to be true. But this assumption lasted well into the twentieth century and was held even by learned professors supposedly questing after the truth in universities (see, for example, Adair, 1988, p. 7).

However, people who were considered unquestionably great national leaders were also regarded as models for leaders in twentieth century organizations in general. One difficulty with this, that had to be glossed over, is that great leaders may be the source of great evil. If leadership means *exercising influence over other people in pursuing collective goals*, then not only were Churchill and Roosevelt great leaders, but so were Hitler and Stalin. If we accept Napoleon and George Washington we also have to accept Attila the Hun.

It is hardly surprising that when psychologists began studying leadership they too accepted the unquestioned assumptions behind the Great Man theory. They therefore set about looking for the personality characteristics or traits that distinguished leaders from other people. That will also be the starting point for our own discussion of leadership. We shall then consider the other major theories of leadership briefly before discussing the issue of *followership*, which is acquiring increasing prominence in research, and the relation of leadership to management in modern organizations.

Formal theories of leadership

I   Trait theory

We came across trait theories earlier in this book, in Chapter 9, when we discussed Personality. You will recall that psychologists who adopted this approach to the study of personality set out to identify and measure all of the relatively stable characteristics or traits of someone's personality, at any given time, by using the methods of statistics and experimentation. We noted that although the same traits are found in everyone people may differ from each other on each trait. Which of these traits were particularly prominent in leaders, was the question they wanted to pursue.

The first problem encountered with this approach was access. Churchill and Roosevelt were hardly likely to sit still for psychologists to study them. So if such leaders were to be the object of study it could only be through biographies and similar documents that were one step removed from their subjects. If psychologists were to study leadership at first hand they had to set their sights lower, much lower. And that is why the vast majority of the thousands of studies of leadership have as their subjects middle and junior managers in work organizations.

To my mind this represents a compromise of such magnitude that one has to wonder about the legitimacy of the whole exercise. Can we seriously be expected to regard Churchill and the foreman in the widget factory as similar examples of leadership? The most obvious difference between the two, of course, is the size and nature of their respective following. It is this factor that is often related to the popular image of a great leader as someone possessing a rare personal quality of magnetism or *charisma*. And it is just this quality that was not contained in the trait studies, though, as we shall see later, the issue has returned in more recent research. Meanwhile I will follow the convention of referring to the work in this area as 'leadership' research.

The vast amount of research effort expended by psychologists on this topic, up to the middle of the twentieth century, was reviewed in a very important article by Stogdill (1948). This research had been dominated by a quest to establish links between personal characteristics and effective performance by people assumed to be in leadership roles in organizations (for example the junior and middle managers). Frank Landy (1989) lists forty of these characteristics that had been studied, ranging from 'adjustment' and 'age' to 'vocabulary usage' to 'insight'.

Stogdill found that such people did tend to be higher in certain characteristics than other people, for example intelligence, level of activity and social participation, but that this relationship was inconsistent, and even where it was found it was a lot less influential than had generally been assumed. He therefore concluded that, while any useful theory of leadership had to say something about personal characteristics, by themselves they explained very little about leadership behaviour in organizations.

Leadership was much more a matter of context and *situation*, Stogdill suggested. People who exhibited leadership behaviour in one situation might not do so in another. He also suggested something I consider absolutely crucial; that the reason for this was that whatever else leadership may be it is always *a relationship between people*. More recent reviews have identified other relevant characteristics, like need for achievement, need for power and goal-directedness, for instance (Stogdill, 1974; House and Baetz, 1979; Bass, 1981). But their conclusions about the usefulness of trait theory remain basically the same. Indeed many psychologists remain unconvinced that there is any link between any specific characteristics and any form of leadership (for example Yetton, 1984).

However fashions change and pendulums swing in everything else so why should leadership research be any different? Even more recent work on trait theory suggests that maybe, after all, 'leaders are not like other people' (Kirkpatrick and Locke, 1991, p. 58). As far as particular characteristics go all the usual suspects are rounded up together with another few, including a couple that I find rather interesting, 'flexibility' plus 'honesty and integrity'.

'Honesty and integrity' is what it says, while 'flexibility' apparently refers to the ability to adapt to the needs of one's followers and to the particular situation one is in, and is regarded as a crucial characteristic. Is there not just a teeny hint of contradiction here? As Groucho Marx put it, 'The secret of life is honesty and fair dealing. If you can fake that you've got it made.' This whole discussion in fact reminds me of the famous dialogue between F. Scott Fitzgerald and Ernest Hemingway:

Fitzgerald: The rich are really different from you and me.
Hemingway: Yes, they've got more money.

In this instance I'm on Hemingway's side.

II Style theories and leader behaviour

Dissatisfaction with trait theories led to an increasing interest in styles of leader behaviour. In other words instead of trying to discover *who* the best leaders *are* the emphasis switched to an examination of *what* the best leaders *do*. The earliest study in this field, and one of the most influential, grew out of the group dynamics tradition that we discussed in Chapter 7. Indeed it took place under the general supervision of Kurt Lewin himself. The study was conducted by Lewin, Lippitt and White (1939: KEY STUDY 14).

(A) AUTOCRATIC AND DEMOCRATIC LEADERSHIP

This study was concerned with the effects of different styles of leadership on group performance. The subjects were eleven year-old members of boys' clubs who were divided into groups to make Halloween masks. Each of the groups had an adult leader, and they were asked to follow one of three styles in performing their role:

Autocratic – where the leader decided what should be done, when, how and by whom.
Democratic – where the work of the group was decided on by group discussion, aided by the leader.
Laissez-faire – where the leader's input was minimal, limited to supplying materials and information.

The findings were that the boys with the Democratic leader were the happiest and most productive of the three group settings. Perhaps the most interesting aspect of the findings is that these boys were much more inclined to continue working effectively than the other two groups when the leader left the room. Does this not raise the question of the need for any leaders at all?

This study was done on the eve of the Second World War, of course, when 'democratic' countries were engaged in an all-out struggle against 'autocratic' countries. For people in countries like the United States these words carried a hefty emotional freight, and it was not surprising that the Lewin, Lippitt and White study should be widely and enthusiastically approved of. After the war it became the basis for a long-term programme on the effects of 'autocratic' and 'democratic' leadership styles, carried out at the Research Centre for Group Dynamics of the University of Michigan. It also occasioned a new definition of leadership as 'the performance of those acts which help the group achieve its preferred outcomes' (Cartwright and Zander, 1968, p. 304).

As well as being heavily influenced by Kurt Lewin's group dynamics ideas this work was also squarely in the Humanist tradition of psychologists like Carl Rogers (whose work on personality we noted in Chapter 9) and Abraham Maslow (whose theory of motivation we considered in Chapter 13). The Michigan researchers examined the leadership styles of many different groups, comparing successful and unsuccessful groups. At the beginning of the 1960s they concluded that, in a great variety of situations, the leadership of the successful groups was invariably democratic in style (Likert, 1961).

Rensis Likert, who was prominent in this work, formulated an influential classification of four systems of leadership styles for use in the management of organizations (1961):

1. Exploitative autocratic
2. Benevolent autocratic
3. Consultative
4. Democratic.

Likert strongly advocated the adoption of a System 4 type of management. He was convinced of its universal applicability to all kinds of organizations and developed specific programmes to help organizations attain that level. These programmes also utilized aspects of motivation that we considered in Chapter 13, such as goal-setting and feedback (Likert, 1961).

Likert's sophisticated approach also took into account the time factor involved in organizational change. To go from System 1 to System 4 could take five years or more to accomplish, he pointed out. But he later produced evidence that the time was well invested, even in purely financial terms, and that short-run measures under autocratic management could be proved counter-productive in the long run. Thus one organization that had an immediate saving of a quarter of a million dollars in cost-cutting lost half a million eventually through staff turnover and work stoppages (Likert, 1977).

Despite the obvious attractions of this approach to leadership in organizations it has been subject to some serious criticism too (well summarised, for example, by Guest, 1987). One major criticism is that the autocratic-democratic dimension is just one aspect of leadership behaviour and that by focussing on it exclusively other important aspects are missed, notably that of task accomplishment and what it requires. Going straight from simple, direct measures of effective leader performance to conclusions about complex, indirect matters like relations between people in organizations has also been considered suspect.

There is also a wider criticism to be made here that I think is particularly telling. From time to time we have seen, throughout this book, that no matter what organizational psychologists and management theorists may get excited about the vast majority of organizations continue to be run as they have always been run – autocratically, from the top down only. When a new system comes along claiming that democratic management based on trust and two-way communication is *always* better it is going right against the grain of vested interests as well as deeply entrenched, unconsciously-held attitudes.

It just takes one piece of contradictory evidence, therefore, to discredit the whole system, and such evidence exists. There are situations in which autocratic leadership, apparently, *can* improve a group's performance (see, for example, Shaw, 1955). The reason seems to be that although the satisfaction of participating in decisions is removed, so also is the burden of responsibility that goes with it, and in some situations the one can outweigh the other. This is an issue that gets to the heart of leadership in its widest context, and we shall return to it later in the chapter.

(B) PARTICIPATIVE AND DIRECTIVE LEADERSHIP

This dimension is clearly similar to the Autocratic-Democratic one, and similar criticisms have been made of it, but it is often considered sufficiently different to rate a mention. It is particularly concerned with the extent to which leaders in organizations encourage their staff to participate in the making of decisions which will affect them directly.

We noted the importance of participation when discussing the dynamics of group decision-making in Chapter 7. This was illustrated by another of Kurt Lewin's studies where he was able to change attitudes, about cooking cheaper cuts of meat, most effectively following participative discussions about the merits of doing so (Lewin, 1958). We saw there that people are more likely to accept and act on a group decision if they have participated in forming that decision.

We also noted that in work groups there is some evidence that participation by workers in decisions affecting their jobs can lead to increased enthusiasm, commitment and productivity (for example Likert, 1961; Lawler and Hackman, 1969; Bass, 1981). But as with the Autocratic-Democratic dimension there *are* situations in which directive leadership appears to be more effective. This seems to be true, for instance, where people know the job inside out and participation would be superfluous (Filley, House and Kerr, 1976). We will pick up this dimension of leadership again in the next section, on contingency theories.

(C) PEOPLE-ORIENTED AND PRODUCTIVITY-ORIENTED LEADERSHIP

A somewhat different approach to leadership style was followed at another American university, Ohio State. As at Michigan psychologists here began a long-term programme of research just after the Second World War. The Ohio State team operated along similar lines to R. B. Cattell's work on personality that I outlined in Chapter 9. They first asked people to describe the behaviour of a leader, a process that yielded some 1800 descriptive phrases. These phrases were then grouped into a number of categories from which, by the technique of factor analysis, two general factors were identified (Halpin and Winer, 1957).

These two factors were called 'consideration' and 'initiating structure'. *Consideration* is the extent to which a leader shows consideration for subordinates and is concerned about their welfare. *Initiating structure* is the extent to which he or she structures the leader's role and the activities of the group around the accomplishment of the group's task.

A great deal of research resulted from this work, reviews of which have been mixed (for example Weissenberg and Kavanagh, 1972; Vroom, 1976). In general terms the consideration dimension seems to be the better established of the two, with high consideration being associated with subordinates' high job satisfaction and low staff turnover. But initiating structure and its apparent effects on subordinates' job satisfaction and work performance seems to vary with the influence of other factors like the type of organization and the size of the work group.

There is also some question about the independence of these two factors from each other and to what extent an effective leader can, or should, be high on both. One interesting finding in this respect is that while leaders think they can operate on both dimensions their subordinates feel that they can't, and they tend to see them as *either* people-oriented *or* productivity-oriented (Weissenberg and Kavanagh, 1972). This is a significant aspect of leadership situations that we shall return to later in the chapter.

III   Contingency Theories

As it became clear that the search for a single all-purpose and universally effective leadership style was as much a mirage as personality traits of leadership, researchers began to focus their attention on the *situation* in which leadership occurred. The question they now asked was what kind of leadership behaviour will produce the most effective response from people *in a given situation*? The most desirable behaviour for a leader, under this formulation, was therefore *contingent* upon the context within which the leader was operating. We shall take a brief look at the main contingency theories below but their fundamental answer to the question of what makes for an effective leader is identical, 'it all depends'.

(A) FIEDLER'S LPC THEORY

Fred Fiedler's contingency theory is probably the best known (Fiedler, 1967). Fiedler was concerned with matching the most appropriate form of leadership with a particular context and to do so he attempted to combine aspects of both trait theory and style theory. In opposition to other theorists he suggested that leadership style grows out of the relatively stable personality traits a person has and is therefore going to be pretty well fixed itself. Fiedler assumed that such leadership styles would be oriented towards one of two positions, being concerned mainly with the *task* in hand or with *interpersonal relationships* among the people trying to perform the task.

In order to assess where a given leader's position was on this dimension Fiedler developed a questionnaire to measure his or her *least preferred co-worker* (LPC). The LPC measure consisted of 16 scales with descriptive adjectives like 'friendly-unfriendly' or 'boring-interesting'. The leader would be asked to rate the co-worker they least preferred to work with on each of these scales, from which a single LPC score was then derived. Leaders with a high LPC score therefore had a positive view of even their least desirable colleague and Fiedler interpreted this to mean that they were particularly considerate and concerned with maintaining harmonious relationships. Conversely a low LPC score implied a greater concern with the task.

So which of these two styles is likely to be more effective? Fiedler's answer is that it depends on three situational factors and the degree to which their combined effect is favourable to the particular leader. These three factors are:

- *relations between leader and group members* (the extent to which the leader has the members' support and trust)
- *task structure* (the extent to which the group's task is clearly defined)
- *leader's position power* (the extent to which the leader has the power to enforce the compliance of group members by controlling rewards and punishments).

When these factors are combined the most favourable context of the leader (that is, in terms of controlling the situation) is where there are good relations with group members, a very structured task and high position power. The least favourable context would have poor relations with group members, a very unstructured task and low position power. Fiedler concluded that in very favourable and very unfavourable situations a group worked best if its leader had a low LPC score and was task-oriented. But if the situation was between these extremes and only moderately favourable then a high LPC-scoring, person-oriented leader was more effective in producing a good group performance.

Fiedler's theory has resulted in a great deal of research and commentary and the results, of course, have been mixed. Reviews of the research have found many exceptions, but also some support for the theory, though more in the laboratory than in the field (Strube and Garcia, 1981; Peters, Hartke and Pohlmann, 1985). The model Fiedler has produced is a complex and ambitious one and there have been some recurrent and serious criticisms of it.

Most of the criticism has been about the LPC measure. This has included both its reliability and validity and the assumption that it measures a stable personality trait (Ashour, 1973). It has been shown that a leader's LPC score can change radically over time (Stinson and Tracy, 1974). In addition it has been shown that changes in group performance can affect relations between leader and group members (Vroom, 1976). These are interesting findings that have implications for later sections of this chapter.

(B) VROOM-YETTON THEORY

The participative-directive conception of leadership which we encountered earlier was formalised by Vroom and Yetton (1974) into a model that is intended to guide leaders in choosing the most effective style to adopt. They used this approach because they found, in opposition to Fiedler, that only about 10 per cent of leaders in organizations appeared to be *either* participative *or* directive, consistently, across different situations. Everyone else had a style that varied, at least to some extent, with the people and the situation involved. Most leaders were usually at the mid-point of the participative-directive dimension, known as 'consultation'.

The original Vroom-Yetton model required leaders to answer seven questions and follow a Yes/No decision tree in arriving at the most effective style to adopt for any given situation. A more recent version of the model uses ten questions with a five point scale for most of them (Vroom and Jago, 1988). The first few questions are:

1. Is there a quality requirement such that one solution is likely to be more effective than another?
2. How important is it that subordinates feel committed to the decision?
3. Do I have sufficient information to make a high-quality decision?

Five decision-making styles were identified, ranging from the most directive or autocratic, through consultative styles, to the most participative or democratic:

Autocratic: Leader makes decision using information available at the time.

Consultative: Leader makes decision unilaterally after sharing the problem with subordinates.

Democratic: Leader shares the problem with the group of subordinates and accepts the group decision on it.

The Vroom-Yetton theory is extremely complex and difficult to put to the test of empirical research. However there has been some support for the (original) model (Crouch and Yetton, 1987; Paul and Ebadi, 1989). Funnily enough the research seems to indicate that a participative style is generally best, *except* where the other work group members do not share the leader's commitment to the organizational goals.

However as we saw in the cases of the Volvo and Volkswagen pilot schemes that we examined in Chapter 7, there are still considerable problems in translating the choice of participative style into the workplace for any length of time and in any far-reaching way. People who had been traditionally autocratic leaders of work groups found it very difficult to let the workers participate to the point where their *own* participation became much less necessary. For workers to participate in making a decision, and then to act on it as a group, often seemed to be just too threatening for these leaders to accept.

(C) PATH-GOAL THEORY

The final contingency theory we will consider focusses on leadership from the viewpoint of motivating subordinates (House, 1971; House and Baetz, 1979). Path-goal theory is based mainly on the expectancy (VIE) theory of motivation that we discussed in Chapter 13. (You will recall that expectancy theory is concerned with the process of motivation and the question of how people decide what behaviour to engage in.) Path-goal theory also uses elements of both the Michigan and Ohio research into leadership style and Fiedler's contingency theory.

According to path-goal theory the leader's job is to make the paths to the goal of rewards easier for subordinates, and in so doing to increase their opportunities for job satisfaction. The theory suggests the existence of four leadership styles:

1. Supportive (such as consideration)
2. Instrumental (such as initiating structure)
3. Participative
4. Achievement-oriented.

Leaders can (and should, to be most effective) adopt different styles in different situations. The key situational factors are more elaborate than those suggested by Fiedler but essentially similar; leader-group relations, task structure and position power.

Research support for path-goal theory has been mixed (but you already guessed that). Some research studies and reviews have been quite positive (for example Schriesheim and De Nisi, 1981). Others have not (Downey, Sheridan and Slocum, 1976). To a large extent it is seen as sharing both the strengths and weaknesses of the expectancy theory of motivation.

Path-goal theory thus has an intuitive appeal, both to behavioural scientists and to managers, because of its objective, rational, quantifying approach. But as we have seen time and again in this book such an approach ignores a large part of our lives and cannot explain a great deal of workplace behaviour. In particular it concentrates on the task in question and in the provision of external rewards to encourage its accomplishment, denying the possibility of internal factors in motivation.

Review of leadership theories

In our brief tour round the major theories of leadership you will doubtless have noticed quite a few similarities between them. Edgar

Schein has summarised these similarities and identified two fundamental issues that virtually all theories of leadership, he claims, have
grappled with. These issues are a concern with *task or people* and the *level
of participation* that subordinates should have in decision making (Schein,
1988).

Examples from the theories we looked at, and the terminology used,
would be:

TABLE 15.1 Summary of leadership theories

(a) *Task or People*

Research group	Task	People
Ohio State	Initiating structure	Consideration
Fiedler	Low LPC (Task)	High LPC (Relationships)
Path-goal	Achievement oriented	Supportive

(b) *Level of Participation*

Research group	Low	Medium	High
Lewin	Autocratic	Laissez-faire	Democratic
Likert	System 1	System 2/3	System 4
Vroom-Yetton	Autocratic	Consultative	Democratic

Schein suggests there are two important differences between theories
regarding Task or People. Does this constitute a single continuum or are
we dealing with two independent dimensions where people could be
high or low on each? Do these dimensions tap into deep-lying attitudes
and values or are they just dealing with conscious behaviour? Schein
himself believes that, given a reasonable level of task competence, being
oriented towards people becomes increasingly important the higher one
goes in an organizational hierarchy.

In terms of Level of Participation Schein believes that no leadership
style is unequivocally the best. Indeed even phrasing the issue in this
way is now rather pointless as current theories of leadership are
practically all moving towards a contingency model.

So after nearly a century of research on leadership and many
thousands of studies we can now conclude, pretty confidently, that
effective leadership depends on a number of things (though we're not
sure which ones), and it seems a good idea for leaders to be interested in
people.

Leadership and management

Given the contribution that formal theories of leadership have made to our understanding of the subject it will not astound you that people with a practical interest in leadership have grown somewhat impatient with them. People who are deeply concerned with organizational effectiveness have often expressed their dissatisfaction with theories that – like the theories of motivation we encountered in Chapter 13 – can offer only a partial and ambiguous explanation of behaviour which they happen to consider crucially important.

This dissatisfaction has increased in recent years and, to be fair, is shared by a growing number of psychologists (for example Kerr and Jermier, 1978; Bennis and Nanus, 1985; Meindl, Ehrlich and Dukerich, 1985). We will look at some of the quite different ways of trying to understand leadership that have been emerging in response to this dissatisfaction. These approaches have grown out of the urgent practical concerns of managers in organizations and a re-appraisal of work organizations in light of structural changes to working life.

First however we need to deal with the terminology of leadership and management, and with the relationship between them. At the beginning of this chapter I pointed out that the subjects in most leadership studies were actually junior and middle managers. In what sense, then, could they be described as leaders? A coherent answer to this question depends on knowing what it is that managers (or supervisors) actually *do* for a living. Empirical research on this basic question has been carried out in the United Kingdom by Rosemary Stewart (1982, 1986) and in the United States by Harvey Mintzberg (1973). Their work also takes account of research done in other countries, and from it a fairly clear picture has emerged of how most managers spend a typical day.

Stewart's work was carried out on the usual junior and middle managers though Mintzberg actually studied chief executives, albeit only five of them. Both writers see leadership behaviour as an integral part of a manager's job. How large a part depends on the circumstances. Managerial jobs across organizations generally seem to be composed of the same elements, and Mintzberg lists ten of them, grouped in three main areas, as is shown in Table 15.2.

Obviously chief executives will spend much more of their time on the interpersonal roles in Table 15.2 than would junior managers. But that doesn't mean they will necessarily be any more effective as leaders. The job titles and descriptions, and the amount of time the job demands for activity defined as leadership, simply tells us *what* is done. It doesn't tell us *how* it is done, and that is where leadership ability and effectiveness would come in. But in any organization we tend to look automatically at

TABLE 15.2 Mintzberg's managerial roles

Interpersonal roles	Figurehead Leader Liaison
Informational roles	Monitor Disseminator Spokesman
Decisional roles	Entrepreneur Disturbance handler Resource allocator Negotiator

the apex for evidence of leadership. Indeed the greatest fallacy of leadership is that it always comes from the top down. It most certainly does not.

We noted in Chapter 11, during our discussion of selection interviewing, that we are prone to making a *fundamental attribution error* of human behaviour in which we overestimate the contribution of personal factors and underestimate that of situational factors. We therefore tend to attribute to people more control over what happens in their lives than is reasonably justified. I would suggest that we do the same with any kind of organizational hierarchy, and there is some research evidence that a group's performance is often attributed to its leader's ability (Phillips and Lord, 1981). From the family to the nation-state and everything in between, I would argue, we tend to associate influence with authority by attributing responsibility for the performance of a family, nation, company or sports team to the person who is the official leader of it. If the organization does well (by whatever criteria) the leader takes the credit; and gets the blame if it doesn't.

There is also some evidence that, as part of our psychological need to make sense, we tend to attribute credit or blame to someone or other for virtually everything that happens. We seem to be very disturbed by the idea that some things (both good and bad) may happen to people randomly, or that things might be out of someone's control (Lerner, 1965). This is especially likely, I would suggest, if that someone is supposed to be in charge. So if the football team does badly the manager/coach gets fired, regardless of injuries, loss of form, disaffected players, fixture congestion, lack of money, lack of time or sheer bad luck.

Moreover, while this looks like a clear case of linking leader behaviour with the subsequent performance I suspect it is nothing of the kind. We have already seen how unlikely it is that leader behaviour *by itself* will make much difference to the performance of a group. And when we consider how many managers are fired by one club then quickly employed by another – sometimes working their way back to the original club that fired them – it looks suspiciously like a ritual sacrifice to appease the gods, or the fans.

In one sense football managers are atypical of managers in general. They are not an integral part of an organization from which they can derive support (regardless of what owners or chairmen might say to the contrary). They are exposed; and it is understood by all that if things go wrong, for whatever reason, they get the chop. But people at the top of an organizational hierarchy only tend to find themselves in this position if they have a high media profile (Meindl, Ehrlich and Dukerich, 1985) and can be clearly linked with the organization.

There are ways of redefining performance, or performance criteria, on the one hand, and shifting the blame for manifest failure on the other, which are routinely employed at the top of organizations. Senior managers have as much need to protect their self-esteem, after all, as anyone else. One of the most striking examples of this process at work has been thoughtfully (and even humorously) analysed by Norman Dixon (1976) who has studied the gross, and murderous, incompetence of British generals, particularly during the First World War.

Transformational leadership and the return of charisma

From the 1970s on more and more attention was paid, both in research and consultancy, to the leader behaviour of senior managers. The impetus for this development was a combination of impatience with the unsatisfactory theories of leadership available and an assumption that highly successful organizations (however defined) had to have better leadership (from the top down of course) than other organizations.

This seemed to be the case from a study of the successful organizations in both the United States (Peters and Austin, 1985) and the United Kingdom (Goldsmith and Clutterbuck, 1984). And it also seemed to hold good when the leaders themselves were studied across a wide variety of organizations, including not only the more usual work organizations but organizations in the realms of sports and the arts (Bennis and Nanus, 1985). The single factor that made the crucial difference for all these authors was *transformational leadership*. This is a description of a type of leadership that was first introduced to social science by J. M. Burns (1978). Burns did not invent the term but he delineated the characteristics of transformational leadership in a way that had a wide appeal to researchers.

Burns contrasted transformational leadership with what he called 'transactional leadership'. The transactional form of leadership, as the name implies, refers to transactions, or interpersonal exchanges, in the workplace. It is concerned with honouring agreements and keeping one's side of the bargain, for instance; with doing one's job responsibly. It arises out of someone's position in the organization and deals with *what* should be done rather than *how*. It is concerned with *means* rather than *ends*. It is in fact the daily stuff of being a manager. In a sense it is about being a manager *rather than* being a leader in the traditional sense.

Transformational leadership is, by contrast, much more dynamic and interested in doing things differently. Such a leader is concerned with ends rather than means, with the future direction of the organization rather than the nuts and bolts of running it right now, and with transforming the way the organization operates.

He or she does this by being concerned to do the right thing for the organization rather than doing things right (that is, by the book). The transformational leader empowers everyone in the organization to achieve much more of their potential, and to open up their horizons by creating and following new objectives. As opposed to the steady state manager who displays transactional leadership, the transformational leader is concerned with a dynamic and changing organizational process. And the most important personality characteristic of the transformational leader is thought to be 'charisma', whatever that might be (Bass, 1985).

Table 15.3 outlines the key differences between being a manager and being a leader that this approach to leadership has fostered. We should note, though, that these are ideal types and *conceptual* distinctions, which may be blurred in actual practice in a given organization at a given time. It is also important to note that both aspects of leadership are considered necessary for organizations to function well.

Transformational leadership and the Loch Ness Monster

A great deal of time and energy has now been expended on looking for it, and some perfectly sober observers claim to have seen it. While I am quite willing to accept that there may possibly be *something* there it's not at all clear what. And I myself have never, to the best of my knowledge, laid eyes on the beast. That's also where I stand on the existence of the Loch Ness Monster.

It might be useful to point out that J. M. Burns, who popularised the notion of transformational leadership, is a political scientist rather than a

TABLE 15.3   **Distinguishing between a manager and a leader**

Manager	Leader
motivates people and administers resources to achieve stated organizational goals	motivates people to develop new objectives
implements	shapes
narrows down horizons	opens up horizons
rational	emotional
does things right	does right thing
TRANSACTIONAL (positional)	TRANSFORMATIONAL
• concerned with *means* for example:	• concerned with *ends* for example:
• responsibility	• future direction of organization
• fairness	• ultimate goals and values
• maintaining agreements	• empowerment of staff
STATIC ORIENTATION	DYNAMIC ORIENTATION

psychologist. There certainly seems to be something familiar about this picture of a heroic leader inspiring people to undreamt-of feats; a leader whose visionary eyes are firmly fixed on the far horizon and who doesn't worry too much about the means used to attain his (or even her) glorious ends.

Yes I'm afraid we're back in Great Man leadership territory again, or as I would prefer it, the Leader as Monster. The Second World War was the last time these great monsters ruled the earth, whether in benevolent (Churchill/Roosevelt) or malevolent (Hitler/Stalin) fashion. But their influence as leader role models is still, I would suggest, very much with us. And the latest swing of the pendulum has brought them back into research fashion again.

When times are particularly difficult or uncertain or changing rapidly the clamour for heroic leadership seems to rise, and behavioural scientists seem to respond by dusting off the Leader as Monster theory yet again. However other strands of research and thinking are also gathering some momentum, perhaps in response to the Monster theory, and it is to these we now turn in the final section of this chapter. These alternative views are concerned primarily with the nature of *followership* as opposed to leadership and focus on the relationships that followers have with their leaders.

Followership

It is a truism, but one we do well to remind ourselves of, that without followers there would be no leaders. So the obvious question then is why do people follow a leader? What does leadership do for them, in other words? And related to this question is the basic issue of whether leaders are always – or ever – necessary.

In the earlier research we discussed there was a hint that, given the right work group conditions, the absence of a leader did not have a detrimental effect on productivity (Lewin, Lippitt and White, 1939: KEY STUDY 14). More recently it has been suggested that in a variety of circumstances individual leaders are quite unnecessary in organizations and may be substituted by factors like providing training for staff, or interesting jobs, or having a variety of experienced people adopt the leadership role as required (Kerr, 1983). And there are the workplace pilot schemes, like those at the Volvo and Volkswagen plants which we discussed in Chapter 7, which show quite clearly that even workers on boring assembly lines can flourish when official leadership is removed and they are given the job to organise for themselves.

Well, what if leaders are not formally appointed, or even elected, do they emerge anyway because of their personal characteristics and/or the situation? Some earlier research by R. F. Bales on the formation of group structure and communication within groups provides a few useful insights into this issue (Bales, 1950; Bales and Slater, 1955). Bales later updated his research methods (Bales and Cohen, 1979). What seemed to happen was that practically everyone in a group made some attempt, at one time or another, to influence the other group members. Some people tried to do so more than others, and some people were more successful at it than others.

However, rather than a single individual emerging as *the* leader of a group, two clear leadership *roles* seem to have emerged. One role was played by the person the group thought had the best ideas and the other was the best-liked member of the group. They were described as the roles of *task* leader and *socio-emotional* leader. What the task leader did for the group was to help it focus effectively on the task it had to perform. The function performed by the *socio-emotional* leader was the care and maintenance of the group's interpersonal relations.

It will not have escaped your notice that these two roles correspond to Schein's Task/People dichotomy of leadership that I mentioned earlier. The difference is that these roles grew out of the interaction of the group and were played out with the agreement and participation of all its members. It might be reasonable enough to talk about task and socio-emotional 'leaders' as a form of shorthand, but we have clearly moved now as far from conventional ideas of leadership as it is possible to get. The concept that was so seriously diluted when junior managers were first used in leadership studies is surely here drained of any useful meaning whatsoever.

In the Bales studies there is no sense in which either the task or socio-emotional 'leaders' had power over the behaviour of other people, and if the term leadership is to retain any meaning I would suggest that it should really be restricted to those situations in which that power – from whatever source – is apparent. That is, we can only talk about leadership sensibly where there exist followers, however willing or unwilling, whose behaviour is directly linked to the actions of an individual leader figure.

There is a different kind of evidence, from a different kind of situation, that provides us with some relevant insight here. Bill Buford is an American writer who spent about eight years closely observing English soccer hooligans. Here is what he says about the leadership of rioting crowds:

> A crowd can never be formed against its will, and it is the great fallacy about the crowd that it can be: this is the leadership fallacy, the rabble-ready-to-be-roused theory. A crowd needs leading and uses leaders, but comes into existence by a series of essential choices made by its members. Muttonchops may have preferred himself as a leader, but it would be for the crowd to decide. Or put another way: a crowd creates the leaders who create the crowd. (Buford, 1991, p. 286)

From all that we have learned in this chapter and in Chapter 7; therefore, I would suggest that there are three propositions about work groups and leadership in organizations that have to be seriously considered:

(i)   work groups have the same needs whether they have officially recognised leaders or not
(ii) they can attend to those needs at least as well when they have no official leaders
(iii) providing work groups with official leaders, whether appointed, or elected, may simply add unnecessary sources of tension and conflict.

Looked at in this light the burden of providing evidence for the beneficial effects of *formal* leadership on work groups now falls on those who support the existence of organizational hierarchies. The unquestioned assumption that formal leadership makes *some* positive difference, let alone the *crucial* difference, in organizational performance is no longer tenable, it seems to me. There is too much evidence to the contrary, and little if any to support it.

I would therefore agree with those psychologists who argue that leadership is in the eye of the beholder (for example Mintzberg, 1973; Calder, 1977). We have already seen in this chapter and others how we seem to have a deep-seated psychological need to attribute qualities of leadership to people just because they occupy leadership positions. But, as we have also seen that this attribution is irrational and in contradiction to all the evidence, we are forced to conclude that it has unconscious origins.

And that brings us back, finally, to the Loch Ness Monster. It was Freud, in his last book *Moses and Monotheism*, who most clearly pointed out the powerful unconscious bond between charismatic leaders and their followers (Freud, 1939). Freud argued that at one level we seem to need some authority or 'father figure' to whom we can subjugate ourselves. We need to adore this authority, even though we also know at some level that, like the case of the Israelites quoted at the beginning of this chapter, he may treat us with contempt.

This powerful need, that has its origin in earliest childhood, is reinforced throughout the process of socialization, at home and in school. By the time we enter the world of work we will inevitably look, suggests this view, for a leader/father figure from somewhere above us in the organizational hierarchy. We will want to project our unconscious needs, desires, wishes and fantasies on to such a person, and the more charismatic or transformational the leader the more successfully can we do so (Kets de Vries, 1989).

If the leader is of the Loch Ness Monster variety it appears that we may identify with him so completely that we are even willing to let him become our Superego and take over all responsibility for deciding between right and wrong in how we behave. Transformational leaders may thus have enormous power, far above that granted them by their organizational position. We do have a need to participate in decision making, but we also have a need to be relieved of the burdens of decision making, and sometimes this need is stronger.

No leader in any sphere can possibly *be* the Loch Ness Monster, of course, and sooner or later they will all be found to be human. They may be more or less admirable – there is after all an enormous gulf between Adolf Hitler and Martin Luther King – but they are all fallible human beings. To treat them as heroic monsters is to deny their humanity, and our own. But dealing with this issue is always very difficult psychologically. It is called growing up, and we probably first encounter it when we discover that our father can't, after all, do absolutely everything.

The managerial viewpoint again

When we looked at the way organizations run, back in Chapter 2, we concluded that they were rather messy things in real life, the products of all the interrelationships between their members. This meant that every member of an organization affects, and at the same time is affected by, the organization. It seemed, therefore, to make more sense to talk of the continuous process of *organizing* rather than of a static, fixed entity called an organization, which could have no separate existence anyway beyond the interrelationships of its members (Hosking and Morley, 1991).

By focussing on the process of organizing we also set aside the managerial viewpoint on organizations which has always dominated both thought and practice in this field. And nowhere is the managerial viewpoint seen more forcefully than in the vast literature on leadership. As a central assumption of this viewpoint is that managers are the 'doers' in an organization and non-managers are there to be managed, or 'done-to', it is quite obvious where one is going to look for evidence of leadership.

Based on this viewpoint any study of leadership reinforces a simple-minded input-output model. Whether we are considering old-fashioned personality trait theories or their more sophisticated Mark II transformational versions, or leadership style, or even contingency theories of leadership, the problem is the same. As Hosking and Morley (1991) say about the latter:

> . . . whatever their precise details, contingency approaches view effectiveness as an outcome of leader inputs in interaction with other inputs from the leaders [sic] setting. (p. 247)

All of these theories simply assume that all the members of an organization have the same view of the organization and of its value to them or, if not, that they can be persuaded (by the appearance of the Loch Ness Monster, for example) to accept, and be committed to, the managerial viewpoint on these matters. As we saw in Chapter 2, and indeed throughout this book, this assumption has only the most tenuous grip on reality.

For me the problems with the manipulative managerial viewpoint are best exemplified by one often-overlooked finding. It seems that managers in organizations tend to use autocratic techniques (however disguised as democratic) to get their subordinates to do what they want while in turn expecting their own boss to be open, considerate and trusting with *them* and genuinely welcome *their* participation (Miles, 1965).

PART IV

THE FUTURE OF WORK

In the final part of the book we examine some of the most important current trends in the world of work and extrapolate from them to consider possible scenarios for the future. In doing so we draw on many of the basic findings and concepts outlined in the preceding fifteen chapters.

We begin by analysing the effects of new technology in general, and the latest information technology in particular, in Chapter 16. Chapter 17 is devoted to the particular experience of women in the world of work, and how and why it differs from that of men. We end, in Chapter 18, by considering the interaction between the topics covered by the previous two chapters, and by taking a long view of psychology and the world of work from the nineteenth century on into the twenty-first.

The effects of new technology

In the following pages, we shall be concerned specifically with people who experience themselves as automata, as robots, as bits of machinery, or even as animals. Such persons are rightly regarded as crazy. Yet why do we not regard a theory that seeks to transmute persons into automata or animals as equally crazy?

R. D. Laing
The Divided Self

Introduction

In the first chapter of this book we reviewed, very briefly, the history of work and noted some of the major developments leading up to the way society has organised work in the twentieth century. These included the Industrial Revolution and the process of industrialization, Frederick Taylor's Scientific Management and Henry Ford's assembly line.

In Chapter 4: 'The time dimension', we saw how something as fundamental, and usually unnoticed, as the way people related to the passage of time at work could reflect radical psychological differences between them. For example we noted that managers and workers often seemed to operate in different time frames, the managers in linear time and the workers in cyclical time. There was never enough time available for managers to do their job, while for workers the problem was to cope with what seemed like an infinite amount. What both were trying to do was exercise control over their workplace, and their goals and methods of doing so were intrinsically opposed to each other.

Finally we have noted throughout this book the constant temptation for managers to treat shopfloor workers as machines – whether it be as a cog in an assembly line or an appendage to a word processor – and the damage this causes both to the individuals involved and their employing

347

organizations. What I would like to do in this chapter is to pull these threads together and use them to outline the effects of introducing new technology into the workplace.

Technology and work

What is technology?

Technology is usually thought of as the practical applications of scientific discoveries or innovations, like steam engines from the discovery of steam power, to take a pertinent example. Sometimes the causal sequence can work the other way round. Thus the recording of tides and planetary movements for practical agricultural reasons led to the study of astronomy in ancient Babylon, and the development of navigational instruments in fifteenth and sixteenth century Europe, had a similar effect.

Often it is a chicken and egg issue, and James Watt himself was a great tinkerer and inventor who went on to become a successful entrepreneur with his scientific discovery. In the successful application of any technology, timing is of the essence. The Ford Motor Corporation found this out painfully in the 1950s when they proudly unveiled their new contribution to automotive safety, seat belts, to a public that would not be ready for them for at least another decade. And of course the ancient Chinese invention of gunpowder did not save them from military defeat and occupation centuries later because, unlike their opponents, they only used the stuff to make firecrackers.

So far we have considered examples from one usage of the term 'technology' the traditional one – but the term is also used in two other ways. These three forms of usage have been classified as follows (Winner, 1977):

apparatus – machines and gadgets: the usage we have been following and the most common one
technique – a standard procedure for achieving a particular purpose: like writing a computer programme or a training manual
organization – social arrangements of the workplace with specific goals; like factories and management hierarchies.

All three usages can occur together, for example where a factory is provided with a training manual for the operation of a new machine.

We tend to think of technology as typical of the post-Industrial Revolution age but in fact it is as old as human history. And indeed no technology that has appeared in the last couple of centuries has had anything like the impact of the wheel for instance or, as we noted in Chapter 4, the invention of the printing press. So when we consider the effects of new technology later we would do well to bear in mind that human societies have frequently had to come to terms with the introduction of some new technology or other. What we will really be looking for are the aspects that make *this* technology different from previous new technologies.

The first Industrial Revolution

We listed some of the major aspects of the Industrial Revolution in Chapter 1. We noted in particular the huge shifts in population that took people off the land and into the cities, forming the large pools of available labour for employment in the new factories that were making such intensive use of James Watt's invention among others. These factories were mainly involved in servicing machines used in industrial processes like the production of steel or coal or textiles, or the manufacture of products from pins to ships.

We observed in Chapter 1 the dreadful conditions and the cruelly long hours that men, women and children had to cope with in these new industries. But what also became apparent was the violence done to the psychological relationship that people had had with their work. Where individuals had formerly produced, or at least worked on, an entire product, they were now required by the minute division of labour demanded by the new technology to perform the same small repetitive task hour after hour, day after day, for the rest of their working lives. Inevitably workers felt themselves divorced from the work they had to do for a living, a process we know as *alienation*.

We examined the psychological effects of this process in Chapter 4 where we discussed the work of people like Donald Roy (1960: KEY STUDY 2). Roy's experience took place just after the Second World War, but in essence the process he describes dates back almost to the beginning of industrialization in the United States. He describes how people staved off terminal boredom by inventing mind games, engaging in *social* games wherever possible, and generally dividing the endless work day up into several artificially created time horizons.

But the discovery of alienation is not a product of twentieth century science. On the contrary it was observed at the very birth of the Industrial Revolution by Adam Smith, and again a couple of generations later by Karl Marx. These two political economists are usually regarded today as being the founding fathers of two diametrically opposed systems; free market capitalism on the one hand and centrally controlled socialism on the other. Yet both Smith and Marx recognised not only the enormous productivity of goods that resulted from organizing work around the factory system, but also the alienation inherent in using people like machines which the process seemed to entail (Marx, 1976; Smith, 1982).

The idea of progress again

Both the simplification and fragmentation of the manufacturing process, and the de-skilling or degradation of the individual's working life have often been regarded as the price that had to be paid for enjoying the fruits of the new technology. Indeed an acceptance of the technology seemed to imply an acceptance of the social and psychological costs that went with it, as though they were implicit in the technology itself. And as new technology was generally regarded, especially in the nineteenth century, as representing progress the costs seemed as inevitable as the benefits.

As we discovered in Chapter 4 'progress' is a seductive idea, especially in the area of technology where it looks so self-evident. In the United States in the century from 1850 to 1950 industrial power from machines as opposed to muscles rose from 14 to 80 per cent (Dubin, 1958). Steam or electric power is obviously stronger than muscle power; a car is obviously faster than a horse. How could any rational, reasonable person be against that? The problem with the question in this form, of course, is that it's a very limited definition of progress, and it assumes an equally limited definition of costs.

Neither people nor horses require non-renewable energy sources, like coal and oil, to fuel them. Neither do they make the atmosphere potentially dangerous to breathe. Obviously this is not by itself a sufficient argument against the introduction of cars or powerful machinery. But it is an argument against being simple-minded about them.

If we had a more sophisticated picture of the costs of a new technology we might still decide to adopt it if the benefits seemed to outweigh the costs. More probably we could try to mitigate the costs. *That* would be a rational decision. Investing heavily in new technology without considering all the aspects of what is a very complex issue is in fact, from a societal point of view, an *irrational* decision. It only makes sense from the viewpoint of making a short-term profit. And perhaps not even then. What would happen to the profits of chemical companies, for example, if governments decided that they should pay for the cost of cleaning up the rivers into which they discharged their waste?

We have already mentioned the human costs of the Industrial Revolution. It is clear that factory owners did not usually consider them when they invested in the new technology of their day, let alone costs to the environment. And because the technology was supported by what amounted to an *ideology* of progress there was neither pressure nor incentive nor much encouragement for them to go against the group norm. The reservations of academic and scholarly writers like Adam Smith or Karl Marx went largely unheeded in the world of work itself, a trend that has continued to the present day. Psychologists and management gurus may think a lot of Maslow or Likert but your average manager is firmly Taylorist in orientation.

This gap between scholarship and practice only closed, I would suggest, when the times were right, that is when the scholarship was in tune with the prevailing ideology of the workplace. Such a time, as we saw in Chapter 1 and Chapter 2, occurred early in the twentieth century with the convergence of Frederick Taylor's scientific management ideas, Henry Ford's assembly line technology, Max Weber's theory of bureaucracy and the psychology of Behaviourism.

So powerful was this union that it set both the prevailing ideology and the practical agenda for defining problems that we are taking into the twenty-first century. And at the heart of both ideology and agenda lies the issue of *control*. But as well as being a crucial issue at the organizational level, it is also, as we discovered in Chapter 5, vital to the individual psychological wellbeing of everyone in the world of work. Control of one's workplace and working life is the key to managing stress.

Control of the workplace

We noted in Chapter 2 that conflicts of interests between groups are built into organizations and part of their normal life. Perhaps the most basic, and certainly the most visible, such conflict started out as being between employers and employees. As industrialization progressed, and individual owners gave way to managers, the conflict took the form of managers versus managed, or 'doers' versus 'done to'. What managers as a group were able to do, in succession to employers, was to have their own interests identified with those of the organization as a whole.

The managerial viewpoint of an organization, where its interests lay and what its problems were, was thus unquestioningly accepted as the legitimate one by most people. This was true by-and-large of industrial psychologists as well, whose work often depended on being hired as consultants by management, or at least being given access to their workers. Indeed as we saw in Chapter 7 it was even true of those psychologists like Elton Mayo who came to reject scientific management in favour of a human relations approach to the workplace.

Workers who seek to further their interests as a group by going on strike or taking other industrial action are therefore generally seen to be doing something illegitimate even though they are a far larger group than management. But such a direct and high profile conflict of interests focusses attention on what this conflict is really about, and that is power, the power to control resources and make decisions on behalf of the organization. That is why management (and media) reaction to a strike is often so virulent. It is a political issue, regardless of what the strike is about, and what is at stake is the power and authority of management (Hyman, 1989).

The introduction of a new technology into the workplace by management can most usefully be seen in this light. As new technologies often imply the use of fewer workers and the de-skilling of others a conflict of interest is practically guaranteed. The decision to introduce such technology therefore has to be a political one, whatever else it might be. For an organization's management to assert that it's the technology that puts people on the dole, and that it has nothing to do with them, is at best ignorant and at worst cynical. This argument is known as *technological determinism* and indeed may be invoked as a cover for the deliberate furthering of management group interests in cutting costs and increasing direct control of the workforce.

Worker cooperation

The situation outlined above is probably the most open and extreme conflict of interests an organization can have. Partly for that reason it is relatively rare. We have already seen that far more work days are lost through stress than industrial action. In fact despite the inherent and ever-present conflict of interests between management and workers the *normal* state of affairs in most organizations is one of cooperation. It is difficult to see how organizations could continue to operate if it wasn't.

There are also times when the interests of workers and the interests of management, within a given organization, are not monolithic. One frequently observed example of this is the gap that may be found between junior management and senior management when new policies are to be implemented or new technology is to be introduced. Junior management will often see their interests lying more in cooperation with the workers they are directly responsible for than with their superiors.

This process has been reported in organizations as diverse as a mid-Western American factory and the London Fire Brigade (Burawoy, 1979; Salaman, 1986). Many observers feel that in the case of private industry and commerce this informal alliance between workers and junior management is actually in the profit-making interests of the organization. It usually entails the ignoring of various company rules, procedures or policies, as laid down by senior management, *in order to get the job done*. That is why 'working to rule' is such a paradoxical form of industrial action for workers to take. It highlights the fact that if they follow the rule book faithfully, and do everything they're supposed to do, production suffers.

But as we saw in the last chapter people in formal leadership positions receive such powerful psychological support from the process of attribution and the fulfilment of unconscious needs that even this obvious irrationality slips by unnoticed, except perhaps by senior managers themselves, who must at some level see in it a challenge to their normally unquestioned authority (Hyman, 1989).

Worker resistance

We have seen how the inherent conflict of interests between workers and management is often masked by a great deal of cooperative behaviour. This can lead senior managers to proclaim that there is no real conflict in their organization. If there is evidence of unrest at a natural crisis point, like the introduction of new technology, it is often put down to one or both of two sources: (1) the Outside Agitator, a cousin of our old friend the Loch Ness Monster, and (2) a problem of communication.

For a senior management group to suggest seriously that outside agitators are the cause of industrial action is to expose the depths of their ignorance about their own organization. It is also a good indication of the contempt they have for their staff. Workers are an easy prey to external influences; managers, of course, are not. The communication argument is just as spurious, but a little more subtle as it is couched in terms of human relations. Indeed it uses the traditional language of the human relations consultants and academics going all the way back to Elton Mayo and the Hawthorne studies. They believed, you will recall, that there was no conflict between groups within any organizations that better human relations practices couldn't overcome.

To continue to believe this in the face of all the accumulated evidence of the twentieth century looks suspiciously like the defence mechanism of *denial* does it not? You might expect psychologists to be a little more aware of this mechanism than senior managers, but then again they also have to earn a living.

The term *structural antagonism* has recently been suggested as a better description of the typical situation in an organization than 'conflict of interests' (Edwards, 1990). This seems to me a more useful description of the way conflicts of interest are built into organizations, without over-emphasizing the overt clashes that only occur at crisis points. It doesn't allow management and consultants to think of the situation in their organization as quite unique, and therefore requiring a one-off, one-time solution, nor to pretend that there isn't really any conflict of interests there at all.

Simply put then, management attempts to control the workplace and the people in it meets, inevitably, with resistance from those people. This resistance will take a variety of forms; overt and covert, active and passive, conscious and unconscious. It ranges from doing less well at the job than one can, to sabotage, to strikes, to trade union organising, to absenteeism. A good early example of a work group defending itself against management control was of course the group norm setting the rate of production discovered during the Hawthorne studies (KEY STUDY 6). The group was resisting the imposition of a management-ordained level of performance arrived at by Taylorist time-and-motion study.

A more recent example is provided by a study of the introduction of new technology. This took the form of installing a computer system in a large retailing company (Pettigrew, 1973). The computer programmers had an important source of power in this situation, their *expertise*. As I suggested in Chapter 2 this source has increased in recent years compared to the formal authority or *legitimate* power of line managers.

In this instance the line management felt directly threatened by the computer professionals and tried to reduce their power, for example by seeking to simplify and fragment their work. And the experts resisted with the weapons they had, a language only they fully understood and important information which they could withhold.

Job design and redesign

Ergonomics revisited

In Chapter 3: 'The work environment' we examined the interaction between workers and their workplace. We saw how an understanding of the way our senses and our processes of perception operate was vital in providing people with a comfortable and efficient working environment. However, although the capacity to design such an environment for any job is available, it is rarely used. Two examples should help illustrate why.

We noted that ergonomics arose out of wartime conditions. From these conditions emerged fighting machines like aeroplanes, tanks, ships and submarines, and systems like radar and sonar. These machines and systems continued to be refined in peacetime and were the ergonomic forerunners of the most carefully designed working environment in human history, the manned (and womanned) spacecraft.

At the other extreme was our old friend Henry Ford. Ford's introduction of the moving assembly line in 1913 was concerned entirely with the technology. In a sense he was the last of the traditional factory owners who presided over the Industrial Revolution. He was so far removed from any concern about ergonomics that he regarded his workers not merely as interchangeable machines but as machine *parts*. As he explained in his autobiography (Ford, 1922):

> The lightest jobs were again classified to discover how many of them required the use of full faculties, and we found that 670 could be filled by legless men, 2637 by one-legged men, two by armless men, 715 by one-armed men, and ten by blind men. (p. 108)

The key to understanding these two extremes is, of course, money. Despite the worker resistance of poor performance, absenteeism and huge labour turnover, Ford was making such vast profits at that point that he could afford to discard his human machines when they broke down rather than worrying about maintaining or repairing them. Astronauts on the other hand were a rare and precious commodity in whom billions of dollars had been invested, to say nothing of the intangible, but powerful, factor of national prestige.

Most other workplaces fall somewhere between these two extremes, though the great majority fall at the Fordist end of the scale. Though there may have been some informal, local attempts to consider the effects of a new technology on its operators *before* it was introduced very, very few workplace environments have ever been ergonomically designed. The research evidence is therefore usually concerned with job *redesign*. In other words this field is dominated by damage limitation exercises carried out after the decision to introduce new technology has been taken. Yet as we will now discover the evidence shows that job satisfaction and productivity are increased when human factors are considered along with the technology.

Socio-technical systems

The concept of a *socio-technical* system dates from the late 1940s and a study of the effects of mechanization on the British coal mining industry

(Trist and Bamforth, 1951). Prior to mechanization two miners plus a couple of assistants formed a work group and each work group was responsible for mining a ten-yard coal face. Each group was autonomous and performed all the tasks necessary to extract the coal in its own place.

When the new technology for cutting the coal and conveying it away was introduced it also entailed changes in the way the work was organized. It was now possible to work a coal face nearly 200 yards long, and a new system for taking advantage of this was devised, known as the 'longwall' method. The former set of tasks needed to extract the coal were divided into three cycles of work, each done by a different shift comprising 40 to 50 miners plus backup plus – for the first time – a supervisor. The three shifts never met. Finally a new and complex pay structure was introduced in parallel with the new tasks which, in effect, produced a hierarchy among the miners.

The immediate effects of introducing the new technology was to produce serious problems of both productivity and industrial relations. Management regarded the problems as so serious that they called in Eric Trist and his associates from the Tavistock Institute in London as psychological consultants (Trist *et al.*, 1963).

Trist realised that the heart of all the problems lay in the disruption of the traditional social organization of the workplace. Under the old arrangement all the miners had a great deal of control over their work together with the close support of their work group colleagues in what was a hard and dangerous job. With the fragmentation of the job, the imposition of a supervisor, the lack of cooperation between groups and the creation of a hierarchy, the basic conditions of Taylorism were introduced, with all the disadvantages we are familiar with. These effects were magnified by the discarding of an existing arrangement which had generally worked so well.

Trist *et al.* modified the new system after observing how the miners themselves tried to cope with it. They reorganized the men into composite teams on each shift so that all the mining tasks were included once more in all the groups. The miners were able to choose which shift they wanted and what task they wanted to work at within a shift. These modifications of the new system were successful in dealing with the problems. The miners regained job satisfaction, cooperation between groups was re-established, and productivity improved. The lesson for the future was that new technology cannot be introduced in a vacuum. For it to be used effectively the social system it will be a part of must be taken into account.

The work of the Tavistock school had a widespread effect on thinking about the complex relationships that exist between organizations and technology. One important such relationship is the one between different technologies and different forms of work organization. This aspect has been extensively studied by social scientists in the United Kingdom, notably Joan Woodward (1965) and the highly influential Burns and Stalker (1961: KEY STUDY 15).

Woodward observed a hundred manufacturing firms in England to analyze the links between their system of production, their social organization and their commercial performance. She had expected to find that the commercially successful organizations would all have the same kind of social structure. But this finding did not occur. What seemed to be much more important was whether the social structure was the most *appropriate* one for the particular technology being used.

1. SMALL-BATCH PRODUCTION

This was used for making small batches of essentially custom-made products, for example in electronics or dressmaking. Companies using this technology had a relatively simple structure with little supervision and a flat management hierarchy.

2. LARGE-BATCH PRODUCTION

This was a form of mass production usually involving some kind of assembly line procedure. Companies using this technology generally had a more elaborate social structure and more layers of management in the hierarchy, especially first-line supervisors. More use was made by management of financial incentives. The technology was used for standardised items like machine parts, cars or television sets.

3. CONTINOUS-PROCESS PRODUCTION

This was the most complex form of production, using the most advanced, automated technology. As the name implies, the production process was in the form of a continuous flow. This kind of technology was used in the petrochemical industry, for instance. The social structure here had relatively small working groups with a fairly loose degree of supervision but more levels of authority. The technology seemed to have a more determining effect on social organization than on small-batch production and much more than large-batch production.

Later work explored the different roles of management in these three socio-technical systems (Dawson, 1986). An important difference was found between the large-batch production system and the other two. In both small-batch and continuous process systems control of the production system was centrally integrated, but in large-batch mass production it was split into different functions, like manufacturing and quality control. We have seen how such structural divisions create scope for conflict of interests within an organization. More recent work has extended Woodward's ideas and applied them to the United States (Hull and Collins, 1987).

At about the same time as Woodward's pioneering work in England Burns and Stalker were producing their classic study on the management of innovation in Britain, focussing on the newly-created Scottish electronics industry (1961: KEY STUDY 15). Burns and Stalker (1961) were quickly struck by how different a successful organization was from the others. In particular its social structure was flexible enough to allow it to adjust its system of production to a rapidly changing market as well as changing technology.

Burns and Stalker concluded that organizations could be placed along a continuum of flexibility in their social organization ranging from *mechanistic* at one end to *organic* at the other. The most important characteristic differences between these extreme points are summarised in Table 16.1.

The Mechanistic type of organization is to be found in large public bureaucracies and large manufacturing companies engaged in the traditional mass production of standard products by 'mature' technologies. Newly introduced modern technologies, such as electronics in the 1950s, require an organic type of flexible social structure if the organizations involved in using them are to be successful.

Essentially the problem from an organizational point of view is to find a way of dealing with the market uncertainty caused by change. But

TABLE 16.1   **Mechanistic and organic organizations**

Mechanistic ⟵────────────────⟶ *Organic*	
Hierarchy of authority	No fixed hierarchy
Communication mainly vertical	Communication mainly horizontal
Information and decision making centralised	Information and decision making decentralised
Much division of labour	Little division of labour
Fixed job description	Changing job description
Low commitment by individual to organization	High commitment by individual to organization
For stable conditions	For changing conditions

from the individual's viewpoint this is also true psychologically, as we have seen throughout this book. The anxiety and stress caused to managers by the disappearance of the familiar, and a perception of losing control, will have to be dealt with head-on if a new socio-technical system is to be created successfully.

Quality of working life

We have seen on several occasions how the Human Relations approach to the world of work became prominent in thinking and research after the Hawthorne studies were published. One strand of this work is concerned with the design and redesign of jobs in such a way that the quality of working life (QWL), rather than the extrinsic financial rewards or fringe benefits, is improved.

QWL programmes for the workplace were intended to increase the worker's commitment to the organization by increasing the *intrinsic* attraction of the job itself and, thereby, the job satisfaction of the person doing it. The expectation was that increased job satisfaction would lead to increased organizational performance, though as we saw in Chapters 13 and 14 the relationship between the two is a little more complex than that. During the 1960s there was an upsurge of interest in QWL throughout the industrialised world (Davis and Cherns, 1975). Most conclusions from research on the effects of Taylor's scientific management during this period were that worker commitment was very low and that physical and mental health suffered, leading to poor productivity (notably Kornhauser, 1965 and Caplan *et al.*, 1975).

While external material rewards were not denied their place, the focus shifted away from their all-important role in Taylorism. The tone was set by the work of Frederick Herzberg, whose theory of motivation we considered in Chapters 13 and 14. Herzberg's distinction between the external rewards of *Hygiene* factors like pay and conditions and the internal *Motivators* like the creativity and challenge involved in the job itself were widely accepted.

In particular Herzberg stressed the importance of applying *job enrichment* to the workplace as a direct counter to the job simplification of Taylorism. Job enrichment implied the reorganization of tasks so that the simplified jobs at the bottom of the hierarchy are given more responsible tasks to do and more discretion in the way they do them.

To a limited extent this may have happened in some occupations, particularly in finance (for example Herzberg, 1966). But more often 'job enrichment' was reduced to a reassertion of managerial control by simply adding more mindless tasks to the existing job. The result for the people whose jobs were thus 'enriched' has been graphically described by a worker in the chemical industry:

> You move from one boring, dirty monotonous job to another boring, dirty, monotonous job. And somehow you're supposed to come out of it all 'enriched'. But I never feel 'enriched' – I just feel knackered. (Nichols and Beynon, 1977, p. 16)

With increasing automation there has been some decline in the traditional use of assembly lines. This is often taken to mean that fewer workers are now tied to an assembly line, but I would suggest caution here. Some of the new industries that have appeared in the last twenty or thirty years make just as much use of assembly line technology as Henry Ford did. Food processing plants for the oven-ready market, for instance, may employ people (mainly women) to stuff the backsides of chickens for seven hours a day. Using both hands simultaneously they can do 2000 chickens an hour, or 14 000 a day. That works out at a cycle time for the job of 3.6 seconds. Henry would be proud.

The most widely used model of job redesign to emerge from the QWL movement is one that we encountered in our discussion of job satisfaction in Chapter 14, the Job Characteristics Model of Hackman and Oldham (1976, 1980). They suggested, you will recall, that there were certain key characteristics of jobs (that could be objectively determined) which were responsible for workers experiencing job satisfaction, and these should be included in the redesign of jobs. They were five in number:

1. Skill variety.
2. Task identity.
3. Task significance.
4. Autonomy.
5. Feedback.

How many of these characteristics do you think apply to our chicken stuffers?

The most significant attempts to improve the quality of life have probably occurred in the European car industry, as we saw when we discussed working-group relationships in Chapter 7. But even the famous Volvo Kalmar plant did not, in the end, make much of an improvement in the general run of Taylorist/Fordist conditions. Volvo have more recently tried again, with a plant opened in 1989 at Uddevalla (Clarke, 1990). This one was designed from the start bearing socio-technical system research in mind. Thus the relevant trade union was a full participant in the design. It is too early for any firm conclusions to be drawn about Uddevalla but in a time of recession and ferocious competition I wouldn't hold my breath.

Elsewhere the myriad job-enrichment-QWL-humanization-of-the-workplace programmes that were hailed in the 1960s and 1970s turned out to be largely public relations exercises (Child, 1984). In fact there were schemes that managers considered very effective where half the workers were totally unaware of anything having changed, and most of the rest didn't think the changes had led to any improvements (Guest, Williams and Dewe, 1980).

Introducing the new 'new technology'

What is it?

When the term 'new technology' is used today it usually refers to developments in *microelectronics* that began in the 1970s. These developments were based on the use of the silicon chip, which allowed a huge number of electrical circuits to be contained on a tiny piece of silicon. It was the use of this technology which encouraged the significant leap in miniaturization necessary to create a new *micro* electronics industry out of the post-war electronics industry that Burns and Stalker had studied.

The most obvious effect of microelectronic technology has been to combine ever-increasing power and complexity of electronic systems with decreased size, weight and, most importantly, cost. A computation that would have cost about $30 000 in 1950 was reduced to one dollar by 1980 (Salvendy, 1982). You can now have available to you on your desk a microcomputer with all the electronic capacity that would have required a large room to contain it a couple of decades ago, and for a tiny fraction of the cost. This enormous increase in availability has in turn led to a greatly expanded range of applications for computers, in the workplace and outside it. These now range from the smallest home computer games to the largest computer-controlled manufacturing processes.

In the workplace the take-up of the new technology has been patchy so far, as it usually is for any new technology (Wall, 1987). Even the steam engine and the assembly line were not universally adopted overnight. These developments are always cost-driven. Some work-places are, however, highly influenced by microelectronics; banks, supermarkets and the mass media for instance. A list of major current types of applications in the three main sectors of the economy – manufacturing, offices and services is given in Table 16.2.

TABLE 16.2   Current microelectronics applications

MANUFACTURING
Computer-aided design (CAD)   ⎫   Computer-
Computer-aided engineering (CAE)   ⎬   integrated (CIM)
Computer-aided manufacturing (CAM)   ⎭   manufacturing
Computer-numerically controlled (CNC) machine tools
Flexible manufacturing systems (FMS)
Monitoring and control of continuous processes
Safety and security systems

OFFICES
Electronic filing
Electronic mail (E-mail)
Electronic transfer of funds
Management information systems (MIS)
Teleconferencing
Word processing

SERVICES
Automatic cash dispensers
Automated laboratory testing
Computerised information systems
Computerised stock control
Electronic point-of-sale systems (EPOS)
Expert diagnostic systems

What's new about it?

What all of this technology is concerned with is the transmission, processing and usage of information in some form, whether as words, numbers or pictures. For that reason it is also referred to as *information technology*. Mankind has, of course, been using information technology since people started signalling to each other with hill-top bonfires. But some people now believe that the application of microelectronics to the process has had a particularly significant effect. Indeed it has been referred to as 'The Second Industrial Revolution', and a British Government Chief Scientist even went so far as to call it 'the most remarkable technology ever to confront mankind' (Forester, 1985).

As I pointed out in Chapter 4 these are huge claims to make and we should be very careful about assessing the evidence for them. To claim that this new technology has *already* had such a unique impact is just silly. As of now it doesn't begin to compare with the impact made by the printing press, or even the telephone. What these claims are really referring to is the *potential* that the new technology has for changing our lives, and that is what we will now consider. But in order to do so we need to take an historical view of the matter.

Shoshana Zuboff has done just that (1988). She is an historian of the Industrial Revolution who was particularly fascinated by its effects on everyday life, and gradually became interested in recording what seemed to her a current transformation in the world of work that might be just as important. Zuboff chose eight companies to study, ranging from financial organizations to paper mills, and considered the working lives of people at various levels of each organizational hierarchy.

What makes the new technology different from what went before, in Zuboff's opinion, can be gleaned from what it does with information:

> For example, computer-based numerically controlled machine tools or microprocessor-based sensing devices not only apply programmed instructions to equipment but also convert the current state of equipment, product, or process into data. Scanner devices in supermarkets automate the checkout process and simultaneously generate data that can be used for inventory control, warehousing, scheduling of deliveries and market analysis. The same systems that make it possible to automate office transactions also create a vast overview of an organization's operations, with many levels of data coordinated and accessible for a variety of analytical efforts. (Zuboff, 1988, p. 9)

Information technology thus has a dimension of *reflexivity* that previous machine technologies did not have. In other words as well as automating the process it deals with, the new technology also acts as a kind of organizational X-ray because it:

> . . . simultaneously generates information about the underlying productive and administrative processes through which an organization accomplishes its work. (Zuboff, 1988, p. 9)

For Zuboff this is the capacity to *informate* and it has radical implications for the future dynamics of organizational life and workplace behaviour, though as yet these have 'not been clearly recognised and remain relatively unexploited' (p. 11). I suspect this is a polite way of saying senior management haven't a clue what's happening. If and when they ever do they will be faced with the problems and opportunities that are always inherent in the introduction of a major new technology. Zuboff sees the key to that contingency (as did Burns and Stalker one generation and one new technology ago) in leadership:

> Will there be leaders who are able to recognize the historical moment and the choices it presents? Will they find ways to create the organizational conditions in which new visions, new concepts, and a new language of workplace

relations can emerge? . . . If not, we will be stranded in a new world with old solutions. We will suffer through the unintended consequences of change, because we have failed to understand this technology and how it differs from what came before. (Zuboff, 1988, p. 12)

If Zuboff is correct in her analysis her questions surely can have only one answer. Indeed I find it a little surprising that an historian has any need to pose them. If you've already read the last chapter on leadership you will know that I would urge you to bet the housekeeping money on 'old solutions' and 'unintended consequences' winning in a canter.

Old solutions and unintended consequences

The most important psychological aspect of introducing new technology is that it inevitably means *change*; change in the way work is performed, in what work is now required, in the way the workplace is organized and in the relationships between different interest groups within the organization. As we have seen at various points throughout this book, and especially in Chapter 6: 'The unconscious at work', change makes people anxious and more prone to clutch at familiar ways of doing things. They reach for old solutions to new problems, if you like, even when the old 'solutions' didn't actually solve the old problems. And this is just as true in the boardroom as on the shop floor.

The anxiety engendered by this looming prospect of change is perfectly rational. People *do* lose their jobs when new technology is introduced. Companies *do* go out of business if they can't adapt to it. But the implications of introducing a new technology can never be predicted in their entirety, and therefore they can never be entirely controlled by any group, no matter how powerful. The negotiation of interests between groups, which is a normal feature of organizational life, does not disappear in the face of new technology. Decisions about the introduction and implementation of any new technology are, as we saw earlier, just as political as any others.

What is different about information technology is the people who are most directly affected by it. Where previous technologies replaced muscle power information technology replaces brain power. Clerical and administrative jobs are affected by it rather than manual jobs. The effects are not all loss, however. A new technology also implies new market opportunities and new jobs. The vast computer industry that seems so much a part of our modern world of work did not exist less than half a century ago. The situation is, of course, changing continuously and it is very difficult to predict the net effects of information technology on job opportunities. Estimates vary between a small gain and a large loss (Burnes, 1989).

The continuing struggle for control of the workplace between management and workers – the 'structural antagonism' we considered earlier – has led some writers to suggest that the most pessimistic scenario is the most likely one (see especially Braverman, 1974; Cooley, 1984). By this account the de-skilling and degradation of jobs that followed from the widespread adoption of Taylorism and Fordism in the early twentieth century is still the dominant ideology and practice of management. Therefore they can be expected, as a group, to use information technology in the same way, deliberately to weaken the influence of the workforce and extend their own control of the workplace.

From all the evidence we have already considered I think it is probably reasonable to conclude that this may well be (at least part of) the *intention* that managements have in introducing new technology. But how successful they are in actually doing so is another matter. We've seen more than once how much psychology there is between intention and actuality. I think Zuboff gets this issue about right:

> The data I have presented suggest a more complicated reality. Even where control or deskilling has been the intent of managerial choices with respect to new information technology, managers themselves are also captive to a wide range of impulses and pressures. Only rarely is there a grand design concocted by an elite group ruthlessly grinding its way toward the fulfilment of some special and secret plan . . . Activities that seem to represent choices are often inert reproductions of accepted practice. (Zuboff, 1988, p. 389)

We should not lose sight of the fact that, as with any other new technology, the most immediate impact that information technology has on jobs is ergonomic. As the technology is invariably installed with no regard whatever to the people who will operate it, it is the people, as usual, who suffer the consequences. One of these is a physical disability called Repetitive Strain Injury (RSI). RSI is a general term for physical disorders in the muscles and tendons of the hand and arm caused by repetitive movements over a long period of time. It is very painful and can frequently disable the affected limb.

RSI has been around for some time in certain industries. For example the (mainly female) chicken stuffers we met earlier are at serious risk from RSI. But the disorder became internationally recognised when it was associated with excessive keyboard use following the introduction of information technology. Moreover it hit not only the 'shop floor' workers – poorly paid low status female secretaries – but also professionals and executives (often male) who used keyboards in their work, such as journalism, for instance.

In 1989 nearly a third of the journalists on *The Financial Times* had RSI symptoms (*Guardian*, 1989). In 1990 a journalist for the Reuters news agency settled an RSI compensation claim for an estimated £250 000 (*Guardian*, 1991). In the United States in 1980 RSI accounted for 20 per cent of occupational injuries. By 1992 the figure was more than 50 per cent (*Newsweek*, 1992). These people were tied to their keyboards as effectively as Henry Ford's assembly line workers were tied to *their* technology. Given the potential size of compensation bills money is now being invested in an ergonomically designed keyboard (*Newsweek*, 1992). But we can be pretty sure that if employers find it cheaper to pay compensation then that's what will happen.

One final development in response to the new information technology is worth considering and that lies in organizational theory. Just as we saw in Chapter 2 that an organization is not a static or a stable entity, so some theorists have suggested recently that the relationship between technologies and organizations is also a more complex and dynamic one than had previously been thought (Scarbrough and Corbett, 1992).

On this view technology does not, of itself, determine the form of an organization. Nor do members of an organization simply choose the latest form of technology as it becomes available. Instead both organizations and technologies are to be seen 'as fluid and interlocking *processes* . . . which . . . evolve and overlap together rather than separately or in opposition to each other' (Scarbrough and Corbett, 1992, p. 3). Depending on how an organization defines its goals at a given point a mix of simple and advanced technologies, and a tailoring of organizational structure in tandem, might successfully evolve to meet the organization's needs.

Scarbrough and Corbett cite the example of the Edinburgh-based Kwik-Fit company. In the 1970s the company discovered a market niche in the United Kingdom by focussing on fitting car exhausts and tyres rather than offering the usual range of (increasingly hi-tech) garage services. Simple services requiring a simple technology, and which were available to the customer while she waited. This specialization and simplification also meant that management could discard skilled (and expensive) garage mechanics in favour of young, cheap and unskilled labour.

As business increased the company opened new depots, but going from 50 depots to 180 in a short time began to pose serious problems. Trying to administer the organization from its central location had become very inefficient and costly. They solved the problem by having an information technology programme tailored especially for their needs.

Each depot was then given a computer terminal which provided all the administrative information and services it needed for dealing with customer transactions, stock control and so on. All this information was then collected centrally by computer every night for the use of senior management. Depot managers thus were relieved of administrative routine and paperwork, and found themselves running what were virtually small businesses. At the same time they were backed by the economies of scale and the level of computerisation available only to a large organization. As of late 1993 they were up to 450 depots.

CHAPTER 17

Women at work

Introduction

As we head for the twenty-first century perhaps the most striking thing a Martian visitor would notice about women in the workplace is that most of them do different jobs from men. As I mentioned near the beginning of Chapter 1 this is a state of affairs that has endured throughout human history, since men first went out hunting and women stayed home to look after the children and perform the domestic chores.

When human social behaviour is so long-lasting and so widespread it takes on, psychologically, an aura of inevitability, and naturalness. The different jobs that men and women do come to be seen, partly by the process of attribution that we have encountered several times before, as being *naturally* men's or women's work because of the natural, biological, differences between men and women. But as we shall see throughout this chapter these differences are actually – indeed literally – man-made.

As I have mentioned from time to time, most of the research and theory dealing with psychology and the world of work has concerned the experience of men. Where women have been included their particular experiences have been, or been seen to be, essentially the same as men. In this chapter I will try to redress the balance by focussing on the world of work from the viewpoint of women's experience. I do this not only because it is right and fair to do so but because it helps us understand psychology and the world of work better. In fact we cannot really understand that world unless we do so.

Women are often regarded as a minority group in this kind of discussion and lumped together with, for example, ethnic groups and people with disabilities. I can understand why this is done; many of the problems and disadvantages that women face in the world of work are also faced by minority groups. But is it not a little incongruous to label as a 'minority' a group of people who are getting on for 54 per cent of the world's population? As a psychologist I can't help feeling that this is an important symptom of the difficulties that women *as women* are uniquely burdened with.

There is no meaningful sense in which women are a minority other than the psychological. People who have no disability and are not a member of an ethnic minority group are only a minority because in the eyes of the (male) people who define these things *they have not yet attained the age of majority*. Psychologically they are still minors in other words. That being the case it would obviously be unwise to treat them as responsible adults – let alone as equals. And we are thereby discouraged from seeing women as a legitimate self-interest group within the world of work.

None of this should be taken to imply that the problems of actual – statistical – minority groups are unimportant. Socially, economically and politically their experience is certainly important. But psychologically, in relation to the dominant (male) groups in the workplace, I would argue that focussing on the experience of women, who may also of course have physical disabilities or be ethnic group members, is a more fruitful way to increase our understanding of the underlying power relationships in the world of work (see also Cockburn, 1991b).

What is women's work?

The origin of gender

When a baby is born the first thing people notice about it is whether it is male or female. From then on the baby is treated as a boy or girl. The effects on the individual of this simple and universally accepted behaviour cannot be overestimated. For quite a while babies themselves are apparently not conscious of any sex differences. Growing children learn about themselves and how they should behave by modelling their behaviour on that of the people around them. Gradually the child perceives that he is a boy or she is a girl and that boys and girls are treated differently, long before there is any understanding of why this is so or what the physical differences are.

Adult expectations of sex differences in behaviour are communicated very quickly to children. As early as age one boys tend to play more vigorously and aggressively than girls (Maccoby and Jacklin, 1980). Children are already acting out what their parents consider to be the masculine and feminine roles in their society, by following their lead and responding to their encouragement or discouragement of various activities (Huston, 1983). Thus boys are typically encouraged to play with blocks but not with dolls, and vice versa for girls. Girls are encouraged to seek help and to offer help to others, but boys are not. By the age of two girls have learned, apparently, that they are supposed to be dependent and conformist while boys know they are supposed to be ruggedly independent.

By the age of four practically all children know what sex they are – although they may still be confused about the genital basis for sex differences. Usually they seem to make judgements of sex from external cues like dress, manner and appearance (Kohlberg, 1966). They now have some definite ideas about appropriate behaviour for boys and girls.

Initially this is very specific, like whether they should go to the boys' or girls' lavatory. By the end of adolescence, however, the idea of sex role differences has permeated their whole lives and developed into either a masculine or feminine *gender identity*, that is, having an image of oneself as a man or a woman. They now accept the unquestioned assumption that men and women are supposed to feel differently and behave differently about virtually everything.

As adults they will react differently to (other people's) infant children depending on what colour of bonnet they're wearing, blue or pink (Nicholson, 1984). And men, in their descriptions of men and women, will use different lists of personality characteristics.

An important aspect of this stereotyping is that along with the 'strong and aggressive' as opposed to 'weak and passive' differences which people learned before they ever went to school, there are mental attributes which bear directly on the modern workplace. Men are now 'logical' and 'scientific' where women are not (Gettys and Cann, 1981). In this they are following a long tradition of Western philosophy in which reason itself was seen as a male but not a female attribute (Lloyd, 1984). Our whole world is therefore gendered, and we will now focus on the way that that process applies specifically to the work of world.

The gendering of work

Differences between people are cognitively easier to spot than similarities. In the Stanford-Binet intelligence test that we discussed in Chapter 10 there is a marked difference in the conceptual ability required to see similarities as opposed to seeing differences. Six-year old children, for instance can usually tell us that *summer* is hot whereas *winter* is cold. But not until they are much older can they tell us the similarity between them, that they are both seasons.

It should be no surprise, therefore, that people tend to see males and females as much more different from each other than similar as people.

And differences, when applied to social groups, invariably take on connotations of 'us' and 'them' and of superiority/inferiority. We saw how easy this was to arrange, even with artificially formed laboratory groups, when we discussed group dynamics in Chapter 7. In the world of work men and women are different and *unequal*, and that inevitably means that men as a group are in positions superior to women as a group. As we shall see this applies in all areas of the world of work, within an organization and also between different kinds of job.

In its crudest form the gendering of work assumes that the biological differences between men and women inevitably mean that men are physically stronger than women and thus the more arduous forms of work, for example in heavy industry, should be done exclusively by men. This assumption does not stand up to any scrutiny.

We noted in Chapter 1 that with the coming of the Industrial Revolution to the United Kingdom whole families, women and children as well as men, worked in the new factories. Nineteen-hour days under the appalling conditions of these early factories does seem fairly arduous does it not? Yet oddly enough few people said that women were biologically incapable of doing it.

By the 1870s the situation had changed. The first serious depression of the industrialised era and the growth of the (mainly male) trade unions combined to exclude many women from the factories (Hakim, 1980). Where jobs were scarce men took, and were given, priority over women. When the next economic boom occurred, in the 1890s, it was based on the development of heavy industry like steelmaking and shipbuilding, and this seems to have been the time when men discovered that women were biologically incapable of such arduous and dangerous labour. This exclusion of women from heavy work was extended to paid work in general:

> Working wives and mothers in particular were regarded as unnatural, immoral, and negligent home-makers and parents. They were also accused of taking work from men. (Abbott and Wallace, 1990)

From this point on the basic pattern was set, psychologically, for most of the twentieth century: the man was the head of the household and the breadwinner, who went out to work for which he was paid, while the woman stayed home and looked after the home and the children – and of course the husband – for which she was not paid. The exceptions were single women, most of whom always had to work, and many working-class women who couldn't afford not to. Historically at least a third of all women have been in paid employment at any given time (Hakim, 1980). But this ideological division between public (male) work life and private (female) domestic life was almost universally accepted – by women as well as men (Davidoff, L'Esperance and Newby, 1976).

In the twentieth century this basic pattern was radically shaken up twice, during each of the World Wars. During these ten years most of the able-bodied men in the industrialised world were called upon to fight for their countries. This resulted in several labour shortages, particularly in agriculture and heavy industry and every government involved exhorted its women to do their patriotic duty and take over the world of work from their menfolk.

So women made tanks and guns and ships, drove buses, tractors and ambulances and did all the other arduous work that only men were biologically capable of handling before the war. Indeed governments went so far as to provide workplace nurseries during the Second World War so that even women with young children could do their bit. (See, for example, Costello, 1985).

All this changed very rapidly when war ended. Yet again the prevailing social dogma was that a woman's place is in the home and that women are biologically unsuited to heavy work. Only towards the end of the twentieth century has this convenient myth, used to regulate female participation in the labour market, been seriously challenged with economic conditions producing a higher proportion of women at work than ever before. With this challenge has gone what was widely seen as the last taboo, the employment of women in fighting units of the military. Though even here there is a convenient amnesia about the women who fought in the Soviet army in the Second World War and in most guerilla armies thereafter.

But the myth of women's work/men's work is so psychologically important to men as a group that it retains a great deal of its vigour even now. The gendering of work in general has led inexorably, and continuously, to the gendering of jobs in particular.

The gendering of particular jobs

The figures really speak for themselves in this case. In the United Kingdom, in the 1980s, some 86 per cent of workers in heavy industry were male while in the retail trade and consumer services sector of the economy 67 per cent were female (EOC, 1987). In the clerical/secretarial field about 73 per cent of workers were female.

While men are numerically dominant in several areas of employment there are very few jobs in which men don't work. They are found in far more jobs than women, who tend to be clustered in just a few. In the United States, for example, three quarters of all women in paid employment work at just five kinds of job, clerical/secretarial, domestic, elementary school teaching, nursing and consumer services (Terborg, 1985). This situation has not come about by chance. It is important to men as a group that the work they do be distinguished from that of women as a group, and they use their power in organizations to make it happen (see for example, Walby, 1988; West, 1990).

This de facto segregation between men's and women's work is known as *horizontal* segregation to distinguish it from another type of segregation, *vertical* segregation (Hakim, 1979). Vertical segregation occurs where one sex is typically in higher status occupations than the other. So it is no great surprise to find that 80 to 90 per cent of managers in Britain are male (EOC, 1987).

But even in occupations that are predominantly female, like hairdressing, catering or social work, the people at the top of the occupational ladder are also usually male. Less than two per cent of all senior executives in the United Kingdom and the United States are female (Alban-Metcalfe and Nicholson, 1984, Marshall 1984). Moreover job segregation is not confined to capitalist societies: it was just as true of the former Soviet Union (Sacks, 1975). It is also true of Cuba where biological differences have been enshrined in law, resulting in 300 kinds of jobs being closed to women (Bengelsdorf and Hagelman, 1979).

Of course there have been some changes in recent years. There are higher and increasing percentages of women in professional and managerial jobs in many countries than there were twenty years ago. There are even a few more women engineers and bus drivers. And there are also more women who own their own businesses. But the basic pattern remains the same and one review, after surveying these changes, concludes succinctly:

> All in all . . . there has been little reduction in the segregation of jobs based on gender over the years. The majority of men work with other men and are supervised and managed by men. Most women work only with other women and are supervised by women, although their employers and senior bosses will probably be male. Very few women occupy positions of power. (Davidson, 1987, p. 230)

Paid and unpaid work

It goes without saying that if women generally have lower-grade work than men they will be paid less for doing it. So women typically earn less than men. But women also typically earn less than men even for doing the *same* kind of work (Coyle, 1982). In recent decades women have generally earned between a half and two thirds of what men earned for doing the same work (Walby, 1988).

In previous years it was even quite common for men and women doing the same *job* in the same *organization* to receive different rates of pay. Legislation in the 1960s and 1970s, in various countries, to enforce the principle of equal pay for equal work has ended this particularly obvious inequity. It is partly for this reason that the pay gap appeared to close slightly in recent years. But (male) employers have become adept at finding loopholes in the fine print of what 'equal work' means exactly (for example EOC, 1991).

The pay difference between men and women is not simply a problem of capitalist or Western societies. Doctors in most industrialised countries generally earn several times the average industrial wage, while in the former Soviet Union they earned less than the average industrial wage. But then most of the doctors there were women (Sacks, 1975).

So far we have been discussing the experiences mainly of women in the full-time labour market. But there are two other important aspects of the typically female relationship to the world of work that we need to examine, part-time employment and the unpaid domestic work that plays a role in the life of virtually every woman regardless of what else she may do.

The 1970s and 1980s saw a marked trend in the industrialised world away from manufacturing and into the service sector of the economy. This meant a switch away from traditionally male and full-time employment towards a traditionally female employment that was deliberately organized to be largely part-time (Beechey and Perkins, 1987). Married women, with or without children, were especially likely to enter this kind of employment rather than full-time work. Some 90 per cent of all part-time jobs in the European Community are now done by women (Davidson, 1987).

But part-time work is usually more poorly paid and insecure than full-time work. There is often no entitlement to pensions and other benefits. However, women returning to the world of work after their children start school are often given little choice. Part-time work may well be all that is available to them given the universal assumption that they (and not the male parents) are primarily responsible for the care of their children. Private day care is very expensive and public or workplace care almost non-existent. So even to work part-time entails a great deal of time pressure on women with children that can lead to stress and ill health (Haw, 1982). For many women therefore the option of having a full-time working career that is the goal of nearly all men, with its opportunities for advancement, for using existing skills and learning new ones, and for earning more money, is simply not available.

The differences between men and women are probably most starkly contrasted when we consider the unpaid domestic labour that is done at home. The vast majority of this work is done by women. In some cases it can be well over 100 hours a week. Marilyn Waring graphically lists what that may entail:

> Cathy, a young middle-class North American housewife spends her days preparing food, clearing food and dishes from the table, washing dishes, dressing and diapering her children, disciplining children, taking the children to day-care or to school, disposing of garbage, dusting, gathering clothes for washing, doing the laundry, going to the gas station and the supermarket, repairing household items, ironing, keeping an eye on or playing with the children, making beds, paying bills, caring for pets and plants, putting away toys, books and clothes, sewing or mending or knitting, talking with door-to-door salespeople, answering the telephone, vacuuming, sweeping, and washing floors, cutting the grass, weeding and shoveling snow, cleaning the bathroom and the kitchen, putting her children to bed. Cathy has to face the fact that she fills her time in a *totally* unproductive manner. She . . . is economically inactive, and economists regard her as unoccupied. (Waring, 1989, pp. 15–16)

Waring's point here is that unless 'Cathy' did all this her husband would be quite unable to do *his* (paid, full-time) job. If she were not there he would be faced with the choice of paying an enormous amount of money for these services – or giving up his job. And no government could afford to pay the market rate for these services either if it wanted to keep husbands and fathers in full-time employment.

Yet the only 'payment' Cathy receives for her work is whatever her husband feels like giving her. She earns nothing as of right. And her skilled labour does not officially exist. Only if she performs these tasks in the formal economy – as a cleaner, caterer, housekeeper or manager – will she count. Because she has pre-school age children Cathy's exclusion from the labour force is generally regarded as right and proper; as 'natural' – unless she or her husband are rich enough to afford a nanny or they live in an extended family.

For most of the twentieth century this state of affairs has been accepted as normal and gone largely unquestioned, certainly by men, in the industrialised world (both capitalist and communist) *and* in the Third World, where if anything women do even more of the housework and sometimes earn money from craftwork as well (Waring, 1989). The different treatment officially accorded to male and female work has often been reflected in pay bargaining where trade unions and employers have agreed on a 'family wage' with the understanding that the man is the breadwinner with a wife and children to care for.

Totalitarian states have not bothered with such niceties. Mussolini and the Italian Fascists in 1929 and Hitler and the German Nazis in 1933 'solved' their countries' unemployment problems by simply ordering all working women back into the home, which was much more suited to their female nature, of course, than the world of work.

As little as a dozen years ago men in full-time employment usually saw their domestic contribution as merely helping out with the chores, even when their wife was also working full-time (for example, Cockburn, 1991a). This attitude may be changing however. In a recent British survey 91 per cent of men agreed with the proposition that 'When both partners work full-time, the man should take an equal share of the domestic chores.' So has the New Man finally arrived? Sorry. Although their *attitudes* may have changed, men's *behaviour* lags far behind: less than 20 per cent actually did the chores equally (Ferri, 1993). But as we have already seen in Chapter 14, and elsewhere, attitudes can change more readily than the behaviour associated with them.

The same survey showed that the work careers of women were still largely determined by the role that reproduction could play in their life cycle – whether they actually had children or not – and how this role was perceived by (mainly male) employers and managers, as well as partners. Though women are spending less and less time out of the labour market in order to bear children and care for them (having fewer children, spaced closer together, and returning to work sooner) the male parent is still generally regarded as the breadwinner.

Work is still regarded as being of secondary importance to women, and employers and trade unions both continue to act on that assumption (see for example Purcell, 1984; Cockburn, 1991b). Yet there is ample evidence that work has a similar meaning for the lives of women as it does for those of men (for example Martin and Roberts, 1983; Dex, 1985). And the loss of their employment can have the same negative consequences for women as it can for men (Martin and Wallace, 1986).

Also in this recent survey more men than women saw themselves as being good with tools and making things, and with organizing and managing, than women (Ferri, 1993). More women than men saw themselves as good at speaking and writing and in caring. All the old stereotypes are very much alive and well. They have a particularly powerful effect at a time of rapid technological change, and that is the issue we will now address.

Women and the effects of the new technology

In the last chapter we examined the effects of new technology on the workplace and on working lives and saw that the introduction of such technology was always a political act, whatever else it was. We noted the structural antagonism between managers and workers in organizations that was expressed in a long-term struggle for control of the workplace.

That struggle was usually perceived as being between different groups of men, and where women were affected it was simply by virtue of being part of the workforce.

During the 1980s research was carried out on the effects of new technology specifically as it affected women. Especially important was the pioneering work of Cynthia Cockburn who studied an important aspect of the new information technology, the computerisation of the printing industry (Cockburn, 1991a). Cockburn's research was centred on London where the printers had been a tightly-organized and close-knit fraternity since the invention of the printing press in the fifteenth century.

For much of the twentieth century printers had been able to earn considerably more money through their trade unions (sometimes vastly more money) than workers in other trades and the prospect of new technology being introduced was a very serious threat to these earnings. This was especially true for the compositors, who actually set the type, and had always regarded themselves as a labour aristocracy. Their jealously guarded craft was to be entirely replaced by the new technology.

Cockburn shows how this blow not only devastated the working lives of the compositors but also their sense of masculine identity which was intimately bound up with it. Throughout their history the print workers had been hostile to the entry of women into their craft. The usual be-whiskered arguments were offered about women not being able to cope with the physical demands of the job. These were rendered even more specious than usual by the fact that, although the technology had always been designed by men for the use of men, there were always *some* women printers who had braved the hostility and entered the craft successfully.

Cockburn also found, both in printing and elsewhere, that where there *were* the occasional heavy physical demands in a job they also taxed the strength of older or weaker men (Cockburn, 1985). But with the help of their colleagues, and/or a little re-organization of the work, they had no trouble in coping. But when this arrangement was suggested as a possibility for any women who might require it it was regarded as favourable treatment and unfair to men as a group. Most of the older compositors accepted redundancy settlements and left the trade with the introduction of the new computer technology. However their trade union was still powerful enough to find jobs (albeit with lower earnings often) for younger members using the new technology. But the new jobs did not have the old 'hot metal' masculine atmosphere of the traditional print room. They were regarded as only semi-skilled.

These jobs involved the use of keyboards and typically were regarded by the men as 'glorified typing'. In other words what they were now reduced to doing (shock! horror!) was 'women's work'. And indeed there was no longer even the tired old strength argument to deny women these jobs any longer. The handful of women in the London printing industry in 1960 had grown to about 10 000 by 1990. And the Apprentice of the Year Award for 1985 was won by a young woman (Cockburn, 1991a).

However these women not only earn a lot less than men in the printing trade used to, they earn a lot less than the men do *now*. Female earnings at the end of the 1980s were 56 per cent of male earnings. Yet Cockburn notes some change in the position of women, and perhaps even a greater awareness on the part of men, arising from the new technology:

> At the beginning of the 1980s women were battling even for the right to express their views. By the early 1990s, even though equality of outcomes in practice is as distant as ever, there is a certain legitimacy in the idea of equality of treatment and of opportunity for women workers. If the men's age-old fear of employers' use of women to degrade their occupation has become a reality, it is a possibility they now know, in their heart of hearts, that they themselves helped to create. (Cockburn, 1991a, p. 247)

But Cockburn has also shown that where men can move out of previously male-oriented jobs that are becoming identified as 'women's work' they will do so (Cockburn, 1985). This may occur *horizontally* as in tailoring where men moved out of sewing jobs when women moved in to them and gravitated to cutting and pattern making. It may also occur *vertically* as in radiography where men tend to be promoted over women because of their greater mobility – wives normally being expected to accompany husbands when they move but not vice versa – and because they don't usually need to take time out from their career to look after children. Men generally escape into management even in occupations that have mainly female workers, like primary school teaching, social work or catering.

The gendering of technology

One of the most important insights thrown up by the work of Cockburn and others is that not only do different jobs become gendered as men's work or women's work but technology itself is gendered, and that gender is, of course, masculine (Cockburn, 1985). As Cockburn says:

> The many technologists and technicians I have interviewed (almost all male) have expressed time and again their identification as men with technology and of technology itself with masculinity. (Cockburn, 1988, p. 38)

Even the new information technology, which in physical terms is clearly just as useable by women as men, very quickly became gendered as male:

> The computer was the brainchild of male engineers and was born into a male line of production technology. The fact that it has a keyboard rather like a (feminine) typewriter confuses no one for long. When a computer arrives in a school, for instance, boys and girls are quick to detect its latent masculinity. Their own relationship to each other and to the new machine quickly confirms this. The boys soon elbow the girls out of the way. But when they use the keyboard they often take care to do so with two fingers only, so that they cannot be thought to be typists. (Cockburn, 1988, p. 32)

That last resonant image (which has been confirmed to me by more than one teacher) gets right to the heart of the matter. It is also the final nail in the coffin of the need-for-male-strength myth. Even young children know that the real issue is one of *control*. Technology means power, and knowing how to use that power lets you feel in control.

In any given job the control may actually be quite illusory; we saw in the last chapter how men could be as tied to the destructive pace of the new information technology as of any other kind. But the *feeling* of being in control is psychologically important in their relation to the people who are kept away from the technology – females. And as the new generation learns the same lessons about control, technology and gender, so the circle is closed and the cycle continues over time.

Organizations and sexuality

Male values

One of the major unquestioned assumptions about organizations is that they are value-free. But we have seen throughout this book that Weber's model (first encountered in Chapter 2) of an unchanging entity which is run objectively according to the rulebook, and where everyone is treated impartially, bears only the most tenuous connection to the world that people actually work in. In fact, as we shall see, the organization's values are distinctly male.

The very fact of organizational hierarchies, with pyramidal structures and a leader at the top is a typically masculine way of regarding the world of work (Hearn *et al.*, 1989). It grew out of the patriarchal hierarchies in which the vast majority of societies have been arranged, with male Popes and Archbishops, with fathers as heads of household and kings and presidents as heads of state (Mann, 1986). And an arrangement as universal as this probably has powerful psychological roots and a great in-built resistance to change (Mitchell, 1975).

That heads of state or household can sometimes be female simply reinforces the arrangement, because they are still generally regarded as exceptional. Take the case of Margaret Thatcher, for example, a renowned head of state but not head of her own household – or even an equal partner in the eyes of the law. For all of the eleven years that she was Prime Minister of the United Kingdom Mrs Thatcher had to ask her husband to sign her annual tax return.

When we look at the way women *as women* are treated in organizations an interesting pattern emerges (Hearn *et al.*, 1989). Women seem to be categorised largely in terms of their biological sex characteristics. At one end of the spectrum are organizations in the twilight world of prostitution and pornography where women's bodies, or their images, are objects and services for sale. The sex industry throughout the world is a vast multi-billion dollar enterprise, employing many people and raising a lot of money for governments through taxes.

In the more respectable world of work are the organizations found in the 'glamour' industries like fashion, modelling, cosmetics and the mass media (in both its advertising and its 'news' role). In these industries images of women are used to sell clothes, cars, eyeliners and newspapers. All these industries are, of course, controlled by men and the images of women that they employ are designed to appeal either directly to men or to women who want to appeal to men.

But how does this relate to the everyday life of office or factory where most people earn their living? Well, when was the last time you were greeted at a company's reception desk by a fat old man? Commercial organizations typically use young women in that role in their office buildings, as do other organizations that have direct contact with the general public like banks, airlines, car rental firms and so on. And following the grey male heads that appear at the front of an organization's glossy literature you will probably find a lot of young and female ones.

Finally it is very important to note here the interaction of work and emotional life, which we explored in Chapter 6: 'The unconscious at work'. We saw there that, however much organizations may want their employees to bring only their hands and brains to work, people come as a package deal. That includes their emotional life, and an important part of anyone's emotional life is their sexuality – regardless of how it may be expressed in terms of behaviour, whether directly or indirectly. Insofar as people at work have interpersonal relationships, therefore, their sexuality may potentially be involved. The behaviour expressed directly can range from mild flirtation to a passionate love affair. And of course many marriages have resulted from work relationships between men and women with estimates, for what they're worth, ranging as high as about a quarter of all marriage partners met in such a context (Hearn and Parkin, 1987).

You can see why organizations would want to discourage such behaviour of course: they can make work life very messy. At the same time there is not much that organizations can, or perhaps should, do to legislate against such behaviour *provided* (and it is a big proviso) that it is dealing with relationships willingly entered into on both sides. If not, we're talking about *sexual harassment*.

Sexual harassment

Running through even the most pin-striped and buttoned-down of organizations, as we have seen, we can usually find the unquestioned assumption that the sexuality of female employees can be used, in ways ranging from crucial to trivial, to further the organization's goals.

The other important unquestioned assumption about sexuality in the organization, as in society at large, is that everybody in it is heterosexual. So the automatic casting of homosexual men and women as not only abnormal but alien, and therefore less human than heterosexuals, is the first and most pervasive aspect of sexual harassment (Hearn *et al.*, 1989). Homosexuals in many organizations can still, in fact, lose their jobs entirely on account of their sexuality.

The term 'sexual harassment' was first used in the United States in the 1970s to describe unwanted sexual activity by men against women. Several public bodies in the United States and the United Kingdom have produced detailed definitions of the term and a typical one would include the following:

> repeated and unwanted verbal or sexual advances, sexually explicit derogatory statements or sexually discriminating remarks which are offensive to the worker involved, which cause the worker to feel threatened, humiliated, patronised or harassed or which interfere with the worker's job performance, undermine job security or create a threatening or intimidating work environment. Sexual harassment can take many forms, from leering, ridicule, embarrassing remarks or jokes, unwelcome comments about dress or appearance, deliberate abuse, the repeated and/or unwanted physical contact, demands for sexual favours, or physical assaults on workers. (Hadjifotiou, 1983)

The activity itself had always existed in organizations, of course. But up until the 1970s the combination of Weber's bureaucracy, Taylor's scientific management and Behaviourist views of human psychology had militated against a serious study of the problem. It was regarded as an aberration; something that shouldn't happen in a well-run organization. It is now clear that it is an integral part of organizational life.

There are perhaps two major reasons for this. One is that organizations are embedded in a society which, as we saw earlier in the chapter, is still largely male-oriented in its values and patriarchal in its social organization. The other reason is that of the way power is distributed in organizations. As we saw in Chapter 2, and again at various times throughout this book, the pursuit of group interests is an important everyday aspect of organizational life.

The most powerful groups are the most successful in satisfying their interests. Men as men rarely form such a group, because they rarely need to. Whether it is the provision of toilet facilities or promotion opportunities, men's needs and interests are invariably seen as being those of the organization (for example Cockburn, 1991b; Hearn *et al.*, 1989; Kanter, 1977). Therefore if women form a group to pursue *their* particular interests within the organization they are immediately seen as seeking more favourable treatment than men. This is as true of the provision of a workplace crèche as removing the need to relocate to obtain promotion.

This combination of organizational power and a male-dominated society means that sexual harassment has been, and largely still is, well-nigh invisible for many men. There are exceptions, of course. The research in this field usually mentions individual men who *are* aware of the problem, and indeed some men suffer sexual harassment from women. But the fundamental problem is a structural one and there is probably little that individual women can do to change organizations in this respect. And psychologically the roots of sexual harassment originate, as we have seen, in earliest childhood where males learn that they are more powerful than females in every way.

In terms of numbers of women directly suffering from sexual harassment the figures vary from study to study, going as high as 96 per cent in some jobs traditionally seen as 'men's work' (Hearn and Parkin, 1987). Other areas of work have produced figures ranging from 48 per cent in the United Kingdom to 80 per cent in the United States, where there is probably more awareness of the problem. It certainly seems safe to say that most working women have suffered from sexual harassment.

And this is not a problem confined to women in low-status jobs or positions in an organization; it also occurs in the professions and in the boardroom (Hearn and Parkin, 1987). Indeed on the very day in October 1993 that I first drafted this paragraph there were newspaper reports from both the British and Austrian parliaments of women members being subjected to the most vicious verbal sexual abuse by male political *colleagues*, as well as opponents.

The female experience of management

When women are promoted or recruited into management they quickly face the problem of role models in knowing how to do a manager's job. For men in the same position the problem is solved by modelling themselves on the behaviour of their supervisors. They may be lousy managers but that's besides the point. What they usually are is male. But what do women managers do if they're newly appointed to that situation? Do they behave the way their male boss does too?

For a start they will have to decide how to dress, something that rarely troubles men. Should they wear a dress, trousers, a suit? We have already seen how important appearance can be to people's judgement of ability. Should they try to look like male managers, and be thought too masculine, or should they look different – with all that that implies. Well they can now be advised by image consultants who will tell them about 'power' dressing and how to cultivate an 'executive' image (Hearn and Parkin, 1987).

The next issue the woman manager faces is the attitude of the men she is supposed to manage. Many men seem to feel threatened by having a woman manager. Expressions of resentment are common, and they seem to centre around the relative organizational power involved. As Cockburn puts it:

> Men . . . have a repertoire of negative representations of women and, significantly, they are criticisms of women *only* in relation to authority. It hinges on two themes, a 'belt and braces' pair. Women are not capable of authority. And they turn into nasty people when in authority . . . Men win in several ways simultaneously. They select women with masculine virtues. They actually succeed in defeminising some women as they filter through. They also, however, condemn even appropriately authoritative behaviour in women as mannish. And they gain a stick with which to threaten other women. 'You wouldn't want to change your nice little personality, would you ?' said one reporting officer . . . to a woman subordinate, to discourage her from seeking promotion. (Cockburn, 1991b, pp. 68–9)

Yet Cockburn also shows that, for all the male resentment of women becoming managers, when it actually happens they may be surprised to find that they quite enjoy the difference. Their experience was that

> . . . women were *nicer* than men . . . women were less autocratic . . . had more sympathy with staff feelings and related better to the public. One man preferred working with women because 'you can smile at each other. With the same sex you don't.' (p. 68, original emphasis)

As opposed to the case of the 'New Man' that we noted earlier in the chapter, what may have been happening here is that attitudes were changing to catch up with behaviour. Women managers were a fact of organizational life, their numbers were increasing and it looked as if they had come to stay. Being faced with a new situation the men either had to quit or come to terms with the changes.

From the viewpoint of senior management the more feminine approach to managing was also welcome, at least in some respects. It fitted in with a more human relations attitude to the organization and where the organization wished to present a caring image, either to its staff or to its customers, women were often ideal for the job. But this approach can only be allowed to go so far, of course. Here is Cockburn again:

> If changes of this kind become widespread and long-lasting . . . it will be a gain for women and will make working life more tolerable for many men too. On the other hand . . . a new line is likely to be drawn. Women may join in the exercise of power: they may even change the style of management: but they are unlikely to be permitted to change the nature of the organization. (Cockburn, 1991b, p. 73)

The relationship between men and women that we have been discussing seems to me to have become one of the most crucial aspects of the world of work and of the way that world is changing. We will examine this issue again, from a somewhat different perspective, in the next (and final) chapter of this book.

CHAPTER 18

Into the twenty-first century

Plus ça change plus c'est la même chose (The more things change the more they stay the same)

French proverb

The Edsel is here to stay

Henry Ford II to car dealers in 1957

Nobody was ever fired for buying IBM

Anonymous, pre-1991

Introduction

A hundred years ago, on the threshold of the twentieth century, blacksmiths and builders of horse-drawn carriages were in steady employment. Even the wisest and most far-sighted of social commentators alive then did not foresee (and could not have foreseen) how the motor car would change the way people lived in the twentieth century.

No one could have predicted that this recently invented novelty, the 'horseless carriage', would soon become the dominant mode of transportation, first in the industrialised West, and then throughout the world. Thirteen years into the new century Henry Ford's stroke of genius would lower the unit cost of production sufficiently to bring what had been a luxury within the reach of most families in the United States.

It may be interesting to predict long-term trends in society and in the world of work, and indeed planners of financial and welfare services have no option but to make the attempt, but for our purposes here it would be a pretty fruitless exercise. About the only thing we can be sure of is that a hundred years from now someone will be writing something very similar to the first paragraph of this chapter. Only the example used will be different. Change, as we saw in Chapter 1, is the condition of the universe. Yet as we have also seen throughout the rest of this book, change often masks continuity at a deeper level. What I would like to do in this chapter is to extrapolate what we know about current trends into the immediate future, and to point up some of the enduring issues that will accompany them.

Even this relatively modest exercise is not without its pitfalls. Only a few years ago nobody *had* ever been fired for buying IBM. And the famous proclamation from Henry Ford's grandson about the car that turned out to be industry's most famous turkey is a salutary reminder to us never to trust an expert's opinion about the future, even on the rare occasions when he *doesn't* have a vested interest at stake.

What is likely to change?

Working lives and the kind of work done

The kind of working life that male workers in industrialised countries expected to have at the beginning of the twentieth century will no longer exist at the beginning of the twenty-first. The prospect of spending the whole of one's working life in the same organization if not in the same job, is now rare and rapidly vanishing. For many people in the course of the twentieth century this was in any case an *ideal model* of a working life rather than their actual experience of one. Work lives interrupted (and sometimes terminated) by periods of unemployment or service in the armed forces, were very common. Nevertheless a working life spent in the same factory or office or coal mine was the generally shared, normal expectation of working men, and of their employers too.

The expectations of women had always been different. As we saw in the last chapter a woman's expectations of her working life throughout the twentieth century has been closely bound up with her reproductive cycle and the attitudes towards that cycle of her menfolk and her male employers. Women have been cajoled, enticed, persuaded and bullied into and out of the world of paid employment as male politicians and employers have thought fit. Unless they were unmarried throughout their working lives women did not have the same model of lifetime employment with a single organization that men had.

With the disappearance of that model women may be better placed than men to deal with the implications of working life in the twenty-first century. Heavy industry has declined precipitately in the older industrialised countries, partly because many manufacturing companies are now multinational and can site their factories in less developed countries (or 'newly industrializing countries' in the current jargon), where labour is cheaper. Manufacturing in industrialised countries will be focussed more on consumer goods and services. Existing jobs are now much more likely to be in the service sector, where women have always found more employment.

In addition the increase in computerisation and the use of information technology has, as we saw in the case of printing in the last chapter, had the effect of providing more opportunities of employment for women. And as we also saw in that chapter the growth of part-time employment and the relative decrease of full-time employment also implies a relative increase of women in the work force. Women will shortly make up half the work force in industrialised countries. The marked trend throughout the 1980s and early 1990s of cutting back on full-time staff in favour not only of part-time staff but of external contract staff, seems set to continue.

One other important change to the ideal model of a working life spent in a single organization is that the organization might not last that long, or if it does it may well have altered quite radically. In the past decade or so many household names have either gone out of business, as markets and world trading conditions changed, or merged with, or been taken over by, other companies. This is perhaps particularly evident in the car industry where very few marques are still owned by the organizations that bear their names.

Even the grandest of companies are no longer immune from these problems. Indeed the largest ones may have a particular difficulty in adapting to changed conditions partly because of the huge success they have previously enjoyed. IBM is perhaps the most notable case in point here. Having invested heavily in supplying expensive mainframe computers for centralised use in organizations, it found itself being out-flanked and losing market share dramatically in the late 1980s to newer companies marketing cheap personal computers for localised use, such as the highly successful Apple. In 1991 IBM in fact decided to cut its losses and come to an agreement with Apple in order to safeguard its very existence. And in the following year General Motors, at one time the largest company in the world, lost a staggering $10 billion.

The clear implication for the future is that organizational size, formerly regarded almost as a good-in-itself, will have to be related to the function and operation of the organization. This is true of the public sector just as much as the private, and both will apparently have a more managerial ethos and closer relations with consumers of services than previously. Then trends towards decentralisation of function and flatter hierarchies in organizations, which we have noted in previous chapters, will presumably continue also.

Another important trend in future working lives is that the uncertainty about the continued existence of employment, which most blue-collar workers have always lived with, will also apply to white-collar workers, and even professionals. Where blue-collar workers have traditionally, and routinely, been fired or made redundant at short notice as employers tried to cut costs, the same fate is now befalling even the most highly trained and experienced professional specialists. A typical prediction is that many American organizations will halve their managerial staff between 1990 and the year 2000 (Miller, 1991). The only difference in their status now is the quality of euphemism applied to their treatment. They are not fired as such but are rather the victims of 'downsizing' or 'delayering', or having their posts 'saved'.

The accountant's 'bottom line' view of organizational priorities looks like being the only one that matters for the foreseeable future. Despite the glowing tributes ritually paid by organizations in their glossy publications to the wonderful qualities of their staff (invariably their 'best asset') they are still seen purely as a *cost* on the balance sheet. Perhaps the situation will only change when an organization has such few staff performing such crucial jobs that they all have (very expensive) expert power, rather like football teams whose major *assets* (as well as costs) appear on both the balance sheet *and* the field of play (Handy, 1985).

How much work will people do?

For all but the 10 to 12 per cent of people who are self-employed, work in an industrialised society means having a job – and therefore an income. Despite the small but steady increase in the numbers of self-employed people in the 1980s and 1990s the links between work-job-income seem to be as firm as ever for most people and the great majority will continue to envisage their working lives in terms of being employed by an organization.

The most immediate problem with this vision of future working lives is that there will not be enough jobs for all the people who want them. The recent 10 to 15 per cent levels of unemployment in the industrialised world look set to continue. Even if governments are not actually encouraging unemployment by their economic policies, and have some idea of how to create jobs (two very big 'ifs'), the ideal of full employment that informed policy and planning for most of the twentieth century has all but been abandoned. So, many people will have their expected working lives curtailed by 10 or even 20 years or more. At the same time there is a serious possibility that many young people may have to wait for years, perhaps indefinitely, before they can even start their working lives.

There has also been a long-term trend for people who *are* employed to work less. Between the end of the nineteenth and the end of the twentieth century the full-time working week for men has decreased by a third, from about 60 hours to about 40 hours. Holiday entitlement has also increased from virtually nothing to over four weeks on average. Together with a shorter working life this means that the total number of hours worked by men in full-time employment has decreased by about half (Armstrong, 1984). It looks as if this process has now halted, if not started to go into reverse. A favourite ploy for organizations wishing to show quick results from restructuring is to have the same amount of work done by fewer people. This leads to instant paper profits and efficiency savings. It also leads to more hours of work, often accompanied by more stress, for the remaining staff.

However as we saw in Chapter 5 this process can also have an expensive downside for the organization, with workers producing diminishing returns beyond a certain point, feeling increasingly angry and frustrated, and even burning out. Even the traditionally workaholic Japanese organizational culture, in which the 'salary men' routinely work far more hours than they are paid for and do not take their fully holiday entitlement, has been forced to recognise the existence of *karoshi*, or death by overwork. And the very low level of stress associated with, for example, librarians in Figure 5.2 has almost certainly increased now because of fewer staff coupled with increasing use of information technology.

Work organizations and the future

The focus on cost-cutting and therefore reduction of full-time staff, which has dominated organizational life during the 1980s and early 1990s, looks at this stage to be irreversible. The services previously performed by many of these staff are now subcontracted out on a fee basis. Cleaning, catering, maintenance, security and so on will be provided by other organizations, often themselves now fairly large companies. But there is also a growing trend for a great variety of professional and technical services to be provided in this way too.

Some industries have always used *some* professional and technical services in this way, for example publishing and the mass media, and here the trend will simply be taken as far as possible. This is particularly true of increased self-employment in these industries. In other industries that had previously employed many technical and professional people, either as line managers or as specialists, staff cuts have often meant the establishment of small businesses, or self-employed consultants who may well find themselves dealing with their previous employers but on a fee basis. The computer and information technology industries are a good example of this trend (Handy, 1984)

Self-employment has the important psychological benefit of *autonomy*, of being one's own boss, but that only applies if the self-employment is freely chosen. Anecdotal evidence and personal experience suggest to me, however, that a lot of this consultancy activity is more of a desperate form of self-defence, and the economic reality for many people in this position may be more *un*employment than *self*-employment. And of course the failure rate of small businesses in most industrialised countries is huge. Most of them can expect to be out of business within a few years.

As we saw in the last chapter there has also been a tremendous growth of part-time employment in recent years, with the great majority of these jobs filled by (poorly paid) women workers. This trend also looks like continuing. So organizations will be generally smaller, therefore, with fewer permanent full-time staff. Organizations will often be considering another important cost-cutting measure, moving the organization – wholly or partly – to cheaper accommodation. The two are often connected of course. Fewer people means that less space is required, but the decision to relocate, often out of major cities like London or New York, usually means leaving behind many people who are unable or unwilling to move – which may, of course, be a major point of the exercise. And it may also mean paying lower rates to staff who do move, even permanent staff.

The fashionable buzzword applied to recent changes in employment practice, from the organizational viewpoint, is *flexibility* of labour. Crucial to this viewpoint is the perceived capacity of the organization to deploy its human resources at very short notice and in any way it chooses. Although the origin of the flexible specialisation of labour *theory* is American (Piore and Sabel, 1984), much of its appeal lies in the key role that this *practice* has played in the spectacular financial success of many large Japanese companies (Kumazawa and Yamada, 1988). In the West this approach has taken various forms.

The concept of *the flexible firm* is the form that flexibility has taken in the United Kingdom, for example (Atkinson, 1984). The concept here implies two forms of flexibility in the use of labour, *functional* and *numerical*. With functional flexibility a small 'core' of well-paid permanent full-time employees provide a set of integrated skills needed to perform the key tasks of the organization. By contrast a large 'periphery' of part-time/temporary/self-employed, and so on, workers will perform the less important tasks and they can, of course, be hired and fired at will. There is also a parallel here with the use of peripheral labour in the Third World that we noted earlier.

For the 'core' workers to function in this way they will need to be highly trained, and as training is usually regarded as a cost by most employers guess what doesn't happen? Because it is popularly seen as a necessary response to rapidly changing market conditions, the *idea* of flexibility will continue to inform the future strategy of many work organizations, but how much change this actually represents in the organization of work is open to question (Thompson, 1989). It has been argued that the major impact of the flexible firm has been the (politically-motivated) removal of workers' rights to wage bargaining and security of employment (Pollert, 1988).

From the individual worker's viewpoint *insecurity* might therefore be a more appropriate term than flexibility. Of course for some people this may be just the stimulus they need, and redundancy may be a springboard to great success. People high on need for achievement and with an internal locus of control would probably be involved here, and their success stories receive wide currency. But what about the majority who are not high achievers and have an external locus of control? Are they to be regarded simply as nature's losers in a re-run of the Victorian Social Darwinism we encountered in Chapter 1?

The individual's relationship to work and non-work

We saw in the last section how more and more people are being forced into part-time employment and/or self-employment and/or unemployment. The lines between these three ways of relating to work are becoming blurred, and it is quite possible for people to be in more than one of these situations at any given time. Indeed in any financial year, when someone loses full-time employment, it is possible to experience all four ways of relating to the world of work. This does mark a change from the previous Great Depression of the 1930s when full-time work or welfare were usually the only options available.

Another important set of orientations towards the world of work lies in what is called the *informal economy*. The formal economy represents the traditional industrial society model of wages paid and taxes collected; of goods and services exchanged for money. The informal economy is much less visible, but no less real for all that. It consists of work activities that are not officially recorded in statistics of earnings and taxes. The housework that we considered in the last chapter would be included in the informal economy as would painting one's own house instead of paying to have it done.

Charles Handy has divided work activity in the informal economy into three different colours, *black, mauve* and *grey* (Handy, 1984).

(A) THE BLACK ECONOMY

This is the most publicised sector of the informal economy. It is essentially illegal because it involves payment for work done by individuals or small businesses that is not declared as taxable income. By its very nature it is therefore very difficult to calculate precisely. Its frequency also differs in different cultures. Thus estimates have ranged from 2 per cent of the Gross National Product in the former West Germany to 20 per cent in Italy, with the United States and the United Kingdom at around 7 to 10 per cent (Mars, 1982; Handy, 1984).

Contrary to political folklore and media stereotype, work in the black economy is usually done by people who are also employed in the formal economy. That is, rather than unemployed people cheating on welfare it is much more likely to be full-time employees 'moon-lighting' from their jobs and cheating the taxman (Pahl, 1984). The reason for this seems to be that they have the wherewithal to do so – capital, access to tools and materials, contacts and so on – denied to the unemployed. The construction trades are the most notable example.

Allied to these activities are a wide variety of underground activities within the formal economy, ranging from systematic fraud and insider dealing in financial centres, like the City of London, to the petty theft of time and resources that are apparently now standard practice in every work organization (Mars, 1982). As Charles Handy puts it:

> Cheating at work is today expected, even condoned, in industries like catering, transport and retailing, while the personal use of office telephones, stationery and secretaries is an accepted perk of every manager. Compared with many of the practices of formal employment, moonlighting is a paragon of honesty and integrity, at least in customer relations. (Handy, 1984, p. 45)

Allowing a controlled amount of theft at work can be quite beneficial from an employer's point of view (Zeitlin, 1971). It can save him paying for decent wages and conditions for a start. It can also allow the employee the chance to exercise some creativity in an otherwise boring environment, which saves the employer the expense and inconvenience of bothering with job enrichment, or any of that other human relations nonsense. The increasing use of information technology at work, such as EPOS and laser scanning devices, will greatly reduce the *presently* known areas of petty theft. But I would never underestimate the power of human ingenuity.

(B) THE MAUVE ECONOMY

The mauve economy was a term coined in 1983 by Helen Chappell to describe small services provided somewhere between the formal and informal economies by people who are often part-time self-employed (Chappell, 1983). They provide mundane services like typing or dressmaking as well as more unusual ones like a dating agency or a telephone reminder service. People providing these services may well declare all or part of their earnings and tend to flit in and out of both formal and informal economies.

In itself the mauve economy may be fairly marginal as yet but it can sometimes provide openings for people to become substantial entrepreneurs, perhaps even with the help of government grants. There are many possibilities and Charles Handy lists 26 of them, ranging from car maintenance to tree pruning (Handy, 1984).

(C) THE GREY ECONOMY

Unlike the black or mauve economics, work in the grey economy is unpaid. It consists of work done in the household or the immediate community in which people live. As well as all the household tasks which, as we saw in the last chapter, are mostly done by women, the grey economy includes performing the same tasks for other people outside the household – whether from love, friendship, duty or reciprocal agreement – plus anything else that people can do for themselves or others without pay. This latter kind of activity can range from looking after a friend's pet in return for his having sorted out a computer bug, to gardening and cooking for disabled relatives or washing the windows of elderly neighbours.

This kind of work activity is far from marginal. Indeed it has been estimated at 51 per cent of all the work done in both formal and informal economies combined (Rose, 1983). Moreover work in this sector of the informal economy is probably growing fastest as people generally spend less time working in the formal economy. People have not regarded work in the grey economy in the same way as working for money, whether for an employer or for themselves. But I suspect that, as the ideal model of lifetime employment with a single employer disappears, the clear distinctions made between the different types of work people do will become blurred, and with that our attitudes towards all kinds of work may well change.

Relationships between men and women

Of all the likely changes in the world of work I would regard this one as the most important and far-reaching in its effects. In the last chapter we noted that the biggest single demographic change in the labour market over recent years was the increased number of women now in it and expected to be in it in the near future. What this means is that dual earning households, where both the man and the woman are in paid employment, have changed from being the exception to being the norm. A recent survey found that more than 60 per cent of households in the United Kingdom were now in this category, and the trend is upwards (Ferri, 1993). This trend will have implications for the future relationships between men and women.

We saw in the last chapter how even where a man and woman worked full-time the woman still ended up doing most of the housework and was normally the one to give up her job if the couple decided to relocate. But there are signs that this might be changing. With so many women now earning, some of them will inevitably earn more than the man they live with. This may be particularly true in the United States. It has been found there that women who earn more than their partner can translate this into an advantage in the domestic 'balance of power' by demanding – and usually receiving – more responsibility and practical help (Ferree, 1987).

The important point of this example is that the behaviour of the men involved changed not because their attitudes towards housework had changed (though they often had) but because the objective financial situation had changed and they had to adapt to it. We have seen more than once in this book the gap between expressed attitudes and actual behaviour, and how if behaviour can be changed first the attitudes will tend to follow.

Changing the behavioural norms in this area will not happen overnight of course: it is a cumulative process. But there are signs that there is a powerful generational phenomenon at work here. Women who are high achievers or who choose to enter traditionally male occupations usually have mothers who were themselves out in the world of work, and at a time when it was less common for women to do so (Sandburg *et al.*, 1987).

There is also some evidence that if fathers do take more responsibility for domestic work, including raising the children, they will tend to produce daughters with a more confident self-image, with fewer stereotypes about what they can and cannot do in the world of work, and probably sons with less macho attitudes towards women (Gilbert and Dancer, 1992). At the same time there is also evidence that men in dual-earner households who manage to have an equitable domestic relationship with their partners suffer less from stress at work than their more traditional male colleagues (Izraeli, 1989).

What is likely to stay the same?

The relationship between men and women

Yes, I think the relationship between men and women at work will change, but it will also stay the same. What will change will be the content of the work done by the different sexes and the perceived importance of women in the labour force. What will change at the margins will be the balance of paid employment and domestic labour. What I suspect will remain largely unchanged is the relative importance attached to men's and women's lives, whether inside or outside the workplace.

The evidence we considered in the last chapter seems to point unequivocally in that direction. The overwhelming difference is that men as a group have power in organizations, and in society in general, and women as a group do not. A few token women on the board of directors, or even a sprinkling of women as Prime Ministers, has made no fundamental difference that I can detect and nor do many observers think it will make any difference in the foreseeable future. Nor can we anticipate any differences when the 'New Men' take over from the old. The words may change, but there is little evidence that men as a group will relate to women as a group any differently.

Even as recently as 1985 it was possible to envisage a different scenario for the twenty-first century:

> ... the conventional attribution of higher status to men's work than to women's work is increasingly coming to be seen as perverse, as the tasks which have typically fallen to women are coming to be seen as more important then many of those which have typically fallen to men ... bearing children ... feeding people ... clothing people ... tending the weak and the sick ... bringing up and educating young children ... being in charge of the household ...
> ... Men have typically shuffled things around in factories, they have shuffled papers around in offices, they have shuffled money around in banks and they have shuffled ideas around in universities. Women, on the other

hand, have been directly concerned with meeting the needs of people. (Robertson, 1985, p. 87)

This does seem to me now, less than a decade later, to be largely wishful thinking unsupported by the most recent evidence.

The problem is at root a psychological one, of course. As we noted in the last chapter it begins at birth – or even before birth, thanks to the wonders of modern medical technology – when parents (and the rest of the world) first become aware of an infant's sex and treat it accordingly. The gendering of jobs and all the other relationships between men and women at work can be traced right back to that moment. Until there is change at this level there can be no real change in the workplace. Waiting for the generational effects of working mothers on their children, which we noted above, may be a very long process indeed, especially with the divorce rate in Western marriages heading for one in two.

The need to work

We began Chapter 8 with a celebrated quotation from former American President Richard Nixon:

> The 'work ethic' holds that labor is good in itself; that a man or woman becomes a better person by virtue of the act of working.

In that chapter we examined the psychological effects of paid employment and the implications for people when that work is lost. One of the ideas we looked at critically was the notion that work is good for mental health and unemployment bad. We found evidence that for many people this simply was not the case, both in the 1930s and over the past fifteen or twenty years. What these people missed most about paid employment was not the 'act of working' itself but the income and the company of others, and, to a certain extent, the social status.

Nixon's version of the work ethic therefore is one that was probably not shared by a sizeable number of his fellow Americans. As we also saw in Chapter 8, and at various other points in this book, what matters more than money to most people, *if they have a choice*, is the content of the work they do. This was borne out by a recent survey conducted in seven countries; Belgium, Britain, Israel, Japan, the Netherlands, the United States and the former West Germany (Harpaz, 1990). The most important work goal (out of 11 possibilities) that people identified in five of these countries was 'interesting work'. In the other two countries it was rated second (Netherlands) and third (West Germany).

An even more recent survey has found that *less than half* of the respondents considered being in paid employment more desirable than being unemployed (Ferri, 1993). As I suggested above this kind of finding probably does not represent a change in people's attitudes towards work, though it is often presented as such.

The people who enjoy their work are, as they always have been and always will be, the people who have enjoyable work. The tiring, dirty, boring, mind-numbing, or soul-destroying work that many (perhaps most) people have to do in order to make a living does nothing to make them 'a better person by virtue of the act of working'. It just makes them angry, depressed and frustrated, something that politicans don't want to know about as they continue to trumpet the work ethic as the official ideology of the industrialised world. What may well change is that people's real feelings about the work ethic will be less easy to suppress.

Work as a social activity

We have seen over and over again how work is a social activity, probably the most important social activity people engage in outside the home. It provides a large part of the meaning of work in everyone's life. Periodically there are debates about the 'flexibility' to be obtained when an organization's staff work from home rather than a central location (Upton, 1984). Certainly the technology is available to make this feasible logistically. Home-workers can be connected with the centre, and with other home-workers, via telephone, fax and personal computer, and they can even communicate as a group via tele- or video-conferencing.

This kind of working obviously lends itself more to some industries than to others. It is widely used in the computer industry and to a lesser extent in a few others, like publishing and financial services. This way of organising work could be extended much more widely, with a little ingenuity, so why does it not happen? In most offices people could either commute physically or electronically, yet working at home is still a comparative rarity for people in full-time paid employment.

One obvious problem is that people can feel physically isolated. Organizations try to counter this by bringing people into the centre at frequent intervals, or arranging a social programme for them. The difficulty with this arrangement as a solution is the formality of it. We have seen throughout this book that it is the very *informality* of social interaction at work that people find attractive, the fact that this interaction is *not* part of the official formal organization but something they provide for themselves. I would therefore suggest that however desirable home-working might look to organizations they will always be faced by this psychological limit to what can be done.

Work psychologists and the struggle for control of the workplace

There is another reason why home-working has had only limited success and it concerns another issue we have met throughout this book: the need for control, which informs the working lives of many managers. Not being able to see in person the people they are supposed to manage is apparently a source of considerable anxiety for managers of 'telecommuting' workers in the computer industry (Clutterbuck, 1985). Any underlying lack of trust that exists is then heightened and exposed.

As with the case of the autonomous work groups in the car industry that we examined in Chapter 7, it was not dissatisfaction with productivity that concerned the managers in question but the fact that they no longer had direct control over their subordinates' *time*. As the psychological relationship between managers and managed shows little signs of changing it is unlikely that telecommuting will be the wave of the future – or for that matter autonomous work groups.

We have seen many instances in this book of the psychological importance of controlling one's working environment. As we saw in Chapter 5, for example, lack of such control is a prime cause of stress. A recent manifestation of problems resulting from such lack of control is known as *Sick Building Syndrome* (Nicholson-Lord, 1990). People who suffer from this syndrome report symptoms such as headaches, eyestrain, sore throats and stuffy noses, for which no likely cause can be found other than the building in which they work.

Many modern office buildings are designed for centralised control of heating, lighting and ventilation. Usually this means that windows are sealed, with heating and air conditioning controlled automatically by (centrally-set) thermostats, and illumination provided by standard strip-lighting in the ceiling space. This environment often contains computers and other kinds of equipment which have not been ergonomically designed and are themselves the source of considerable strain on the individual's capacities. Most importantly from a psychological view-point, neither the working environment nor much of the equipment it contains is subject to individual control, or even adjustment. It is the people concerned who have to adjust, much as people have to adjust to assembly lines. It should not be totally surprising therefore, even to employers, that the resulting stress will inevitably have physical repercussions such as Sick Building Syndrome.

As always, one standard way for employers to react when evidence of work-related illness appears is to deny any responsibility for it. Despite the fact that the United Nations recognises the existence of Sick Building Syndrome, sufferers are often classed as 'malingerers' looking to get off work (Nicholson-Lord, 1990). As up to 80 per cent of office workers may have suffered from it this does seem to represent management denial on a quite heroic scale.

Experts on stress, like the work psychologist Professor Cary Cooper, advise people to get out of their building for twenty minutes when they begin to show symptoms of Sick Building Syndrome (Nicholson-Lord, 1990). This seems like good advice – for managers who have the organizational seniority to act on it. But what about the people who are tied to the end of a word processor all day and suffer disciplinary measures if they don't achieve a certain number of key strokes per hour?

Moreover Cooper's advice does not deal with the central issue: why should individuals be solely responsible for dealing with the working conditions provided by their organization? By putting the onus on the individual to adjust, no matter what the conditions, employers and senior managers are allowed to evade any responsibility for providing an unhealthy working environment in the first place.

This episode neatly encapsulates the relationship of psychologists to the world of work that has existed for the whole of the twentieth century (Hollway, 1991). A workplace problem is defined as the problem of the individuals affected, and individual problems are, of course, the psychologist's prime area of expertise. This allows the organization to hire the psychologist and be seen as helping its employees, without the need for it to change in any meaningful way (Thompson and McHugh, 1990).

There have been suggestions that the concerns of psychologists studying the world of work have been changing, with new trends emerging that will continue into the twenty-first century. The traditional focus of psychologists on psychometrics, for example, is coming under serious attack, as we saw in Chapter 11, with doubts being raised both among researchers and practitioners about the way tests are constructed and used. More attention seems to be devoted now, runs this argument, to the importance of such topics as time and the ahistorical nature of much organizational thinking, and to the importance of relationships at work and the role of the unconscious (see, for example, Hollway, 1991; Thompson and McHugh, 1990).

As these topics have formed the major themes of this book I would like to believe in the existence of these trends, and their possible influence in the future. I remain, however, sceptical. The prevailing managerial ideologies of this century have had great difficulty with such ideas and these ideologies, moreover, are increasingly being applied to the very institutions of higher education that usually employ work psychologists. It would be unrealistic to expect either this relationship or the ongoing struggle within organizations for control of the workplace to change as we go into the twenty-first century.

The worker's view of work

All the evidence that we have considered up to this point leads me to suggest, finally, that what will be least likely to change in the future workplace is the *realism* with which people generally view their work. Time and again we have noted how workers see through attempts to manipulate them whether it be by the carrot and stick of Scientific Management, or the official concern for their welfare that usually denotes a more Human Relations-oriented approach. The most sophisticated recent attempt at manipulation of the workforce has gone under the banner of changing the 'organizational culture'. By 'organizational culture' is usually meant a *sharing* by everyone in the organization of the same ideas, values, assumptions, beliefs and, crucially, *meanings* (for example Bate, 1984; Schein, 1984). We have already come across organizational cultures in the London Fire Brigade (KEY STUDY 10) and the study of Banana Time (KEY STUDY 2). The idea is that if the workforce can be persuaded to accept a changed organizational culture as their own they will then identify with the new image of the organization and be optimally motivated to do their best for both themselves and their employers.

And that is the crucial point, because this kind of organizational culture and attempted culture change does not arise from the normal interactions of people at work, or from an openly negotiated agreement between competing interest groups. On the contrary, it is provided for the workforce by senior management. As one writer in this field has put it:

> As far as top management is concerned, what is important is the articulation and channelling of the culture in directions which supply employees with guidelines and which promote a system of strongly-held, shared values . . . conscious attempts must be made to dispense the culture in ways that are perceived as helpful in achieving the goals of corporate leaders. Put another way, the effects of culture should not be left to chance. (Ray, 1986, p. 289)

The engineering of change via organizational culture is thus simply the latest expression of the century-long struggle for control between senior management and workforce. And even where it is apparently successful, at least in the short-term, it is quite clear to most people that the organization's values, practices, goals and so on have precisely the meaning that senior management wish them to have. Organizational culture, therefore, is generally something that workers conform to rather than identify with, as the recent case of British Airways demonstrates.

British Airways was losing money heavily until it had a change of senior management, and organizational culture, in the early 1980s. It then officially became a caring, sharing organization in which everyone was devoted to customer service. The airline reduced its staff at the same time from 60 000 to 38 000, and went into profit. But few of the 22 000 people who lost their jobs as a result of the change to the new caring, sharing organizational culture expected the organization to act any differently. They did not even feel that the organization had acted hypocritically (Gowler, Legge and Clegg, 1993). It is, they seemed to feel, in the nature of organizations that the people who run them will use rewards or punishments when they can and human relations hype when they can't. So what else is new?

The problem is not that senior managers are naturally devious – any more than workers are naturally lazy. The way the world of work is organized encourages managers at all levels to think in terms of technique and manipulation in dealing with their subordinates. The powerful and universal seduction of the managerial quick fix will still be with us in the twenty-first century. While individual managers may have the personal qualities to see beyond it they will be swimming against the tide.

The best help for everyone in this situation is an objective and critical appraisal of how and why people behave as they do in work organizations. In this respect a thorough psychological analysis is the enemy of the quick fix and that role, ultimately, may one day be seen as the most important contribution psychology can make to the world of work.

Key studies

The fifteen KEY STUDIES referred to throughout the text are described in this section. In selecting these necessarily few, but very diverse, studies I have been guided largely by my teaching experience. Students seem to have found them particularly helpful in illuminating important concepts and wanted to know more about how the studies were done. Many of these studies are difficult to obtain, and most would cause intellectual indigestion if taken in their raw state. These accounts are therefore concise summaries, in a standard format, leavened where possible by quotations from the original to give readers at least a flavour of the thinking and approach of their authors.

All of the studies here described have been criticised on methodological and/ or theoretical grounds by specialists in their field. I have not attempted the huge task of dealing with, or even listing, these criticisms. That would have required a hefty volume by itself. And in a sense it doesn't matter. I can't think of a single important study in the social and behavioural sciences that has *not* been criticised on grounds of theory or methodology. That, after all, is how the academic game is played, and business is business.

But all of the studies listed here, with publication dates from 1911 to 1985, have contributed notably to our understanding of psychology and the world of work in the twentieth century. Whatever their faults they were imaginative in their day and have been influential since.

KEY STUDY 1

TITLE: *The Principles of Scientific Management*
AUTHOR: Frederick W. Taylor
SOURCE: New York: Harper, 1911. Reprinted by Harper and Row, 1964
AREA: Management theory
PROBLEM: Managing work practices of industrial workers
SUBJECTS: Principally labourers in Bethlehem Steel Company, Pennsylvania, USA
METHODS and DATA:
    Time-and-motion study involving detailed observation of individual workers as they went about their tasks, for example shovelling. 'For a first-class shoveler there is a given shovel load at which he will do his biggest day's work ... By first selecting two or three first-class shovelers, and paying them extra wages for doing

trustworthy work, and then gradually varying the shovel load and having all the conditions accompanying the work carefully observed for several weeks by men who were used to experimenting, it was found that a first-class man would do his biggest day's work with a shovel load of about 21 pounds.

. . . instead of allowing each shoveler to select and own his own shovel, it became necessary to provide 8 to 10 different kinds of shovels, and so on, each one appropriate to handling a given type of material; not only so as to enable the men to handle an average load of 21 pounds, but also to adapt the shovel to several other requirements which became perfectly evident when this work is studied as a science . . . This made it possible to issue to each workman a shovel which would hold a load of 21 pounds of whatever class of material they were to handle: a small shovel for ore, say, or a large one for ashes . . .

. . . thousands of stop-watch observations were made to study just how quickly a laborer, provided in each case with the proper type of shovel, can push his shovel into the pile of materials and then draw it out properly loaded . . .

. . . a similar accurate time study was made of the time required to swing the shovel backwards and then throw the load for a given horizontal distance, accompanied by a given height. This time study was made for various combinations of distance and height.' (pp. 65–7)

FINDINGS:

1. The 'science' of time-and-motion study was the basis for scientific management.
2. The systematic application of scientific management by managers used a worker's abilities most efficiently and allowed him to earn the maximum wage he was capable of.
3. Each worker should be dealt with as an individual with different mental and physical abilities, in the interests of both worker and organization.
4. A fair day's work should be determined by the 'scientific' investigation of time-and-motion study rather than the collective bargaining of labour and employers.

KEY STUDY 2

TITLE: Banana time: job satisfaction and informal interaction
AUTHOR: Donald F. Roy
SOURCE: *Human Organization*, 18 (1960) 156–68 [Reprinted in *People and Organizations*, G. Salaman and K. Thompson (eds), London: Longmans, 1973]
AREA: The time dimension; group dynamics
PROBLEM: What can workers in mind-numbing jobs do about job satisfaction?
SUBJECTS: A small group of workers in a 'clicking-room' machine shop of a mid-Western American factory in 1945
METHODS: Largely participant observation by the author, who worked with the subject group for a few months.
DATA: The informal interactions of the subject group, for example the daily ritual that involved one man stealing his colleague's lunchtime banana.

FINDINGS:

1. '. . . one key source of job satisfaction lies in the informal interaction shared by members of a work group. In the clicking-room situation the spontaneous development of a patterned combination of horseplay, serious conversation, and frequent sharing of food and drink reduced the monotony of simple, repetitive operations to the point where a regular schedule of long work days became liveable' (p. 217).

2. By these means the workers introduced 'job satisfaction, at least job endurance, to work situations largely bereft of creative experience' (p. 218).

3. 'In regard to another managerial concern, employee productivity, . . . I obtained no evidence to warrant a claim that banana time, or any of its accompaniments in consummatory interaction, boosted production . . . However I did not obtain sufficient evidence to indicate that, under the prevailing conditions of laissez-faire management, the output of our group would have been more impressive if the playful cavorting of three middle-aged gentlemen about the barred windows had never been' (p. 218).

N.B. Thirty years after Roy's experiences another social scientist, an Englishman called Michael Burawoy, found himself also working temporarily in the same factory. Burawoy took advantage of this coincidence to produce a rare follow-up study. His findings were broadly similar to those of Donald Roy, though his work is more detailed and has a wider scope. See *Manufacturing Consent: Changes in the Labor Process Under Monopoly Capitalism* (Chicago: University of Chicago Press, 1979).

KEY STUDY 3

TITLE: Job longevity as a situational factor in job satisfaction

AUTHOR: Ralph Katz

SOURCE: *Administrative Science Quarterly*, 23 (1978) 204–23

AREA: The time dimension

PROBLEM: Measuring the effect of time spent in a job on an individual's level of job satisfaction

SUBJECTS: Employees of city, county and state governments in the United States

METHODS: Four organizations were selected, representing four different regions of the United States. A stratified random sample was drawn from each organization. Questionnaires on job satisfaction were then administered to a total of 3085 subjects, representing about 40 per cent of the people employed by the four organizations. The questionnaires were based on the Job Diagnostic Survey of Hackman and Oldham (1975). The five factors contained in the JDS are:

- Skill variety
- Task identity
- Task significance
- Feedback
- Autonomy

FINDINGS:
1. Job satisfaction varies with length of time spent in a job and in an organization. People obtain satisfaction in different ways at different points in their experience.
2. In the first few months in the job employees found job satisfaction in the significance of the task and in receiving feedback on their performance.
3. Between six months and five years in the job the other three aspects of the JDS also become important for job satisfaction, that is the variety of skills required, being responsible for a whole task, and having autonomy in the job.
4. After five years in the job all five factors began to have less effect on job satisfaction, until after 15 years none of them had much effect at all. What did matter at this point were the social and situational factors of the job such as pay and benefits and relationships with colleagues and supervisor.

KEY STUDY 4

TITLE: *Type A Behaviour and Your Heart*
AUTHOR: M. Friedman and R. Rosenman
SOURCE: Greenwich, Conn.: Fawcett, 1974
              London: Wildwood House, 1974
AREA: Stress
PROBLEM: The contribution of behaviour patterns to the incidence of coronary heart disease
SUBJECTS: Mainly male American clinical patients and healthy subjects
METHODS: Clinical diagnosis and observation of coronary heart disease patients. Analysis of epidemiological statistical patterns
DATA: *Stage 1*
              ● initial questionnaire to 150 San Francisco businessmen regarding the behaviour that preceded a friend's heart attack
              ● Questionnaire to 100 physicians who treated coronary patients
              Stage 2
              ● 80 San Francisco businessmen who appeared to exhibit Type A behaviour and 80 who appeared to exhibit Type B behaviour were studied
              ● samples of similar types of (white) American women were studied
              Stage 3
              ● over 3500 healthy men for long-term study (over 10 years)
FINDINGS:
1. 'In the absence of Type A Behaviour Pattern, coronary heart disease almost never occurs before seventy years of age, regardless of the fatty foods eaten, the cigarettes smoked, or the lack of exercise. But when this behaviour pattern is present, coronary heart disease can easily erupt in one's thirties or forties' (Preface).
2. 'Type A Behaviour Pattern is an action-complex that can be observed in any person who is *aggressively* involved in a *chronic, incessant* struggle to achieve more and more in less and less time, and if required to do so, against the opposing efforts of other things

or other persons. It is not psychosis or a complex of worries or fears or phobias or obsessions, but a socially acceptable – indeed often praised – form of conflict. Persons possessing this pattern also are quite prone to exhibit a free-floating but extraordinary well-rationalized hostility (p. 67).

3. 'Type B Behaviour Pattern is the exact opposite of Type A, even though a Type B person may have at least as much ambition as a Type A person. He may also have a considerable amount of 'drive', but its character is such that it seems to steady him, give confidence and security to him, rather than to goad, irritate, and infuriate, as with the Type A man' (p. 68).

4. Urban Americans seem to fall into one or other behaviour pattern with more than half being Type A, about 40 per cent Type B and only a few per cent mixed.

KEY STUDY 5

TITLE: A case-study in the functioning of social systems as a defence against anxiety

AUTHOR: Isabel E. P. Menzies

SOURCE: *Human Relations*, 13 (1960) 95–121

AREA: Organizations and the unconscious

PROBLEM: To understand the reasons for the chronically high levels of anxiety and stress among nurses in a hospital

SUBJECTS: Student nurses in a high-status general teaching hospital in London

METHODS: The organization was treated as if it was the subject of a psychoanalytic relationship. The 'presenting symptom' (which the hospital brought to the therapist) was the administrative difficulty it was having in training nurses as it wished because of the priority given to staffing needs for patient care. Out of 700 nurses at the hospital only 150 were fully trained. The other 550 were at various stages of a four-year training course. The situation was exacerbated by the nurses' unusually high rate of sickness and dropping out of training. The drop-out rate was about one-third.

DATA: ● Interviews were held with about 70 nurses, either individually or in small groups
            ● Interviews were held with senior medical and non-medical staff
            ● Observation of operational units
            ● Informal contacts with nurses and other staff

FINDINGS:

1. The very high levels of anxiety and stress could not be accounted for solely by the inherent difficulties of the nurse's job but had to include the way the hospital defined the nurse's role.

2. The social system of defence against this basic anxiety and stress of the job which the organization fostered was psychologically a very primitive one, amounting to an evasion of the problem and even a denial of its existence. Nurses had to deny the powerful feelings they felt, were discouraged from forming any relationships with patients by being moved frequently, and felt their work lives were severely constricted by strict rules and regulations that allowed for no discretion and lacked common sense.

3. The social structure was so rigid and controlling that the radical changes necessary to deal with the underlying anxiety and stress would have required a complete re-structuring of the organization, to which its members were very resistant. The fear of facing the unknown with no defence mechanisms was just too threatening.

KEY STUDY 6

TITLE: *Management and the Worker* (the Hawthorne studies)
AUTHOR: F.J. Roethlisberger and W.J. Dickson (Harvard Business School) (Western Electric Company)
SOURCE: Cambridge, Mass.: Harvard University Press, 1939
AREA: Work group relationships; group dynamics; human relations
PROBLEM: The effects of work-group interactions on employee morale and productivity
SUBJECTS: Workers in the Hawthorne (Chicago) plant of the Western Electric Company employed to make telephone equipment
METHODS and DATA:

'The experimental studies of human relations . . . were begun in the spring of 1927, when five employees were segregated from a regular operating department for special study. At the beginning of the inquiry the general interest was primarily in the relationship between conditions of work and the incidence of fatigue and monotony among employees. It was anticipated that exact knowledge could be obtained about this relationship by establishing an experimental situation in which the effect of variables like temperature, humidity and hours of sleep could be measured separately from the effect of an experimentally imposed condition of work. Little was it doubted that within a year, or perhaps less, definite answers to questions could be obtained. But the inquiry developed in an unexpected fashion. In most cases the result obtained, instead of giving definite answers to the original questions, demanded a restatement of them . . . As a result, the inquiry continued for five years, from 1927 to 1932, when for reasons unconnected with the experiment it was suspended. From the original observation of five workers, the investigation during one phase of its development had expanded until it included studies of about 20000 individual employees' (p. 3).

The human relations studies grew out of a previous set of studies carried out at the Hawthorne plant from November 1924 to April 1927 on the effects of illumination on productivity. These studies, carried out by engineers from the National Academy of Sciences, came up with some unexpected findings. They discovered that level of illumination had little effect on productivity. For example they found that output increased in both experimental groups where illumination was lowered and in control groups where it was kept at a constant level.

  (i) *Relay Assembly Test Room*

     In the first phase of the Hawthorne human relations experiments the Harvard experimenters studied a group of five self-selected 'girls' plus a female supervisor. The group was observed assembling relays by a man who had been involved in the previous illumination studies. His task was to record what happened and 'maintain a friendly atmosphere'. The assumption was that by isolating a work group and systematically examining the relevant variables they would be able to establish the relationship between illumination (and other environmental variables like rest breaks and temperature) and productivity.

(ii) *Second Relay Assembly Group and Mica Splitting Test Room*
This phase concentrated on the effects of wage incentives using small groups of female workers as before.

(iii) *Interviewing Programme*
'The program started essentially as a plan for improving supervision' (p. 189). The idea was to obtain from the employees a frank expression of their opinions and attitudes about their work environment. This information could then be used to take corrective action as well as training supervisors in human relations at work. A total of 21 126 people were interviewed over three years, out of a total workforce of about 30 000. During this period interviews changed from 30 minutes of structured questioning to non-directive interviews of about one and a half hours.

(iv) *Bank Wiring Observation Room*
One important discovery from the vast mass of interview data was that the individual's attitudes towards work and productivity were heavily influenced by the other members of his work group. Thus the final phase of the Hawthorne experiments, beginning in November 1931, were concerned with observing the dynamics of a work group. Fourteen men were engaged in wiring, soldering and inspecting a bank of terminals.

FINDINGS:

1. Changes in working conditions were followed by increased productivity, even when the change was back to the original conditions.

2. The effects of financial incentives on individual productivity were very limited.

3. Social aspects of work were of paramount importance to individuals.

4. Work groups maintained an informal norm of output which largely fixed productivity at a constant level, regardless of external management attempts to increase it by offering group and individual incentives. In this the group was helped by the acquiescence of its immediate supervisor.

KEY STUDY 7

TITLE: *Group Conflict and Cooperation*
AUTHOR: Muzafer Sherif
SOURCE: London: Routledge and Kegan Paul, 1966
AREA: Social psychology; group dynamics
PROBLEM: Reducing inter-group conflict

SUBJECTS: Eleven-year-old American boys, all from white, middle-class, Protestant backgrounds. The boys were selected to be healthy, well-adjusted and from stable home backgrounds.

METHODS and DATA:

Field experiments were conducted at summer camps over a number of years:' . . . every effort was made so that the activities and the flow of interpersonal interaction as they occurred were as natural as possible . . . the subjects were not aware that data were being collected or that the sequence of events was experimentally planned. All research staff appeared in the role of personnel in a usual camp situation . . . In these capacities, they observed the boys throughout their waking hours, recording symbols and other notes only when out of the subjects' sight and expanding them into a report later each day.' (p. 73)

Phase I

Initially all the boys were housed together. After they had begun to form friendships they were split into two groups, housed separately, whereupon each boy found that most of his friends were now in the other groups. But after the groups had been formed the pattern of friendships were found to be reversed, with most friends now being found in the same group.

Phase II

Competitive games were arranged between the teams, with the eager participation of the boys. This started out as good-natured fun but then gave way to hostility and even physical conflict, even between boys who had been best friends in the first phase of the camp.

Phase III

To overcome this hostility and produce cooperation between the groups several conditions for the emergence of superordinate goals were created, 'superordinate goals being those that have a compelling appeal for members of each group, but that neither group can achieve without participation of the other' (p. 89).

The first of these situations involved the camp's water supply breaking down. Each of the two groups offered to help. 'They explored separately, then came together and jointly located the source of the difficulty. But despite the good spirits aroused, the groups fell back on their old recriminations once the immediate crisis was over' (p. 89).

The next situation required the boys to pay for a movie they all wished to see. 'The two groups got together, figured out how much each group would have to contribute, chose the film by a common vote, and enjoyed the show together' (p. 89).

Finally on an outing a problem developed with the truck bringing the food. '. . . when everyone was hungry and ready to eat, it developed that the truck would not start (the staff had taken care of that). The boys got a rope – the same rope they had used in their acrimonious tug of war – and all pulled together to start the truck' (p. 89).

FINDINGS:

    1. 'Joint efforts in situations such as these did not *immediately* dispel hostility. But gradually, the series of activities requiring interdependent action reduced conflict and hostility between the groups. . . . New friendships developed, cutting across group lines' (pp. 89–90).

    2. Such techniques for reducing hostility seem to work best 'when employed within a framework of cooperation among groups working toward goals that are genuinely appealing to all and that require equitable participation and contributions from all groups' (p. 93).

KEY STUDY 8

TITLE: *The Authoritarian Personality*

AUTHOR: T.W. Adorno, E. Frenkel-Brunswik, D.J. Levinson and R.N. Sanford

SOURCE: New York: Harper & Brothers, 1950

AREA: Personality; social psychology

PROBLEM: Uncovering the individual psychological roots of social prejudice and hatred of other ethnic groups

SUBJECTS: A total of 2099 men and women in California and Oregon.

    ● 449 of them were university students (some of them adults)
    ● 121 of them were male and female psychiatric patients
    ● 110 of them were male prison inmates
    ● the remaining 1419 came from a variety of working-class and middle-class backgrounds

METHODS and DATA:

    (i) *Questionnaires*

    Groups of subjects filled out questionnaires consisting of three aspects (a) factual, (b) opinion-attitude, (c) open-ended projective questions.

    (a) Factual questions dealt with the individual's group memberships, like church, political party and so on.

    (b) Opinion-attitude scales were used in an attempt to obtain measures of authoritarian ideologies like anti-Semitism and ethnocentrism. This resulted in a single scale of anti-democratic tendencies, the California F – (for Fascism) scale. People were asked whether they agreed or disagreed with statements like:

    Obedience and respect for authority are the most important virtues children should learn
    If people would talk less and work more, everybody would be better off
    There are two kinds of people in the world, the weak and the strong
    Nobody ever learned anything really important except through suffering

    (c) Projective questions were deliberately ambiguous and had emotional overtones like, 'What would you do if you had only six months to live, and could do anything you wanted?'

    (ii) *Clinical Techniques*

    These were administered to the 25 per cent highest and 25 per cent lowest scorers on the opinion-attitude scales.

(a) *Interviews*

Subjects were encouraged to talk as freely as possible about issues involved in politics, religion, minority groups and so on. They were then asked about their biographies in more detail, then about their emotions and personal relationships and finally about their childhood.

(b) *Thematic Apperception Test (TAT)*

Subjects were administered a slightly modified TAT.

FINDINGS:

1. 'The most crucial result ... is the demonstration of close correspondence in the type of approach and outlook a subject is likely to have in a great variety of areas, ranging from the most intimate features of family and sex adjustment through relationships to other people in general, to religion and to social and political philosophy. Thus a basically hierarchical, authoritarian, exploitative parent-child relationship is apt to carry over into a power-oriented, exploitively dependent attitude towards one's sex partner and one's God and may well culminate in a political philosophy and social outlook which has no room for anything but a desperate clinging to what appears to be strong and a disdainful rejection of whatever is relegated to the bottom.' (p. 971)

2. People who agreed with the statements on the F-scale tended to be anti-Semitic, racist and generally prejudiced in their attitudes towards members of other social groups.

3. The characteristic attributes of the 'authoritarian personality' were identified. Such a person was likely to be rigid, conventional, moralistic, impersonal, simplistic and judgemental.

4. The childhood of the 'authoritarian personality' is likely to have been unhappy. His parents were invariably harsh and demanding, highly punitive yet arbitrary in their rules and regulations for home life and quite intolerant of any expression of resentment by their children. The hostility, and even hatred, aroused by this kind of treatment was often generalised to authorities in general. But these feelings could not be openly expressed, because parents and authorities were too powerful and menacing, so they tended to identify with authority figures for security while projecting their repressed feelings onto outgroups.

KEY STUDY 9

TITLE: *The Achieving Society*
AUTHOR: David C. McClelland
SOURCE: New York: Van Nostrand, 1961
AREA: The time dimension; personality; motivation
PROBLEM: The links between social psychological processes and economic development
SUBJECTS: ● businessmen and government administrators in the USA, Italy, Poland and Turkey.
● adolescent boys in Brazil, (West) Germany, India and Japan
● villagers in Mexico and India
METHODS: The identification and measurement of achievement imagery across contemporary cultures and across historical eras from Ancient

Greece to England in the Industrial Revolution. This was done to find 'the broadest possible test of the hypothesis that a particular psychological factor – the need for Achievement – is responsible for economic growth and decline' (p. vii).

DATA: Content analysis of interviews designed to highlight achievement imagery

● content analysis of cultural artefacts such as literature, children's books and vase design
● statistics on societal measures of economic development, such as trade, productivity, amount of public building, patents issued and use of electricity

FINDINGS:

1. Significant economic and technological development in a culture is preceded, a generation earlier, by widespread evidence of achievement imagery. A decline in such imagery heralds an economic decline.
2. Children – especially boys – raised in families and in cultures which stress the importance of achievement (including self-reliance and independence) in all aspects of life will be more likely to follow entrepreneurial pursuits as adults. The prime example would be the Protestant countries of Europe at the time of the Industrial Revolution.
3. These findings can produce 'a plan for accelerating economic growth through mobilizing more effectively the high n Achievement resources of a developed country to select and work directly with the scarcer high n Achievement resources in underdeveloped countries' (p. 437).

KEY STUDY 10

TITLE: Work relations and group solidarity : the London Fire Brigade
AUTHOR: G. Salaman
SOURCE: *Working* (London: Tavistock, 1986)
AREA: Recruitment; group dynamics; work group relationships
PROBLEM: How the pattern of work relationships affects the functioning of an organization, particularly as regards the entry of new members.
SUBJECTS: Mainly station officers (first line supervisors) in the London Fire Brigade
METHODS: Group interviews with station officers about the effects of the Equal Opportunities (EO) legislation to encourage women and ethnic minorities to enter largely white male organizations like the London Fire Brigade
DATA: Transcripts of interviews

● figures on distribution of Brigade employees by sex and ethnic group
● figures on distribution of job applicants to the Brigade by sex and ethnic group

FINDINGS:

1. 'When faced with the suggestion that EO law and policy were intended to achieve fairness – treating people in terms of their abilities and merits, and work-relevant characteristics rather than in

terms of their sex or their race – the vast majority approved in principle . . . But even those who agreed with the principle of fairness so qualified the conditions under which this principle could be exercised that it emerged as relatively useless and irrelevant . . . It was defined in terms of doing nothing to disturb existing patterns of power and access' (pp. 40–1).

2. 'Any initiative which was clearly (and justifiably) intended to redress some of the existing and historical imbalances of knowledge, attitudes, confidence, qualification within the population of the London area, was seen as unfair to the extent that it addressed one section rather than another. The existing inequity . . . was seen not as representing an inherently unfair situation, but a normal, natural one which the policy was unfairly disturbing' (p. 41).

3. 'The officers were convinced that women firefighters were not able properly to do the work of firefighting. They were highly resistant to arguments on this point. Even if, in a discussion group, there was a station officer who was currently acting as an officer of a watch with a woman in it, and this officer was prepared to admit that she was in fact competent – as certainly happened – this information would be ignored by the rest of the group or defined as exceptional' (p. 42).

4. A more subtle resistance took the form of accepting that theoretically women *could* be competent firefighters but that in *practice* the ones currently employed were incompetent. They had only gained entry to the Brigade because of the cowardice and political opportunism of senior management who were willing to lower standards in order to admit them.

5. '. . . the vigour of station officers' attitudes towards the EO policy . . . was probably the most striking feature of their reactions: they were angry, sometimes to the point of incoherence, often to the point of obscenity. Their anger and distress were real. Frequently officers insisted that their pride and confidence in their work was destroyed, that they personally were diminished' (p. 43).

KEY STUDY 11

TITLE: *The Motivation to Work*
AUTHORS: F. Herzberg, B. Mausner and B. Snyderman
SOURCE: New York: Wiley, 1959
AREA: Motivation
PROBLEM: What factors motivate people's behaviour in the world of work?
SUBJECTS: People in nine small, large and medium-sized companies in Pittsburgh, Pennsylvania and within a thirty-mile radius. The 203 subjects chosen were engaged in engineering and accounting. It was felt that these two professions were particularly important to industry, that they were both 'rich in technique' and could provide 'exceptionally vivid accounts of their work experiences' though they were very different professions attracting, it was presumed, very different kinds of people.

METHODS and DATA:
Structured interviews were carried out with all the subjects. A set of 14 questions was introduced by the following paragraph:

'Think of a time when you felt exceptionally good and exceptionally bad about your job, either your present job or any other job you have had. This can be either the "long-range" or the "short range" kind of situation, as I have just described it. Tell me what happened' (p. 141).

FINDINGS:

1. Different factors are responsible for increasing job satisfaction and for decreasing job satisfaction.
2. ' . . . the job satisfiers deal with the factors involved in doing the job, whereas the job dissatisfiers deal with the factors that define the job context. Poor working conditions, bad company policies and administration, and bad supervision will lead to job dissatisfaction. Good company policies, good administration, good supervision and good working conditions will not lead to positive job attitudes. In opposition to this . . . recognition, achievement, interesting work, responsibility and advancement all lead to positive job attitudes. Their absence will much less frequently lead to job dissatisfaction' (p. 82).
3. ' . . . as an affector of job attitudes salary has more potency as a job dissatisfier than as a job satisfier' (p. 82)

KEY STUDY 12

TITLE: Toward a Theory of Task Motivation and Incentives
AUTHOR: Edwin A. Locke
SOURCE: *Organizational Behaviour and Human Performance,* (1968) 157–89
AREA: Motivation
PROBLEM: 'the relationship between conscious goals and intentions and task performance' (p. 157)
SUBJECTS: 1171 American college students
METHODS and DATA:

A: Goal difficulty and level of performance

Twelve experimental studies (most followed up by interviews) 'concerned with the relationship between the level of difficulty of the goal the subject is trying for and the quantitative level of his performance (amount of output, speed of reaction time, school grades, etc.' (p. 161)

B. Relationship of Qualitatively Different Goals to Level of Performance

Eight experimental studies comparing the instruction 'do your best' with specifically assigned hard goals.

FINDINGS:

1. ' . . . hard goals produce a higher level of performance (output) than easy goals
2. specific hard goals produce a higher level of output than a goal of "do your best".
3. behavioral intentions regulate choice behaviour' (p. 157)
4. 'Subjects who had the same output goals produced the same amount whether they were paid a bonus for reaching the goal or not.' (p. 175)
5. Similarly, knowledge of results and the existence of time limits 'do not affect performance level independently of the individual's goals

and intentions' (p. 157). However, 'giving knowledge (of results) in relation to the different standards in effect influenced the difficulty of the goals subjects tried for.' (p. 177)

KEY STUDY 13

TITLE: Cognitive Consequences of Forced Compliance
AUTHORS: Leon Festinger and James M. Carlsmith
SOURCE: *Journal of Abnormal and Social Psychology*, 58 (1959) 203–10
AREA: Attitude change; social psychology
PROBLEM: 'What happens to a person's private opinion if he is forced to do or say something contrary to that opinion?' (p. 203)
SUBJECTS: 71 male students in introductory psychology at Stanford University
METHODS and DATA:

Serving as experimental subjects was a requirement of the introductory psychology course. At the beginning of the course the students were told that '. . . since they were required to serve in experiments, the department was conducting a study to evaluate these experiments in order to be able to improve them in the future. They were told that a sample of students would be interviewed after having served as subjects. They were urged to cooperate in these interviews by being completely frank and honest' (p. 204).

The experiment the students had signed up for in this case was called 'Measures of Performance'. It consisted of two tasks, each lasting for 30 minutes. The first task involved filling and emptying a tray with spools, the second called for turning square pegs in a board. The experimenter busied himself conspicuously with note-taking and stop watch. At the end of the hour the subject believed the experiment was over.

The experimenter then told the subject a story about how he was part of Group A which was not given a preamble to the experiment whereas subjects in another group, Group B, were told what the experiment was like by someone who had just done it. This person, continued the experimenter, was actually his assistant and he was instructed to tell people how interesting, enjoyable, intriguing and exciting this (mind-numbingly boring) task was. Unfortunately he had not turned up that day, would the subject be willing to take his place – a job for which he would be paid? This was the heart of the real experiment. In one condition the subject was offered one dollar to be the experimenter's assistant and in the other, twenty dollars.

Each of the subjects in the experiment agreed to be the experimenter's assistant, regardless of how much he was paid. The experimenter then introduced the subject to the next student waiting to do the experiment. This was a young woman who really *was* the experimenter's assistant. She '. . . said little until the S made some positive remarks about the experiment and then said that she was surprised because a friend of hers had taken the experiment the week before and had told her that it was boring and that she ought to try to get out of it. Most S's responded by saying something like "Oh no, it's really very interesting. I'm sure you'll enjoy it . . ." The discussion . . . was recorded on a hidden tape recorder.' (p. 206)

The final part of the experiment then involved the subject in meeting a supposed interviewer from the psychology department who was ostensibly evaluating all the experiments. The subject was asked his opinion on several issues including the extent to which the tasks were interesting and enjoyable.

FINDINGS:

1. 'If a person is induced to do or say something which is contrary to his private opinion, there will be a tendency for him to change his opinion so as to bring it into correspondence with what he has done or said.

2. The larger the pressure used to elicit the overt behaviour (beyond the minimum needed to elicit it) the weaker will be the above-mentioned tendency.' (p. 210)

KEY STUDY 14

TITLE: Patterns of aggressive behaviour in experimentally created 'social climates'

AUTHORS: K. Lewin, R. Lippitt and R. White

SOURCE: *The Journal of Social Psychology*, 10 (1939) 271–299

AREA: Group Dynamics

PROBLEM: The effects on the behaviour of groups of boys of different leadership styles

SUBJECTS: Groups of 10-year-olds in boys clubs in Iowa, USA

METHODS: The boys formed four five-member groups for the purpose of making theatrical masks. Each group had an adult leader. The adult leaders exhibited three different types of leadership style, Authoritarian, Democratic and Laissez-faire.

  (i) The *Authoritarian* leader decided what each member would do, how he would do it and with whom he would work, in a step-by-step fashion. His comments on each member's work, whether positive or negative, were personal and he did not get involved with the group as a whole.

  (ii) The *Democratic* leader was oriented towards dealing with the group as a whole rather than individuals. He encouraged the group to decide for itself how to proceed, who would do what and with whom, while he provided technical advice and outlined alternatives.

  (iii) The *Laissez-faire* leader did not participate at all in the work of the group, but merely supplied information when asked. Individuals, and groups as a whole, were left to make their own decisions.

In each of the groups the leader left the room at some point and observers analysed the group dynamics following his exit.

DATA: ● Stenographic records of conversations

              ● Quantified records of group structure and social interactions

              ● Qualitative interpretation

              ● Interviews with parents and teachers

              ● Rorschach Ink Blot test administered to each boy

              ● Sociometric questionnaire administered to each boy

              ● Three interviews conducted with each boy

FINDINGS:
1. Hostility in autocratic group 30 times as frequent as democratic group.
2. Aggression in autocratic group 8 times as frequent as democratic group, most of it directed against scapegoats rather than leader.
3. Aggression in autocratic group rose sharply when leader left the room.
4. Out of the 20 boys in the study 19 liked the democratic leader better than the autocratic leader. Liking for the laissez-faire leader fell between the two.

KEY STUDY 15

TITLE: *The Management of Innovation*
AUTHORS: Tom Burns and G. M Stalker
SOURCE: London: Tavistock, 1961
AREA: Effects of new technology; organizations
PROBLEM: The effects on industrial business organizations used to relatively stable conditions of new developments in markets and technology
SUBJECTS: 20 British industrial companies, 15 of them in electronics, involving interviews with about 300 individuals
METHODS and DATA:

'The methods of study . . . are those common to . . . field sociology and to social anthropology. These are simply directed towards gaining acquaintance, through conversation and observation, with the routines of behaviour current in the particular social system being studied, and trying thereafter to reach an appreciation of the codes of conduct which are supposed by the members of the system to underlie behaviour. All this emerged fairly slowly in the course of interviews, meetings, lunch-time conversations, and the like . . .

Our usual procedure, after the first interview with the head of a firm, was to conduct a series of interviews with as large a number of persons as possible in managerial and supervisory positions. Such interviews lasted anything from one hour to a whole working day. They would start as a general description of the informant's position and function in the concern and of the way in which his job linked with other people's. They would then develop along fairly free lines, taking as their point of departure a request to the informant to be more explicit about some point . . .

It was during this stage that it proved possible to create a more productive relationship than . . . one person's seeking information from another' (pp. 12–13).

FINDINGS:
1. Commercial success in different types of market (and to a lesser extent technological) environments was directly related to the system of management used.
2. There was a continuum of management system from 'mechanistic' at one end to 'organic' at the other. The former was most appropriate for operating in a relatively stable environment (like textiles), and the latter for a relatively unstable and changing environment (like electronics). The mechanistic system was formal,

hierarchical and bureaucratic, where the organic system was much more informal, less hierarchical and less bound by strict rules and regulations.

3. Both types of management may operate in an organization at any particular time.
4. An organic system of management may lead to increased anxiety in its managers because of their need for structure in their working environment and for certainty in predicting their future and definiteness in knowing what role is expected of them.

References

Abbott, P. and C. Wallace (1990) *An Introduction to Sociology: Feminist Perspectives* (Routledge: London and New York).

Adair, J., (1988) *Effective Leadership* (London: Pan).

Adams, J. S. (1965) 'Inequality in social exchange', in L. Berkowitz (ed.), *Advances in Experimental Social Psychology*, Volume 2 (London and New York: Academic Press).

Adorno, T. W., E. Frenkel-Brunswik, D. J. Levinson and R. N. Sanford (1950) *The Authoritarian Personality* (New York: Harper and Brothers).

Alban-Metcalfe, B. M. and N. Nicholson (1984) *The Career Development of British Managers* (London: British Institute of Management).

Albee, G. W. (1978) 'IQ tests on trial', *The New York Times*, February 12, E13.

Alderfer, C. P. (1972) *Existence, Relatedness and Growth: Human Needs in Organizational Settings* (New York: Free Press).

Allen, V. and D. A. Wilder (1979) 'Group categorization and attribution of belief similarity', *Small Group Behaviour*, 110, 73–80.

Allport, G. W. (1963) *Pattern and Growth in Personality* (London: Holt, Rinehart & Winston).

Allport, G. and L. Postman (1947) 'The Basic Psychology of Rumor', in *Readings in Social Psychology*, T. Newcomb and E. Hartley (eds) (New York: Holt, Rinehart and Winston).

Anastasi, A. (1990) *Psychological Testing*, 6th ed. (New York: Macmillan).

Anderson, E. W. (1941) 'Hysteria in wartime', *Journal of the Royal Navy Medical Services*, 27, 141–9.

Anderson, J. R. (ed.) (1981) *Cognitive Skills and Their Acquisition* (Hillsdale, New Jersey: Lawrence Erlbaum Associates).

Annett, J. (1969) *Feedback and Human Behaviour* (Harmondsworth: Penguin).

Argyle, M. (1983) *The Psychology of Interpersonal Behaviour*, 4th ed. (Harmondsworth: Penguin).

Argyle, M. (1987) *The Psychology of Happiness* (London: Methuen).

Argyle, M. (1988) *Bodily Communication*, 2nd ed. (London: Methuen).

Argyle, M. (1989) *The Social Psychology of Work*, 2nd ed. (London: Penguin).

Argyle, M. and H. Cook (1976) *Gaze and Mutual Gaze* (Cambridge: Cambridge University Press).

Argyle, M., F. Alkema and R. Gilmour (1971) 'The communication of friendly and hostile attitudes by verbal and nonverbal signals', *European Journal of Social Psychology* (1), 385–402.

Argyle, M., G. Gardner and F. Cioffi (1958) 'Supervisory methods relating to productivity, absenteeism and labour turnover', *Human Relations* 11, 23–45.

Armstrong, P. (1984) 'Work, rest or play? Changes in time spent at work', in P. Marstrand (ed.) *New Technology and the Future of Work and Skills* (London: Pinter).

Armstrong, P. (1986) 'Management Control Strategies and Inter-Professional Competition: the Cases of Accountancy and Personnel Management', in D. Knights and H. Willmott (eds) *Managing the Labour Process* (Aldershot: Gower).

Arnold, J., I. T. Robertson and C. L. Cooper (1991) *Work Psychology: Understanding Huamn Behaviour in the Workplace* (London: Pitman).

Aronson, E. (1992) *The Social Animal*, 6th ed. (New York: Freeman).

Aronson, E., J. Turner and J. Carlsmith (1963) 'Communication credibility and communication discrepancy as determinants of opinion', *Journal of Abnormal and Social Psychology*, 67, 31–6.

Aronson, E., T. Chase, R. Helmreich and R. Ruhnke (1974) 'A two-factor theory of dissonance reduction: The effect of feeling stupid or feeling "awful" on opinion change', *International Journal for Research and Communication*, 3, 59–74.

Arvey, R. D. and J. E. Campion (1982) 'The employment interview: a summary and review of recent literature', *Personnel Psychology*, 35, 281–322.

Asch, S. E. (1946) 'Forming impressions of personality', *Journal of Abnormal and Social Psychology*, 41, 258–90.

Asch, S. E. (1956) 'Studies of independence and conformity: A minority of one against a unanimous majority' *Psychological Monograph*, 70(9) Whole Issue 416.

Ashkenasy, N. M. (1985) 'Rotter's internal-external scale: confirmatory factor analysis and correlation with social desirability for alternative scale formats', *Journal of Personality and Social Psychology*, 48, 1328–41.

Ashour, A. S. (1973) 'The contingency model of leadership effectiveness: An evaluation', *Organizational Behavior and Human Performance*, 9, 339–55.

Atkinson, J. (1984) 'Manpower strategies for flexible organizations', *Personnel Management*, August.

Austin, J. T. and P. Bobko (1985) 'Goal-setting theory: Unexplored areas and future research needs', *Journal of Occupational Psychology*, 58, 289–308.

Austin, W., N. C. McGinn and C. Susmilch (1980) 'Internal standards revisited: effects of social comparisons and expectancies on judgements of fairness and satisfaction', *Journal of Experimental Social Psychology*, 16, 426–41.

Babbage, C. (1835) *On the Economy of Machinery and Manufacturers* (London: Charles Knight).

Bacharach, S. B. and E. J. Lawler (1980) *Power and Politics in Organizations* (London: Jossey-Bass).

Bachrach, P. and M. S. Baratz (1962) 'Two Faces of Power', *American Political Science Review*, 56, 947–52.

Back, K. (1973) *Beyond Words: The Story of Sensitivity Training and the Encounter Movement* (Baltimore: Penguin).

Baddeley, A. D. (1986) *Working Memory* (Oxford: Oxford University Press).

Bagby, E. (1923) *The Psychology of Personality* (New York: Holt, Rinehart and Winston).

Bakke, E. W. (1933) *The Unemployed Man: A Social Study* (London: Nisbet).

Bakke, E. W. (1940a) *Citizens Without Work: A Study of the Effects of Unemployment Upon the Workers' Social Relations and Practices* (New Haven: Yale University Press).

Bakke, E. W. (1940b) *The Unemployed Worker: A Study of the Task of Making a Living Without a Job* (New Haven: Yale University Press).

Bales, R. F. (1950) *Interaction Process Analysis: A Method for the Study of Small Groups* (Reading, Mass.: Addison-Wesley).

Bales, R. F. and S. P. Cohen (1979) *SYMLOG: A System for the Multiple Level Observation of Groups* (New York: Free Press. London: Collier Macmillan).

Bales, R. F. and P. E. Slater (1955) 'Role differentiation in small decision-making groups', in T. Parsons and R. F. Bales (eds), *Family, Socialization and Interaction Process* (New York: Free Press).

Bandura, A. (1986) *Social Foundation of Thought and Action: A Social Cognitive Theory* (Englewood Cliffs, New Jersey: Prentice-Hall).

Bandura, A. (1987) 'Self-regulation of motivation and action through goal systems', in V. Hamilton and N. H. Fryda (eds), *Cognition, Motivation and Affect: A Cognitive Science View* (Dordrecht: Martinus Nijholl).

Banks, M. H. (1988) 'Job Components Inventory', in S. Gael (ed.), *Job Analysis Handbook* (New York: Wiley).

Banks, M. H. and P. R. Jackson (1982) 'Unemployment and risk of minor psychiatric disorder in young people: cross-sectional and longitudinal evidence', *Psychological Medicine*, 12, 789–98.

Barnard, C. I. (1938) *The Functions of the Executive* (Boston: Harvard University Press).

Baron, R. A. (1986) *Behaviour in Organizations* (Boston: Allyn and Bacon).

Baron, R. A. (1987) 'Interviewer's moods and reactions to job applicants: The influence of affective states on applied social judgments', *Journal of Applied Social Psychology*, 17, 911–26.

Barsoux, J. and P. Lawrence (1990) *The Challenge of British Management* (London: Macmillan).

Bass, B. M. (1981) *Stogdill's Handbook of Leadership* (London: Collier Macmillan. New York: Free Press).

Bass, B. M. (1985) *Leadership and Performance: Beyond Expectations* (New York: Free Press).

Bate, P. (1984) 'The impact of organizational culture on approaches to organizational problem solving', *Organization Studies*, 5, 1, 43–66.

Bateman, T. and D. Organ (1983) 'Job satisfaction and the good soldier: the relationship between affect and employee "citizenship" ', *Academy of Management Journal* 26, 587–95.

Baumgartel, H. J., J. I. Reynolds and R. Z. Pathan (1984) 'How personality and organizational climate variables moderate the effectiveness of management development programmes: a review and some recent research findings', *Management and Labour Studies* 9, 1–16.

Bavelas, A. (1968) 'Communication patterns in task-orientated groups', in D. Cartwright and A. Zander (eds), *Group Dynamics: Research and Theory*, 3rd. ed. (New York: Harper and Row).

Beck, R. C. (1983) *Motivation: Theory and Principles* (Englewood Cliffs, New Jersey: Prentice-Hall).

Beechey, V. and T. Perkins (1987) *A Matter of Hours: Women, Part-time Work and the Labour Market* (Oxford: Polity Press).

Beehr, T. A. (1986) 'The process of retirement: a review and recommendations for future investigation', *Personnel Psychology*, 39, 31–55.

Bengelsdorf, C. and A. Hagelman (1979) 'Emerging from underdevelopment. Women and work in Cuba', in Z. R. Eisenstein (ed.), *Capitalist Patriarchy and the Case for Socialist Feminism* (London: Monthly Review Press).

Bennis, W. G. and G. Nanus (1985) *Leaders* (New York: Harper and Row).

422   References

Berggren, C. (1989) 'New production concepts in final assembly', in S. Wood (ed.), *The Transformation of Work?* (London: Unwin Hyman).

Berkman, L. F. and S. L. Syme (1979) 'Social networks, host resistance and mortality: a nine-year follow-up study of Alameda Country residents', *American Journal of Epidemiology* 109, 186–204.

Berkowitz, L. and A. Le Page (1967) 'Weapons as aggression-eliciting stimuli', *Journal of Personality and Social Psychology* 7, 202–7.

Bernardin, H. J. and D. A. Bownas (eds) (1985) *Personality Assessment in Organizations* (New York: Praeger).

Bernardin, H. J. and E. C. Pence (1980) 'Effects of rater training: Creating new response sets and decreasing accuracy', *Journal of Applied Psychology* 65, 60–6.

Berne, E. (1964) *Games People Play: The Psychology of Human Relationships* (London: Penguin).

Beveridge, W. E. (1980) 'Retirement and life significance: a study of the adustment to retirement of a sample of men at management level', *Human Relations* 33, 69–78.

Bhagat, P. (1982) 'Conditions under which stronger job performance – job satisfaction relationships may be observed: a closer look at two situational contingencies', *Academy of Management Journal* 25, 722–89.

Bingham, W. V. (1932) 'Making work worthwhile' in *Psychology Today*, 262–4 (Chicago: University of Chicago Press).

Birnbaum, M. H. (1983) 'Perceived equity of salary policies', *Journal of Applied Psychology* 68, 49–59.

Blackler, F. and S. Shimmin (1984) *Applying Psychology in Organizations* (London: Methuen).

Blauner, R. (1960) 'Work satisfaction and industrial trends in modern society', in W. Galenson and S. Lipset (eds), *Labor and Trade Unions* (New York: Wiley).

Blinkhorn, S. and C. Johnson (1990) 'The insignificance of personality testing', *Nature* 348, 671–2.

Blyton, P., J. Hassard, S. Hill and K. Starkey (1989) *Time, Work and Organization* (Routledge: London).

Boettcher, E. G., S. F. Alderson and M. Saccucci (1981) 'A comparison of the effects of computer-assisted instruction versus printed instruction on student learning in the cognitive categories of knowledge and application', *Journal of Computer-Based Instruction* 3 (1) 13–17.

Bossard, J. H. S. (1932) 'Residential propinquity as a factor in mate selection', *American Journal of Sociology* 38, 219–24.

Bower, G. H. and E. R. Hilgard (1981) *Theories of Learning*, 5th ed. (Englewood Cliffs, New Jersey: Prentice-Hall).

Braverman, H. (1974) *Labor and Monopoly Capital* (New York: Monthly Review Press).

Brehm, J. (1956) 'Postdecision changes in the desirability of alternatives', *Journal of Abnormal and Social Psychology* 52, 384–9.

Brenner, M. H. (1973) *Mental Illness and Economy* (Cambridge, Mass.: Harvard University Press).

Brenner, M. H. (1979) 'Influences of the social environment on psychopathology: the historic perspective', in J. E. Barrett, R. M. Rose and G. L. Klerman (eds) *Stress and Mental Disorder* (New York, Raven).

Breslow, L. and P. Buell (1960) 'Mortality from coronary heart disease and physical activity of work in California', *Journal of Chronic Diseases* 11, 615–25.

Broadbent, D. E (1987) 'Skill and Workload', in P. Warr (ed.) *Psychology at Work*, 3rd ed. (Harmondsworth: Penguin).

Broadbent, D. E., P. F. Fitzgerald, M. H. P. Broadbent (1986) 'Implicit and explicit knowledge in the control of complex systems', *British Journal of Psychology* 77, 33–50.

Brockner, J. and L. Adsit (1986) 'The moderating effect of sex on the equity-satisfaction relationship: a field study', *Journal of Applied Psychology* 71, 585–90.

Brown, G. W. and T. Harris (1978) *Social Origins of Depression* (London: Tavistock).

Buchanan, D. and A. Huczynski (1985) *Organizational Behaviour* (London: Prentice-Hall International)

Buford, B. (1991) *Among the Thugs* (London: Secker and Warburg).

Burawoy, M. (1979) *Manufacturing Consent: Changes in the Labor Process Under Monopoly Capitalism* (Chicago: University of Chicago Press).

Burnes, B. (1989) *New Technology in Context* (Aldershot: Gower).

Burns, J. M. (1978) *Leadership* (New York: Harper and Row).

Burns, T. and G. M. Stalker (1961) *The Management of Innovation* (London: Tavistock).

Burtt, H. (1941) 'An experimental study of early childhood memory', *Journal of Genetic Psychology* 58, 435–9.

Cadbury, E. (1914) 'Some principles of industrial organization: the case for and against Scientific Management', *Sociological Review* 7, 2, 99–117.

Calder, B. J. (1977) 'An attribution theory of leadership', in B. M. Staw and G. R. Salancik (eds), *New Directions in Organizational Behaviour* (Chicago, Ill.: St. Clair Press).

Campbell, D. P. (1971) *Handbook for the Strong Vocational Interest Blank* (Stanford: Stanford University Press).

Campbell, J. P., M. D. Dunnette, E. E. Lawler and K. E. Weick (1970) *Managerial Behaviour, Performance and Effectiveness* (New York: McGraw-Hill).

Caplan, R. D., S. Cobb, J. R. P. French, R. Van Harrison and S. Pinneau (1975) *Job Demands and Worker Health* (Ann Arbor, Michigan: Institute for Social Research, University of Michigan).

Carmichael, L., H. P. Hogan and A. A. Walter (1932) 'An experimental study of the effect of language on the reproduction of visually perceived form', *Journal of Experimental Psychology* 15, 73–86.

Carrell, M. R. and J. E. Dittrich (1978), 'Equity theory: the recent literature, methodological considerations and new directions', *Academy of Management Review* 3, 202–10.

Carter, R. C. and M. C. Cahill (1979) 'Regression models of search time for color-coded information displays', *Human Factors* 21, 293–302.

Cartwright, D. and A. Zander (eds) (1968) *Group Dynamics: Research and Theory*, 3rd ed. (New York: Harper and Row).

Cattell, R. B. (1965) *The Scientific Analysis of Personality* (London: Penguin).

Cattell, R. B., H. W. Eber and M. M. Tatsuoka (1970) *Handbook of the Cattell 16 Personality Factor Questionnaire* (Champaign, Ill: Institute of Personality and Ability Testing).

Chadwick-Jones, J., N. Nicholson and C. Brown (1982) *The Social Psychology of Absenteeism* (New York: Praeger).

Chapanis, A. (1976) 'Engineering Psychology', in M. D. Dunnette (ed.) *Handbook of Industrial and Organizational Psychology* (Chicago: Rand McNally).

Chappell, H. (1983) 'The mauve economy', *New Society*, 28 July.

Cherry, F. and D. Byrne, (eds) (1977) 'Authoritarianism', in *Personality Variables in Social Behaviour* (Hillsdale, New Jersey: Lawrence Erlbaum Associates).

Chesney, M. A. and R. Rosenman (1980) 'Type A behaviour in a work setting', in: C. L. Cooper and R. Payne (eds) *Current Concerns in Occupational Stress* (Chichester: Wiley).

Child, D. (1990) *The Essentials of Factor Analysis* (London: Cassell).

Child, J. (1984) *Organization*, 2nd ed. (London: Harper and Row).

Christie, R. C. and F. Geis (eds) (1971) *Studies in Machiavellianism* (New York: Academic Press).

Clarke, T. (1990) 'Automation and craftwork', Paper presented to World Congress of the International Sociological Association (Madrid).

Clutterbuck, D. (ed.) (1985) 'Telecommuting', in *New Patterns of Work* (Aldershot: Gower).

Cobb, S. (1973) 'Workload and coronary heart disease', in American Statistical Association *Proceedings, Social Statistics Section* December.

Cobb, S. (1976) 'Social Support as a Moderator of Life Stress', *Psychosomatic Medicine* 3, 5, 300–14.

Cobb, S. and S. V. Kasl (1977) *Termination; The Consequences of Job Loss*, (Cincinatti: U.S. Department of Health, Education and Welfare).

Coch, L. and J. R. P. French (1948) 'Overcoming resistance to change', *Human Relations* 512–32.

Cockburn, C. (1985) *Machinery of Dominance: Women, Men and Technical Knowhow* (London: Pluto Press).

Cockburn, C. (1988) 'The gendering of jobs: workplace relations and the reproduction of sex segregation', in: S. Walby (ed.), *Gender Segregation at Work* (Milton Keynes and Philadelphia: Open University Press).

Cockburn, C. (1991a) *Brothers: Male Dominance and Technological Change* (London: Pluto Press).

Cockburn, C. (1991b) *In the Way of Women: Men's Resistance to Sex Equality in Organizations* (Basingstoke: Macmillan).

Concise Oxford Dictionary (1976) 6th ed. (Oxford: Oxford University Press).

Cook, T. D. C. L. Gruder, K. M. Hennigan and B. R. Flay (1979) 'History of the sleeper effect: Some logical pitfalls in accepting the null hypothesis', *Psychological Bulletin*, 86, 662–79.

Cooley, M. (1984) 'Problems of automation' in T. Lupton (ed.) *Proceedings of the First International Conference on Human Factors in Manufacturing* (Amsterdam: North-Holland).

Cooper, C. L. (1985) 'Your place in the stress league', *The Sunday Times*, 24 February.

Cooper, C. L. and M. J. Smith (1985) *Job Stress and Blue Collar Work* (Chichester: John Wiley).

Costello, J. (1985) *Love Sex and War: Changing Values 1939–45* (London: Collins).

Coyle, A. (1982) 'Sex and skill in the organisation of the clothing industry', in J. West (ed.) *Work, Women and the Labour Market* (London: Routledge and Kegan Paul).

Crouch, A. and P. W. Yetton (1987) 'Manager behavior, leadership style and subordinate performance: An empirical extension of the Vroom-Yetton conflict rule', *Organizational Behavior and Human Decision Processes* 39, 384–96.

Crutchfield, R. S. (1955) 'Conformity and character', *American Psychologist* 10, 191–8.

Csikszentmihalyi, M. (1975) *Beyond Boredom and Anxiety* (San Francisco: Jossey-Bass).

Curran, J., R. Burrows and M. Evandrou (1987) *Small Business Owners and the Self-Employed in Britain* (London: Small Business Research Trust).

Dahl, R. A. (1957) 'The concept of power', *Behavioral Science* 2, 201–18.

Danziger, K. (1973) *Socialization* (Baltimore: Penguin).

Davidoff, L., J. L'Esperance and H. Newby (1976) 'Landscape with figures: home and community in English society', in J. Mitchell and A. Oakley (eds) *The Rights and Wrongs of Women* (Harmondsworth: Penguin).

Davidson, M. (1987) 'Women and Employment', in P. Warr (ed.) *Psychology at Work*, 3rd ed., (Harmondsworth: Penguin).

Davis, L. E. and A. B. Cherns (eds) (1975) *The Quality of Working Life* (New York: Free Press).

Dawson, S. (1986) *Analyzing Organizations*, (Basingstoke: Macmillan).

De Board, R. (1978) *The Psychoanalysis of Organizations* (London: Tavistock).

Delaney, E. and T. Hopkins (1987) *Stanford-Binet Intelligence Scale – Examiner's Handbook: An Expanded Guide For Fourth Edition Users* (Chicago: Riverside).

Dell, T. (1989) *How to Motivate People: A Guide for Managers* (London: Kogan Page).

De Man, H. (1929) *Joy in Work* (New York: Henry Holt).

Dex, S. (1985) *The Sexual Division of Work* (Brighton: Harvester Wheatsheaf).

Dion, K. and E. Berscheid (1992) 'Physical attractiveness and sociometric choice in nursery school children', mimeographed research report quoted in: Aronson, op. cit.

Dion, K., E. Berscheid and E. Walster (1972) 'What is beautiful is good', *Journal of Personality and Social Psychology* 24, 285–90.

Dipboye, R. L. and J. W. Wiley (1977) 'Reactions of college recruiters to interviewee sex and self-presentation style', *Journal of Vocational Behaviour* 10, 1–12.

Dipboye, R. L., H. L. Fromkin and K. Wilback (1975) 'The importance of applicant sex, attractiveness and scholastic standing in evaluation of job applicant résumés', *Journal of Applied Psychology* 60(1), 39–43.

Ditton, J. (1979) 'Baking Time', *Sociological Review* 27 157–67.

Dixon, N. F. (1976) *On the Psychology of Military Incompetence* (London: Cape).

Dobb, M. (1963) *Studies in the Development of Capitalism* (London: Routledge & Kegan Paul).

Dollard, J. and N. E. Miller (1950) *Personality and Psychotherapy: An Analysis in Terms of Learning, Thinking and Culture* (New York: McGraw-Hill).

Downey, H. K., J. E. Sheridan and J. W. Slocum (1976) 'The path-goal theory of leadership: A longitudinal analysis', *Organizational Behaviour and Human Performance* 16, 156–76.

Dror, Y. and T. Romm (1988) 'Politics in organizations and its perception within the organization', *Organization Studies* 9(2), 165–80.

Drucker, P. F. (1954) *The Practice of Management* (New York: Harper and Row).

Drucker, P. F. (1988) *Management* (London: Heinemann).

Dubin, R. (1958) *The World of Work* (Englewood Cliffs, New Jersey: Prentice-Hall).

Duncan, J. (1983) 'Perceptual selection based on alphanumeric class: Evidence from partial reports', in *Perception and Psychophysics*, 33, 533–47.

Eagly, A. and S. Chaiken (1975) 'An attribution analysis of the effect of communicator characteristics on opinion change: The case of communicator attractiveness', *Journal of Personality and Social Psychology*, 32, 136–44.

Earley, P. C., T. Connolly and G. Ekegren (1989) 'Goals, strategy development and task performance: Some limits on the efficacy of goal-setting', *Journal of Applied Psychology* 74, 24–33.

Edwards, P. K. (1990) 'Understanding conflict in the labour process: the logic and autonomy of struggle', in D. Knights and H. Willmott (eds) *Labour Process Theory* (Basingstoke: Macmillan).

Ehrlich, D., I. Guttman, P. Schonbach and J. Mills (1957) 'Postdecision exposure to relevant information', *Journal of Abnormal and Social Psychology*, 57, 98–102.

Eisenberg, P. and P. F. Lazarsfeld (1938) 'The psychological effects of unemployment', *Psychological Bulletin*, 35, 358–90.

Ekman, P. (ed.) (1982) *Emotion in the Human Face*, 2nd ed. (Cambridge and New York: Cambridge University Press).

Elder, G. H. (1974) *Children of the Great Depression* (Chicago: University of Chicago Press).

Elder, G. H. (1981) 'History and the life course' in D. Bertaux (ed.) *Biography and Society* (Beverly Hills: Sage).

Elder, G. H. and J. K. Likert (1982) 'Hard times in women's lives: historical influences across forty years', *American Journal of Sociology*, 88, 241–69.

English, H. B. and A. C. English (1958) *A Comprehensive Dictionary of Psychological and Psychoanalytical Terms* (New York: Longmans).

Equal Opportunities Commission (1987) *Women and Men in Britain: A Statistical Profile* (London: HMSO).

Equal Opportunities Commission (1991) *Pay and Gender in Britain* (London: HMSO).

Erikson, E. (1963) *Childhood and Society*, 2nd ed. (New York: Norton).

Exner, J. E. (1974) *The Rorschach: A Comprehensive System* (New York: Wiley).

Eysenck, H. J. (1952) *The Scientific Study of Personality* (London: Routledge and Kegan Paul).

Eysenck, H. J. (1967) 'Personality patterns in various groups of businessmen', *Occupational Psychology* 41, 449–50.

Eysenck, H. J. (1976) *Case Studies in Behaviour Therapy* (London: Routledge and Kegan Paul).

Farh, J. and G. H. Dobbins (1989) 'Effects of comparative performance information on the accuracy of self-rating and agreement between self and supervisor ratings', *Journal of Applied Psychology* 74, 606–10.

Feather, N. T. and G. E. O'Brien (1986) 'A longitudinal study of the effects of employment and unemployment on school-leavers', *Journal of Occupational Psychology* 59, 121–44.

Feldman, D. C. and H. J. Arnold (1983) *Managing Individual and Group Behaviour in Organizations* (New York: McGraw-Hill).

Ferree, M. M. (1987) 'The struggles of superwoman', in C. Bose, K. Feldberg and N. Sokoloff (eds) *Hidden Aspects of Women's Work* (New York: Praeger).

Ferri, E. (ed.) (1993) *Life at 33: The Fifth Follow-up of the National Child Development Study* (London: National Children's Bureau, and the Economic and Social Research Council).

Festinger, L. (1957) *A Theory of Cognitive Dissonance* (Stanford: Stanford University Press).

Festinger, L. and J. M. Carlsmith (1959) 'Cognitive consequences of forced compliance', *Journal of Abnormal and Social Psychology* 58, 203–10.

Festinger, L., S. Schachter and K. Back (1950) *Social Pressures in Informal Groups* (New York: Harper and Bros).

Fiedler, F. E. (1967) *A Theory of Leadership Effectiveness* (New York: McGraw-Hill).

Fiedler, F. E. (1970) 'Leadership experience and leader performance – another hypothesis shot to hell', *Organizational Behaviour and Human Performance*, 5, 1–14.

Filley, A. C., R. J. House and S. Kerr (1976) *Managerial Process and Organizational Behavior* (Glenview, Illinois.: Scott, Foresman).

Fincham, R. and P. Rhodes (1992) *The Individual, Work and Organization*, 2nd ed. (London: Weidenfeld and Nicolson).

Fineman, S. (1983) *White Collar Unemployment* (Chichester: Wiley).

Firth, J. and D. A. Shapiro (1986) 'An evaluation of psychotherapy for job-related distress', *Journal of Occupational Psychology* 59, 111–19.

Fiske, E. B. (1977) 'An issue that won't go away', *The New York Times Magazine* March 27, p. 58.

Fleishman, E. A. (1975) 'Toward a taxonomy of human performance', *American Psychologist* 30, 1127–49.

Fleishman, E. A. and J. C. Hogan (1978) *A Taxonomic Method for Assessing the Physical Requirements of Jobs* (Washington, DC: Advanced Research Resources Organization).

Fleishman, E. A. and M. K. Quaintance (1984) *Taxonomies of Human Performance: The Description of Human Tasks* (Orlando, Florida: Academic Press).

Folkard, S. (1987) 'Circadian Rhythms and Hours of Work', in Peter Warr (ed.) *Psychology of Work*, 3rd ed. (London: Penguin).

Fontana, D. (1989) *Managing Stress* (London: Routledge/British Psychological Society).

Forbes, R. J. and P. R. Jackson (1980) 'Non-verbal behaviour and the outcome of selection interviews', *Journal of Occupational Psychology* 53, 65–72.

Ford, H. (1922) *My Life and Work* (New York: Doubleday Page).

Forester, T. (ed.) (1985) *The Information Technology Revolution: The Complete Guide* (Oxford: Blackwell).

Forsythe, S., M. F. Drake and C. E. Cox (1985) 'Influence of applicant's dress on interviewer's selection decisions', *Journal of Applied Psychology* 70, 374–8.

Fraisse, P. (1964) *The Psychology of Time* (London: Eyre and Spottiswoode).

Freedman, J. and D. Sears (1965) 'Warning, distraction and resistance to influence', *Journal of Personality and Social Psychology* 1, 262–6.

French, J. R. P. and R. D. Caplan (1970) 'Psychosocial Factors in Coronary Heart Disease', *Industrial Medicine* 39 383–97.

French, J. R. P. and B. H. Raven (1968) 'The bases of social power', in: D. Cartwright and A. Zander (eds) *Group Dynamics*, (3rd ed.) (New York: Harper & Row).

French, J. R. P., R. D. Caplan and R. Van Harrison (1982) *The Mechanisms of Job Stress and Strain* (Chichester: Wiley).

Freud, S. (1939) *Moses and Monotheism* (London: Hogarth. Reprinted in The Standard Edition, J. Strachey (ed.), 1953–1974, Volume 23).

Freud, S. (1953) *The Interpretation of Dreams* (London: Hogarth).

Freud, S. (1953–1974) *The Standard Edition of the Complete Psychological Works of Sigmund Freud* J. Strachey (ed.) (London: Hogarth).

Friedman, M. and R. H. Rosenman (1974) *Type A Behavior and Your Heart* (Greenwich, Connecticut: Fawcett. London: Wildwood House).

Fryer, D. and R. Payne (1984) 'Proactive behaviour in unemployment', *Leisure Studies* 3, 273–95.

Furnham, A. (1982) 'Explanations for unemployment in Britain', *European Journal of Social Psychology*, 12, 335–52.

Furnham, A. (1984) 'Getting a job: school leavers' perceptions of employment prospects', *British Journal of Educational Psychology* 54, 295–305.

Furnham, A. and R. Schaeffer (1984) 'Person-environment fit, job satisfaction and mental health', *Journal of Occupational Psychology* 57, 295–307.

Gagné, R. M. (1977) *The Conditions of Learning*, 3rd ed. (New York: Holt, Rinehart and Winston).

Galton, F. (1869) *Hereditary Genius* (London: Macmillan).

Garner, W. and A. Wigdor (1982) *Ability Testing: Use, Consequences and Controversies* (Washington, DC: National Academy Press).

Gergen. K. J. and S. J. Morse (1967) 'Self-consistency: measurement and validation', *Proceedings of the American Psychological Association* 207–8.

Gerstein, M. and M. A. Amos (1986) 'Implementation and evaluation of adult career development programs in organizations', *Journal of Career Development* 12, 210–18.

Gesell, A. and C. Amatruda (1947) *Developmental Diagnosis*, 2nd ed. (New York: Hoeber).

Gettys, L. D. and A. Cann (1981) 'Children's perceptions of occupational sex stereotypes', *Sex Roles* 1, 301–8.

Gilbert, L. A. and L. S Dancer (1992) 'Dual earner families in the United States and adolescent development', in S. Lewis, D. Izraeli and H. Hootemans (eds) *Dual Earner Families: International Perspectives* (London: Sage).

Gilloran, A. J. T. McGlew, K. McKee, A. Robertson and D. Wight (1993) 'Measuring the quality of care in psychogeriatric wards', *Journal of Advanced Nursing* 18, 269–75.

Goffman, E. (1971) *The Presentation of Self in Everyday Life* (Harmondsworth: Pelican).

Goldsmith, W. and D. Clutterbuck (1984) *The Winning Streak* (London: Weidenfeld and Nicolson).

Goldstein, I. L. and V. M. Buxton (1982) 'Training and human performance', in M. D. Dunnette and E. A. Fleishman (eds) *Human Performance and Productivity: Human Capability Assessment* (Hillsdale, New Jersey: Lawrence Erlbaum Associates).

Goldthorpe, J., D. Lockwood, F. Bechhofer and J. Platt (1968) *The Affluent Worker: Industrial Attitudes and Behaviour* (Cambridge: Cambridge University Press).

Gonzales, M., E. Aronson and M. Costanzo (1988) 'Increasing the effectiveness of energy auditors: A field experiment', *Journal of Applied Social Psychology* 18, 1049–66.

Goodale, J. C. and D. T. Hall (1976) 'Inheriting a career: the effects of sex, values and parents', *Journal of Vocational Behavior* 8, 19–30.

Goodworth, C. T. (1979) *Effective Interviewing for Employment Selection* (London: Business Books).

Gorsuch, R. L. (1983) *Factor Analysis*, 2nd ed. (Hillsdale, New Jersey: Lawrence Erlbaum Associates).

Gouldner, A. W. (1958) 'Organizational Analysis', in R. K. Merton, L. Brown and L. S. Cottrell (eds) *Sociology Today* (New York: Basic Books).

Gowler, D., K. Legge and C. Clegg (1993) *Case Studies in Organizational Behaviour and Human Resource Management*, 2nd ed. (London: Paul Chapman Publishing).

Guardian, The 'FT Injury test case looms' (London, 7 December 1989).

Guardian, The 'Technology's toll on staff welfare threatens health of balance sheets' (London, 4 January 1991).

Guest, D. E. (1987) 'Leadership and management', in Peter Warr (ed.) *Psychology of Work* 3rd ed. (Harmondsworth: Penguin).

Guest, D., R. Williams and P. Dewe (1980) 'Workers' perceptions of changes affecting the quality of working life', in K. D. Duncan, M. M. Gruneberg and D. Wallis (eds) *Changes in Working Life* (Chichester: Wiley).

Guilford, J. P. and J. I. Lacey (eds) (1947) *Printed Classification Tests* (AAF Aviation Psychology Program, Research Reports, Report No 5) (Washington DC: US Government Printing Office).

Guion, R.M. and R.F. Gottier (1965) 'Validity of personality measures in personnel selection', *Personnel Psychology* 18, 135–64.

Guthrie, E.R. (1938) *The Psychology of Human Conflict* (New York: Harper and Row).

Gutteridge, T.G. (1986) 'Organizational career development systems: The state of the practice', in: D.T. Hall (ed.) *Career Development in Organizations* (London: Jossey-Bass).

Gyllenhammar, P.G. (1977) 'How Volvo adapts work to people', *Harvard Business Review* 55, 102–13.

Hackman, J.R. and G.R. Oldham (1975) 'Development of the Job Diagnostic Survey', *Journal of Applied Psychology* 60, 159–70.

Hackman, J.R. and G.R. Oldham (1976) 'Motivation through the design of work: test of a theory', *Organizational Behaviour and Human Performance* 16, 250–79.

Hackman, J.R. and G.R. Oldham (1980) *Work Redesign* (Reading, Massachusetts: Addison-Wesley).

Hadjifotiou, N. (1983) *Women and Harassment at Work* (London: Pluto Press).

Hagestad, G. and B.L. Neugarten (1985) 'Age and the Life Course', in R.H. Binstock and E. Shanas (eds) *Handbook of Aging and the Social Sciences* 2nd ed. (New York: Van Nostrand Reinhold).

Hakim, C. (1979) *Occupational Segregation* Research paper No. 9 (London: Department of Employment).

Hakim, C. (1980) 'Census reports as documentary evidence: the Census Commentaries 1801–1951', *Sociological Review* 28, 551–80.

Hall, C.S. and Lindzey, G. (1978) *Theories of Personality*, 3rd ed. (New York: Wiley).

Halpin, A.W. and B.J. Winer (1957) 'A factorial study of the leader behaviour descriptions', in R.M. Stogdill and A.E. Coons (eds) *Leader Behavior: Its Description and Measurement* (Columbus, Ohio: Ohio State University, Bureau of Business Research).

Halsey, A.H., A.F. Heath and J.M. Ridge (1980) *Origins and Destinations: Family, Class and Education in Modern Britain* (Oxford: Clarendon).

Handy, C.B. (1984) *The Future of Work: A Guide to a Changing Society* (Oxford: Blackwell).

Handy, C.B. (1985) *Understanding Organizations*, 3rd ed. (London: Penguin).

Handy, C.B. (1987) 'Management training: perk or prerequisite?', *Personnel Management* May, 28–31.

Hansen, J.C. and D.P. Campbell (1985) *Manual for the SVIB-SCII* 4th ed. (Stanford: Stanford University Press).

Harlow, H. (1949) 'The formation of learning sets', *Psychological Review* 56, 51–65.

Harpaz, I. (1990) 'The importance of work goals: An international perspective', *Journal of International Business Studies* 21, 75–93.

Harré, R. and R. Lamb (eds) (1986) *The Dictionary of Personality and Social Psychology* (Oxford: Blackwell).

Harrell, T.W. and M.S. Harrell (1945) 'Army classification test scores for civilian occupations', *Educational and Psychological Measurement* 5, 229–39.

Hartley, J. 'The personality of unemployed managers: myth and measurement', *Personnel Review* 9 (1980) 12–18.

Hathaway, S.R. and J.C. McKinley (1940) 'A multiphasic personality schedule (Minnesota): I. Construction of the schedule', *Journal of Psychology* 10, 249–54.

Haw, A.H. (1982) 'Women, work and stress: a review and agenda for the future', *Journal of Health and Social Behaviour* 23, 132–44.

Hayes, J. and P. Nutman (1981) *Understanding the Unemployed* (London: Tavistock).

Hearn, J. and W. Parkin (1987) *'Sex' at 'Work': The Power and Paradox of Organization Sexuality* (Brighton: Wheatsheaf).

Hearn, J., D. Sheppard, P. Tancred-Sheriff and G. Burrell (eds) (1989) *The Sexuality of Organization* (London: Sage).

Hearnshaw, L. S. (1987) *The Shaping of Modern Psychology* (London: Routledge & Kegan Paul).

Hearnshaw, L. and R. Winterbourn (1945) *Human Welfare and Industrial Efficiency* (Wellington, New Zealand: Reed).

Heider, F. (1958) *The Psychology of Interpersonal Relations* (New York: Wiley).

Heider, F. and M. Simmel (1944) 'An experimental study of apparent behavior', *American Journal of Psychology* 57, 243–59.

Henderson, M. and M. Argyle (1985) 'Social support by four categories of work colleagues: relationships between activities, stress and satisfaction', *Journal of Occupational Behaviour* 6, 229–39.

Herriot, P. (1987) 'The Selection Interview', in P. Warr (ed.) *Psychology at Work* (Harmondsworth: Penguin).

Herzberg, F. (1966) *Work and the Nature of Man* (Cleveland: World Publishing Company).

Herzberg, F., B. Mausner and B. Snyderman (1959) *The Motivation To Work* (New York: Wiley).

Hickson, D. J. (1990) 'Politics permeate', in D. C. Wilson and R. H. Rosenfeld, (eds) *Managing Organisations* (Maidenhead: McGraw-Hill) pp. 175–81.

Higgins, E. T., G. A. King and G. H. Mavin (1982) 'Individual construct accessibility and subjective impressions and recall', *Journal of Personality and Social Psychology* 43, 35–47.

Hilgard, E. R., R. C. Atkinson and R. L. Atkinson (1975) *Introduction to Psychology* 6th ed. (New York: Harcourt Brace Jovanovich).

Hill, J. M. M. (1978) 'The psychological impact of unemployment', *New Society* 43, (798), 118–20.

Himmelweit, H. and J. Whitfield (1944) 'Mean intelligence scores of a random sample of occupations', *British Journal of Industrial Medicine* I, 224–6.

Hochschild, A. R. (1983) *The Managed Heart* (Berkeley: University of California Press).

Hofstede, G. (1980) *Culture's Consequences: International Differences in Work-Related Values* (Beverly Hills: Sage).

Hogan, R. (1990) quoted in: 'Unmasking Incompetent Managers', *Insight* May 21, 42–4.

Holland, J. L. (1985) *Making Vocational Choices: A Theory of Careers*, 2nd ed. (Englewood Cliffs, New Jersey: Prentice-Hall).

Hollenbeck, J. R. and A. P. Brief (1987) 'The effects of individual differences and goal origin on goal setting and performance', *Organizational Behavior and Human Decision Processes* 40, 392–414.

Hollenbeck, J. R. and H. J. Klein (1987) 'Goal commitment and the goal-setting process: Problems, prospects, and proposals for future research', *Journal of Applied Psychology* 72(2), 212–20.

Hollway, W. (1991) *Work Psychology and Organizational Behaviour* (London: Sage).

Holmes, T. H. and R. H. Rahe (1967) 'The social readjustment rating scale', *Journal of Psychosomatic Research* 11, 213–18.

Horne, J. A., C. G. Brass and A. N. Pettit (1980) 'Circadian performance differences between morning and evening types' *Ergonomics* 23, 129–36.

Hosking, D. and I. Morley (1991) *A Social Psychology of Organizing* (London: Harvester Wheatsheaf)

Hough, L. M., N. K. Eaton, M. D. Dunnette, J. D. Kamp and R. A. McCloy (1990) 'Criterion-related validities of personality constructs and the effect of response distortion on those validities', *Journal of Applied Psychology* 75, 581–95.

House, R. J. (1971) 'A path goal theory of leader-effectiveness', *Administrative Science Quarterly* 16, 321–38.

House, R. J. and M. L. Baetz (1979) 'Leadership: Some empirical generalizations and new research directions', in B. M. Staw (ed.) *Research in Organizational Behavior* (Greenwich, Connecticut: JAI Press).

Hovland, C. and R. Sears (1940) 'Minor studies of aggression: correlation of lynchings with economic indices', *Journal of Psychology* 9, 301–10.

Hovland, C., A. Lumsdaine and F. Sheffield (1949) *Experiments on Mass Communication* (Princeton, New Jersey: Princeton University Press).

Hoxie, R. F. (1915) *Scientific Management and Labor* (New York: Appleton).

Hull, F. M. and P. D. Collins (1987) 'High-technology batch production systems: Woodward's missing type', *Academy of Management Journal* 30, 786–97.

Hunter, J. and H. Hirsch (1987) 'Applications of meta-analysis', in C. Cooper and I. Robertson (eds) *International Review of Industrial and Organizational Psychology* (Chichester: Wiley).

Hunter, J. E. and R. F. Hunter (1984) 'Validity and utility of alternative predictors of job performance', *Psychological Bulletin* 96, 72–98.

Huseman, R. C., J. D. Hatfield and E. W. Miles (1987) 'A new perspective on equity theory: The equity sensitivity construct', *Academy of Management Review* 12, 222–34.

Huston, A. C. (1983) 'Sex-typing', in P. H. Mussen (ed.) *Handbook of Child Psychology*, 4th ed. (New York: Wiley).

Hyman, H. H. (1942) 'The psychology of status', *Archives of Psychology* No. 269.

Hyman, R. (1989) *Strikes*, 4th ed. (Basingstoke: Macmillan).

Ingleton, C. (1988) *Management Interviewing* (South Luffenham: Special Interest Publications).

Israeli, N. (1935) 'Distress in the outlook of Lancashire and Scottish unemployed', *Journal of Applied Psychology* 19, 67–9.

Izraeli, D. (1989) 'Burning out in medicine', in E. Goldsmith (ed.) *Work and Family: Theory, Research and Applications* (Newbury Park, California: Sage).

Jackofsky, E. and L. Peters (1983), 'Job turnover versus company turnover: Reassessment of the March and Simon participation hypothesis', *Journal of Applied Psychology* 68, 490–5.

Jahoda, G. (1954) 'A note on Ashanti names and their relation to personality', *British Journal of Psychology* 45, 192–5.

Jahoda, M. (1979) 'The impact of unemployment in the 1930s and the 1970s', *Bulletin of the British Psychological Society* 32, 309–14.

Jahoda, M. (1982) *Employment and Unemployment: A Social Psychological Analysis* (Cambridge: Cambridge University Press).

Jahoda, M., P. F. Lazarsfeld and H. Zeisel (1972) *Marienthal: The Sociography of an Unemployed Community* (London: Tavistock, New York: Aldine-Atherton (1933, trans.)).

Janis, I. L. (1982) *Groupthink* (Boston: Houghton Mifflin).

Jenkins, D. (1985) 'The West German humanisation of work programme: A preliminary assessment', (WRU Occasional Paper No 8, 1978) cited in C. Littler (ed.) *The Experience of Work* (Aldershot: Gower/Open University Press).

Jensen, A. (1969) 'How much can we boost IQ and scholastic achievement?', *Harvard Educational Review* 31, 1–123.

Johnson, D.W., G. Maruyama, R. Johnson and L. Skon (1980) 'Effects of cooperation, competition, and individualistic goal structures on achievement: a meta-analysis', *Psychological Bulletin* 89, 47–62.

Kamin, L. (1976) 'Heredity, intelligence, politics and psychology', in N.J. Block and G. Dworkin (eds), *The IQ Controversy* (New York: Pantheon).

Kanter, R. (1977) *Men and Women of the Corporation* (New York: Basic Books).

Kasl, S.V. (1978) 'Epidemiological contributions to the study of work stress', in: C.L. Cooper and R. Payne (eds), *Stress at Work* (Chichester: Wiley).

Kasl, S.V. (1980) 'The impact of retirement', in: C.L. Cooper and R. Payne (eds) *Current Concerns in Occupational Stress* (Chichester: Wiley).

Katz, R. (1977) 'Job enrichment: some career considerations', in J. Van Maanen (ed.), *Organizational Careers: Some New Perspectives* (London, New York, Sydney, Toronto: Wiley).

Katz, R. (1978) 'Job longevity as a situational factor in job satisfaction', *Administrative Science Quarterly* 23, 204–23.

Katz, A.M. and R. Hill (1958) 'Residential propinquity and marital selection: A review of theory, method and fact', *Marriage and Family Living* 20, 27–35.

Katz, D. and R.L. Kahn (1978) *The Social Psychology of Organizations*, 2nd ed. (New York: Wiley).

Kelley, H.H. (1950) 'The warm-cold variable in first impressions of persons', *Journal of Personality* 18, 431–9.

Kelly, G.A. (1955) *The Psychology of Personal Constructs* (New York: Norton).

Kelvin, P. and J.E. Jarrett (1985) *Unemployment: Its Social Psychological Effects* (Cambridge: Cambridge University Press).

Kemp, N., T. Wall, C. Clegg and J. Cordery (1983) 'Autonomous work groups in a greenfield site: a comparative study', *Journal of Occupational Psychology* 56, 271–88.

Kempner, T. (ed.) (1987) *The Penguin Management Handbook*, 4th ed. (London: Penguin).

Kerkhoff, G.A. (1985) 'Inter-individual differences in the human circadian system: A review', *Biological Psychology* 20, 83–112.

Kern, S. (1983) *The Culture of Time and Space, 1880–1918* (London: Weidenfeld and Nicolson).

Kerr, S. (1983) 'Substitutes for leadership: Some implications for organizational design', in J.R. Hackman, E.E. Lawler and L.W. Porter (eds), *Perspectives on Behavior in Organizations* (New York: McGraw-Hill).

Kerr, S. and J.M. Jermier (1978) 'Substitutes for leadership: Their meanings and measurement', *Organizational Behavior and Human Performance* 22, 375–403.

Kets de Vries, M.F.R. (1989) *Prisoners of Leadership* (Chichester: Wiley).

Kets De Vries, M.F.R. and D. Miller (1984) *The Neurotic Organization: Diagnosing and Changing Counterproductive Styles of Management* (San Francisco: Jossey-Bass Inc).

Kiesler, C. (1971) *The Psychology of Commitment* (London: Academic Press).

Kilpatrick, R. and K. Trew (1985) 'Life-styles and psychological well-being among unemployed men in Northern Ireland', *Journal of Occupational Psychology* 58, 207–16.

Kirkpatrick, D.L. (1967) 'Evaluation of training', in R.L. Craig and L.R. Bittel (eds) *Training and Development Handbook* (New York: McGraw-Hill).

Kirkpatrick, S.A. and E.A. Locke (1991) 'Leadership: Do traits matter?', *Academy of Management Executive* 5, (2), 48–60.

Klein, D. B. (1977) *The Unconscious: Invention or Discovery* (Santa Monica, California: Goodyear)

Klein, K. E., H. M. Wegmann and B. I. Hunt (1972) 'Desynchronization of body temperature and performance circadian rhythm as a result of outgoing and homegoing transmission flights', *Aerospace Medicine* 43, 119–32.

Klimoski, R. J. and W. J. Strickland 'Assessment centers: Valid or merely prescient?', *Personnel Psychology* 30, (1977) 353–63.

Kline, P. (1981) *Fact and Fiction in Freudian Theory*, 2nd ed. (London: Methuen).

Kline, P. (1983) *Personality: Measurement and Theory* (London: Hutchinson).

Klineberg, O. (1944) *Characteristics of the American Negro* (New York: Harper).

Kogan, N. and M. A. Wallach (1967) 'Risk taking as a function of the situation, the person and the group', in G. Mandler *et al.* (eds) *New Directions in Psychology* vol. 2 (New York: Holt, Rinehart and Winston).

Kohlberg, L. (1966) 'A cognitive-developmental analysis of children's sex-role concepts and attitudes', in E. E. Maccoby (ed.) *The Development of Sex Differences* (Stanford, California: Stanford University Press).

Kohler, W. (1925) *The Mentality of Apes* (New York: Harcourt Brace Jovanovich).

Kolodner, J. L. (1983) 'Maintaining organization in a dynamic long-term memory', *Cognitive Science* 7, 243–280.

Komarovsky, M. (1940) *The Unemployed Man and His Family: The Effect of Unemployment on the Status of the Man in 59 Families* (New York: Dryden).

Kornhauser, A. (1965) *Mental Health of the Industrial Worker* (New York: Wiley).

Kossoris, M. D., R. F. Kohler and Associates (1947) 'Hours of Work and Output', US Department of Labor, Bureau of Labor Statistics, *Bulletin* Number 917.

Kotter, J. (1982) *The General Manager* (New York: Free Press).

Kraut, A. (1965) 'A Study of Role Conflicts and their Relationships to Job Satisfaction, Tension and Performance', Doctoral dissertation, University of Michigan, Ann Arbor, USA, University Microfilms, 67–8312.

Kumazawa, M. and J. Yamada (1988) 'Job and Skill under the Life-long Nen-ko Employment Practice', in: S. Wood (ed.) *The Transformation of Work* (London: Hutchinson).

Kundi, M., M. Koller, R. Cervinka and M. Haider (1979) 'Consequence of shift work as a function of age and years on shift', *Chronobiologica* 6, 123.

La Benz, P., A. Cohen and B. Pearson (1967) 'A Noise and Hearing Survey of Earth-moving Equipment Operation', *American Industrial Hygiene Association Journal* 28, 117–28.

Laing, R. D. (1967) *The Politics of Experience* (London: Penguin).

Lamm, H. and D. G. Myers (1978) 'Group induced polarization of attitudes and behavior', in L. Berkowitz (ed.), *Advances in Experimental Social Psychology*, Volume 2 (New York: Academic Press).

Landy, F. (1989) *Psychology of Work Behaviour*, 4th ed. (Belmont: Wadsworth).

Landy, F. (ed.) (1986) *Readings in Industrial and Organizational Psychology* (Chicago: The Dorsey Press).

Latané, B., K. Williams and S. Harkins (1979) 'Many hands make light work: the causes and consequences of social loafing', *Journal of Personality and Social Psychology* 37, 822–32.

Latham, G. P. and E. A. Locke (1979) 'Goal-setting – a motivational technique that works', *Organizational Dynamics* 8, (2), 68–80.

Latham, G. P. and L. M. Saari (1979) 'Application of social learning theory to training supervisors through behavioral modeling', *Journal of Applied Psychology* 64 (3) 239–46.

Latham, G. P., M. Erez and E. A. Locke (1988) 'Resolving scientific disputes by the joint design of crucial experiments by the antagonists: Application to the Erez-Latham dispute regarding participation in goal setting', *Journal of Applied Psychology* 73, 753–72.

Lawler, E. E. and J. R. Hackman (1969) 'Impact of employee participation in the development of pay incentive plans: A field experiment', *Journal of Applied Psychology* 53, 467–71.

Lawshe, C. H., R. A. Bolda and R. L. Brune (1959) 'Studies in management training evaluation: Chapter II. The effects of exposure to role playing', *Journal of Applied Psychology* 43, 287–92.

Lee, R. M. and C. C. Harris (1985) 'Redundancy studies: Port Talbot and the future', *Quarterly Journal of Social Affairs* 1, 19–27.

Leishman, K. (1987) 'Heterosexuals and AIDS', *The Atlantic Monthly* (February) 39–58.

Lerner, M. (1965) 'Evaluation of performance as a function of performer's reward and attractiveness', *Journal of Personality and Social Psychology* 1, 355–60.

Leventhal, H. (1970) 'Findings and theory in the study of fear communications', in L. Berkowitz (ed.) *Advances in Experimental Social Psychology*, Volume 5 (New York: Academic Press).

Leventhal, H., D. Meyer and D. Nerenz (1980) 'The common sense representation of illness danger', in S. Rachman (ed.), *Contributions to Medical Psychology*, Volume 2 (New York: Pergamon Press).

Lewin, K. (1958) 'Group decision and social change', in E. E. Maccoby, T. Newcomb and E. L. Hartley (eds) *Readings in Social Psychology*, 3rd ed. (New York: Holt, Rinehart and Winston).

Lewin, K., R. Lippitt and R. White (1939) 'Patterns of aggressive behavior in experimentally created "social climates" ', *Journal of Social Psychology* 10, 271–99.

Likert, R. (1961) *New Patterns of Management* (New York: McGraw-Hill).

Likert, R. (1967) *The Human Organization* (New York: McGraw-Hill).

Likert, R. (1977) 'Management styles: the human component', *Management Review* 66, 23–8, 43–5.

Lindsay, P. H. and D. A. Norman (1977) *Human Information Processing* (2nd ed.) (London: Academic Press).

Lindsley, D. B. (1952) 'Psychological phenomena and the electroencephalogram', *Electroencephalography and Clinical Neurophysiology* (4), 443–56.

Little, C. B. (1976) 'Technical-professional unemployment: Middle-class adaptability to personal crisis', *Sociological Quarterly* 17, 262–74.

Littler, C. R. and G. Salaman (1985) 'The Design of Jobs', in Littler, C. R. (ed.) *The Experience of Work* (Aldershot: Gower)

Livesley, W. J. and D. B. Bromley (1973) *Person Perception in Childhood and Adolescence* (London and New York: Wiley).

Lloyd, G. (1984) *Man of Reason: "Male" and "Female" in Western Philosophy* (London: Methuen).

Locke, E. A. (1968) 'Toward a theory of task motivation and incentives', *Organizational Behavior and Human Performance* 3, 157–89.

Locke, E. A. (1976) 'The nature and causes of job satisfaction', in M. Dunnette (ed.), *Handbook of Industrial and Organizational Psychology* (Chicago: Rand McNally).

Locke, E. A. and G. P. Latham (1990) *A Theory of Goal Setting and Task Performance* (Englewood Cliffs, New Jersey: Prentice-Hall).

Locke, E. A., K. N. Shaw, L. M. Saari and G. P. Latham (1981) 'Goal setting and task performance 1969–1980', *Psychological Bulletin* 90, 125–52.

Loehlin, J.C., G. Lindzey and J.N. Spuhler (1975) *Racial Differences in Intelligence* (San Francisco: Freeman).

Louis, M.R. (1980) 'Surprise and sense-making: What newcomers expect in entering unfamiliar organizational settings', *Administrative Science Quarterly* 25, 226–51.

Luthans, F. and R. Kreitner (1985) *Organizational Behavior Modification and Beyond* (Glenview, Illinois: Scott, Foresman).

McCall, R.B., M.I. Appelbaum and P.S. Hogarty (1973) 'Developmental changes in mental performance', *Monographs of the Society for Research in Child Development* 173.

McClelland, D.C. (1961) *The Achieving Society* (New York: Van Nostrand).

McClelland, D.C. (1978) 'Managing motivation to expand human freedom', *American Psychologist* 33, 201–10.

McClelland, D.C. and R.E. Boyatzis (1982) 'Leadership motive pattern and long-term success in management', *Journal of Applied Psychology* 67, 737–43.

McClelland, D.C. and D.G. Winter (1969) *Motivating Economic Achievement* (New York: Free Press).

McClelland, D.C., J.W. Atkinson, R.A. Clark and E.L. Lowell (1953) *The Achievement Motive* (New York: Appleton-Century-Croft).

McCormick, E. and D. Ilgen (1987) *Industrial and Organizational Psychology* 8th ed. (London and Winchester, Massachusetts: Unwin Hyman).

McCormick, E.J., P.J. Jeanneret and R.C. Mecham (1972) 'A study of job characteristics and job dimensions as based on the position analysis questionnaires', *Journal of Applied Psychology* 36, 347–68.

McGoldrick, A. (1982) 'Early retirement: a new leisure opportunity', *Work and Leisure* (Leisure Studies Association Series) 15, 73–89.

McGregor, D.M. (1960) *The Human Side of Enterprise* (New York: McGraw-Hill).

McGuire, W.J. (1985) 'Attitudes and attitude change', in G. Lindzey and E. Aronson (eds), *Handbook of Social Psychology*, 3rd ed., Volume 2, 233–346 (New York: Random House).

McGuire, W. and D. Papageorgis (1961) 'The relative efficacy of various types of prior belief defence in producing immunity against persuasion', *Journal of Abnormal and Social Psychology* 62, 327–37.

McKenna, E.F. (1987) *Psychology in Business* (London: Lawrence Erlbaum Associates).

Mabe, P.A. and S.G. West (1982) 'Validity of self-evaluation of ability: A review and meta-analysis', *Journal of Applied Psychology* 67, 280–296.

Maccoby, E.C. and C.N. Jacklin (1980) 'Sex differences in aggression: A rejoinder and reprise', *Child Development* 51, 964–80.

Machungawa, P. and N. Schmitt (1983) 'Work motivation in a developing country', *Journal of Applied Psychology* 68, 31–42.

Makin, P.J., C.L. Cooper and C.J. Cox (1989) *Managing People at Work* (London: Routledge/British Psychological Society).

Mangoine, T. and R. Quinn (1975) 'Job satisfaction, counterproductive behaviour and drug use at work', *Journal of Applied Psychology* 60, 114–16.

Mann, M. (1986) 'A crisis in stratification theory?', in R. Compton and M. Mann (eds) *Gender and Stratification* (Cambridge: Polity).

Marglin, S.A. (1974) 'What do bosses do? The origins and functions of hierarchy in capitalist production', *Review of Radical Political Economics* 6, 33–60.

Marlowe, D. and K. Gergen (1969) 'Personality and social interaction', in G. Lindzey and E. Aronson (eds) *Handbook of Social Psychology*, 2nd ed., Volume 3 (Reading, Mass.: Addison-Wesley).

Mars, G. (1982) *Cheats at Work* (London: Allen and Unwin).

Marsh, P. (1982) 'Rules in the organization of action', in M. von Cranach and R. Harré (eds) *The Analysis of Action* (Cambridge: Cambridge University Press).

Marshall, J. (1984) *Women Managers – Travellers in a Male World* (Chichester: Wiley).

Martin, J. and C. Roberts (1983) *Women and Employment: A Lifetime Perspective* (London: HMSO Books).

Martin, R. and J. Wallace (1986) *Working Women in Recession: Employment, Redundancy and Unemployment* (Oxford: Oxford University Press).

Marx, K. (1976) *Capital* Volume 1 (Harmondsworth: Penguin).

Maslach, C. and S. E. Jackson (1982) 'Burnout in health professions: a social psychological analysis', in G. S. Sanders and J. Suls (eds), *Social Psychology of Health and Illness* (Hillsdale, New Jersey: Lawrence Erlbaum Associates).

Maslow, A. H. (1943) 'A theory of motivation', *Psychological Review* 50, 370–96.

Maslow, A. H. (1954) *Motivation and Personality* (New York: Harper and Row).

Maslow, A. H. (1970) *Motivation and Personality*, 2nd ed. (New York: Harper and Row).

Matsui, T., A. Okada and A. Inoshita (1983) 'Mechanism of feedback affecting task performance', *Organizational Behavior and Human Performance* 31, 114–22

Matsui, T., A. Okada and R. Mizuguchi (1981) 'Expectancy theory prediction of the goal theory postulate "the harder the goals the higher the performance"', *Journal of Applied Psychology* 66, 54–8.

Mayer, R. E. (1977) 'The sequencing of instruction and the concept of assimilation-to-schema', *Instructional Science* 6, 369–88.

Mayo, E. (1946) *Human Problems of an Industrial Civilization* (Macmillan: New York).

Meichenbaum, D. H. and M. E. Jaremko (eds) (1983) *Stress Reduction and Prevention* (New York: Plenum Press).

Meindl, J. R., S. B. Ehrlich and J. M. Dukerich (1985) 'The romance of leadership', *Administrative Science Quarterly* 30, 78–102.

Mento, A. J., R. P. Steel and R. J. Karren (1987) 'A meta-analytic study of the effects of goal-setting on task performance: 1966–1984', *Organizational Behavior and Human Decision Processes* 39, 52–83.

Menzies, I. E. P. (1960) 'A Case-Study in the Functioning of Social Systems as a Defence Against Anxiety', *Human Relations*, 13, 95–121.

Merton, R. K. and A. K. Rossi (1949) 'Contributions to the theory of reference group behavior' in R. K. Merton (ed.), *Social Theory and Social Structure* (Glencoe, Illinois: Free Press).

Merton, R. K., G. G. Reader and P. L. Kendall (1957) *The Student-Physician* (Cambridge, Massachusetts: Harvard University Press).

Meyer, J. P. and I. R. Gellatly (1988) 'Perceived performance norm as a mediator in the effect of assigned goal on personal goal and task performance', *Journal of Applied Psychology* 73, 410–20.

Michotte, A. (1954) *The Perception of Causality* (New York: Basic Books).

Miles, R. E. (1965) 'Human relations or human resources?', *Harvard Business Review* 43, 148–63.

Miles, G. H. and O. Skilbeck (1944) 'An Experiment on Change of Work', *Occupational Psychology* 18, 192–5.

Milgram, S. (1963) 'Behavioral study of obedience', *Journal of Applied Psychology* 67, 371–8.

Milgram, S. (1974) *Obedience to Authority* (New York and London: Harper and Row/Tavistock).

Miller, W. H. (1991) 'A new perspective for tomorrow's workforce', *Industry Week* May 6, 7–9.

Miller, E. J. and G. V. Gwynne (1972) *A Life Apart* (London: Tavistock).

Miller, G. A. (1956) 'The magical number seven, plus or minus two: Some limits on our capacity for processing information', *Psychological Review* 63, 81–97.

Miller, N. and D. Campbell (1959) 'Recency and primacy in persuasion as a function of the timing of speeches and measurements', *Journal of Abnormal and Social Psychology* 59, 1–9.

Miller, N., G. Maruyama, R. J. Beaber and K. Valone (1976) 'Speed of speech and persuasion', *Journal of Personality and Social Psychology* 34, 615–24.

Mintzberg, H. (1973) *The Nature of Managerial Work* (New York: Harper & Row).

Mischel, W. (1973) 'Toward a cognitive social learning reconceptualization of personality', *Psychological Review* (80), 252–83.

Mitchell, J. (1975) *Psychoanalysis and Feminism* (Harmondsworth: Penguin).

Moore, W. E. (1963) *Man, Time and Society* (New York: Wiley).

Morris, J. N., J. A. Heady and R. G. Barley (1952) 'Coronary heart disease in medical practitioners', *British Medical Journal*, 1, 503.

Morrison, R. F., W. A. Owens, J. R. Glennon and L. E. Albright (1962) 'Factored life history antecedents of industrial research performance', *Journal of Applied Psychology*, 46, 281-4.

Moscovici, S. (1985) 'Social influence and conformity', in G. Lindzey and E. Aronson (eds), *Handbook of Social Psychology*, 3rd ed., Volume 2 (New Jersey: Erlbaum).

Mowday, R., C. Koberg and A. McArthur (1984) 'The psychology of the withdrawal process: A cross-validational test of Mobley's intermediate linkages model of turnover in two samples', *Academy of Management Journal* 27, 79–94.

Muchinsky, P. M. (1986) 'Personnel selection methods', in C. L. Cooper and I. T. Robertson (eds), *International Review of Industrial and Organizational Psychology* (Chichester: Wiley).

Mumford, A. (ed.) (1986) *Handbook of Management Deveopment*, 2nd ed. (Aldershot: Gower).

Mumford, L. (1934) *Technics and Civilisation* (New York: Harcourt, Brace and World).

Murray, H. A. (1938) *Explorations in Personality* (New York: Oxford University Press).

Murray, O. (1986) 'Life and society in classical Greece', in J. Boardman *et al.* (eds) *The Oxford History of the Classical World* (Oxford: Oxford University Press).

Nadien, M. (1989) *Adult Years and Aging* (Dubuque, Iowa: Kendall/Hunt).

Neff, W. S. (1985) *Work and Human Behaviour*, 3rd ed. (New York: Aldine).

Neimeyer, G. J. and J. E. Hudson (1985) 'Couple's constructs: personal systems in marital satisfaction', in D. Bannister (ed.) *Issues and Approaches in Personal Construct Theory* (London: Academic Press).

Nelson, T. M. and S. H. Bartley (1968) 'The pattern of personnel response arising during the office work day', *Occupational Psychology* 42 (1), 77–83.

Nemeroff, W. F. and J. Cosentino (1979) 'The benefits of combining feedback and goal setting', *Academy of Management Journal* 22, 566–76.

Newsweek 'Typing without keys' (New York: 1 December 1992).

Nichols, R. G. (1962) 'Listening is good business', *Management of Personnel Quarterly* 4, 4.

Nichols, T. and H. Beynon (1977) *Living with Capitalism* (London: Routledge and Kegan Paul).

Nicholson, J. (1984) *Men and Women – How Different Are They?* (Oxford: Oxford University Press).

Nicholson-Lord, D. (1990) 'Some buildings simply make you sick', *Independent on Sunday* 25 March, 3–5.

Nicholson, N. and J. Arnold (1989) 'Graduate early experience in a multinational corporation', *Personnel Review* 18 (4), 3–14.

Nicholson, N. and M. A. West (1988) *Managerial Job Change: Men and Women in Transition* (Cambridge: Cambridge University Press).

NIOSH (1987) *Stress Management in Work Settings* (Cincinatti: National Institute for Occupational Safety and Health).

Nisbett, R. and L. Ross (1980) *Human Inference: Strategies and Shortcomings of Social Judgment* (Englewood Cliffs, New Jersey: Prentice-Hall).

O'Brien, G. E. (1986) *Psychology of Work and Unemployment* (Chichester: Wiley).

O'Brien, G. E. and B. Kabanoff (1981) 'Australian norms and factor analyses of Rotter's internal-external control scale', *Australian Psychologist* 16, 184–202.

O'Leary, V. E. (1972) 'The Hawthorne effect in reverse: Effects of training and practice on individual and group performance', *Journal of Applied Psychology* 56, 491–4.

Orpen, C. (1978) 'Work and non-work satisfaction: a causal-correlational analysis', *Journal of Applied Psychology* 63, 530–2.

Pahl, J. M and R. E (1971) *Managers and Their Wives* (London: Allen and Unwin).

Pahl, R. E. (1984) *Divisions of Labour* (Oxford: Blackwell).

Park, B. and M. Rothbart (1982) 'Perception of out-group homogeneity and levels of social categorization: memory for the subordinate attributes of in-group and out-group members', *Journal of Applied Psychology* 42, 1051–68.

Parker, S. (1987) 'Retirement in Britain', in K. S. Markides and C. L. Cooper (eds), *Retirement in Industrialized Societies* (Chichester: Wiley).

Pasmore, W., C. Francis and J. Haldeman (1984) 'Sociotechnical systems: a North American reflection on empirical studies of the seventies', *Human Relations* 35, 1179–1204.

Patton, W. and P. Noller (1984) 'Unemployment and youth: a longitudinal study', *Australian Journal of Psychology* 36, 399–413.

Paul, R. J. and Y. M. Ebadi (1989) 'Leadership decision-making in a service organization: A field test of the Vroom-Yetton model', *Journal of Occupational Psychology* 62, 201–11.

Pavlov, I. (1927) *Conditioned Reflexes: An Investigation of the Physiological Activity of the Cerebral Cortex* (London: Oxford University Press).

Payne, R. L., P. B. Warr and J. Hartley (1984) 'Social class and the experience of unemployment', *Sociology of Health and Illness* 6, 152–74.

Pearson, K. (1924) *The Life, Letters and Labours of Francis Galton*, Volume II (Cambridge: Cambridge University Press).

Pearson, K. and M. Moul (1925) 'The problem of alien immigration into Great Britain, illustrated by an examination of Russian and Polish Jewish children', *Annals of Eugenics* 1, 5–127.

Peter, L. J. (1969) *The Peter Principle* (New York: William Morrow).

Peters, L. H., D. D. Hartke and J. T. Pohlmann (1985), 'Fiedler's contingency theory of leadership: An application of the meta-analysis procedures of Schmidt and Hunter', *Psychological Bulletin* 97, 274–85.

Peters, T. J. (1989) *Thriving on Chaos* (London: Pan).

Peters, T. J. and N. Austin (1985) *A Passion for Excellence: The Leadership Difference* (London: Collings; New York: Random House).

Pettigrew, A. (1973) *The Politics of Organizational Decision-Making* (London: Tavistock).

Phillips, J.S. and R.G. Lord (1981) 'Causal attribution and perceptions of leadership', *Organizational Behavior and Human Performance* 28, 143–63.

Piaget, J. (1953) *The Origin of Intelligence in the Child* (London: Routledge and Kegan Paul).

Piliavin, I., J. Rodin and J. Piliavin (1969) 'Good Samaritans: An underground phenomenon?', *Journal of Applied Psychology* 13, 289–99.

Piore, M.J. and C.F. Sabel (1984) *The Second Industrial Divide: Possibilities for Prosperity* (New York: Basic Books).

Platt, S. (1984) 'Unemployment and suicidal behaviour: a review of the literature', *Social Science and Medicine* 19, 93–115.

Platt, S. (1986) 'Recent trends in parasuicide ("attempted suicide") and unemployment among men in Edinburgh' in S. Allen *et al.* (eds) *The Experience of Unemployment* (Basingstoke: MacMillan).

Pollert, A. (1988) 'The "flexible firm": fixation or fact?', *Work, Employment and Society* 2, 3, 281–316.

Porter, L.W and E.E. Lawler (1968) *Managerial Attitudes and Performance* (Homewood, Illinois: Dorsey Press).

Porter, L. and R. Steers (1973) 'Organization, work and personal factors in employee turnover and absenteeism', *Psychological Bulletin* 80, 151–76.

Pugh, D.S. (ed.) (1971) *Organization Theory: Selected Readings* (Harmondsworth: Penguin).

Purcell, K. (1984) 'Militancy and acquiescence among women workers', in J. Siltanen and M. Stanworth (eds) *Women and the Public Sphere* (London: Hutchinson).

Rachman, S.J. (1978) *Fear and Courage* (San Francisco: W.H. Freeman).

Ray, C.A. (1986) 'Corporate culture: The last frontier of control?', *Journal of Management Studies* 23, 3, May, 287–97

Reason, R. (1987) 'The Chernobyl errors', *Bulletin of the Psychological Society* 40, 201–6.

Reber, A. (1985) *Dictionary of Psychology* (London: Penguin).

Reinberg, A., P. Andlauer, J. De Prins, W. Malbec, N. Vieux and P. Bourdeleau (1984) 'Desynchronisation of the oral temperature circadian rhythm and intolerance to shift work', *Nature* 308, 272–274.

Richards, E.W. (1984) 'Undergraduate preparation and early career outcomes: a study of recent college graduates', *Journal of Vocational Behavior* 24, 279–304.

Rimm, D.C. and J.C. Masters (1979) *Behavior Therapy: Techniques and Empirical Findings*, 2nd ed. (London and New York: Academic Press).

Rivera, A.N. and J.T. Tedeschi (1976) 'Public versus private reactions to positive inequity', *Journal of Personality and Social Psychology* 34, 895–900.

Robertson, I.T. and S. Downs (1989) 'Work sample tests of trainability: A meta-analysis', *Journal of Applied Psychology* 74, 402–10.

Robinson, D. (1976) *An Intellectual History of Psychology* (New York: Macmillan).

Robertson, J. (1985) *Future Work* (Aldershot: Gower).

Roethlisberger, F. and W. Dickson (1939) *Management and the Worker* (Cambridge: Harvard University Press).

Rogers, C.R. (1961) *On Becoming a Person* (Boston: Houghton Mifflin).

Rogers, C.R. (1974) 'In retrospect: Forty-six years', *American Psychologist* 29, 115–23.

Rorschach, H. (1942) *Psychodiagnosis: A Diagnostic Test Based On Perception* (New York: Grune and Stratton).

Rose, R. (1983) *Getting by in Three Economies* (Glasgow: Centre for the Study of Public Policy, University of Strathclyde).

Rosenmann, R.H., R.J. Brand, C.D. Jenkins, M. Friedman, R. Straus and M. Wurm (1975) 'Coronary heart disease in the Western collaborative group study: Final follow-up experience of 8½ years', *Journal of American Medical Association* 8, 872–7.

Ross, L. (1977) 'The intuitive psychologist and his shortcomings: distortions in the attribution process', in L. Berkowitz (ed.) *Advances in Experimental Social Psychology* Volume 10, 174–220 (New York: Academic Press).

Rotter, J. (1966) 'Generalized expectancies for internal versus external control of reinforcement', *Psychological Monograph* 80, No 1.

Roy, D. F. (1973) 'Banana time: job satisfaction and informal interaction, *Human Organization* 18, (1960) 156–68 (Reprinted in G. Salaman and K. Thompson (eds), *People and Organizations* (London: Longman).)

Rush, M. F. and P. S. McGrath (1973) 'Transactional analysis moves into corporate training: a new theory of interpersonal development becomes a new tool for personal development', *The Conference Board Record*, 10, 38–44.

Russek, H. I. (1960) 'Emotional stress and coronary heart disease in American physicians', *American Journal of Medical Science* 240, 711.

Rust, J., P. Sinclair and S. Barrow (1992) 'The RPQ: validation of the five-factor model in the workplace', in *Proceedings of the Occupational Psychology Conference* (Leicester: British Psychological Society).

Ryan, T. A. (1970) *Intentional Behavior* (New York: Ronald Press).

Sacks, M. P. (1975) *Women's Work in Soviet Russia: Continuity in the Midst of Change* (New York: Praeger).

Salaman, G. (1986) *Working* (London: Tavistock).

Salancik, G. R. and J. Pfeffer (1977) 'An examination of need-satisfaction models of job attitudes', *Administrative Science Quarterly* 22, 427–56.

Sales, S. M. (1969) 'Differences among individuals in affective, behavioral, biochemical, and physiological responses to variations in workload', *Dissertation Abstracts International* 30, 2407–B.

Salvendy, G. (1982) 'Human-computer communication with special reference to technological development, occupational stress, and educational needs', *Ergonomics* 25, 435.

Sandburg, D. F., A. A. Ehrhardt, C. A. Mellins, S. E. Ince and H. F. Meyer-Bahjburg (1987) 'The influence of individual and family characteristics on career aspirations of girls during childhood and adolescence', *Sex Roles* 16, 649–67

Scarbrough, H. and J. M. Corbett (1992) *Technology and Organization* (London: Routledge).

Scarr, S. (1981) *Race, Social Class and Individual Differences in IQ* (Hillsdale, New Jersey: Lawrence Erlbaum Associates).

Scarr-Salapatek, S. (1971) 'Unknowns in the IQ equation', *Science* 174 1223–8.

Schachter, S. and J. Singer (1962) 'Cognitive, social and physiological determinants of emotional state', *Psychological Review* 69, 379–99.

Schein, E. H. (1984) 'Coming to a new awareness of organizational culture', *Sloan Management Review*, Winter, 3–16.

Schein, E. (1985) *Organizational Culture and Leadership* (San Francisco: Jossey Bass).

Schein, E. (1988) *Organizational Psychology*, 3rd ed. (Englewood Cliffs, New Jersey: Prentice-Hall Inc).

Schermerhorn, J., J. Hunt and R. Osborn (1985) *Managing Organizational Behaviour* (New York: Wiley).

Schmidt, F. L. (1985) 'Review of Wonderlic Personnel Test', *Ninth Mental Measurement Yearbook* Volume 2, 1755–57.

Schmitt, N. (1976) 'Social and situational determinants of interview decisions: Implications for the employment interview', *Personnel Psychology* 29, 79–101.

Schmitt, N., R. Z. Gooding, R. A. Noe and M. Kirsch (1984) 'Meta-analyses of validity studies published between 1964 and 1982 and the investigation of study characteristics', *Personnel Psychology* 37, 407–22.

Schriesheim, C. A. and A. S. De Nisi (1981) 'Task dimensions as moderators of the effects of instrumental leadership: A two-sample replicated test of Path-Goal leadership theory', *Journal of Applied Psychology* 66, 589–97.

Schwab, D., J. Olian-Gottlieb and H. Heneman (1979) 'Between-subjects expectancy theory research: A statistical review of studies predicting effort and performance', *Psychological Bulletin* 86, 139–47.

Shackleton, V. J. and S. Newell (1991) 'Management selection: A comparative survey of methods used in top British and French companies', *Journal of Occupational Psychology* 64, 23–36.

Shaw, M. E. (1955) 'A comparison of two types of leadership in various communication nets', *Journal of Abnormal and Social Psychology* 50, 127–34.

Shaw, M. E. (1976) *Group Dynamics: The Dynamics of Small Group Behavior* (New York: McGraw-Hill).

Sherif, M. (1936) *The Psychology of Social Norms* (New York: Harper and Brothers).

Sherif, M. (1966) *Group Conflict and Cooperation* (Boston: Houghton Mifflin).

Shields, J. (1962) *Monozygotic Twins* (New York: Oxford University Press).

Silver, M. (1991) *Competent to Manage* (London: Routledge).

Singleton, W. T. (ed.) (1983) *Social Skills* (Lancaster: MTP Press).

Skinner, B. F. (1938) *The Behavior of Organisms* (New York: Appleton Century Croft).

Skinner, B. F. (1971) *Beyond Freedom and Dignity* (Harmondsworth: Penguin).

Slovic, P., B. Fischoff and S. Lichtenstein (1977) 'Behavioral decision theory', *Annual Review of Psychology* 28, 1–39.

Small, C. (1982) *The Printed Word: An Instrument of Popularity* (Aberdeen: Aberdeen University Press).

Smith, A. (1982) *On the Wealth of Nations* (Harmondsworth: Penguin).

Smith M. (1952) *An Introduction to Industrial Psychology* (London: Cassell).

Smith, R. 'Occupationless health', *British Medical Journal* Issues from 12 October 1985–25 January 1986.

Social Trends, (London: HMSO, volumes 12–17, 1982–7).

South, S. J. (1984) 'Economic conditions and the divorce rate: a time-series analysis of the post-war United States', *Journal of Marriage and the Family* 47, 31–41.

Spence, K. W., I. E. Farber and H. H. McFann (1956) 'The relation of anxiety (drive) level to performance in competitional and non-competitional paired-associates learning', *Journal of Experimental Psychology* 52, 296–305.

Springbett, B. M. (1958) 'Factors affecting the final decision in the employment interview', *Canadian Journal of Psychology* 12, 13–22.

Stahl, M. J. and A. M. Harrell (1981) 'Effort decisions with behavioral decision theory: Toward an individual differences model', *Organizational Behavior and Human Performance* 27, 303–25.

Stammers, R. (1987) 'Training and the Acquisition of Knowledge and Skill', in Peter Warr (ed.) *Psychology at Work*, 3rd ed. (Harmondsworth: Penguin).

Star, S. A., R. M. Williams and S. A. Stouffer (1965) 'Negro infantry platoons in white companies', in: H. Proshansky and B. Seidenberg (eds) *Basic Studies in Social Psychology* (New York: Holt, Rinehart and Winston).

Statt, D. A. (1972) 'National Identity in United States and Canadian Children', in: B. Massialas (ed.) *Political Youth, Traditional Schools* (Englewood Cliffs, New Jersey: Prentice-Hall).

Statt, D. A. (1977) *Psychology: Making Sense* (New York: Harper and Row).

Statt, D. A. (1990) *The Concise Dictionary of Psychology* (London and New York: Routledge).

Staw, B. and J. Ross (1985) 'Stability in the midst of change: A dispositional approach to job attitudes', *Journal of Applied Psychology* 70, 469–80.

Stebbins, R. A. (1979) *Amateurs* (Beverly Hills: Sage).

Steers, R. M. and S. R. Rhodes (1984) 'Knowledge and speculation about absenteeism', in P. S. Goodman, R. S. Atkin *et al.* (eds) *Absenteeism* (San Francisco: Jossey-Bass).

Stevenson, A. W. (1980) *Planned Safety Management* (London: Osborne).

Stewart, R. (1967) *Managers and Their Jobs* (Macmillan: London).

Stewart, R. (1982) *Choices for the Manager: A Guide to Managerial Work and Behaviour* (London: McGraw-Hill).

Stewart, R. (1986) *The Reality of Management*, 2nd ed. (London: Pan).

Stinson, J. E. and L. Tracy (1974) 'Some disturbing characteristics of the LPC score', *Personnel Psychology* 24, 477–85.

Stogdill, R. M. (1948) 'Personal factors associated with leadership: a survey of the literature', *Journal of Psychology* 25, 35–71.

Stogdill, R. M. (1974) *Handbook of Leadership: A Survey of Theory and Research* (New York: Free Press).

Strube, M. J. and J. E. Garcia (1981) 'A meta-analytic investigation of Fiedler's contingency model of leadership effectiveness', *Psychological Bulletin* 90, 307–21.

Suls, J. (ed.) (1982) *Psychological Perspectives on the Self* (Hillsdale, New Jersey: Lawrence Erlbaum Associates).

Sundstrom, E. (1986) *Work Places* (Cambridge: Cambridge University Press).

Super, D. E. and M. J. Bohn (1971) *Occupational Psychology* (Belmont, California: Wadsworth Publishing Company; 1970 London: Tavistock Publications).

Sutherland, V. and C. L. Cooper (1987) *Man and Accidents Offshore* (London: Lloyds).

Tasto, D., M. Colligan, E. Skjei and S. Polly (1978) *Health Consequences of Shiftwork* (Washington DC: NIOSH US Government Printing Office).

Tavris, C. and C. Offir (1977) *The Longest War* (New York: Harcourt Brace Jovanovich).

Taylor, F. W (1911) *The Principles of Scientific Management* (New York: Harper).

Terborg, J. R. (1985) 'Working women and stress', in T. A. Beehr and R. S. Bhagat (eds) *Human Stress and Cognition in Organizations* (Chichester: Wiley).

Terkel, S. (1974) *Working* (New York: Random House).

Tesser, A. and D. Shaffer (1990) 'Attitudes and attitude change', in M. Rosenzweig and L. Porter (eds), *Annual Review of Psychology*, Volume 41 (Palo Alto, California: Annual Reviews Inc.).

Thomas, K. (1964) 'Work and leisure in pre-industrial society', *Past and Present* 29, 50–66.

Thompson, E. P. (1967) 'Time, work, discipline and industrial capitalism', *Past and Present* 38, 55–97.

Thompson, P. (1989) *The Nature of Work*, 2nd ed. (London: Macmillan).

Thompson, P. and D. McHugh (1990) *Work Organizations* (London: Macmillan).

Thorndike, R. L. and E. Hagen (1959) *Ten Thousand Careers* (Wiley: New York)

Thornton, G. C. and W. C. Byham (1982) *Assessment Center and Managerial Performance* (New York: Academic Press).

Trew, K. and R. Kilpatrick (1983) *The Daily Life of the Unemployed* (Department of Psychology: Queen's University of Belfast).

Triplett, N. (1897) 'The dynamogenic factors in pacemaking and competition', *American Journal of Psychology* 9, 507–33.

Trist, E. L. and K. W. Bamforth (1951) 'Some social and psychological consequences of the Longwall method of coal-cutting', *Human Relations* 4 (1), 3–38.

Trist, E. L., G. W. Higgin, H. Murray and A. B. Pollock (1963) *Organizational Choice* (London: Tavistock).

Tubbs, M. E. (1986) 'Goal-setting: a meta-analytic examination of the empirical evidence', *Journal of Applied Psychology*, 71, 474–83.

Tucker, F. D. (1985) 'A study of the training needs of older workers: Implications for human resources development planning', *Public Personnel Management*, 1 (3), 273–302.

Turner, J. C. (1975) 'Social comparison and social identity; some prospects for intergroup behaviour', *European Journal of Social Psychology* 5, 5–24.

Uhrbrock, R. S. (1961) 'Music on the job: its influence on worker morale and productivity', *Personnel Psychology* 14, 9–38.

Ulrich, L. and D. Trumbo (1965) 'The selection interview since 1949', *Psychological Bulletin* 63, 100–116.

Umstot, D., C. Bell and T. Mitchell (1976) 'Effects of job enrichment and task goals on satisfaction and productivity: implications for job design', *Journal of Applied Psychology* 61, 4, 379–94.

Upton, R. (1984) 'The "home office" and the new homeworkers', *Personnel Management* September, 39–43.

Vernon, P. (1941) 'Psychological effects of air raids', *Journal of Abnormal and Social Psychology* 36, 457–76.

Vroom, V. H. (1959) 'Some personality determinants of the effects of participation', *Journal of Abnormal and Social Psychology* 59, 322–7.

Vroom, V. H. (1964) *Work and Motivation* (New York: Wiley).

Vroom, V. H. (1976) 'Leadership', in M. D. Dunnette (ed.) *Handbook of Industrial and Organizational Psychology* (Chicago, Illinois: Rand McNally).

Vroom, V. H. and A. G. Jago (1988) *The New Leadership: Managing Participation in Organizations* (Englewood Cliffs, New Jersey: Prentice-Hall).

Vroom, V. H. and P. W. Yetton (1974) *Leadership and Decision-making* (New York: Wiley).

Walby, S. (ed.) (1988) *Gender Segregation at Work* (Milton Keynes and Philadelphia, Penn.: Open University Press).

Walker, A. (1985) 'Early retirement: release or refuge from the labour market?', *Quarterly Journal of Social Affairs*, 1, 211–29.

Wall, T. D. (1987) 'New Technology and Job Design', in P. Warr (ed.) *Psychology at Work* 3rd ed. (Harmondsworth: Penguin).

Wall, T. D., N. J. Kemp, P. R. Jackson and C. W. Clegg (1986) 'An outcome evaluation of autonomous work groups: a long-term field experiment', *Academy of Management Journal* 29, 280–304.

Walster, E., E. Aronson and D. Abrahams (1966) 'On increasing the effectiveness of a low prestige communicator', *Journal of Experimental Social Psychology* 2, 325–42.

Wanous, J. P. and A. Zwany (1977) 'A cross-sectional test of need hierarchy theory', *Organizational Behavior and Human Performance* 18, 78–9.

Waring, M. (1989) *If Women Counted: A New Feminist Economics* (London: Macmillan, 1988; Harper and Row, 1988).

Warr, P. B. (1974) 'Inference magnitude, range and evaluative direction as factors affecting relative importance of cues in impression formation', *Journal of Personality and Social Psychology* 30, 191–7.

Warr, P. B. (1982) 'A national study of non-financial employment commitment', *Journal of Occupational Psychology* 55, 297–312.

Warr, P. B. (1984) 'Work and unemployment' in P. J. D. Drenth *et al.* (eds), *Handbook of Work and Organizational Psychology* (Chichester: Wiley).

Warr, P. B. (ed.) (1987a) *Psychology at Work*, 3rd ed. (Harmondsworth: Penguin).

Warr, P. B. (1987b) *Work, Unemployment, and Mental Health* (Oxford: Clarendon).

Warr, P. B. and P. R. Jackson (1984) 'Men without jobs: some correlates of age and length of unemployment', *Journal of Occupational Psychology* 57, 77–85.

Warr, P. B. and P. R. Jackson (1985) 'Factors influencing the psychological impact of prolonged unemployment and of re-employment', *Psychological Medicine* 15, 795–807.

Warr, P. B. and G. Parry (1982) 'Paid employment and women's psychological well-being', *Psychological Bulletin* 91, 498–516.

Warr, P. B. and R. Payne (1982) 'Experience of strain and pleasure among British adults', *Social Science and Medicine* 16, 1691–7.

Watson, J. B. (1913) 'Psychology as a Behaviorist Views it', *Psychological Review* XX, 158–177.

Watson, J. B. (1928) *Psychological Care of Infant and Child* (New York: Norton).

Watson, J. B. and R. Rayner (1920) 'Conditioned emotional reactions', *Journal of Experimental Psychology* 3, 1–14.

Watson, R. I. (1978) *The Great Psychologists*, 4th ed. (Philadelphia: Lippincott).

Weaver, C. (1980) 'Job satisfaction in the United States in the 1970s', *Journal of Applied Psychology* 65, 364–7.

Weber, M. (1922) *The Theory of Social and Economic Organization* (Oxford: Oxford University Press).

Webster, E. C. (1982) *The Employment Interview* (Schomberg, Ontario: Special Interest Publications).

Weiss, H. M. and S. Adler (1984) 'Personality and organizational behaviour', in B. M. Staw and L. L. Cummings (eds), *Research in Organizational Behaviour*, Volume 6 (Greenwich, Connecticut: JAI Press).

Weissenberg, P. and M. Kavanagh (1972) 'The independence of initiating structure and consideration: A review of the evidence', *Personnel Psychology* 25, 119–30.

Weitz, J. and S. Adler (1973) 'The optimal use of simulation', *Journal of Applied Psychology* 58 (2) 219–24.

Wernimont, P. F. and J. P. Campbell (1968) 'Signs, samples and criteria', *Journal of Applied Psychology* 52, 372–6.

West, J. (1990) 'Gender in the labour process', in D. Knights and H. Willmott (eds), *Labour Process Theory* (Basingstoke: Macmillan).

Wexley, K. N. and G. P. Latham (1981) *Developing and Training Human Resources in Organizations* (Glenview, Illinois: Scott, Foresman).

Wicker, A. (1969) 'Attitudes versus actions: the relationship of verbal and overt behavioural responses to attitude objects', *The Journal of Social Issues* 25, 41–78.

Willis, P. E. (1977) *Learning to Labour* (Farnborough: Saxon House).

Winner, L. (1977) *Autonomous Technology: Technics-Out-of Control as a Theme in Political Thought* (Cambridge, Massachusetts: MIT Press).

Woodward, J. (1965) *Industrial Organization: Theory and Practice* (Oxford: Oxford University Press).

Yerkes, R. M. and J. D. Dodson (1908) 'The relationship of strength of stimulus to rapidity of habit formations', *Journal of Comparative Neurology and Psychology* 18, 459–82.

Yetton, P. W. (1984) 'Leadership and supervision', in M. Gruneberg and T. Wall (eds), *Social Psychology and Organizational Behaviour* (Chichester: Wiley).

Zajonc, R. B., (1965) 'Social facilitation' *Science* 149, 269–74.

Zeitlin, L. (1971) 'A little larceny can do a lot for employee morale', *Psychology Today* June.

Zellner, M. (1970) 'Self-esteem, reception, and influenceability', *Journal of Personality and Social Psychology* 15, 87–93.

Zimbardo, P. G., W. C. Banks, C. Haney and D. Jaffe (1973) 'The mind is a formidable jailer: a Pirandellian prison', *The New York Times Sunday Magazine* 8 April, 38–60.

Zuboff, S. (1988) *In the Age of the Smart Machine* (New York: Basic Books).

Author index

Subject index